FRAMED BY WAR

NATION OF NATIONS:
IMMIGRANT HISTORY AS AMERICAN HISTORY

General Editor: Matthew Jacobson
Founding Editors: Matthew Jacobson and Werner Sollors

Beyond the Shadow of Camptown: Korean Military Brides in America
Ji-Yeon Yuh

Feeling Italian: The Art of Ethnicity in America
Thomas J. Ferraro

Constructing Black Selves: Caribbean American Narratives and the Second Generation
Lisa D. McGill

Transnational Adoption: A Cultural Economy of Race, Gender, and Kinship
Sara K. Dorow

Immigration and American Popular Culture: An Introduction
Jeffrey Melnick and Rachel Rubin

From Arrival to Incorporation: Migrants to the US in a Global Era
Edited by Elliott Barkan, Hasia Diner, and Alan M. Kraut

Migrant Imaginaries: Latino Cultural Politics in the US-Mexico Borderlands
Alicia Schmidt Camacho

The Force of Domesticity: Filipina Migrants and Globalization
Rhacel Salazar Parreñas

Immigrant Rights in the Shadows of Citizenship
Edited by Rachel Ida Buff

Rough Writing: Ethnic Authorship in Theodore Roosevelt's America
Aviva F. Taubenfeld

The Third Asiatic Invasion: Migration and Empire in Filipino America, 1898–1946
Rick Baldoz

Race for Citizenship: Black Orientalism and Asian Uplift from Pre-Emancipation to Neoliberal America
Helen Heran Jun

Entitled to Nothing: The Struggle for Immigrant Health Care in the Age of Welfare Reform
Lisa Sun-Hee Park

The Slums of Aspen: Immigrants vs. the Environment in America's Eden
Lisa Sun-Hee Park and David Naguib Pellow

Arab America: Gender, Cultural Politics, and Activism
Nadine Naber

Social Death: Racialized Rightlessness and the Criminalization of the Unprotected
Lisa Marie Cacho

Love and Empire: Cybermarriage and Citizenship across the Americas
Felicity Amaya Schaeffer

Global Families: A History of Asian International Adoption in America
Catherine Ceniza Choy

Who's Your Paddy? Racial Expectations and the Struggle for Irish American Identity
Jennifer Nugent Duffy

Islam Is a Foreign Country: American Muslims and the Global Crisis of Authority
Zareena Grewal

Soft Soil, Black Grapes: The Birth of Italian Winemaking in California
Simone Cinotto

African & American: West Africans in Post–Civil Rights America
Marilyn Halter and Violet Showers Johnson

Citizens of Asian America: Democracy and Race during the Cold War
Cindy I-Fen Cheng

From the Land of Shadows: War, Revolution, and the Making of the Cambodian Diaspora
Khatharya Um

The Cultural Politics of US Immigration: Gender, Race, and Media
Leah Perry

Whiteness on the Border: Mapping the US Racial Imagination in Brown and White
Lee Bebout

Strange Fruit of the Black Pacific: Imperialism's Racial Justice and Its Fugitives
Vince Schleitwiler

The New Immigrant Whiteness: Neoliberalism, Race, and Post-Soviet Migration to the United States
Claudia Sadowski-Smith

Colonial Phantoms: Belonging and Refusal in the Dominican Americas, from the 19th Century to the Present
Dixa Ramírez

Girlhood in the Borderlands: Mexican Teens Caught in the Crossroads of Migration
Lilia Soto

Returns of War: South Vietnam and the Price of Refugee Memory
Long T. Bui

Framed by War: Korean Children and Women at the Crossroads of US Empire
Susie Woo

Framed by War

Korean Children and Women at the
Crossroads of US Empire

Susie Woo

NEW YORK UNIVERSITY PRESS

New York

NEW YORK UNIVERSITY PRESS
New York
www.nyupress.org

An earlier version of chapter 2 was published as "Imagining Kin: Cold War Sentimental-
ism and the Korean Children's Choir," *American Quarterly* 67, no. 1 (March 2015): 25–53,
© 2015 The American Studies Association. Portions of chapter 3 were previously published
as "Transpacific Adoption: The Korean War, US Missionaries, and Cold War Liberalism,"
in *Pacific America: Histories of Transoceanic Crossings*, edited by Lon Kurashige (Honolulu:
University of Hawaiʻi Press, 2017), 161–77.

References to Internet websites (URLs) were accurate at the time of writing. Neither the
author nor New York University Press is responsible for URLs that may have expired or
changed since the manuscript was prepared.

Library of Congress Cataloging-in-Publication Data
Names: Woo, Susie, author.
Title: Framed by war : Korean children and women at the crossroads of US empire /
Susie Woo.
Description: New York : New York University Press, [2019] | Series: Nation of nations:
immigrant history as American history | Includes bibliographical references and index.
Identifiers: LCCN 2019007705 | ISBN 9781479889914 (cl ; alk. paper) | ISBN 9781479880539
(pb ; alk. paper)
Subjects: LCSH: Korean War, 1950–1953—Children—Social conditions. | Korean War, 1950–
1953—Women—Social conditions. | Koreans—United States—History—20th century. |
Koreans—Cultural assimilation—United States. | Korea (South)—Emigration and
immigration—Social aspects.
Classification: LCC E184.K6 W658 2019 | DDC 951.904/2083—dc23
LC record available at https://lccn.loc.gov/2019007705

New York University Press books are printed on acid-free paper, and their binding materials
are chosen for strength and durability. We strive to use environmentally responsible suppli-
ers and materials to the greatest extent possible in publishing our books.

Manufactured in the United States of America

10 9 8 7 6 5 4 3 2 1

Also available as an ebook

For my parents,
Moon Sook and Do Keun Woo

CONTENTS

List of Figures   xi

Preface   xiii

Introduction: Cold War Empire   1

PART I. IMAGINED FAMILY FRAMES   31

1. GIs and the Kids of Korea   33

2. US Aid Campaigns and the Korean Children's Choir   57

PART II. INTERNATIONAL COLD WAR FAMILIES   83

3. Missionary Rescue and the Transnational Making of Family   86

4. Producing Model Korean Adoptees   112

PART III. ERASING EMPIRE   143

5. Mixed-Race Children and Their Korean Mothers   148

6. Managing Korean War Brides   174

Conclusion: Broken Family Frames   205

Acknowledgments   217

Notes   225

Bibliography   279

Index   303

About the Author   325

FIGURES

I.1. Korean adoptee Lee Kyung Soo comes to America.   2

I.2. US Navy boatswain Vincent Paladino carries his adopted son.   3

I.3. Children of recent US territories come to school in the United States.   7

1.1. A Korean orphan huddles on the side of the road.   44

1.2. Stookie Allen's cartoon of Jimmy Pusan as a "Keen Teen."   46

1.3. American sailor gives Jimmy Pusan a GI buzz cut.   47

1.4. Three Korean boys read *Roy Rogers*.   49

2.1. Korean Children's Choir sings at the Statue of Liberty.   72

2.2. Korean Orphan Choir rehearses.   76

3.1. Harry Holt arrives in the United States with mixed-race adoptees in his inaugural "babylift."   87

3.2. Drawing by an adoptive mother of two Korean-white children from South Korea.   103

4.1. War orphan Kang Koo Rhee in a Korean orphanage.   132

4.2. Adopted Kang Koo Rhee rides a carousel in Los Angeles.   133

P.1. Cartoon of Asian women awaiting a US military search.   144

6.1. Korean bride makes gravy for her US military husband.   175

6.2. Charles Kapitzky watches his wife eat an *aisu kuriimu* cone.   187

6.3. Album cover, *The Kim Sisters: Their First Album*.   195

6.4. Kim Sisters watch television, "in pony-tails."   198

6.5. Kim Sisters pose in hanboks with their Korean instruments.   199

PREFACE

I remember the day that Elvis died. My appa was driving and listening to news of the singer's death on the radio. From the back seat of our family station wagon and through the rearview mirror, I could see that he was crying. What I did not know then is in part what I am trying to understand now—how so much was bound up in my father's love for Elvis. From the first time he heard "Love Me Tender" on Armed Forces Radio Korea to the concert he attended in Phoenix, Arizona, where Elvis was the "size of an ant" given his distance from the stage, Elvis connected his childhood in Korea with his adult life in America in subtle yet profound ways. That my father came to the United States in 1969 with America in his heart signaled a relationship many years in the making, one that had deep and deeply complicated roots in Korea.

A second-generation Korean American, I did not live through the Korean War, but I am tied to the migration of peoples who moved because of it. Ji-Yeon Yuh importantly argues that nearly all Korean migration since 1950 links back to that war, if not immediately as in the case of adoptees, then to the trauma left in its wake. My parents were what Yuh refers to as "refuge migrants," a group "motivated by a deep psychological need to leave behind chaos, and insecurity, and trauma . . . [who] seek out emotional/mental peace and a stable environment."[1] Growing up, I avoided asking my parents about the war because I was afraid of what I might hear and of the pain that I could cause by asking them to remember. This may have been why they themselves waited until I was in college to begin sharing their experiences. Once they started recounting the war, the stories steadily unfolded: My father recalled the time he spent as a young boy on US bases, where American soldiers gave him chewing gum, chocolate bars, and weathered copies of *Life* and *Look*. My mother told me how North Korean soldiers dragged her father from their home as she watched from a hiding place above the rafters and how the men returned for her older sister, neither of whom she would ever see again.

She spoke of her mother, who placed her two youngest siblings in a local orphanage not for the purpose of adoption, but because it was the only place where they were guaranteed a meal. As I listened to these stories, I realized that their memories of the war were sharp and the wounds fresh. They are but two of millions of survivors for whom the war remains what Chungmoo Choi describes as a "deep scar" that has shaped the very fabric of who they are, and has come to complicate their place in the United States and their relationship to a Korea forever changed by US military, political, and economic intervention.[2]

Their experiences prompted my interest in writing a social history of the Korean War. Military and political histories describe the events of the war, but few center on what happened to Korean civilians. As I began searching through pamphlets, guides, government and missionary records, as well as an array of cultural sources including magazines like *Life* and the *Saturday Evening Post*, one figure consistently appeared across all of them—the Korean child. The statistics that marked children's needs, protocols to manage their health, and photographs that placed them in the company of Americans who gave them candy, clothes, prosthetics, and Bibles raised questions about the place of children in, and their centrality to, US-South Korea relations. As I continued with my research, I saw that the history of Korean children was also about Korean women, the hidden half of the story. These two figures came to anchor the project for what they revealed about US power in South Korea during and after the war, and for how they exposed the intimate fallout of US empire, which landed squarely on the shoulders of Korea's most vulnerable populations.

At the start of this project, I contacted adoptees who came to the United States immediately following the war and were now mostly in their sixties. Among the responses that I received was one who said that her story was American through and through and another who stated that he did not wish to open past wounds. One response came as a phone call from the spouse of an adoptee. She saw my letter and wanted to explain why I would likely not hear from her husband, who was adopted at the age of three. She relayed that he rarely talked about his life growing up as a Korean adoptee in an East Coast suburb because it brought back painful memories. These responses made me think about the years of silence from my parents, especially my mother, on the topic of war. Memories are not always available, nor should they have to be, and perhaps I was not in a position to ask them to recall.

That phone call changed the course of my research, though not the questions at its core. I wanted to better understand the circumstances that produced war migrants, and how it was that thousands of Korean children and women found themselves suddenly in America living with families that were foreign to them. My research took me to military, government, missionary, and welfare organizations across the United States, and to national archives, welfare agencies, and wartime orphanages in South Korea. I also looked to US and South Korean newspapers and magazines for what they could tell me about the production of Korean children and women at this time. The photographs that appeared in public media told stories that were vastly different from the private records kept in administrative files, a disjuncture between visibility and erasure shared across projects of empire. These wide-ranging sources helped me piece together a fragmented history that has been excised from the national memories of both the United States and Korea.

In this book, I try to see those who were lost in one of America's many "forgotten wars." In the flashes when they appeared in US media as Korean children loved by American parents and brides adored by US servicemen, perspective radically altered the story that was being told. Americans who looked at these images saw hopeful beginnings; yet for the Korean children and women pictured, their arrival to the United States also meant their departure from Korea—a migration sparked not by the American Dream, but by the nightmare of war.

NOTE ON LANGUAGE

For Korean names, I list the family name first followed by the given name in accordance with Korean conventions, except for commonly used English transliterations, like Syngman Rhee. For individuals in the public record, I use their names as they appear in print. To protect the identities of children, women, and adoptive parents whose records are private, I use an initial instead of their names. Nearly all of the interviews were conducted in Korean, for which I provide the English translations. For the transliteration of Korean to English, I follow the McCune-Reischauer system.

When describing geographic spaces and political divisions, I use "North Korea" and "South Korea." However, when referring to people from South Korea, I use "Korean," since this is how they would have viewed themselves, as part of one Korea.

Introduction

Cold War Empire

In November 1953, *Life* magazine introduced readers to a "new American," three-year-old Lee Kyung Soo.[1] In the leading photograph, readers saw the Korean boy wearing a tailored US Navy uniform to match that of his adoptive father, US Navy boatswain Vincent Paladino (figure I.1). Paladino and a group of reporters ushered the child toward the camera and into America. The tall men may have dwarfed the boy, but Lee remained center stage. For some viewers, his steady gait and military uniform gestured toward the resolve of Lee and fellow Koreans in their fight against communism. Still others may have seen in the boy's downturned gaze, hands thrust deep in his pockets, the emotions of a child who had recently lost his parents in the war and now found himself far from Korea. Regardless of how *Life* readers interpreted the story, all eyes were trained on "little Lee," whose first steps on US soil opened a new chapter in US-South Korea relations and repositioned America's place in the world more broadly.

Lee's story reached American audiences five months after delegates from the United Nations, North Korea, and China signed an armistice to suspend fighting in the Korean peninsula. The 1953 agreement brought an end to the air, land, and sea assaults that claimed over thirty-six thousand American, one million Chinese, and an estimated three to four million Korean lives.[2] The Korean War ended in a stalemate; the country remained divided along the 38th parallel and communists maintained a hold of the North. In this context, little Lee carried with him the political weight of nations. He was what the United States purportedly fought for—Korea's future democracy—and what South Korea was presumed to be—an ally of the United States. Placing a small orphan under the care of a US serviceman helped to cushion the blow of the costly war. Given the scarcity of and barriers to overseas adoptions at this time, the story was less an advertisement for adoption than a geopolitical script.[3]

1

Figure 1.1. Korean adoptee Lee Kyung Soo comes to America. "A New American Comes 'Home,'" *Life*, November 30, 1953, 25. Photograph by Jon Brenneis. Getty Images.

When paired together, Vincent Paladino and Lee helped narrate America's role in South Korea. Here, the United States was the father to South Korea, the latter a child who was innocent, vulnerable, and in need of US protection. The article about Lee in *Life* welcomed continued US intervention, while eclipsing the US military's role in the recent violence that orphaned Lee and others like him. The curated story privileged US perspectives over Korean ones, helping to position the United States as a benevolent superpower in a global landscape dramatically changed after World War II.

In addition to introducing the international dimensions of US-South Korea relations, this story also edified Americans with domestic Cold War lessons. The next four pages of the article chronicled Lee's first days in the United States. Photographers captured the boy playing with a reporter's microphone, enjoying his first "too cold" ice cream cone, and pointing toy pistols. In the article's closing shot, a stoic Paladino, dressed in a suit with patches that marked his heroism, carried a gleeful Lee, who wore his new "favorite dress," a cowboy outfit (figure I.2). Using his adoptive father's hand as a saddle, Lee symbolized a new kind of American staking claim to the West. Visions of the interracial father-son duo at home in a cosmopolitan city replete with broad sidewalks and shiny cars overflowed with Cold War sentiment. The photograph suggested that Americans cared about their Korean neighbors, even enough to make them family.

Figure I.2. US Navy boatswain Vincent Paladino carries his adopted son. "A New American Comes 'Home," *Life*, November 30, 1953, 29. Photograph by Jon Brenneis. Getty Images.

Though seemingly too small for the stuff of politics, Lee bridged vast cultural and political gaps between the United States and South Korea. In one fell swoop, he embodied democratic visions of internationalism, racial harmony, and happiness bound up in consumer capitalism.

When millions of *Life* magazine readers first met Lee in 1953, it must have been curious for them to see a Korean child in the United States, especially in the context of kin.[4] The population of Koreans living in the United States remained relatively small, at around eight thousand (with an estimated seven thousand in Hawai'i and less than a thousand in California), and existing immigration laws continued to restrict their entry.[5] The Immigration and Nationality Act of 1924 banned the entry of aliens ineligible to citizenship. Since the Naturalization Act of 1790 excluded people of Asian descent, Koreans could not enter the United States. While the McCarran-Walter Act of 1952 ended Asian exclusion, it continued the national origins quota system, which limited the number of visas allotted to each Asian country to around a hundred per year.[6] At this time, most Americans knew little about Koreans save for wartime images that pictured them frail and far away. After the war, however, Americans would become increasingly familiar with Koreans on US soil in ways both imagined and real. Korean children flashed up suddenly and with great fanfare in magazines, on television, and in auditoriums across the country. In these public displays, Americans witnessed Koreans singing Christmas jingles, eating hot dogs, watching television, and doing other "American" things. The hypervisibility of Korean children made political sense. Their age and the attendant scripts of assimilation made them ideal representatives of US-South Korea relations.

Alongside media representations came the actual arrival of Korean children and women. Between 1953 and 1965, over 6,000 Korean and mixed-race adoptees and an estimated 7,700 Korean military brides immigrated to the United States, more than doubling the existing Korean population.[7] Their immigration was first made possible through individual acts of Congress and temporary legislation that circumnavigated existing restrictive immigration laws. They arrived as the sons, daughters, and wives of predominantly white American families. Since their ability to immigrate to the United States was predicated upon their adoption by or marriage to an American, the moment that they set foot in the United States they transgressed the racial boundaries of one of the most fiercely protected spaces—the white nuclear family home. While mainstream media may have celebrated the arrival of Korean adoptees, they often evaded and at times fully eclipsed the arrival of Korean military brides, the latter complicated by their age, gender, and assumed connection with prostitution. Whether celebrated or hidden, tensions surrounded these newly arrived immigrants who formed interracial families that embodied Cold War internationalism in practice, not theory.

How did Korean children and women come to the United States in the 1950s and 1960s ahead of the 1965 Immigration Act, which opened immigration from Asia more broadly? How was it that they arrived as ready-made members of predominantly white families during a time of continued Jim Crow in the South and amidst visibly heightened struggles for racial equality nationally? How was this immigrant group intimately tied to US actions and interests in South Korea, relations that intensified as a result of the Korean War? In addressing these questions, this book traces how Korean children and women became crucial to the transnational making of American empire in the early Cold War. The study centers upon US interactions with and policies surrounding Korean children and women during the war and the recovery period that followed.[8] Though historical accounts have left Korean children and women as the largely forgotten population of a forgotten war, they were essential to the work of the US military, government, and private sector in ways that both enabled American power and forced its unraveling. At the heart of these processes was the US militarized production of the Korean orphan, GI baby, adoptee, birth mother, prostitute, and bride.[9] These strained and unstable embodiments emerged as a result of US geopolitical needs during the Cold War that brought Americans into Korea and Koreans into the United States, intimate crossings that defined, and at times defied, American empire in the postwar Pacific.

Children of American Empire

American empire had its beginnings well over a century before the United States divided and occupied the Korean peninsula. The transatlantic slave trade, the Louisiana Purchase and forced removal of Native Americans, the US annexation of Texas in 1845, the Mexican War of 1848, and territorial expansion to the Southwest evidenced the imperialist impulses that drove US expansionism. Jodi A. Byrd reminds readers that it is through the study of American Indians and other indigenous peoples that US empire became possible at all.[10] This history acts as a reminder that US imperialism was well underway domestically prior to 1898, at which point the United States reached across the Pacific to annex Hawai'i and the Philippines, and expand its territories to Cuba, Guam, Puerto Rico, and Samoa. The material benefits of American empire came in the form of new markets for the feared overproduction of American goods, military outposts and stepping stones across the Pacific toward the fabled China market, and imported natural resources, like rubber, coffee, and sugar. US expansion also served ideological needs. It opened up new frontiers beyond the purportedly closed West, enabling Americans to fulfill their Manifest Destiny. It made robust adventurers out of men, helping to reaffirm a white masculinity destabilized by mechanized industrialization.[11] US expansion to the Pacific helped America redefine itself at a moment when the changes wrought by rapid industrialization and the massive influx of immigrants needed to fuel it required Americans to look forward to a postindustrial future rather than nostalgically hold on to a pastoral (and for Southerners, antebellum) past.

For all of its benefits, material and otherwise, US expansion to the Pacific posed a domestic problem. Anti-expansionists warned that the doors of imperialism would swing both ways, and that soon the inhabitants of its newest territories would seek entry into the United States. Vociferous nativist and union organizer Samuel Gompers predicted that US expansion would result in "an inundation of Mongolians" flooding the mainland to take the jobs of white laborers.[12] A slew of American "experts" used science to back claims that expansion threatened the health of the nation. Eugenicist Herbert Spencer asserted that US subjects in the Pacific embodied "the minds of children and the passion of adults," a deviant combination that could threaten the Victorian order of things should they be granted entry.[13]

Images of swarthy subjects from the far-off Pacific making their way to the United States circulated in the popular press. In January 1899, the political satire magazine *Puck* included as its centerfold a cartoon titled "School Begins" (figure I.3). A large Uncle Sam leaned over his desk to give the children seated in the first row, "Cuba, Porto Rico [*sic*], Hawaii,

Figure 1.3. Children of recent US territories come to school in the United States. "School Begins," *Puck*, January 25, 1899. Courtesy of Library of Congress Prints and Photographs Division, call no. AP101.P7 1899 (Case X) [P&P].

and the Philippines," their first lesson on "self-government." He repri-
manded them, "Now, children, you've got to learn these lessons whether
you want to or not!" The children of America's newest territories, with
their downturned mouths, bodily fidgets, unkempt hair, half-dress, and
dark skin, were the class troublemakers. The unruly and visibly foreign
children were juxtaposed against the well-behaved students seated behind them. Holding books labeled California, Texas, New Mexico, Arizona, and Alaska, these children sat upright at their desks, the girls with
their hair neatly tied back, the boys dressed in pressed blue uniforms, all
reading quietly. They had become model citizens of the republic in the
decades since their annexation.

There were others in and around the classroom who were unlike
the rest. The African American man cleaning the windows, the Native
American male sitting alone in the back of the room, and a Chinese boy
peeking in through the door represented those who had been in the
United States for some time, but lay permanently outside the American
polity. The African American individual was relegated to servitude, the
Native subject with his upside-down reader was summarily dismissed,
while the Chinese figure, standing outside with his queue blowing in the
wind, was excluded from the classroom altogether. Here and in other
images circulating at this time, subjects of US territories were placed in
relation to nonwhite peoples at home, a slotting of imperial subjects into
an existing domestic racial order that placed whites firmly at the top.[14]
The cartoon relayed the current dilemma of America's foray into the
Pacific in these racialized terms. Would America's most recent imperial
subjects go the way of the three children arrested in progress due to their
race? *Puck* readers were left to wonder whether or not the visibly impetuous children of the Pacific would be able to follow in the footsteps
of the annexed class that came before them.

It made sense to work out the tensions of empire via children. Dis-
tanced from labor or sex, the baggage of adult subjects, children provided a purportedly less complicated slate upon which to ponder the
problems and possibilities of empire. The narratives that they conveyed
shifted with the needs of the state. For domestic imperialisms, assimilative scripts helped to manage subjects already within US borders.
For example, Laura Wexler shows how administrators at the Hampton
Normal and Agricultural Institute in the late nineteenth century used

photographs to prove the merits of their boarding school for Native American and African American children. A "before" photograph of three Native American girls on their first day at school, wrapped in blankets and sitting on the floor, was juxtaposed against an "after" shot of the same children a year later, two sitting upright in chairs playing checkers, all three with their braids shorn and dressed in pinafores.[15] Staged productions like these were useful to promote the school and green-light intervention, but also important for how they made Native Americans, for whom North America was already home, into good and useful US subjects. These assimilative scripts did not usually apply to imperial charges who lived outside the mainland United States.

During US expansion at the turn of the twentieth century, imagining people of the Pacific as children permitted a familiar brand of paternalism used to justify intervention and dominance, yet these children seemed particularly resistant to US governance. Indeed, as shown in the *Puck* cartoon, they appeared to repel civilizing efforts, thus supporting nativist appeals to keep them out. Imperial wards of the Pacific were added to an existing list of Asian undesirables, a project with legal beginnings in the 1875 Page Act, which barred the entry of Chinese contract laborers, felons, and women for the purpose of prostitution, language that marked Chinese bodies as both dangerous and immoral. The series of restrictive Asian immigration laws that followed culminated in the 1924 Immigration and Nationality Act, which prohibited the entry of nearly all peoples from Asia. Filipinos were the only exception, a direct—and, for nativists, unwelcome—outcome of American empire. As US subjects, they could not be denied entry, though forcing them into low-wage agricultural labor and other needed fields of employment ensured the unequal conditions of their immigration.[16] Thus, while US expansion to the Pacific benefitted the economic, military, and political growth of the nation, it also foiled America's gatekeeping efforts. At the end of the nineteenth century, American empire resulted in an immigration breach—a problem that would arise again fifty years later when the United States occupied South Korea.

In 1945 Korea was at once liberated, divided, and reoccupied. With Japan's defeat in World War II and its subsequent loss of imperial holdings in Asia, Koreans, who had been under Japanese rule since 1910, were eager to establish their sovereignty. However, before they could enact plans for independence, the United States and the Soviet Union intervened. On the evening of August 10, 1945, the day after the United States dropped a second atomic bomb in Japan, the State-War-Navy Co-ordinating Committee asked Dean Rusk and Charles H. Bonesteel to divide the Korean peninsula. It is rumored that the young US colonels spent less than thirty minutes deciding upon the 38th parallel, a then invisible line that would cleave a division so deep and permanent that the chasm can now be seen from space.[17] Between 1945 and 1948, US occupying forces established military bases and implemented economic aid programs in the south, while the Soviet Union administered control of the north. US officials billed the military occupation of South Korea as a temporary trusteeship, a postwar measure to stabilize the region.

If the Truman administration was initially unsure about the level or duration of its commitments in Korea, the war solidified its indefinite place in the peninsula, making South Korea a central location of American empire. On June 25, 1950, North Korean soldiers fired across the demilitarized zone. The United States entered the war unilaterally, committing US air and naval forces with President Truman's verbal support, but in advance of United Nations, Pentagon, or congressional approval.[18] What began as a "limited police action" turned into a full-scale war once China entered in October 1950. International audiences, particularly those from recently decolonized or decolonizing countries, watched with great concern. In 1952 Chester Bowles, American ambassador in New Delhi and close friend of the president, told Truman that America should heed its international reputation. Bowles explained, "Throughout our history we have demonstrated our consistent opposition to colonialism in any form. And yet, tragically enough, the Cold War has forced us necessarily into compromises which have laid us open to the charge, particularly here in Asia, of having changed our basic policies." Writing from the newly independent India, he warned that Asians were "totally unable to think clearly on this subject" because Western dominance triggered an "almost automatic . . . bitter reaction to any colonial situation."[19] US administrators shared Bowles's amnesiac view of US history, a strategic disremembering of US imperial conquests past and present. However, Bowles's report indicated that the colonized most certainly did not forget, and saw clearly the far-reaching implications of US power in Asia as the war raged on.

The critique of Western powers came at a time of global change and reflected a rising collective Third World consciousness. The recent world war highlighted the right to self-determination and threw into question the very meaning of humanity. During World War II, America's support of anti-fascism clashed with the continuation of Jim Crow policies and the incarceration of Japanese Americans at home, contradictions that opened the United States to critiques of its own imperial practices.[20] The terrors of that war—the holocaust that exposed the unfathomable dangers of racial policies and the remarkable devastation caused by atomic bombs dropped on Hiroshima and Nagasaki—required a meaningful reconfiguration of power in its wake. Between 1945 and 1960, forty countries that together accounted for more than a quarter of the world's population revolted against colonizers and gained their independence.[21] Radical shifts in the years following World War II resulted from and intertwined with the growing pressures of the Cold War, forcing the United States to navigate its newfound power under increased global scrutiny.

This proved difficult given the scale of the Korean War and America's use of force to fight it. By the war's end, the US military had dropped 635,000 tons of bombs in a peninsula the size of Minnesota and utilized new devastating technologies, like napalm, to rout out guerrilla fighters.[22] When the armistice was signed in July 1953, more than half of the Korean population had been killed, wounded, or permanently separated from their families. From the outside looking in, US actions deeply challenged American claims that it had liberated Korea from Japanese oppression, exhibiting instead imperial imposition at its worst.[23] Amidst global pressures, US war violence needed a corrective antidote. The child, once again, offered a useful location through which to navigate and also narrate US intentions in Asia. Sharon Stephens has urged us not to view childhood as universal but rather as contested sites that operate differently across time to meet specific political needs. She has used critical approaches to childhood to reveal how the state utilized children for global disciplining and moralizing purposes.[24] Paternalism continued to underwrite scripts of US intervention as it had at the turn of the century, but because of the circumstances of the Korean War and the emergent needs of the Cold War, rather than being kept at a distance, Korean children were placed in intimate proximity with Americans.

During the war, news of entire battalions "adopting" Korean mascots, and, after the war, visions of model Korean children happy in their new American homes brought Americans together with Asians in ways not seen before. Fifty years on from the first episode of US territorial expansion to the Pacific, empire's children were no longer unruly, but were now deserving objects of rescue. What explained the transformation from the impetuous child with dangerous adult-like inflexibility to the innocent, malleable, and Americanizing child? What accounted for the shift in responsibility for empire's wards from the authoritative figure of the teacher to the tender care of Americans who played parents to Korean children? How did popular constructions of imperial wards move from the undesirable savage "over there" to the rapidly assimilating Korean child at home in America? The shift from the incorrigible child-subject in 1898 to the adoptable son or daughter after 1953 was significant. It signaled the importance of the optics needed to make it appear as though the United States was not an imperialist power, a task made difficult by the facts of the war itself and the extent of US military, economic, and political embroilments in South Korea afterwards. Placing Americans with Korean children in the context of family produced the right kind of Cold War script, one that configured US-South Korean relations in the framework of care and kin, not violence and force.[25] These representations also came with new ways for Americans to participate in a transnational project. No longer on the sidelines waiting to see how US expansion would affect the national polity, as was the case at the turn of the century, average Americans were given ample opportunities to take part in Korea by extending familiar domestic roles across the Pacific.

Global Family Frames

After World War II, constructions of the American family reordered the domestic realm, providing an anchor for the nation in uncertain times. As Elaine Tyler May and others have shown, the American family took on new meaning after World War II, when public policy, government legislation, and popular culture converged to make the heteronormative, middle-class white family a prime location of US national security. These structures helped to stabilize gender norms disrupted by World War II;

as Rosie the Riveter was expected to return home to fulfill the important duty of wife and mother, men were to reclaim their place as breadwinners at the head of the family. The family offered additional reassurances during a time of nuclear threat. May reveals how the danger of the bomb converged with representations of the titillating but volatile independent woman, each a peril that could be contained through marriage, a family, and its capitalist companion—a suburban home filled with appliances and other mass-produced goods.[26]

Constructions of the family that solved domestic problems also proved portable abroad, making them effective ways to grapple with the international challenges of the Atomic Age. After the US military deployed atomic bombs, Americans had to contend with the guilt and global ramifications of its nuclear capabilities. Norman Cousins, editor of the *Saturday Review*, offered one response in his highly publicized Hiroshima Maidens Project. In 1948 he brought twenty-five Japanese women disfigured by the bombs to the United States for reconstructive surgery by American doctors. During the yearlong project, Cousins asked donors to imagine themselves as part of a single global family reaching out to help those whom they may have never met, but toward whom they felt "love" and a sense of "duty."[27] While the "maidens" were at the heart of this effort, the project said as much if not more about Americans who repaired the damage wrought by bombs that Americans also produced and deployed. The Western features given the Japanese women—ones for which they were maligned when they returned to Japan—signaled the extent to which Americans did not always recognize the US-centric parameters of their actions even in the midst of helping others.[28]

Edward Steichen, the director of photography at the Museum of Modern Art in New York, organized two exhibits hoping to promote similar ideas of global understanding. His 1951 show *Korea—The Impact of War in Photographs* included close-up images of US servicemen and Korean civilians, as well as of bombs and the evacuation of Korean children. The conflicting images of humanity amidst violence from a war still underway complicated Steichen's intended message. He found greater success in his 1955 exhibition of 503 family portraits from sixty-eight countries, *The Family of Man*. In the first fifteen weeks, the show drew 270,000 visitors, who could see themselves reflected in the portraits from around the world. Even dark-skinned, impoverished "Third World" families registered as recognizable when positioned in a family frame that included grandparents, parents, children, and grandchildren. Marianne Hirsch describes how these intimately familiar juxtapositions helped to "transform a global space of vast differences and competing interests into a domestic space structured by likeness and specularity."[29]

During the Cold War, family frames were symbolic, aspirational, and illusory representations that prescribed for Americans everything from how to behave at home to how they should see themselves in relation to the world. Imagined family frames, with children anchored at the center, proved particularly useful when it came to navigating US involvement in Korea. Visions of the US-Korean family were evoked to support the geopolitical needs of the United States as it made its debut as a superpower after World War II. Part 1 of this book describes how these intimate relationships were first introduced during and immediately following the war. US media figured American servicemen as surrogate fathers who fed, clothed, and sheltered orphaned children of war, while US aid campaigns asked Americans at home to take up a similar parental role through donations for Korean children. These constructions helped to reframe the unpopular war as a rescue mission in which the United States saved innocent children from the clutches of communism. Also during the war, news of the first Korean war brides reached American audiences, furthering familial scripts of love that knew no bounds. Together, these family frames served important state functions. For international audiences, they helped allay accusations of US imperialism. For Americans, they offered a lens through which to understand why US soldiers fought and died for Asian others thousands of miles away. The scripts also altered existing postwar conceptions of the global family. More than suggesting a broad imagined kinship with international others, narratives that emerged from Korea asked Americans to see Koreans as an intimate part of their own family.

After the war, transnational family frames served as the ideological foundation upon which nongovernmental US actors created paths to the actual formation of US-Korean families. Part 2 of this book considers what happened when hundreds of American missionaries, doctors, nurses, philanthropists, and social workers entered South Korea to spearhead postwar recovery efforts. The estimated 100,000 children left homeless by the war became the primary focus of their work. As in other colonial contexts, populations deemed in-need justified access. In US postwar aid campaigns, the children were no longer under the protection of American soldiers and instead appeared heartbreakingly alone, the latter a construction that asked American citizens to intervene.[30] Missionaries and philanthropists asked Americans to rescue the children through their sponsorship and donations, which Americans readily did, sending supplies and millions of dollars. Postwar aid campaigns effectively shifted the responsibility for Korea's children from US servicemen in South Korea to a wide range of Americans in the United States. The change expanded the emotional and material connections between Americans at home and the children of South Korea, while the structure of family frames engendered the participation of American women specifically.

While white men headed up major US aid organizations in postwar South Korea, daily operations were carried out primarily by women. The geopolitical needs of the Cold War converged with the destruction of the Korean War to create opportunities for white women to implement their domestic expertise abroad. Their presumed innate ability to mother became a tool of Cold War internationalism, opening up prospects for travel and influence.[31] In South Korea, American women administered care and carried out the day-to-day functions of hundreds of US-operated orphanages. And when it came to adoptions, American women assessed the children, kept track of the medical records, visa applications, and reports needed to process them, and taught Koreans how to do this work. They arrived armed with Western lessons on childcare, nutrition, hygiene, and the Bible. Even American women who remained home in the United States could participate in the international project of rescue by donating money and needed supplies such as powdered milk. When missionary organizations and prominent adoption proponents presented their American constituents the option to enact the ultimate form of rescue by bringing Korean children into their homes, thousands of women filled out applications, placed their names on waiting lists, and prepared their homes for the arrival of a Korean child.[32] Their reasons for adoption were varied and overlapped, from resolving issues of infertility to enacting Christian duty. Yet most Americans who adopted Korean children understood their actions in clear Cold War terms—by creating international and interracial families, they worked to secure democracy in domestic and now also global ways.

In the end, the wide-reaching public relations effort that figured Koreans as part of the American family coupled with the "remarkable mobilization of [US] voluntary child welfare agencies" made it impossible for the US government to deny the formation of US-Korean families.[33] In 1961 US policy makers reluctantly established permanent adoption legislation. This law, coupled with the amended War Brides Act of 1947, which permitted the entry of Korean brides, resulted in the formation of close to fourteen thousand US-Korean families between 1953 and 1965. These families marked a turning point in American empire. The war, Cold War geopolitics, and internationalist Americans converged to make South Korea the logical, if unintended, location for the production of international and interracial families. The unprecedented scale and publicness of these integrated families challenged long-standing segregationist policies in the United States.

Because their arrival destabilized the white nuclear family norm, Korean children and women had to be managed and made safe for immigration. This US project of transformation had its beginnings in South Korea. Institutional processes assured that Koreans were made good American subjects *prior* to their arrival. In US missionary-run orphanages, Americans taught children lessons in godliness and cleanliness; and in United Service Organization (USO) brides schools, Korean women learned how to cook American meals and sew American fashions. This transnational project with white Americans at the helm had a dual purpose. For Korean women and children who remained in South Korea, the democratizing project made Koreans productive, Christian, and manageable subjects. For those who came to the United States, these lessons helped to make them an acceptable immigrant, a docile and unthreatening addition to the nation who in behavior, if not appearance, left existing constructions of the American family intact.

When Korean adoptees and brides came to the United States, they landed upon an Orientalist stage not of their own making. Upon arrival, they were placed into an existing hierarchy that envisioned the West as powerful and civilized, in contrast to a feminized, exoticized, and sexualized East.[34] While Orientalist constructions historically lumped Asians together, the US racial state also differentiated Asians from one another to meet changing domestic and foreign policy needs. Some of the most dramatic shifts occurred during and after World War II. After the bombing of Pearl Harbor in 1941, the need to differentiate between Japanese enemies and Chinese allies became a matter of national security.[35] After the war, when the United States occupied a defeated Japan, the Japanese had to be transformed from threatening enemy to democratic ally almost overnight.[36] It was in this context that reporters and scholars honed in on Japanese Americans' economic and educational success following their wartime incarceration to evidence their model behavior. The characterization failed to consider the few choices Japanese Americans had outside of resettlement programs aimed at assimilation, not to mention the silencing effects of fear and trauma.[37] The model minority myth that was applied to postwar Japanese American families was soon extended to other Asian American groups. Chinese American adherence to middle-class nuclear family ideals in the 1950s also supported model minority scripts.[38] The myth was further advanced in popular culture, as in the 1958 musical *Flower Drum Song*, wherein Asian actors performed the Asian American family for the masses—singing and dancing their assimilation while maintaining an exotic Orientalist flair that made them worth watching.

Korean War immigrants arrived within this cultural milieu, but the circumstances of their immigration both advanced and altered postwar scripts of the Asian model minority. Narratives circulating around Korean adoptees and brides figured them as distinct immigrants who were already well on their way to becoming American. Like model Asian Americans, they too were part of a normative family—only theirs was interracial and they were foreign-born. The possible threat that their arrival posed to the protected realm of the white nuclear family was simultaneously solved by those same family frames. In the case of adoptees, placement within and under the care of predominantly white, Christian American couples made them appear to be pliable immigrants. Korean military brides, on the rare occasions that they appeared in US media, arrived apparently well-versed in American ways, while still fitting gendered Orientalist expectations of the lotus blossom. As children and wives, Koreans became additive to the core foundation of the white nuclear family. They were subsumed into the private space of the American home under the tutelage of white parents or husbands. The circumstances of their arrival contributed to their disappearance. They lived in scattered locations in suburbs along the East and West Coasts and in rural towns across the Midwest, separated from one another as well as from Asian American communities. Placed in predominantly white neighborhoods, Korean War immigrants were left few options outside of assimilation. Media constructions that applauded their rapid Americanization brought them closer to honorary whiteness, while the private family home served to contain their lingering differences.

With the majority of decolonized countries inhabited by nonwhite peoples, the United States needed to convince international audiences that it had resolved deep-rooted racial inequality, a difficult task given ongoing segregation at home. News of violence that reached international audiences marred American claims to democracy. As Thomas Borstelmann, Mary Dudziak, and Penny Von Eschen have described, African American civil rights activists leveraged the Cold War needs of the United States to force their government to make changes at home.[39] The US government came to see civil rights as integral to its foreign policy needs, but looked primarily to symbolic rather than substantive solutions to racial inequality. In this context, newly formed US-Korean families helped to bolster US claims of racial pluralism with minimal actual change. Their integration did not disrupt the status quo since it left white Americans, in this case adoptive parents and military husbands, in positions of power and placed the onus upon Korean children and women to fit themselves into an expected white, middle-class ideal. Still, and conveniently, these Cold War families gave US administrators and cultural producers a way to tout successful integration during a time of continuing racial strife.

Rather than highlight the tenaciousness with which the US military and US policy makers tried to keep Americans from adopting or marrying Koreans, once these families were formed, they were harnessed to exemplify a liberal modernity.[40] The assembling of families across racial difference and geographic distance was framed not as an immigration problem, but rather as a technology that evidenced the power of American domesticity, a worldliness on the most intimate scale. In the context of the Cold War, Korean adoptees and brides became commodities in service to the post–World War II construction of benevolent US power. Stories of model Korean children and rapidly adjusting Korean brides, and the white American families that loved them, relayed ideal visions of racial democracy and internationalism, making these families another useful node in America's cultural Cold War efforts.[41] They also adhered to a very specific kind of integration, where, soon after the public fanfare surrounding their initial arrival, Korean children and women quite literally disappeared into the private space of the home. More absorbed than accepted, Koreans modeled for nonwhite others at home and abroad the parameters of a universal freedom that upheld middle-class white Americans as the standard bearers of democracy.[42]

Just beyond media representations that celebrated the supposed ease with which white American families crossed racial, cultural, biological, and national divides were the necessary erasures that revealed the limits of racial liberalism. To begin, media constructions highlighted primarily one kind of international family: "full" Korean adoptees in white American homes. Mixed-race children and military brides remained in the shadows of this internationalist narrative, even though they together made up 85 percent of all Korean immigrants at this time.[43] When it came to mixed-race children, US administrators in South Korea and the United States upheld existing black-white boundaries. Social workers in the United States placed those deemed part-white with white American couples and part-black with African American couples. The flexibility and modelness of Koreans did not apply to those who were half-black, the latter whom some welfare workers actively tried to keep out of the United States, arguing that local African American children should be adopted first before bringing in black bodies from afar.[44] For military brides, the 71,043 US servicemen still stationed in South Korea in 1957, years after the unsuccessful war, meant the continuation of military marriages.[45] No longer a novelty of war, the Korean bride signaled an ongoing problem of Korean immigration. For all its claims to liberalism, the United States tried to control which Koreans could enter and who was denied, as well as how those who did arrive were made to adhere to assimilative scripts that furthered state aims.

Behind generative constructions of the US-Korean family, there existed populations that were pushed permanently outside of Cold War family frames. Part 3 of this book centers upon those who necessarily had to remain unseen in order to sustain scripts of the US-Korean family. Korean prostitutes and Korean mothers of mixed-race children were left outside of the possibility of family and hence ineligible for rescue. Most remained hidden in US-established institutions in South Korea, including camptowns, segregated schools, and orphanages. Whereas the United States became the geographic location of family formation, South Korea remained a site where family was impossible, a location of persistent brokenness. The social, legal, and cultural place of Korean women and children who found themselves in the margins of both US and South Korean societies exposed the violence that lay at the heart of America's intimate empire.

America's Intimate Empire and the Cold War

In this book, I use the terms "imperial" and "empire" to place US actions in Korea as part of a longer continuum of US domestic and international power. As in previous imperialist episodes, the US military occupied South Korea, while the government imposed economic and political policies to procure a democratic stronghold in Asia at the expense of Korean sovereignty. Administrators layered US imperial practices upon the existing structures of Korea's previous colonizer, Japan. These intersecting imperialisms served as the foundation for US power in South Korea. While the primary components of imperial rule were not new, the United States reworked the cultural framework to appear non-imperial in a rapidly decolonizing world.[46] US actions in South Korea were a case study in what Kwame Nkrumah, Ghana's first post-independence president, would in 1965 coin "neo-colonialism." Nkrumah warned that in Ghana and other African countries, independence and sovereignty were token gestures that did not in any substantive way alter the relationship between the colonial power and the colonial state. He cautioned that instruments of indirect control, such as international monetary bodies that created systems of debt and a variety of other educational and cultural nongovernmental organizations, made it more difficult to detect and resist neocolonial rule.[47] In South Korea, insidious forms of rule operated through the realm of the intimate, seemingly apolitical encounters that enabled intervention while simultaneously providing cover behind which US power could operate.

What makes South Korea a revealing place to study the making of US postwar power is the extent to which administrators made it up as they went along. The suddenness with which the United States entered Korea, divided it, militarily occupied it, and went to war in it—all events that occurred within five years of World War II—set the stage for America's reactionary approach to nation-building in the postwar era. The rapidly changing political landscape of Korea, which was both caused and exacerbated by US involvement, required flexibility. Cold War pressures made it critical that the United States fight the war, while also winning hearts and minds—two projects that did not align together easily. Washington struggled to uphold liberal representations of the United States as an altruistic leader of the world. US administrators managed the dilemma with dual strategies of military force and widely publicized humanitarian aid. It was during the Korean War that these contradictory approaches first found institutional expression, actively bringing Americans together with foreign subjects as kin, in ways both imagined and real.

Postcolonial scholars have explored the "intimate frontiers" of empire, cultural spaces that expose the "human dimension" of the colonial encounter.[48] They have shown that rather than a supreme domination, empire is made up of many moving parts, including the quotidian practices of individuals—colonizers and the colonized—who actively shape and often confound the parameters of rule.[49] Americans in South Korea did the work of the state by fighting the war and then aiding Koreans afflicted by it. The spike in Korean civilian needs after the war gave a wide range of Americans increased access to Koreans. Uneven power structures dictated these intimate day-to-day interactions, but were cloaked by scripts of care that made US power difficult to detect. The intimate scale of empire in Korea bore echoes of imperial relationships in other sites. As Laura Briggs describes, midcentury US attempts to manage the sexuality and reproduction of Puerto Rican women turned that island into a social laboratory for an array of American "experts." Megan Vaughan illuminates how illness and disease validated the intervention of Christian missionaries in African countries; Warwick Anderson observes similar patterns among American medical officers in the Philippines.[50] Vernadette Vicuña Gonzalez examines the tandem rise in and seamless merging of US militarism and tourism in Hawai'i and the Philippines to consider how the dominance of the US military, especially upon female bodies in both of these locations, blurred the distinctions between military and civilian life and politics; these manufactured attachments enabled and helped mitigate the historical violence of military occupation in the islands.[51] Through the management of private spaces and public spaces where people were privately managed, which included orphanages, schools, churches, and hospitals, colonial authorities gained access to subject populations, imbricating US power by disseminating control in diffuse and seemingly innocuous ways.[52]

As they did in other sites of intimate empire, Americans used cultural scripts of rescue to validate their unfettered access to Koreans. Throughout the 1950s and 1960s, US aid and Korean child welfare became synonymous. Americans quickly dominated Korea's welfare system, a legacy that can be seen today through South Korea's implementation of Western welfare institutions, orphanages, and the practice of transnational adoptions.[53] Scripts of rescue also triggered an outpouring of support from Americans back home, who gave millions to aid Korean children, which, in turn, sustained the work of US missionary and aid organizations abroad. The remarkable scale of Americans who participated in the transnational project of rescue made the Korean case unique. Unlike in previous episodes of US imperialism, the work of nongovernmental actors in South Korea also granted hundreds of thousands of Americans at home access to Korean populations in ways both figurative and real. For those who responded to US aid campaigns by giving money, affective ties bound them to Korea's children; and for the thousands who adopted Korean and mixed-race children, their daily interactions with sons and daughters at home in America cemented international bonds between the United States and South Korea.

While the practices of US nongovernmental missionaries, social welfare workers, and philanthropists effectively furthered the needs of American empire, they were also the very reason for its unraveling. As was true in other cultural fronts of the Cold War, US administrators quickly lost a handle on Americans who had initially helped bolster its democracy-building efforts.[54] Intimate and daily interactions between Americans and Koreans transgressed borders of the nation-state. When military men adopted Korean children and married Korean women, and when Americans in the United States, encouraged and facilitated by US missionaries in South Korea, brought Korean and mixed-race children into their homes, national, racial, and ideological boundaries were crossed in ways that the US government neither intended nor desired. In the end, transnational families formed because of Cold War needs that required the United States to appear internationalist after a war in which it inflicted the bulk of the damage. It was not happenstance that the first large-scale formation of transnational, interracial families came out of Korea, the first hot war of the Cold War era, which required that the United States act on its liberal claims.

Dual—and at times competing—US and South Korean nationalisms played out upon the bodies of Korean children and women. South Korea also had a stake in the successful construction of the transnational family, a cultural display of an emergent modernism. In particular, public scripts of the democracy-loving, well-behaved Korean adoptee allowed Koreans to leverage the tragic outcomes of American empire to communicate Korean cosmopolitanism and democratized futures. Korean children who went to America were figured as young ambassadors who helped to politically align the two countries. Yet behind these constructions lingered the material needs of a Korean nationalism that was fundamentally altered by US empire. As in other colonial contexts, US military, governance, and economic aid dramatically changed the parameters of sovereignty. In the case of Korea, the US government divided the peninsula and then intervened in the civil war, causing great destruction in the process. It is from this starting point at the end of the war that Koreans had to reconfigure new paths to unification and sovereignty. Before it could make plans for independence, Korea had to stabilize a population ravaged by war. In addition to having lost an estimated 17 percent of the country's population, Koreans grappled with new kinds of subjects. From the birth of mixed-race children to the establishment of militarized prostitution, the US military had produced Koreans who could not be included in the Korean polity. The visibly mixed-race child and the "fallen" Korean woman were summarily written out of Korea's national identity for their intimate ties to the United States. Sending these children and women to the United States as adoptees and brides supported South Korea's nation-building efforts in the wake of American empire. The resulting erasure of these people, whether by placement into American homes or hidden away in institutions throughout South Korea, is but one example of how America's intimate empire persists through the lives of Korea's women and children.

The public rarely saw the US structures established to manage Korean civilians. Indeed, as argued by Hannah Arendt, imperial projects worked best at the hands of an "invisible government."[55] By positioning average Americans as noble rescuers of Koreans who happened to be suffering, the US government and military could excuse themselves from culpability, past and present. Visibility and erasure worked in tandem to rewrite US actions in Korea; Korean children and women often found themselves at the center of these scripts, helping to soften the look of American empire.

Piecing Together a Fragmented Past

From the Fourth of July to war memorials, national memory enacts a selective remembrance, highlighting certain dimensions of the past at the expense of others.[56] In labeling it a "forgotten war," the United States has excused itself from addressing the enduring legacies of the Korean War. By placing Korean children and women at the center of this war and its aftermath, this book attempts to challenge the national memory of the United States, as well as to reinstate thousands of marginalized Koreans into the national memory of Korea.

Scholars have worked to address these absences. Katherine H. S. Moon, Ji-Yeon Yuh, Grace M. Cho, and Seungsook Moon pioneered a shift in existing scholarship with their work on Korean camptowns, prostitution, and military brides. Each of these scholars privileges the perspectives of women to reveal the transnational effects of power and the inequity of these intimate exchanges, as well as unveil women's activism and resistance in South Korea and the United States.[57] Scholars have built upon their work and the groundbreaking feminist projects of Cynthia Enloe to reveal the radiating and lasting effects of US militarization upon women around the world.[58] US militarized presence in South Korea, which today hovers at around 28,000, and the continued arrival of Korean military brides, who now number over 100,000 in the United States, embody the corporeal legacies of US militarization in South Korea that began with US occupation in 1945 and continues today.[59]

Critical adoption studies scholars place Korea at the origins of transnational adoption processes. Tobias Hübinette, Arissa Oh, Catherine Ceniza Choy, SooJin Pate, and others trace the historical beginnings of Korean transnational adoptions to the war and consider the broader politics involved in moving children across borders.[60] Korean transnational adoptions have continued since the war; Eleana Kim illuminates the emergence of a collective adoptee identity, and Kim Park Nelson conducts extensive oral history interviews with Korean adoptees. Both significantly expand current understandings of transnational adoptees from the perspectives of adoptees themselves.[61] Elise Prébin and Hosu Kim address the far-reaching impact of transnational adoptions upon Korean birth mothers and families, as well as adoptees in the United States, where over 150,000 Korean adoptees reside, and European countries, where an estimated 50,000 Korean adoptees currently live.[62] Through oral history, documentary film, memoir, novels, and art, Korean adoptees are telling their own stories that critique the work of US and South Korean states, while offering new forms of kinship that extend beyond staid notions of family. Their interventions show the other side of public representations that tout the rapidly assimilating Korean adoptee. In her memoir, Jane Jeong Trenka explains that she tried to be the perfect daughter for fear that she would be given up again. Deann Borshay Liem, who recounts her story in the documentary *First Person Plural*, believed as a child that she would be able to go back to Korea if she pleased her adoptive parents.[63] What these works poignantly show are the lives lived before and after adoptees became visible to the United States, ones shaped and deeply complicated by the needs of American empire. Without an understanding of the processes responsible for producing their circumstances, we cannot begin to comprehend the depth of these experiences, which combined violence and opportunity, trauma and love, loss and kinship. This study is indebted to these works, and looks to contribute to the conversation by tracing the historical and social foundations upon which these identities first emerged.

Korean military brides and adoptees who came to the United States immediately following the war were unlike contemporary populations in part because they were also refugees. The conditions of their arrival were predicated upon their inability to survive in war-torn Korea, a situation made worse for children who had lost their parents in the war or were mixed-race. Critical refugee studies scholars point to the discrepancies between national narratives and lived realities that prove essential to thinking about Korean War migrants. Yên Lê Espiritu notably argues that model minority constructions of Vietnamese Americans rely upon scripts that credit the benevolence of the United States for their rescue, while simultaneously denying the reality that they were made refugees at the hands of the US military.[64] Eric Tang uses the phrase "refugee exceptionalism" to describe how refuge is never found for those who had no option but to leave Cambodia. The violence of resettlement is masked by US constructions of Cambodians as the beneficiaries of American liberal freedoms.[65] And Mimi Nguyen urges a closer look at liberal empire claims to the "gift of freedom" that has become the rationale for continued governance and violence.[66] Like refugees of other US wars in Asia, Korean children and women became screens for American actions; it was through them that the United States could lose the war on the battlefield, yet still win the moral war by acting as their saviors.

Behind the veil that served Cold War needs, Korean women were ostracized from Korean society because of their links to the US military, leaving them few options outside of emigrating; and for young Korean adoptees, the choice was often made for them. When considered in these terms, their transnational existence was not a choice. They came to occupy a space between two nations by circumstances that have set them outside of US and South Korean communities. Given the historical context of their arrival to the United States, it becomes clear that it is not enough to expand the category of "Korean American" to include adoptees and brides; instead, it is imperative that we reconfigure a belonging not bound by race, kinship, citizenship, or nation.[67] This book attempts to contribute to this effort by making the after-effects of US militarization and war transparent, a historical project that lays bare how the work of governments, militaries, and institutions came to intimately affect the lives of thousands of children and women on both sides of the Pacific.

In this book, I search across a range of sources to find the perspectives and processes that were made to go missing from national narratives. Utilizing approaches from postcolonial studies, ethnic studies, and social and cultural history, this book casts a wide net to examine disparate sources that when placed together help suture a fragmented past. To understand the inner workings of American empire and to see how Korean children and women were central to these operations in ways that were both intended and unintended, I looked to the places where they appeared—in US and South Korean government documents and military correspondence; missionary, philanthropic aid organization, social welfare, and orphanage records; US and South Korean newspapers and media; and photographs intended for public consumption and those used privately for administrative purposes. When brought together, these sources reveal the anxieties, violence, trauma, and care that circulated through America's intimate empire in South Korea.

Many of the sources that contain information about Korea's women and children were produced and used by those in power. US and South Korean discussions about what to do about Korean orphans, prostitutes, and especially mixed-race GI babies cropped up across both state archives from military records to reports on public health. I read these documents alongside and against the grain. Ann Laura Stoler argues that colonial administrative records are ones of "uncertainty and doubt," reflecting "anxious efforts to 'catch up' with what was emergent and 'becoming' in new colonial situations."[68] US and South Korean military and government records are revealing for what they tell us about state intentions, as well as the state's response to circumstances that it neither planned for nor wanted. When it came to the interpersonal bonds that had formed between Americans and Koreans, the documents reveal the excesses of intimate empire that threatened to unravel imperial aims, ones that US administrators were forced to address and scrambled to manage, but could never fully control. The records of US missionaries and American social workers demonstrate how individuals put the ideals of internationalism into practice, efforts that the US government condoned at first but later tried to curtail when they tried to bring Koreans into the United States. Their correspondence reflects a mix of state, proselytizing, and professionalizing goals alongside care and aid that came to characterize America's postwar presence in South Korea and ultimately caused empire's return. While state and institutional records explain what happened to Koreans and why, it is in the gaps and silences that we can begin to imagine the experiences of Korean children and women. In administrator records, when we see notes that "pictures mean a great deal to our mothers who have given up their [mixed-race] children" or mentions of a child who cries less frequently, these are signs of trauma, not adjustment.[69]

To layer on top of these revelatory moments in the archives, this book looks across a variety of cultural sources that narrated Korean children and women for US and South Korean publics. In imperial contexts, representation is key to navigating control, producing identities of colonizer and colonized, and furthering what Mary Louise Pratt has described as anti-conquest narratives, strategies of innocence used to assert dominance.[70] Amy Kaplan has importantly shown that in colonial encounters, stereotypes do not simply impose hierarchies between the civilized and the savage, but become themselves unstable sites of ambivalence that "distort and challenge the bedrock divisions on which they are founded."[71] Time and again, representations of Korean children and women produced inconsistencies and breaks. Media productions of Americanized Korean adoptees or brides were riddled with expressions that betrayed their internationalist intentions. Staged photographs could not always contain the strains of the immigrants' new existence in the United States or the pain of their recent past and uncertainty of their future.

For what they can reveal in the absence of written records, I turn to published and unpublished photographs to find what LaKisha Michelle Simmons describes as the "spaces of dynamic encounter."[72] Photographs, even the ones produced to serve US nation-building efforts, revealed the subjectivity of Korean children and women. By reading what is visible to imagine what is not, we can come to understand Korean and Korean American subjectivity as a process; see it in the moment of its making rather than assume that identity as predetermined, stable, or fixed. As we know from our experiences in taking photographs and consuming media, the way images are framed—what is placed at the center, from what angle the image is shot, what is cropped outside—determines what story the image tells. For Korean children and women, it is important to remember that they did not choose to be seen. And for the Korean adoptees and brides who were summoned by the United States to help navigate the war and US empire, their identities emerged in relation to US family frames that were imposed upon them. Images of Korean children, whether alone or with adoptive parents or missionary administrators, were situated within the context of a caretaking family; those of Korean women with American husbands were placed in the frame of marriage. What other experiences could not be told within US-prescribed family frames? What is captured in the frames thus also suggests what lies outside of them—the experiences of children and women before and after the moment caught on camera, the unseen interactions where the drama of empire unfolds. When it came to Korea, what remained out of public view was more than an incompleteness; it was an active erasure. Marianne Hirsch explains the space of contradiction "between the myth of the ideal family and the lived reality of family life," which shows us "what we wish our family to be, and therefore what, most frequently, it is not."[73] Published and unpublished photographs show this slippage between intention and reality, thus offering glimpses into the inner workings of America's intimate empire.

The chapters in this book trace the arc of intimate relations between Koreans and Americans, and the symbolic and material outcomes of these encounters. Part 1, "Imagined Family Frames," considers how Americans in South Korea came to imagine Korean children as part of the American family. Chapter 1 describes how US military officials mandated serviceman visits to orphanages and the Department of Defense efforts to capture these moments on film. The pairing of American GIs and Korean children boosted soldier morale and gave the public a heartening lens through which to make sense of the war, though they soon posed a problem for the US military when its men tried to make these bonds permanent. Chapter 2 centers upon the work of US aid organizations that produced everything from waif appeals to Korean "songbirds" to raise money for wartime and postwar relief. In 1954, the American-Korean Foundation's Korean Children's Choir toured fifty cities, giving Americans an opportunity to imagine what it might be like to have these children in the United States permanently.

Part 2, "International Cold War Families," traces the transnational and legal makings of the Korean adoptee. Chapter 3 examines the work of US missionaries on the ground in postwar South Korea. Their efforts to aid Korean children-in-need transformed into campaigns to bring them to the United States. The very same individuals that US government officials supported for their internationalist work soon became the root of an immigration problem. Chapter 4 examines the social and cultural processes put in place to manage the arrival of Korean adoptees. It describes the transnational dimensions of making model adoptees, a project that began in US-run institutions in South Korea and ended with public visions of rapidly Americanizing adoptees in the United States. These scripts also relied upon the racialized management of mixed-race children, who made up an estimated 70 percent of Korean adoptions during the 1950s.[74]

Part 3, "Erasing Empire," centers upon the people and experiences placed outside of acceptable international family frames. US attempts to manage and disappear certain populations produced by the US military in Korea reflected the need to hide damning evidence of imposition, and to sustain positive visions of US internationalism. Chapter 5 reveals how American missionaries coerced Korean mothers into giving up their children, and how mixed-race children who remained in South Korea, children whom welfare studies labeled "social handicaps," were segregated in orphanages and schools. Stateless and without protection or resources, both populations remained out of view and on the fringes of South Korean society. Chapter 6 centers on the figure of the Korean war bride. The assumed connection between camptown prostitution and Korean brides made Korean women untenable and thus in need of public erasure. To mitigate the threat of the Korean prostitute/bride, cultural constructions of the Japanese bride and the family singing sensation, the Kim Sisters, helped to supplant, rewrite, and ultimately erase the Korean military bride in the United States.

Together, these chapters demonstrate how the United States was able to expand its reach to South Korea under the guise of familial care. The making of US power amidst decolonization required conflicting processes of visibility and erasure, enabling and preventing, making and destroying. It was ultimately the pressures of the Cold War that forced the United States to follow through on its internationalist claims by making room for interracial families of war. For the Korean children and women who became the focus of US government administrators, US servicemen, and American missionaries, social workers, and philanthropists, their lives changed course when they encountered American empire in its many forms. From the war that brought with it unfathomable destruction to the aid of Americans who tried to help repair that damage, Korean children and women found themselves bound to geographies that they did not choose, but were forced to navigate in South Korea, the United States, and spaces in between.

PART I

Imagined Family Frames

The United States first established diplomatic relations with Korea in 1882 under the Treaty of Peace, Amity, Commerce, and Navigation, a part of its larger quest for new markets and increased influence in the Pacific. The uneven terms of the treaty, which benefitted US trade and granted Americans extraterritorial rights, reflected the Orientalist lens through which US administrators viewed Korea, and how they placed Koreans alongside an existing compendium of undesirable Asian others. US delegates reported that Koreans were "lazy" and "incredibly ignorant," much like other inhabitants of the Pacific.[1] The US government readily left the peninsula in 1905, as soon as Japan took control of Korean foreign affairs. The US government's swift exit and decision not to honor the treaty's mutual friendship and assistance clause was an Orientalist dismissal, and reflected the tangential place of Korea in US policy at this time.

Things took a turn after World War II, when Korea became geopolitically important to US Cold War policy in Asia. When the United States divided and occupied South Korea in 1945, US administrators sought to bring South Korea and its people into closer alignment with the United States, a way to help render its sudden interest to the tune of $300 million in economic aid to Korea legible to the American public. No longer the backwards, ignorant Koreans of the early 1900s, Koreans in the post–World War II era were said to be rapidly Christianizing and eager to embrace US-style democracy. Some commentators even likened Koreans to Americans. Homer B. Hulbert, a US educator who lived in Korea for twenty years, wrote that while they were neither good merchants like the Chinese nor good fighters like the Japanese, Koreans were "far more like Anglo-Saxons in temperament than either, and [were] by far the pleasantest people in the Far East to live amongst."[2] In 1948 Robert Oliver, the US advisor to President Syngman Rhee, explained that Koreans descended from the nomadic tribes of Mongolia and the Caucasian people of Western Asia, a combination of strains that gave Koreans "both Occidental and Oriental characteristics."[3] In 1951 missionary Horace Horton Underwood observed that, as a whole, Korean "people [were] much lighter in color than either the Japanese or the Chinese."[4] According to these sources, potential Western blood ties and Anglo features made Koreans more like Americans. These scripts helped further US goals to establish a democratic stronghold in Korea, a project that began by convincing Americans that Koreans were capable of adhering to democratic ideals culturally, socially, and even racially.

US involvement in the Korean War both heightened and altered what was at stake in the cultural productions of Korea and Koreans. Extensive US military commitments that included over 1.7 million Americans who served in the theater of war and $67 billion spent between 1950 and 1953 required that Koreans appear worthy, while the damage wrought by the US military during the war necessitated explanations.[5] When China entered the war, the US military relentlessly bombed North Korea, creating a wasteland between the 38th parallel and the Chinese border. On a single day in November 1950, seventy B-29s dropped 550 tons of incendiary bombs on Sinuiju, "removing [it] from off the map."[6] The bombs often came at night. Upon hearing the explosions, mothers grabbed their babies who slept next to them. As they ran away from burning villages, some realized that they were gripping a rice pillow instead of the child, a grave mistake made in the panic and darkness of night.[7] North Koreans and the Chinese also used bombs, but the United States caused the bulk of the damage, which left nary a building standing and a disturbingly high civilian death toll in its wake.[8]

The US military could not easily hide its destruction of Korea. US power had to be remade to mitigate America's violent role in the war. Domestically, a rescripting was necessary to convince Americans to support a war that was supposed to be a "limited military action," but soon dragged on with no clear end in sight. Internationally, decolonizing nations needed proof that the United States practiced the democracy that it preached. Amidst these pressures, the Korean child emerged as a possible solution on both fronts. When placed under the care of the United States, Korean children could be seen as part of America's imagined family, an innocent in need of rescue.

1

GIs and the Kids of Korea

The proximity of the Korean War to World War II made for easy, if unflattering, comparisons. Pulitzer Prize–winning World War II cartoonist Bill Mauldin remarked that the Korean War was an "unglorious" one, where news of soldiers killed in action might appear only in hometown papers "on page 17 under a Lux [soap] ad." Mauldin predicted that the Korean War veteran would not come home to a parade, but rather would return quietly and alone, for "there's no victory in the old-fashioned sense, anyway, because this [wasn't] that kind of war. It [was] a slow, grinding, lonely, bitched-up war."[1] What began as a "pint-sized" military action quickly escalated, causing some to fear that this was the start of World War III.[2] The US military faced new challenges in Korea. US soldiers could not distinguish friend from foe, a problem made worse by North Korean guerrilla fighters who hid guns under women's robes. Panicked allied soldiers opened fire, killing thousands of innocent Korean civilians.[3] US fighter planes strafed refugees walking along roads and bombed dams to flood entire villages suspected of harboring guerrilla fighters.[4] At No Gun Ri in July 1950, US soldiers indiscriminately killed several hundred civilians, including infants and the elderly.[5] News from the front made it difficult for Americans to embrace its servicemen who were responsible for the death of countless Korean civilians. War had indeed taken a turn in Korea.

As the United States emerged a new superpower after World War II, the Korean War acted as a litmus test used to gauge America's behavior in the Pacific and the world more broadly. It was in this context that the US soldier fighting in Korea became a liability. If American men in Korea conjured visions of detached violence, how could they represent the integrity of American democracy? The American GI had to be re-made to conceal his most abject elements. Aaron Belkin describes how the US military asks its soldiers to embody traits that are framed as binary

opposites—strong/weak, dominant/subordinate, victor/victim, civilized/
barbaric, stoic/emotional—and how these irreconcilable paradoxes have
to be smoothed over to extend the reach of American empire. Mary
Renda considers how during the US occupation of Haiti from 1915 to
1934, paternalism did more than veil US military violence, it served as a
vehicle for it.[6] In Korea, to meet the conflicting needs of US Cold War
policy, American soldiers were asked to communicate proper manhood
and humanity, while committing unprecedented violence.

Amidst these pressures emerged a corrective antidote: the Korean
child. When placed in relation to American GIs, the child helped to recast US violence into acts of rescue. The children did what the military
alone could not—they transformed military force into tales of salvation,
redemption, and even love. This chapter centers upon the making of
these relationships—ones that were mandated by US military officials
and filmed by the Department of Defense for the world to see—as well
as the unintended bonds that developed from these points of contact,
intimate relationships that ran counter to the needs of a military that
wanted its men to fight a war, not play fathers to Korean children.

US Militarization from Occupation to War

In 1945, at the start of US occupation in South Korea, US officials
scrambled to get their bearings in a country with which they had minimal previous contact. The Supreme Commander for the Allied Powers
(SCAP) and the Armed Forces Assistance to Korea (AFAK) explained
that occupation occurred "so rapidly that preparations for civil affairs
activities in the area were far from complete, both in terms of policy
directives and personnel."[7] Mass migration to the south exacerbated the
problem. Between 1945 and 1949, nearly two and a half million people
flooded into South Korea. According to the United Nations Korean
Reconstruction Agency (UNKRA), by 1946 the American zone contained almost 70 percent of Korea's entire population, about seventeen
million people. The US military, the largest US entity in South Korea,
helped occupation administrators stabilize and monitor the growing
population. The US military collected census data and executed emergency health measures, like DDT dusting and smallpox vaccinations;
it worked alongside AFAK and the Korea Civil Assistance Command

(KCAC) to build schools and manage agricultural production. These activities linked the US military to Korean civil affairs, a connection that would grow in the years to come.[8]

While the US military helped with a broad range of US occupation needs, it remained steadfast in its primary duty—to train and build a Korean army. During occupation, US military administrators transformed the small Korean army trained under Japanese rule into the Republic of Korea (ROK) army, numbering 100,000 men. US military officers taught Korean cadets US-style combat, military organization, and discipline, and set up a school modeled after West Point Academy. At the end of occupation in 1948, when US and Soviet troops were supposed to leave the peninsula, US military advisors stayed on. They deemed it necessary, claiming that Koreans were incapable of administering their own army and not yet strong enough to face a possible Soviet attack.[9] The Orientalist pretext that justified continued US military presence soon found political backing.

In 1950 Paul Nitz, the chief of the Policy Planning Staff of the State Department, drafted National Security Council Report 68 (NSC-68), which outlined Soviet plans to carry out nuclear attacks in Alaska, Canada, and the United States.[10] Claiming that the USSR sought to "impose its absolute authority over the rest of the world," the writers of NSC-68 demanded the extension of US policies and influence to decolonizing countries in Africa, Asia, and Latin America.[11] Months after its publication, Dean Acheson, then acting secretary of state and one of the policy paper's advisors, committed US air and ground forces to Korea's civil war. During the Korean War, President Truman implemented the policies outlined in NSC-68 by increasing US defense expenditures, atomic capabilities, and military aid to Korea fourfold.[12] By 1952, the United States had committed 350,000 ground troops to add to 448,000 South Korean soldiers. United Nations allies committed 12,000 British, 8,500 Canadian, 5,000 Turkish, and 5,000 Filipino soldiers, and fewer than 1,000 from each of the other eleven allied nations.[13] The rapid buildup and extent of US military commitments in wartime Korea cemented the indefinite place of the US military in the peninsula.

At the outset, 81 percent of Americans were in support of the war. However, a couple of months into the conflict, when China entered, 49 percent of the American population deemed the war misguided.[14] By January 1, 1951, two-thirds of the American public wanted to remove

US troops, and 50 percent believed that President Truman had made a mistake when he decided to enter Korea.[15] The drop in public support had much to do with news coming from the front. For the first six months of the war, scores of Western journalists reported from the battlefield without formal censorship.[16] A February 1951 *New York Times* article described in grim detail how US bombers unleashed napalm on unsuspecting villagers, who were killed while going about their daily routines—children playing in an orphanage, a housewife ordering from a Sears Roebuck catalogue, all frozen in death by napalm.[17] This was the first time that many had heard of the gelling agent that would become all too familiar when the United States waged war in Vietnam a decade later.[18] North Korean news outlets broadcast reports of women and children slain by American bombs. It was difficult to refute the accusations. By December 1952, the United States had dropped upon North Korea almost twice the tonnage of bombs used in Japan during all of World War II.[19]

In May 1951, Truman tried to address the harrowing outcomes of war. Echoing the anti-communist language of the Truman Doctrine and Marshall Plan, he declared that US military action in Korea was guided by a "universal human wish" for Koreans to be as "independent, and united—as they want to be." Positioning the United States as a mere supporter in Korea's quest for freedom from communism, Truman claimed that the United States was a secondary player in their war. In his speech, Truman also defended America's broader Asia policy. He assured the public that his administration did "not want Formosa or any part of Asia for ourselves," reiterating that "we believe in freedom for all the nations of the Far East . . . [and] want to help them secure for themselves better health, more food, better clothes and homes, and the chance to live their own lives in peace."[20] Truman's words addressed international accusations of US imperialism, while the parallel that he drew between freedom and material goods promoted the capitalist goals of an American empire seeking to secure global markets.

In Korea, few saw the United States in these idealistic terms. Beginning with US occupation in 1945, US forces imposed an uneven mix of colonial management and heavy-handed oppression. The US Army Military Government in Korea (USAMGIK) controversially filled top-level positions with Koreans who had worked for the previous Japanese colonial government. US administrators refused to recognize the Korean People's Republic and suppressed protests.[21] The relationship between the US military and local Koreans continued to deteriorate during the war. News of servicemen behaving badly circulated in the US and South Korean press. In December 1950, the *New York Times* reported that some American GIs responded to the "heartbreak of retreat" by looting stores in Seoul. A spokesman for the US Eighth Army in Korea corroborated these reports, noting an increase in the number of homicides and crimes committed by American soldiers.[22] US servicemen started drunken brawls, brandished guns, and "molested" women on the streets, incidents that led the Provost Marshal in Seoul to close dance halls and change the curfew for American servicemen from 9:00 to 7:00 p.m.[23]

The permeating presence of the US military and the extreme devastation of war complicated Korea's path to sovereignty. Once China entered, it became clear that Korea would need the US military to fight the war and US aid to help Korean civilians harmed by it. President Rhee's visit to an orphanage reflected the contradictions of Korea's growing dependence upon the United States. On August 15, 1951 to commemorate Korea's Independence Day, Rhee visited 463 children housed at Joyful Mountain orphanage.[24] That Rhee invited Korean journalists to report on this event held at an orphanage operated by a US Army officer was not happenstance, and in fact revealed the fraught relationship between the nations. While the United States was one of the reasons why Korea was divided and not independent in the first place, and its bombs a primary contributor to the need for Korean orphanages, Korea had little choice but to rely even more heavily upon the United States during and after the war.[25] This was especially true when it came to the welfare of its children. According to *Kyŏnghyang sinmun*, in February 1952 over 100,000 children were orphaned by the war.[26] While the Korean National Assembly increased its welfare budget, it could hardly maintain the existing orphanages and failed to meet the growing needs of children as the war progressed.[27]

The ROK government recognized its reliance upon US military and economic aid, and harnessed the relationship between US servicemen and Korean children to garner additional US military support.[28] In 1951 the Republic of Korea's Office of Public Information (OPI) published letters from Korean children who thanked UN soldiers for their war efforts. Translated into English and printed alongside photos of the child authors and images of Korean palaces, parks, and pictur-esque landscapes, *Letters to Tall Soldiers from Small Koreans* brimmed with gratitude. Children thanked soldiers for leaving their homes to defend Koreans from communism, and assured them that the "blood shed in Korea [would] not be in vain" as Korean children would "repay [their] kindness" when they grew up.[29] The booklet conveyed to American soldiers, who made up 90 percent of the UN armed forces, that Korea was a promising bet for democratic futures.[30]

The thinly veiled propaganda of the letters served both the ROK and US governments by framing the war as necessary to protect Korea's chil-dren. The elementary and middle school–age children who purportedly wrote the letters had an unusually firm grasp of the political stakes of this war. Ahn Jung Ai wrote, "I am anxious to go back to my home in Seoul. But I don't worry about my house being destroyed by bombing. Bomb as you wish so that the bad men of the Communist party may be wiped out of this land. I hope Korea will be made free and democratic."[31] While the OPI's use of Korean children to bolster US military support was over-wrought, it built upon an existing framework that placed Korean chil-dren under the protection of American men, the latter a relationship that proved useful for a US military intent upon assuaging its violent participa-tion in the war.

From Battlefront to Orphanage

Bringing American GIs together with local children was a strategy employed in US-occupied Japan to help transform the recent enemy into a nonthreatening ally. Naoku Shibusawa describes how American GI relationships with Japanese children paved the way for US control of Japan's postwar rehabilitation. In December 1949, the SCAP ordered all of the army units in Osaka to visit an area orphanage. Master Sergeant Hugh O'Reilly went a step further, convincing his regiment to adopt a local orphanage. Shibusawa explains how the story that was later turned into a Hollywood film, *Three Stripes in the Sun* (1955), came to represent American GIs "on their very best behavior," helping Americans forget the horrors of war, including the air raids responsible for turning many children into orphans in the first place.[32]

When US servicemen stationed in Japan were transferred to Korea at the outset of war, they arrived already accustomed to interacting with local children, but in Korea the US Eighth Army created policies to make these points of contact a formal and regular part of their duties. US military chaplains coordinated opportunities for men to play with children and deliver food and supplies to local orphanages. US Army chaplain Robert Sherry's log from December 1950 describes the kinds of activities carried out by the men in his unit: host the "orphan girls" of St. Paul's Orphanage midnight Christmas mass at army headquarters; transport money, food, and clothing to a local orphanage; bring gifts to orphanages near Taegu; deliver a thirteen-year-old "orphan girl" to an orphanage; arrange for an orphan group to put on a Christmas program at the army chapel; distribute apples and hot chocolate to four hundred orphans; and organize a party where "orphans sang and danced to show their appreciation."[33] Extending the work started by the US occupation military, the US Army Corps also sponsored and helped build school-houses and playgrounds near its units.[34] Orphanage signs that prominently displayed the sponsoring US military division in English and Korean evidenced the institutionalized structures that actively brought US military men together with Korean children.

For the US military, these kinds of connections served two important functions: they boosted soldier morale and improved the reputation of the US military with locals. The children gave American GIs hope and something concrete for which to fight in the ideological contest of the Cold War; they were the "symbols of the clean and decent things the homesick soldier have [sic] left behind."[35] News of US servicemen coming to the aid of Korean children helped Koreans see the US military in a more positive light.[36] In February 1952, Dong-A Ilbo, one of South Korea's premier newspapers, described how Koreans were heartened by US soldiers who built orphanages near bases. In July 1952, the daily newspaper published a story about a new US military-constructed orphanage that gave three hundred orphans a chance to start a new life off the streets. Dong-A Ilbo explained that US military men wrote home to family and friends, who gave generously to help fund construction projects and supply food and clothing for the children, a description that extended the generosity of US soldiers to Americans living in the United States.[37] In 1953 Kyŏnghyang sinmun praised a US soldier for adopting a war orphan.[38]

News of American men helping Korean children also offered a way for Americans to make sense of the war. US censorship fluctuated from few restrictions at the outset of war to a formal code instituted in December 1950 to more loosened control by the end of 1952.[39] Regardless of censorship rules, heartwarming stories of children with American GIs were always welcome. In fact, Korean children took center stage in the comprehensive public relations program rolled out by the US government during the war. Edward R. Barrett, former executive editor at *Newsweek* and propaganda chief during World War II, headed up the US State Department Office of Public Affairs and was put in charge of managing news from Korea. He placed public relations officers in various fields, including the Eighth Army in Korea, while the US government supplied needed funds and camera equipment to produce footage from the front.[40] The Department of Defense (DoD), which in 1947 brought the army, navy, and air force together under the direct control of the secretary of defense, contributed to the public relations effort. In addition to executing military strategy, the DoD took on the task of producing countless hours of footage for public consumption.

Paramount News, *Movietone News*, and *The Big Picture*, the latter a weekly report on the US Army that aired on 320 television stations, spliced DoD footage into their newsreels.[41] Judging from the content of these newsreels, the DoD and AFAK, which did much of the filming, had two favorite subjects: US machines of war, including tanks, planes, and ships; and soldiers providing aid to Korean civilians. Unpublished reels included clips of American GIs playing with Korean orphanage children, unloading boxes of donated goods from large trucks, and dropping money onto donation plates. In one scene, a US soldier held up a sweater to a young Korean boy to gauge sizing. Much of the footage showed American men helping Korean civilians, especially children.

Universal-International Newsreel producers selected from the DoD raw footage for its twice-weekly news reports that were shown in theaters across the United States. In many of the edited segments, US military prowess appeared alongside humanitarian efforts, making GIs look both fierce and bighearted. For instance, the April 26, 1951 newsreel began with battle scenes from Korea and then segued into a story about Korean orphans. "Spring is a bloody time in Korea," the announcer remarked as the camera cut to an orphanage, "but the spirit of spring is unbound in the hearts of these South Korean War waifs. They line up in one of the most heartwarming fashion shows this uncertain spring season." The ensuing shots show US servicemen piling clothes into the arms of Korean children, who formed a long, orderly line that stretched out the door. Marine Corps League members from across the United States gathered the clothing for that particular drive. As two marines pulled a dress over the existing tattered clothes of a young girl, the narrator reassured viewers that the "war is a long way from their minds . . . for a while."[42] The joy with which the US Marines distributed the clothes and interacted with the children worked in tandem with the previous footage of tanks and bombs; from battlefront to orphanage, the men fulfilled their dual duty in Korea as rugged fighters of war and kindhearted caretakers of children.

While DoD cameramen captured these moments of exchange to communicate positive images of the war to audiences at home and abroad, they also caught responses of children that did not always fit the intended narrative. A look at Christmas celebrations in local orphanages, footage that appears frequently across DoD film reels, revealed the imperial tensions underlying American rescue.[43] At Christmas, US Army chaplains and orphanage directors had the children put on shows for US servicemen who came bearing gifts.[44] A 1953 unpublished DoD reel captures Christmas Eve in an auditorium filled with over a hundred Korean children. A US serviceman dressed as Santa Claus waves at the crowd and pats several children on the head as he walks by. The boys and girls look bewildered, having never seen Santa Claus before or known anything about him. One girl furrows her brow in concern. The children are curious as they strain to get a better glimpse of the man in red, now sitting on stage. The next scene takes place outside the orphanage, where three young Korean girls sit on the laps of two white servicemen. The men smile and talk to them, but the girls sit still and stare at the camera, unable to understand what the men are saying. It is not until one of the soldiers gives them hot cocoa that the girls begin to smile. Footage from the Yong Dong Po orphanage similarly reveals the strains of military-mandated interactions with Korean children. In the first shot, children line up to receive gifts. A tall serviceman dressed as Santa hands one boy a stuffed animal and points to the camera, encouraging him to smile. The boy stands motionless. After some more prompting, he holds up the little cat, but is still unable to smile.[45] At another orphanage, small Korean girls dressed in white frilly dresses and boys in miniature US Navy uniforms perform a dance for US servicemen. The children move stiffly through the choreographed moves; their seriousness is in stark contrast to the American men sitting in the audience, who smile easily and speak animatedly with one another.

The camera captured the extent to which relationships between American GIs and Korean children were forged. That the interactions were not organic was evidenced by the children who seemed unclear about the intentions of US soldiers and perplexed by Christmas traditions. These gatherings, while they came with toys and clothing for the children, were also for the servicemen, a way to bring a little bit of home to far-off Korea. The films were supposed to balance the violence wrought by US servicemen with visions of domestic care at the hands of these same men. Yet the moments caught on film could not contain the US imperialist structures that framed these interactions. While Americans brought much-needed support to the children, they also imposed Western, Christian traditions. The men appeared to be blind to the children's tentativeness. Caught up in the festivities that were bright spots in an otherwise bleak war, the men did not seem to recognize how in the context of war, they may have appeared strange and perhaps even frightening to the children. For the youngsters, bombs were delivered by the very same men who now arrived bearing gifts. The children were in the orphanage because their parents were killed or because they were separated from their families amidst the chaos of evacuation. While the children's faces conveyed this trauma, the American men around them carried on with their merrymaking; they laughed boisterously and spoke to the children, who were muted amidst all of the commotion.

The uneven power dynamics in these films are stark. Korean children were a necessary part of the US rescue narrative, and this need trumped a critical engagement with their pain and loss.[46] Even more, and to complete their scripts of rescue, military officials hoped to capture the happy faces of Korean children. The fissures within this project appeared in the unpublished footage. The children did not choose the circumstances that resulted in their placement in the orphanage, nor did they have the power to deny the soldiers or cameramen access to that space, but they could choose not to perform the desired responses of joy and gratitude. Even at the prompting of American men, many children refused to smile. These unscripted reactions that were caught on film complicated US narratives of rescue, and tellingly never made it past the cutting room floor.

Korean Boy Mascots and Democratic Futures

While the DoD primarily compiled stock footage that could be easily spliced into newsreels, it also tried its hand at scripting mini-films with complete story arcs. Using a clipboard as a makeshift Hollywood clapperboard, the DoD displayed the title of one of these shorts, "Orphanage Story." The tale opens with a small Korean boy crouched alongside a country road, rubbing his hands together as he tries to keep warm (figure 1.1). Two Korean women carrying large bundles on their heads walk past the child, but do not stop to help him. A moment later, a jeep enters the scene and stops. An American GI climbs out and squats down to talk to the boy. The previous scene shows the same GI introducing the presumed orphan to his new caretakers at an orphanage. While filmed out of sequence, the scenes together told a complete story. While the Korean women, the assumed natural caretakers, passed the child by, it was the American GI who stopped to bring him out of the cold and into the warm shelter of a local orphanage. In this film, the DoD made American men the unequivocal saviors of Korea's children, the only ones who could help them in the midst of war.

The DoD short dovetailed with stories published in mainstream media outlets, like *National Geographic* and the *Saturday Evening Post*, that also typically centered upon the relationships between American GIs and Korean boys. While images of servicemen holding little girls was prevalent in DoD footage, where the sheer number of orphanage children made it impossible for the men not to interact with both genders, popular stories often circulated around Korean boys. Korean girls complicated narratives of rescue. Cho Kyu Hwan, director of Angel's Haven Social Welfare Foundation in Seoul, recalled that few girls could be found on US military bases because their parents and caretakers forbade them to be around military men. Incidents of rape throughout the war made Koreans vigilant about protecting young girls.[47] This context and the added benefit that boys could convey a soldiering nationalism

Figure 1.1. A Korean orphan huddles on the side of the road before an American GI stops to help. US Department of Defense, "Orphanage Story," 1952 (raw footage). National Archives, College Park, MD.

made the Korean boy a logical figure through which to communicate democratizing scripts of rescue.

In these narratives, American men did more than rescue the boys, they also instilled in them US lessons on masculinity and loyalty. One popular story took place aboard the USS *Whitehurst* in 1951. In a DoD short, the film opens with a shot of the ship from afar with a Republic of Korea flag blowing in the wind. The camera then cuts to a young Korean boy aboard the navy vessel scrubbing the hull of the ship, hammering on the deck, and wiping down large guns. He wears a perfectly tailored US Navy uniform and smiles freely at the camera. In one scene, he takes his place alongside US sailors lined up for inspection. Though he stands tall with his chest puffed out, he is considerably smaller than the other men. The colonel stops to fix the boy's crooked lapel and give him a smile before moving down the line. The camera then cuts to a "liberty card" that includes the boy's signature and his newly given American name, "Jimmy."[48] In the final scene, earnest and proud, Jimmy salutes the camera with a large, undulating American flag as his backdrop.

The boy in this story was Pon Sun Se, whom the seamen nicknamed Jimmy Pusan. *Stars and Stripes* regaled readers with his valiant story. During the "Red Invasion," Jimmy's parents were killed and he was injured. He managed to climb onto the roof of a southbound train. When he reached Pusan, two US servicemen found "the little refugee that went straight to their hearts" and decided to bring him aboard the USS *Whitehurst* for a shower and a good meal. Major General Evans arranged for Jimmy to go to the S.O.S. Orphanage and Clinic, but by morning Jimmy found his way back to the ship. From that day forward, the crew made the boy an "honorary seaman" and member of the gunnery department. Jimmy dutifully swept his compartment and shined shoes, and every payday the crew saw to it that something went into Jimmy's special account. The army writer ruminated that the Navy took the child in, but in reality, the "bright-eyed Korean orphan . . . adopted the Navy."[49]

Together, DoD footage and photographs printed in the *Stars and Stripes* evidenced a marked change in the boy during his time aboard the *Whitehurst*. The film starts with the Korean flag but ends with the young Korean boy standing at attention in front of a larger American flag. In less than a minute, the DoD film transformed Jimmy from a Korean child to an American sailor; an orphan to a member of the US military family; a nonwhite other won to American democracy. At times, he was figured as even better than his American counterparts. In one scene, Jimmy walks up to a young naval officer sitting on the deck. Pointing to the three stripes on his own uniform, he smiles and pokes good fun at the white naval officer, who has only two. The short film chronicled how American sailors taught Jimmy the most important lessons of US militarism: masculinity, discipline, and loyalty. Much more than a navy mascot, this film suggested that Jimmy had been transformed into a son of American militarized democracy.

In 1952 Americans at home got to meet Jimmy Pusan. Benjamin "Stookie" Allen, well-known cartoonist and recent World War II veteran, selected Jimmy to be one of his "Keen Teens." Allen started the cartoon series in 1947 to showcase the good work of American teens, and to counter news of juvenile delinquents circulating at this time.[50]

Figure 1.2. Stookie Allen's cartoon of Jimmy Pusan as a "Keen Teen." Stookie Allen, "Keen Teens," *Miami Daily News*, April 1952.

The cartoon appeared in fifty newspapers. Alongside his illustrations of Anglo-Americans like Paul Nielsen, the eighteen-year-old photographer who worked for a "big-time newspaper," and Donna Marxer, the sixteen-year-old fashion editor of the youth page in the *Miami Daily News*, came Jimmy Pusan, the "Korean waif" turned American GI (figure 1.2).[51] Allen illustrated Jimmy saluting, mirroring his parting shot in the DoD reel, and asking a sailor to "cut it like GI!," replicating the photograph that appeared in the *Stars and Stripes* a year earlier (figure 1.3).

Jimmy was able to demonstrate American loyalty that passed the muster of men aboard the USS *Whitehurst* even though he was not a serviceman, and became a model American teenager even though he lived in Korea. Jimmy not only embodied core American ideals, he excelled at them. According to "Keen Teens," he learned to speak English in just two months. His exceptional ability to be American told a story that extended well beyond himself. It was through Jimmy that the success, generosity, and commitment of US sailors could be conveyed. As Jimmy's mentors, the young men fighting in Korea assumed the role of older brother or father, a designation that made them at once responsible and mature. When seen alongside Jimmy, these men were not the deliverers of violence, but rather American representatives capable of winning the hearts and minds of Korea's youth. Beyond the cultural optics, the project of Americanization had additional material benefits. Jimmy acted as a valuable spy and translator for the US military, a role often given to Korean mascots during the war. Jimmy furthered military strategy in ways both symbolic and concrete.

That Jimmy's story circulated via the DoD, *Pacific Stars and Stripes*, and US newspapers signaled the value and portability of the Korean

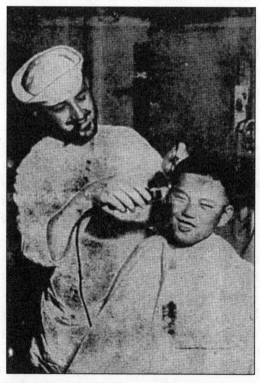

Figure 1.3. American sailor gives Jimmy Pusan a GI buzz cut. *Pacific Stars and Stripes*, June 30, 1951, 3.

mascot narrative. On April 14, 1953, the *Reporter* told of another boy who was found crying over the body of his mother. US marines tried to console him with a chocolate bar, hence giving him the nickname "Chocoletto" for how the child pronounced the sweet treat. The young boy followed the battalion to the base, where he stayed with the men. He sat alongside them to watch American movies and mimicked the marines who whistled at the pretty girls on screen.[52] Like many of the Korean boys who were temporarily adopted by individual US servicemen or entire battalions, Chocoletto became a houseboy who washed clothes, shined shoes, tidied the barracks, and guarded the servicemen's belongings in exchange for shelter, a portion of food rations, clothing, and gear.[53] Like Jimmy Pusan, Chocoletto was an invaluable translator who helped US soldiers communicate with Korean locals. And, as was the case for Jimmy, military men became Chocoletto's new family, saving him from homelessness, while the boy saved them right back by providing comfort and giving them purpose in the war.

In May 1953, *National Geographic* introduced readers to Kim, a Korean boy who lost his father in the war. The American GI who wrote the article, Robert Mosier, found Kim roaming the streets in search of a job and took him in to help around the base. Although Kim's widowed mother lived nearby, Mosier emphasized that he had adopted the fifteen-year-old houseboy. During his time at the base, Kim referred to spaghetti, ice cream, and candy as "No. 1 chow," plastered his portion of the tent with pictures cut from American magazines, learned English quickly, marveled over the concept of free school for American children, and became convinced that "all Americans either rode horses or drove Cadillacs" or held up banks and "peppered each other with six-guns on the street."[54] The cowboy analogy regularly made its way into stories about Korean mascots, from what they wore to what they played. A photograph of three "young cowboys, just off the Korean range" who enthusiastically peruse a *Roy Rogers* comic book appeared in same article (figure 1.4). The youngest boy in the middle wears cowboy boots and a broad smile. The fact that they could probably not read the comic was beside the point. The gendered symbolism of the cowboy made them seem less foreign, and aligned them with typical American boys who played out western fantasies. This staged photograph, which appeared in several wartime publications alongside other articles featuring children

Figure 1.4. Three Korean boys read *Roy Rogers*. "Young Cowboys, Just off the Korean Range, Relax with Roy Rogers." Robert H. Mosier, "The GI and the Kids of Korea," *National Geographic*, May 1953, 649.

in cowboy outfits, cultivated the trope of the Americanizable Korean child, a precursor to postwar productions of the quickly assimilating Korean War adoptee.[55]

Media depictions of Korean mascots introduced Americans at home to Koreans in new and meaningful ways. Touching narratives of "soft-hearted marines" who could not pass the children by, of a Korean child "who refuse[d] rice after tasting GI food," and of a boy "adopted" by a US Navy battalion who treasured a US care package that included "two authentic Hopalong Cassidy six-shooters, a pair of high Texas boots, and a Mexican sombrero"—a kit that ironically recalled America's past hostile conquests that some argued was now happening in the Pacific—helped to humanize the war for a doubtful American public.[56] Personal interest stories like those of Jimmy Pusan, Chocoletto, and Kim said as much about Korean children—and, given the dearth of information about Koreans in the United States at this time, about Koreans in general—as they did about US servicemen. The children helped to transform the American GI. It was through their fatherly relationship with Korean children that the young men displayed kindness, capability, and responsibility. The popular constructions mitigated the consequences of violent warfare by focusing instead on the recuperative ability of servicemen to save Korean children from homelessness and hunger, while instilling core American values of democracy and US militarism along the way. By the war's end and through his relationship to the Korean child, the US military man was redeemed.

Exceeding the Bounds of Sentiment

According to an American bishop stationed in Korea, the American GI quickly "[lost] his heart" to the children. Bill Powers described the Korean baby boy that he and the crew of the Point Cruz aircraft adopted as "a little godsend" who gave the men a chance to "reminisce about the things [they] missed at home."[57] During the war, soldiers with the help of the US military raised $34 million to help orphans in the Seoul vicinity alone.[58] The level of support had grown so considerably by the war's end that one Korean journalist wondered who would aid the children in the absence of the US military.[59]

US servicemen began to assist local orphanages on their own outside of the regular points of contact facilitated by military administrators. One serviceman explained that he "fell completely in love with [the children] and . . . began to visit them every spare moment [he] had."[60] Sŏng Kyŏ Hŭi, whose father founded and acted as the director of Friendship Orphanage located near a US base in Pusan during the war, remembered that as soon as American GIs took notice of her father's efforts, they delivered lumber so that he could build a larger orphanage. The men regularly brought food scraps to be re-boiled for the hungry children and, though milk was scarce, supplied it whenever they could.[61]

GIs wrote home relaying stories about the smallest victims of the war that tugged at the sensibilities of Americans who lived in a country of plenty, especially during the post–World War II consumerist boom.[62]

The personalized appeals for help spurred hundreds of communities into action, and women often led the call. Upon hearing of a "local boy" from Idaho who took seventy orphans under his wing in Korea, Pocatello residents collected enough clothes, toilet articles, and food to fill up a large truck.[63] In New Jersey, women's clubs knit sweaters and collected used clothing and canned food for the orphans of South Korea.[64] While nationwide campaigns sponsored by organizations, like the Cooperative for American Relief Everywhere (CARE), sought donations for Korean people more broadly, many of the local efforts rallied around a particular orphanage or group of children that Americans learned about from a hometown boy fighting in Korea. With just one degree of separation, the plight of Korean children quickly became a community matter best solved by women, for whom it was their presumed innate ability to nurture the children of war-torn Korea.

Whether military-mandated or initiated by individual servicemen, relationships between GIs and Korean children furthered military goals, but also confounded them. Though these relationships proved useful for a US government eager to redeem the negative image of its military men, officials were less thrilled when an increasing number of men invited Korean boys to live with them in the barracks. These requests were so widespread that teenaged houseboys could soon be found on nearly every US base.[65] Some of the boys had living parents who could not afford to care for them, others had lost their families in the war, but all shared a desperate need for food and shelter. For houseboys, the US military provided options amidst the ruins of war; some were able to receive much-needed medical care, while others received money that helped them survive.[66]

The Department of the Army (DoA) was displeased by these living arrangements. To begin, preexisting constructions of the Asian houseboy conjured visions of perversity, contamination, and unnatural gender inversions of the domestic realm.[67] A long history of houseboys in colonial settings and of Chinese male servants in white middle-class American homes at the turn of the century came to bear on understandings of Korean houseboys who cleaned barracks and tidied bunks in line with these familiar pejorative scripts. Yet the context of war expanded the role of the houseboy. Korean houseboys often also served as valuable interpreters and spies for the US military. A 1956 Red Cross pamphlet described a seventeen-year-old houseboy as "well-liked and admired for his ambition and apparently excellent native intelligence."[68] On the heels of World War II, amidst public trials that accused the Japanese of being spies, Korean houseboys figured as both loyal and critical to the success of the US military.[69] More than an Oriental supplicant, the Korean houseboy became an integral part of US military strategy.

While houseboys were deemed loyal, it remained problematic that they lived with American soldiers in the barracks. In the nearly all-male space of the US military, the intimate addition of the Korean houseboy raised the specter of pedophilia or pederasty and homosexual relations. To solve the lurking problem of homosexuality in the homosocial context of the military, soldiers passed along the very same lessons in hypermasculinity that they had followed while in the service. GIs brought the boys to American films and encouraged them to whistle at Hollywood starlets. They taught them the swagger of a heterosexual American man—expressively chewing gum, winking at ladies, and speaking in slang. The mature lessons, while not always appropriate for the young boys, who mimicked the behavior to the great amusement of the servicemen, proved critical to maintaining military scripts of heterosexuality.[70]

For Korean houseboys seeking adoption, the overt lessons in masculinity became a liability. One social worker described a former houseboy as being "sophisticated in sex matters" and using the "free and extravagant speech" typical of an American GI, behaviors that made it difficult for her agency to find an American couple who wished to adopt him.[71] The reputation of houseboys was well known. In a 1955 Steve Roper comic that appeared in the *Pacific Stars and Stripes*, a social worker whose job it was to remove a child from the barracks found the boy sitting next to smoked pipes and an open copy of a novel titled *Murder in the Mist*. The social worker urged the GI to place the already corrupted child in foster care so that he could have the proper guidance of two parents.[72] The intimate pairing of the GI and the Korean houseboy, even when adhering to heteronormative and gendered expectations, proved problematic when placed in the barracks, the soldiers' "home" on the military base.

Indeed, it was the fact that men played house with Korean boys that caused US military officials the greatest concern. Administrators grew wary of the emotional bonds that formed between its men and Korean houseboys when bunking together. The paternal role taken on by soldiers was not conducive to military goals; they were there to fight a war, not act as fathers to Korean children, commanders argued.[73] By taking up nurturing roles traditionally reserved for women, servicemen threatened the image of the military. A year into the war, men began making requests to formally adopt their houseboys and other children whom they met on and around the base.[74] US military commanders concluded that the men, many under the age of twenty, made rash decisions colored by the circumstances of war and their homesickness, and predicted that they would regret the life-changing decision to adopt once they returned to the States.[75] Hoping to sever these bonds, military administrators periodically evacuated houseboys and mascots living on the bases and moved the children to local orphanages. Men on the bases knew when the sweeps were coming and tried to prepare their little charges for the changes to come.[76]

Despite these obstacles, servicemen continued to request adoptions of Korean children. In 1945 Truman had set up a directive to allow for the entry of a certain number of "eligible orphans" to address the calamity of World War II, but there were no formal provisions for Korean children during the Korean War.[77] Complicating matters, given existing restrictive US immigration laws, the race of Korean children further limited their entry. This was largely uncharted territory, which explains in part the spotty correspondence and general confusion about how to handle military adoption requests. Records indicate that military commanders did not keep regular tabs on these requests during the war. Lists of servicemen who requested information about adoptions appeared sporadically in the US Department of State records. These notes were handwritten, reflecting the absence of an established protocol.[78] A 1955 memorandum lists the names of thirty-six servicemen who wished to adopt, suggesting that there were more on other bases who hoped to do the same. Starting that year, the commanding general of the Eighth Army began to collect more standardized records, typing the names of the servicemen and children undergoing the process of adoption.[79]

While it is difficult to ascertain exactly how many military men successfully adopted children during the war, army memos suggest that visa problems and other obstacles barred most adoptions from going through.[80] The process was purposely drawn out to make it challenging for soldiers to succeed. Young military men who wished to adopt needed their parents to act as the official guardians.[81] If parents agreed, they had to undergo home studies to assess whether or not they were financially stable and to determine whether the "Mongolian race [was] accepted in their circle of friends and acquaintances."[82] Some GIs worked around the barriers stacked against them by making spurious documents that declared children with still living parents in Korea to be true orphans, and faking the age of older boys so that they could be brought to America and avoid conscription into the Korean army, the latter mandatory for boys aged eighteen beginning in 1957.[83] Servicemen who successfully waded through the process explained that it took months to get through the red tape. When one American GI ran into continual delays while trying to adopt two Korean girls, a US official told him that it was "deliberate—just as in mixed marriages—to discourage impetuous boys who might regret their decisions later."[84]

Some military men were able to navigate the obstacles. On July 14, 1952, Mr. and Mrs. Victor Beauchamp of Orinda, California, carried out the wish of their son who died in battle by adopting the Korean boy whom their son had befriended.[85] On September 23, 1952, a *United Press* telegram announced the arrival of ten-year-old Rhee Song Wo, who came via special permission from Presidents Truman and Rhee. In April 1953, *Kyŏnghyang sinmun* announced that the mayor of Seoul granted an American soldier permission to adopt an orphan whom he grew to know during the conflict; he brought his adopted son to Oregon.[86] Melvin L. Clow brought "Roger" to Henderson, Nevada, on October 19, 1953.[87] Choi Kyung Hyun, renamed "Jimmy," came with GI Paul Raynor to live with him and his mother on December 9, 1953.[88] Sergeant Ravil B. Branham and his wife adopted "Little Ernie Joe," the three-foot-tall mascot who had stayed with Brown in Korea a full year prior to coming to Texas on June 15, 1954.[89] In 1954, army officer Dr. Ray Paull formally adopted a then sixteen-year-old Korean houseboy; named Paull Shin, the adoptee later became a Washington state senator and honorary president of the Global Overseas Adoptees' Link [90]

While stories of men with Korean boys dominated the mainstream press, around half of all military adoptions were of girls; and a portion of the children adopted were mixed-race children of American GIs.[91] Lieutenant Hugh C. Keenan adopted a "blue-eyed, blond" eight-month-old child "obviously of Caucasian parentage" just after the war. The child, "Little George," had lived aboard his navy ship beginning July 1953.[92] Mixed-race children were not widely adopted until after 1955, when figures like Harry Holt publicly advocated for their adoption, a topic discussed in part 2. Given military efforts to carefully narrate the stories of its men reaching the American public, it is unsurprising that news of mixed-race adoptions did not make the headlines. Such adoptions more readily highlighted the failures of the US military men who abandoned their children, and alluded to the more complicated figure of the Korean mother, an assumed prostitute.

The Department of the Army's uneasiness with the widespread live-in situation of Korean houseboys on US bases and its more active resistance to formal adoptions point to its inability to control the actions of its men. While it had initiated points of contact between soldiers and Korean orphans to promote a gentler side of American power, the military did not intend for the men to form permanent relationships with them, the latter a bond that signaled *too much* sentiment. In their involvement with the children, the military men crossed the line between being a fighting soldier and being an emotionally attached father to Korean children. These connections had implications beyond the military. The relationships between GIs and the kids of Korea cultivated affective ties between Americans at home and Korean children of the war. This and news of successful military adoptions introduced Americans to the possibility of overseas adoptions.

From bureaucratic hurdles that made it extremely difficult to procure visas to quickly expiring medical examinations required of all children leaving Korea, the DoD worked actively to prevent these adoptions. Yet most Americans and others who came to understand the military's relationship to Korea through mainstream media would know little of these efforts, as the stories that reached the public heralded boundless familial love made possible through American democracy, even in the midst of war.

The Korean Child as Healer and Bridge

On May 28, 1953, a US newsreel chronicled Song Yŏng Cho's arrival in the United States.[93] The Department of Defense footage captured the twelve-year-old boy walking confidently through a US airport, despite the fact that he had lost both feet from frostbite during the war. Mrs. Richard Gormanson waited for him on the tarmac and embraced Song the moment he stepped off the plane. It was her husband and several other GIs who "took the little waif in hand after finding him crawling through the streets of Seoul." In Korea, Sergeant Gormanson supplied Song with prosthetic feet, and the boy was now headed to Father Flanagan's Boys Town in Omaha. The narrator triumphantly reports that the boy is "smiling and happy. . . . The horrors of war are behind, and he walks confidently into a future where kindness prevails." Wearing a cowboy hat and a huge grin as he chewed vigorously on a piece of gum, Song signaled that he was well on his way to becoming American.

The newsreel brought the conflict to a tidy close, depicting for American audiences the generosity of American servicemen, as well as the technological and ideological power of the United States. When this newsreel reached the American public, the war was winding down and an armistice was in sight. By this point, it was clear that attempts to rout out communism from the Korean peninsula had failed, and Americans needed to grapple with the losses of war. Much like that of Lee Kyung Soo at the opening of this book, Song's story was less about him than it was about the nation. His ability to walk and the swagger with which he did so marked the success of Sergeant Gormanson specifically and the US military more broadly.

In this newsreel segment, what came home to America was not a military and political failure, but a young Korean boy who in spirit, culture, and politics signaled democratic futures. By telling stories of GIs who "lost their hearts" to Korean children, like Gormanson did to Song, the US military could spin the violence of war into a tale of salvation. Song embodied the changed American soldier who saved and repaired Koreans, body and soul. At the end of the segment, viewers were left with an image of Song waving and smiling as he walked out of the airport terminal. In that moment, Song bridged nations—he was the proxy through which Americans were asked to see the transformed US military man who in spite of war became a responsible caretaker. Song and fellow Korean mascots invited those at home to look upon Korea with sympathy and hope, as a soldier would a child.

2

US Aid Campaigns and the Korean Children's Choir

By 1952, over 2.6 million refugees flooded across the 38th parallel, adding to the 3.4 million war sufferers already in South Korea who needed
food, shelter, clothing, and medical care.[1] Cho Kyu Hwan, the orphanage director of Angel's Haven Social Welfare Foundation, recalled that
after the war "children were coming out of the eaves" and that there
were no structures or systems in place to help them.[2] According to Im
Yong Ok, head of overseas affairs at the Social Welfare Society (formerly Child Placement Service) in Seoul, the Korean government could
not afford to fund existing orphanages.[3] The stark needs of Koreans
after the war opened the door wide to aid workers from Australia, Britain, Canada, and other allied nations, but Americans led the charge,
arriving by the hundreds. The Eisenhower administration enthusiastically welcomed US missionaries, philanthropists, doctors, nurses, and
social workers who came to the aid of Koreans. Their efforts to help
Koreans freed up the US and ROK governments to focus on security
and reconstruction.[4] Stabilizing the Korean populace was a first step to
recovery and a necessary condition for the US government to implement its strategies to maintain a democratic stronghold in South Korea.
Non-military American citizens who fostered collaboration and cooperation with Koreans in their recovery efforts were critical to extending
US power in South Korea. Not only did they do important work for the
US government by aiding Koreans in need, they did so while promoting
visions of benevolent US leadership on the world stage.[5] In this project,
US missionaries led the way. Having already established roots in Korea
through proselytizing efforts dating back to the late nineteenth century,
US Presbyterian and Methodist missionaries operated schools, hospitals, churches, and orphanages that they had built over the first half of
the twentieth century, an extensive foreign mission project described
in part 2 of this book. Alongside US missionaries, an array of nongovernmental agencies that included the Christian Children's Fund,

American-Korean Foundation, CARE, Foster Parents Plan, and American Relief for Korea rushed to aid Korea's most vulnerable population, its children.

This chapter centers on the years immediately following the Korean War, when the responsibility of rescue shifted from US servicemen to average Americans. In the aftermath of an unsuccessful and costly war, US-South Korea relations needed to be reconfigured once again. Korean children remained the bridge that safely connected Americans to Koreans, yet shifting postwar politics required a distancing from the US military. To begin, the US military was responsible for much of the wartime destruction and maintained a large military presence afterwards; four years after the armistice was signed, 71,000 US servicemen were still stationed in South Korea. The United States also remained economically embroiled in South Korea. During the Eisenhower administration from 1953 to 1961, US appropriations for South Korea ranged from $200 million to $300 million annually.[6] Logistically, the scale of postwar needs far exceeded the abilities of US servicemen to address; constructions of military men rescuing Korean children had served their purpose, which was to garner support during the war. In this context, the shifting needs of the postwar era were met by aid organizations that took up the call to rescue Korea's children, producing new scripts that placed Americans at home at the heart of Cold War imagined family frames.

Making the American Rescuer

In March 1953, Howard A. Rusk, a physician, associate editor of the *New York Times*, and board chairman of the American-Korean Foundation (AKF), organized a committee to assess South Korea's postwar needs. His report estimated that there were a hundred thousand war orphans and eight to ten thousand "beggar street children."[7] One small hospital in Seoul cared for over four thousand children, which, the AKF explained, led to a massive spread of tuberculosis since children had to share beds. Rusk and his team doubted that fifty of the approximately four hundred existing orphanages in South Korea offered the "quality of care that would be comparable to the lowest standards tolerated in the United States."[8] Since many Americans first came to know Korea through the war, Rusk's postwar assessment corroborated existing Orientalist imaginings of Korea, made worse by the war. Yet Rusk assured readers that Koreans, "who [had] fought, suffered and died to be free," deserved to feel US "compassion of the warm person-to-person friendship and admiration which they ha[d] earned."[9]

After the war, US administrators, policy makers, and philanthropists connected Korea's child welfare crisis directly to the ongoing threat of communism. Leonard W. Mayo, director of the Association for the Aid of Crippled Children, stated that "the children of Korea offer[ed] a gild-edged investment. . . . Korea's young people [were] democracy's opportunity for a winning bet."[10] Even a decade after the war, the US Army Human Factors and Operations Research Unit maintained that children were critical to US foreign policy aims. The unit determined that humanitarian aid, particularly for children, remained the best way to gain the trust of Korean civilians and to allow the US Army to carry out its mission to control the area, maintain military force, and "win the Cold War."[11] While helping children could further democratizing projects, not helping them could prove catastrophic. The United Nations Korean Reconstruction Agency warned that "unless we all help, Korea's children will become like the lost generation of the Russian revolution who 30 years ago made history as the most terrifying example of childhood ruined by calamity and indifference."[12]

Cold War needs bolstered the efforts of religious and secular aid organizations, as well as their access to Korean civilians. The political benefits of aid allowed them to operate freely and expansively in South Korea. The agencies honed in on the needs of Korean children, so much so that their appeals often displaced the needs of Korean women, widows, and especially prostitutes, who were marginalized despite their victimization. In these constructions, the Korean children were no longer under the protection of American soldiers as they had been during the war. Rather than situating orphans alongside GIs, postwar scripts anchored their campaigns around the frail, solitary child to emphasize the desperation of children in need of American intervention. The appeals invited Americans to enact global citizenry from afar by donating to help the children pictured in their campaigns.

Photography, with its assumed authority to depict real events, was central to the making of the Korean waif-in-need. Photographs of Korean children with dirt-smudged faces and beseeching eyes drew Americans intimately into the tragedy caused by war, while asking them to help solve the problems that they saw therein. Close-up shots of a single child framed amidst the rubble of war made the child's needs all the more pressing. Just months after the armistice, a photograph appeared in *McCall's* magazine with the following caption: "This young girl, whose entire family may have been killed, clings desperately to all that she has left—the ruins of her home in Seoul."[13] The women's magazine pulled at the heartstrings of its American readership with this photograph of a child in an oversized shirt that made her appear even smaller against the broken remnants of what was once her home. With its subject positioned outside, alone, and under no one's supervision, the photograph insisted that viewers do something. American women wrote Young Han Choo, the consul general of the Republic of Korea, who was listed in the article as the person to whom packages could be sent, asking how they could adopt the children pictured in the article.[14]

The photographs communicated ready-made scripts—a child alone signaled homelessness, poverty, and the absence of parents, problems that could be partially solved through American donations.[15] Americans were already familiar with these kinds of appeals. Laura Briggs explains how during World War II, images of waifs in war-torn Europe and Asia encouraged the public to practically demand US entry into the war. Briggs argues that photographs of solitary children "recast international politics as family drama," whereby the United States could rescue a child from his "dreadful aloneness [and] incompleteness."[16] Korean War waif campaigns operated along this same trajectory, imploring Americans to see another's pain, and then act to help them.

Visualizing Korea's children was a necessary component of rescue, for it was through seeing the child in pain that viewers could envision themselves as rescuers. Photographers aimed for impact; the pictures were so devastating, so intimate, so uncomfortable that viewers were not to linger.[17] They were asked to see the immediate needs of the child rather than engage with the trauma that caused the child to be homeless in the first place.[18] Elaine Scarry explains that the effectiveness of an aid organization depends upon its ability to "communicate the reality of physical pain to those who are not themselves in pain."[19] She continues that the appeal must convey to the reader that suffering is happening "inside the body of someone whose country may be far away, whose name can barely be pronounced, and whose ordinary life is unknown." Rendering pain visible in these ways, Scarry concludes, is an "absolute claim for acknowledgement [that] contributes to its being ultimately unacknowledged."[20] When it came to Korean children, relief photographs asked Americans to step in at a moment *after* the events responsible for that child's condition had already transpired. What was the outcome of a series of wartime actions that resulted in the child's aloneness became the starting point for Americans who were seeing the child for the first time. The child was seen and unseen; her or his pain was made visible to incite a reaction that might solve that pain, not grapple with the possibility that US war machines and soldiers might have caused it.

The spectacle of the photograph itself foreclosed a deeper engagement with the experiences of the child pictured. The images worked within a familiar Orientalist framework, where looking was knowing. One need not spend much time with these photographs to become an expert on Korea and its inhabitants, and to determine one's relationship to (and above) those pictured. Through binary opposition, the photographs exposed the uneven power structures at play not only between Americans and Koreans, but also between the United States and South Korea. The photographs that pictured Korean children told the viewer more about themselves (and what they were not) in relation to that child than about the child himself or herself. These were the power dynamics that framed transnational American rescue after the war, ones that carried forth existing Orientalist practices of looking and knowing, but for purposes newly tailored to the evolving needs of the nation. Different from US Orientalism at the turn of the century, intended to keep Asians out of the United States, Orientalism of the Cold War era took an internationalist turn using the same binary logic, only this time to convince Americans that Orientals desperately needed and also deserved help.

Often left nameless, the anonymous children pictured in waif appeals allowed for a generic war sufferer that broadened who could participate in the rescue by also creating a generic American savior. Relief campaigns produced generalized scripts that positioned the West as the presumed rescuer of the East, binaries that naturalized delineations between wealthy and impoverished, powerful and weak. In these appeals, where the private pain of Third World children was made the public business of the First World, the rescuer was significantly better off, so much so that even a small offering carried the potential to alter the life of the child in need. Photographs confirmed the unequal relationships, while downplaying the imperialist traces inherent in these constructions. Furthering these scripts of First versus Third World, the campaigns placed the situation in clear economic terms, typically asking for US dollar amounts and then explicating how far that money could go in Korea. The American-Korean Foundation declared that a Korean orphan could be "maintained for about 20 cents a day."[21] Another appeal informed potential donors that a gift of one dollar could feed and house a Korean orphan for one day, while five dollars would provide a week's subsistence for a destitute family.[22] The amounts listed made it possible for any American, even the poor, to make a radical difference in the Third World.

According to these appeals, by US standards it took very little to sustain the life of a Korean. The comparisons evoked Orientalist logic that fueled anti-Chinese sentiment in the second half of the nineteenth century, when union leaders argued that rat-eating Chinese laborers undercut the wages of Irish workers, who needed meat and potatoes to subsist.[23] Determining the minimum amount of food needed to sustain life demarcated normal from abnormal, healthy from abject.[24] Though this time for the purpose of helping Asians, the postwar ads supported the same logic that the capacity of inherently weaker Asian bodies required less food. In the late 1950s, General Mills' Clifford E. Clinton introduced Multi-Purpose Food (MPF), a vegetable-base concentrate that claimed to "satisf[y] hunger, ha[d] a pleasing, nut-like flavor, [and could] be eaten dry or with liquids." Foreign medical doctors, like Dr. Albert Schweitzer and Dr. Tom Dooley, as well as political leaders like Richard Nixon and Eleanor Roosevelt promoted MPF, calling it "Friendship Food." A two-week supply for one adult took up less than one cubic foot of space and could be stored for up to five years, useful characteristics for what was intended to be lifesaving nutrition for Third World people. Just six ounces of MPF, which could be mixed in with ground beef to make "Oompf-Burgers," supplied the US daily allowance of protein, calcium, phosphorus, iron, iodine, vitamins A and D, thiamine, riboflavin, and niacin.[25] Beginning in 1960, the Meals for Millions program partnered with General Mills to send tens of thousands of pounds of MPF to South Korea, the "3 cent meals" for which the Korean government thanked the United States.[26] General Mills made great efforts to market MPF to Americans, but the product never took off—though apparently sufficient for ailing Third World bodies, it failed to meet the more rigorous biological needs of American ones.

The Christian Children's Fund (CCF), a well-known aid organization that garnered millions in donations for Third World children, illustrates the above described strategies of representation. J. Calvitt Clarke founded the organization, originally called the China Children's Fund, in 1938 to help Chinese children in the wake of the Sino-Japanese War.[27] The organization was among the first to monetize and systematize the symbolic "adoption" of children, a tactic that would be used in rescue appeals across the second half of the twentieth century.[28] Donors were invited to sponsor a child for a year, a long-term commitment that deepened the donor's level of engagement and sustained support for CCF operations. After World War II, the CCF politicized its appeals in the context of the Cold War. Clarke wrote that hungry children of the Third World were more dangerous than the atomic bomb.[29] Close-up photographs of thin children appeared alongside narratives that described the desperation of Third World children, who if left alone to suffer would be vulnerable to communist aggression. The heavy politicization of this religious organization's appeals linked the CCF with the broader goals of the state. The photographs became effective vehicles for these messages, what John Tagg describes as "wordless power." Tagg clarifies how the camera has the "authority to arrest, picture and transform daily life," while the photographer constructs and implements the photograph as a "register of truth," often for the intended purposes of the state.[30] The relationship between the US government and the work of internationalists like Clarke was symbiotic. In CCF photographs, Christian morality merged with the Cold War cultural needs of the state to appear non-imperialist and anti-racist, while communist fears underlying CCF appeals made the work of the religious organization politically relevant. The blurring of church and state helped showcase humanitarian aid over US militarization and governance in South Korea and other Asian countries.

The organization grew exponentially, and by the late 1950s boasted two thousand volunteers who helped raise $30 million. The CCF expanded its operations to South Korea, and added the country to its already long list of Third World peoples-in-need. Yet the recent war in Korea made its needs both unique and more acute. As well, the Korean children seen in CCF campaigns resonated with American donors, who catalogued these images alongside an existing compendium of recent wartime and postwar recovery appeals that pictured Korean waifs. One CCF brochure featured a photograph of a "starved Korean child, belly bloated, arms and legs like match sticks"—the single image raised nearly $500,000.[31] The stark difference between the child and the American looking at the image significantly increased the kinds of people who could participate in this international project of rescue. Donations came from a range of groups and individuals, including Sunday school classes, a "lonely government gal, living in a Washington hotel," and the "inmates of an institution for the criminally insane in Wisconsin."[32] The campaign emphasized that any American—even unmarried career women and the incarcerated—could help save the lives of those who were less fortunate.

The popularity of the CCF spurred the development of similar national campaigns, as well as more homegrown local efforts. At Halloween, UNICEF encouraged children to forgo candy and trick-or-treat for pennies and dimes for Korean children.[33] Local schools adopted Korean orphans, sending them money, food, and clothing in return for updates from the orphanage that included the children's pictures and report cards.[34] Nitro High School in Charleston, West Virginia, sponsored two Korean orphans who, according to letters, were excited to hear that they had been "adopted" by their "good friends" in the United States. In describing the children, the orphanage letter stated that though they practiced Buddhism, "they [were] eager to learn more about the western world."[35] Letter writing was a shared component of many of these campaigns, including the CCF, intimate personal connections that worked in tandem with President Eisenhower's People-to-People program, launched in 1956.[36]

In the years following the Korean War, US aid organizations produced and circulated images of the Korean waif that figured average Americans as the presumed saviors of these children. These campaigns gave Americans a way to enact international cosmopolitanism, an opportunity to materially connect with nonwhite peoples of the Third World, to cross divides of nation, race, and class.[37] The programs were structured expressly so that Americans could help Korean children over there, a way for them to be non-racist internationalists without having to confront these divisions at home. With the problems faced by Korean children taking place thousands of miles from the United States, Americans could safely participate in global integration without having to alter the practices of their daily lives.

For the Republic of Korea government, US-led aid campaigns garnered much-needed monetary support in the wake of the war, but the ubiquity of the waif imagery used to achieve these ends ran counter to the aims of the South Korean state. President Rhee and his administration were aware of how representations of a frail and impoverished Korea hampered the nation's sovereignty goals. South Korean administrators looked for alternative representations that would bring in postwar aid, but also figure Korea as distinctly on its way to becoming an independent nation. Administrators found its answer in the Korean Children's Choir, a healthy group of singing youngsters who had the potential to replace existing constructions of the waif at the center of current aid campaigns.

The Korean Children's Choir of 1954

During the postwar recovery period, Koreans were eager to represent themselves. While aware of the global reordering efforts underway at the 1955 Afro-Asian conference in Bandung, Koreans still suffering from the war focused primarily upon the immediate needs of their war-torn nation.[38] An array of Korean cultural producers aimed to replace negative images from the war with ones that proved Korea's capability for independence. The International Publicity League of Korea produced annual English-language photobooks called *Pictorial Korea* in which they portrayed Korea as a modern, sovereign nation.[39] In 1956, South Korean guidebook author Kyung Cho Chung stated that the Korean people were "struggling to restore their unity, liberty, and national dignity. . . . The Korean people [felt] that they, and not the major powers, should make decisions concerning their own destiny."[40] A year later, Chae Kyung Oh set out to produce the "most authoritative and comprehensive work on Korea ever published in the English language" because he was unhappy with the "florid and reflective fiction, hastily written 'guides' . . . [and] polemical non-fiction" written by Americans.[41]

In 1957 the ROK government spent over $41,000 for a sixteen-page spread in the *New York Times* that advertised Korean industrialization, economic recovery, and new business opportunities for US investors.[42] The piece outlined South Korea's progress in the four years since the war. President Rhee assured Americans that Korea would repay the United States by "attaining a level of economic self-sufficiency . . . where help no longer will be required."[43] Replacing images of "delousing operations, squalor and poverty" with those of tungsten factories, power plants, and reconstructed buildings, the newspaper ad demonstrated that South Korea, with the help and guidance of America, was well on its way to becoming an industrialized nation that would soon be able to stand on its own.[44]

South Korean cultural producers appealed to US readers' Orientalist expectations, while also strategically emphasizing Korea's difference from other Asian countries.[45] The Korea-sponsored *Times* spread described Korea in the following way:

> Korea . . . has cultural and historical attractions of the first order. Its music and its dancing are unique, related to the rest of the Orient, but, on the whole, much more appealing to Western tastes. Costumes and customs are colorful and also different from those of China, Japan and the rest of Asia. Particular fascination is to be found in the fact that Korea is in flux, a mixture of the old and the new. Both are observable everywhere, in country as well as city.[46]

Understanding the political liability of association, the ad distinguished Korea from communist China and recent US enemy Japan, instead aligning South Korea squarely with the United States. Political affinity with and loyalty to the United States, in concert with its striking Asian qualities, made South Korea the perfect place for Americans to "travel . . . , spend money, and increase Korea's dollar supply."[47] As Shirley Jennifer Lim argues, while reorientalization can reproduce some aspects of hegemonic power relations, it also presents "an opportunity to reracialize and reconfigure" them.[48] South Korea's ad rendered Korea as still exotic, but also modern, democratic, and desirable for US investors and visitors.

The Korean Children's Choir fit squarely with the ROK's broader strategy to modernize South Korea, while still representing the otherness that intrigued American audiences. The choir was a source of terrific national pride in Korea since before the war. Ahn Byŏng Wŏn, secretary of the Seoul Young Men's Christian Association, and Chung Dal Bin, chief chaplain of the Korean navy, founded the Korean Children's Choir in 1945 to celebrate independence from Japanese colonization.[49] After the Korean War, the choir came to represent endurance and hope for a unified future. James A. Van Fleet, retired general of the United Nations forces in Korea and chairman of the American-Korean Foundation, was so deeply moved by the children when he saw them perform in Korea that he asked if he could make them the headliners of the American-Korean Foundation's 1954 fundraising campaign. President Rhee enthusiastically agreed.[50] The choir became a savvy foray into transnational cultural politics that established Korea on a path in line with US democracy, but with its sights set upon eventual sovereignty and unification. In Rhee's estimation, the healthy choir was physical proof that although Korea needed US assistance, its resilient youth were a worthwhile investment.[51]

The choir also readily met the political and cultural needs of the US government. The singing children on US soil evidenced a Cold War exchange where Americans welcomed and generously donated to support South Korea, an outpouring of aid that Rusk likened to a "spontaneous eruption, like Vesuvius."[52] US reports of the children's tour situated them firmly in the context of US internationalism, making them ideal representatives that evidenced the benefits of US democracy. In April 1954, numerous news outlets announced the arrival of twenty-five "small-fry fresh from their war-shattered homeland" of Korea. Within minutes of landing at New York International Airport, the children sang songs in Korean and English, to the great delight of awaiting reporters and other onlookers. New York City representatives, the Korean consul, and members of the American-Korean Foundation enthusiastically welcomed the children. Even Lee Kyung Soo, the Korean War adoptee made famous by a recent spread in *Life* magazine, was there to welcome his fellow countrymen. Five-year-old Lee waved a Korean flag and chatted excitedly in Korean with the other children. Richard C. Patterson Jr., the chairman of Mayor Robert F. Wagner's reception committee, praised the children by telling them and the attendant press, "We are very proud to welcome you as a representative of a great country which has fought so bravely and so well against the Communists."[53]

The high-profile US military and government representatives who headed up the AKF made the political stakes of the choir transparent. James Van Fleet personally oversaw the children during their tour, and the AKF's director at the time was Milton Eisenhower. The president's brother avidly promoted the foundation's objective for "the warm, personal assistance of people to people."[54] Military and government connections to this organization positioned the AKF to bridge the cultural politics of wartime and postwar Korea. While the Department of Defense framed US military men as the primary rescuers of Korean children during the war, the baton was smoothly passed to the private sector via the AKF, a nongovernmental agency that was far from disconnected from the state. The extreme success of the AKF cannot be separated from the US government backing that it received, state support that receded into the background in order to highlight the benevolent work of American civilians in South Korea.

Van Fleet's military background made him an ideal representative of the postwar shift that moved the responsibility for Korea's children from the military to average Americans. The military general-turned-philanthropist advanced wartime narratives by embodying the full transformation of the American soldier into the internationalist caretaker. He appeared alongside the singing children throughout the tour wearing a suit, not his military uniform. By dressing as a civilian, Van Fleet reframed white men in relation to Korea via their dedication to Korean children, rather than their participation in the recent war. When he turned in his uniform to embrace his role as a Cold War citizen, he became an everyday ambassador of democracy.

The Cold War aims of the AKF were showcased at the kick-off party for the choir at New York's Astor Hotel. Two hundred and fifty attendees listened to the singing children dressed in hanboks, "brightly colored silk costumes, decorated with gold characters signifying long life, blessings and joy." The children regaled guests with a repertoire that included everything from the Korean national anthem to "Jingle Bells." A *New York Times* photograph offered a glimpse of the exchange for broad audiences. Five young Korean girls dressed in hanboks stood arm in arm with Van Fleet's grandson. One of the girls, Sin Jou Mi, handed a tie pin to the former general, who kneeled down to accept the gift with an upturned, welcoming hand and a broad smile.[55] The gentle exchange between a Korean child and the former US general put wartime violence far behind, and instead looked toward a future of US-South Korean trust and cooperation.

At the party, leaders of the AKF spelled out the political aims of the tour. In his speech, Howard Rusk explained that while the United States failed to remove communists from the peninsula during the war, investment in South Korea's children would "help build a cornerstone of peace in the Far East." In a short film screened at the party, President Eisenhower enthusiastically praised the AKF's campaign and the organization's alignment with his administration's foreign policy aims.[56] The children became useful vehicles for political Cold War scripts since they came packaged in an appealing, youthful, and seemingly pre-political stage. More than the centerpiece of a fundraising drive and quite unlike the waif campaigns circulating at this time, the choir children came to symbolize an emerging South Korean democracy in ideological alignment with the United States.

The age and gender of the choristers further advanced the choir's ability to bring to America a palatable vision of postwar Korea. Twenty-two of the twenty-five choristers were girls, and the entire troupe was between the ages of six and twelve. Most were known to be "double orphans who lost their parents in the fight of South Korea against the Communists."[57] Too young to be associated with Korean military brides, the girl choristers symbolized a childlike and feminized South Korea in need of American protection. Unlike the boy mascots of war, who were framed as American soldiers-in-the-making, the girls because of their gender were decoupled from politics. Their visibility as gendered, innocent subjects welcomed and warranted US paternalism as well as civilian intervention.

The Korean Children's Choir offered a strikingly different view of Korean children than those that appeared in concurrent aid campaigns. The sentiment that brought Korea's youngsters into US consciousness during the war drove thousands of Americans to want to see the children up close and personal. In the tradition of what historian John Kuo Wei Tchen describes as "edifying curiosities," many rushed out to witness the children firsthand.[58] But when they entered auditoriums, audience members did not see the waifs whom they had come to know. Singing Korean folk songs and American favorites like "Oh! Susanna," the robust, smiling children standing before them jarred previous representations and were appealing in new ways.

From April to June 1954, the Korean Children's Choir performed for thousands of Americans across the nation. The choir traveled to over fifty cities and visited iconic American sites along the way. In addition to serenading the Statue of Liberty, the children performed for First Lady Mamie Eisenhower in the White House and brought the Senate "to its feet in applause" with Korean and English versions of "Clementine."[59] These decidedly democratic settings affiliated Korean children with the United States and helped make them appear less foreign. Their participation in consumer culture further tied the tiny choristers to the American way. The AKF signed a record deal with Urania Records, making it possible for anyone to experience the children that they had "seen and heard . . . on television [and in] Life Magazine" by purchasing the album that was "capturing America's heart!"[60] US media constructions made the Korean choristers modern, democratic, and a part of the United States in ways not possible when the children were visualized far away and alone in Korea.

The popularity and marketability of the choir relied in part upon the fantasy of transition. The story of the foreign and destitute on their way to becoming domesticated and healthy bolstered the power of US democracy. Yet, while the children appeared to be on a path to rapid Americanization, they importantly remained othered by their Asian faces and Korean dress, a racialization necessary to support Cold War internationalist scripts. The importance of Oriental exoticism was not lost on the AKF. Even after American clothing designer Vera Maxwell gifted gabardine coats, quilted skirts, and corduroy pants for the children to wear during the winter tour months, photographs did not show the children in anything but their hanboks.[61] This provided just the difference needed to invite hundreds of thousands of donors to provide the financial and emotional support that could help complete the transformation.

Geography also played a critical role in the narrative of transition. News of the children coupled with their actual performances intimated that merely being on US soil improved their situation. In the United States, there was no famine or destruction, just warmth and acceptance. That the children thrived in America was seemingly rooted in simple geography—the United States was not only not Korea, but was unquestionably better for the children. American viewers witnessed the effortless ease with which US intervention could improve the lives of Korea's youth. By extension, the choir children imbued average citizens with the confidence that they, by virtue of their residence in the modern United States as opposed to a backwards Korea, could do the same. As described in the next chapter, this Orientalist framework helped to underwrite emerging adoptee narratives that assumed the inherent superiority of the United States over South Korea and assured prospective adoptive parents that the children would be better off under their care.

Existing constructions of global family frames helped the AKF cast the relationship between donors and the choir children as an intimate family affair. Like other images circulating at this time, global family frames helped Americans see across difference to recognize and embrace the universal qualities of people from around the world. Yet choir scripts revised the parameters of global family frames. The tangible proximity of the choir coupled with the fact that many of the children were known to be "double orphans" reified their availability and need of a new family. Connections between the choristers and actual adoptees, like James Lee Paladino, who welcomed the choir at the airport, solidified the identification of the choristers as Korean orphans and potential adoptees, constructions that were further cemented by photographs published throughout the tour.

In April 1954, the New York Times pictured the choir sitting with Van Fleet at the foot of the Statue of Liberty (figure 2.1). Mouths open in song as they performed the American and Korean national anthems, the children huddled together under the iconic US symbol of freedom. These children were no longer helpless and alone. In this image, the military general-turned-caretaker, Van Fleet, became the father of the children, while Lady Liberty took her place as the mother of the foreign brood. The all-American family—with white parents, if not white children— reified the dominance and paternalism of the United States over South Korea. While Van Fleet and Lady Liberty acted as placeholders, in this construction any American could ostensibly take up the parental role by

Figure 2.1. Korean Children's Choir sings at the Statue of Liberty. "Korean Children's Choir Tunes Up for US Tour," *New York Times*, April 16, 1954. Photograph by Neal Boenzi.

donating to the cause. This image and others like it taught average viewers that they too could be caretakers of their newest neighbor, Korea, replacing imperialist imposition abroad with familial love at home.[62]

In US news coverage, the children often appeared next to Van Fleet, Rusk, and dignitaries for whom the children sang, including President Eisenhower and First Lady Mamie Eisenhower. The choir director, Ahn Byŏng Wŏn, as well as the liaison officer, Chung Dal Bin, and the nurse Ahn Hi Ok, who accompanied the children during their tour, went largely missing from the photographs. Some articles mentioned their names, but few, if any, included them in pictures.[63] The absence of Korean adults who could be construed as primary caretakers or biological parents permitted American audiences to take up figurative roles as the children's guardians. For the choristers who were in the United States temporarily, their status as "double orphans" demonstrated the absolute need of the parentless children. When figured in these ways, whether pictured with white custodians, like Van Fleet, or in groups not under the supervision of any adult, the photographs left room for American audiences to step in to complete the imagined family frame.

The choir children suggested no trace of pain, only hope, constructions that further disconnected them from Korea and the trauma of war. Photographs of smiling and finely dressed girls and boys separated them from the war that created the need for the fundraising campaign in the first place. Unlike the CCF and other waif campaigns, the AKF invited Americans to help the Korean children standing before them, who were already well on their way to becoming American. Narratives of quickly Americanizing children who thrived on US soil worked alongside the absence of a Korean past. A New York Times special report titled "25 Koreans Turn American for Day" offered readers a glimpse of the choir in between performances. At an Easter picnic in Mamaroneck, New York, the Korean children "sang for their supper of frankfurters and ham cooked on an outdoor grill, buttered rolls, cookies, candy and cola beverage." Korean boys "raced around the school playground on American bikes, [while] their sisters became . . . entranced with rope-skipping." Some of the choristers attended church services at the local Methodist church and the Roman Catholic Church of the Holy Trinity before the festivities began. From food to activities to religion, the children "'lived American' [that day]—and liked it."[64]

Finally, the Korean Children's Choir of 1954 introduced Korean children as commodities within reach. Sold-out concerts across the country, record sales, and media exposure, like their appearance on the popular game show *Name That Tune*, made Korean children available for public consumption.[65] The ability of average Americans to easily access and come to know Korean children refigured this relationship. No longer donating to help a foreign child in a faraway land, Americans were now able to save the child who stood on the stage in front of them, a proximity that deepened existing affective ties and extended the possibilities of rescue to include adoptions, which would increase significantly in the coming years. In the end, what the choir proposed was not just any global family, but an Americanized international family made possible by the power of democracy.

When the tour concluded, the children were welcomed back to Seoul with open arms. Seoul's mayor and other Korean dignitaries greeted the children at the airport. Before returning to their orphanage homes, the children visited President Rhee's residence to receive praise.[66] The president and mayor commended the children for acting as foreign ambassadors, and Korean newspapers thanked the children for helping to raise $22 million during their four-month tour in the United States.[67] Given the success of the Korean Children's Choir, it came as little surprise that the ROK government would support subsequent iterations of children's choirs under the new sponsorship of World Vision.

World Vision's Korean Orphan Choirs

Between 1958 and 1968, World Vision, an interdenominational organization, sponsored five choir tours, for which a new group of children always under the age of sixteen was selected from orphanages throughout South Korea.[68] The children trained at the Music Center in Seoul, which was established by World Vision in 1964. Adding religious hymns like "He Sent My Sins a' Rolling" and "The Lord Is My Shepherd" to the usual lineup of Korean and American folk songs, World Vision tours aligned the Korean children with Christianity, furthering scripts of their Americanization. During the Christmas holiday season, newspapers reported that the children sang delightful "Western Christian chants and carols."[69] In 1963 the children recorded an album with folk singer

Burl Ives titled *Faith and Joy*. In 1968 the children performed on Billy Graham's evangelical television program.[70]

The choristers and Christianity converged in unmistakable ways when World Vision assembled the Korean Orphan Choir. The overt similarities with the recent AKF Korean Children's Choir—from the age of the children to the kinds of songs they sang to where they performed— made World Vision's choir immediately recognizable. Yet the insertion of "Orphan" in the World Vision choir name did additional work. First, the word affirmed concurrent narratives about Korean waifs and adoptees, making it difficult to imagine a Korean child who was not orphaned. The homogenization of Korean children as presumed orphans made World Vision's use of the word appear a foregone conclusion. Second, the re- named troupe mirrored the rise in Korean intercountry adoptions, and World Vision helped sponsor many of the placements.[71]

Under World Vision, and alongside the increased visibility of Korean adoptees, the choir reached a new level of popularity and marketability. World Vision hired a public relations firm, Hamner Bellows, to promote the choir.[72] The popularity of the Orphan Choir soared. In 1961 the children appeared on a float at the famous Rose Parade in Pasadena, California, and performed live on *The Ed Sullivan Show*.[73] At a New York 1962 performance, Carnegie Hall reached capacity, and disappointed crowds were turned away at the door.[74] To thank a generous Jewish donor, the children sang a Hanukkah song in Hebrew to thunderous applause at Rockefeller Plaza.[75] In Minnesota, ten thousand people filled the Minneapolis Auditorium and another two thousand packed an overflow meeting hall, while an estimated four thousand were turned away.[76] Los Angeles mayor Pat Brown declared January 1, 1963, World Vision Orphan Choir Day. Between the traveling Korean Orphan Choirs and media representations of model Korean adoptees, by the mid-1950s the American public had come to know Korean children in an American context, far removed from war-torn Korea.

By the 1960s, the Korean Orphan Choir cemented its place in American consciousness alongside adoptees as the bridge between the United States and South Korea. During holidays, the Korean choirs were among several international children's choirs visiting from afar. While singing children from other countries, like Czechoslovakia and Germany, also communicated Cold War internationalism, the Korean

Figure 2.2. The Korean Orphan Choir rehearses music that they will sing in five languages. Ellen Shulte, "From South Korea with Love," *Los Angeles Times,* December 15, 1965. Photograph by Harry Chase.

Orphan Choir more clearly demonstrated the permanence of Korean children in the United States. Various aspects of the Korean Orphan Choirs marked the shift from visitor to potential American citizen. During the 1962 tour, the children performed in western-style red and blue blazers, conveniently the national colors of both the United States and South Korea.[77] Spiritually and physically the children reflected an increasing alignment with the United States. The 1965 *Los Angeles Times* article "From South Korea with Love" showed just how much the choir had changed since the AKF's choir visited the United States in 1954. No longer in hanboks, the girls wore dresses with rounded collars and the boys sported bow ties, button-down shirts, and striped sweaters (figure 2.2). Lined up in orderly rows with neatly brushed hair and picture-perfect smiles, the children offered proof of transformation. Reporters marveled at how the children were "just as much at home in foreign tongues as their own." Not only did they quickly learn languages, they "also showed how well they adapt themselves to their changing locations."[78] Though they had learned English lyrics phonetically, not knowing the meanings of songs, this was hardly the point.[79] Their behavior, dress, and spirit marked them as newly American. Other photographs underscored these characteristics. One shot pictured two children who added Korean hot pepper paste to hot dogs, inviting viewers to smile at the childhood innocence that overlay the serious business of Cold War internationalism. In another image, two girls beamed as they played "American" games. Judging from the photographs and descriptions, the children had become decidedly more American in the short time that they were touring the United States.

Hollywood's Orphan: Melding the Waif, Chorister, and Adoptee

In 1958 Universal-International Pictures released the film *Battle Hymn*. Based on a true story, the film starred Rock Hudson as the ordained minister-turned-pilot Dean Hess, who with Chaplain Russell L. Blaisdell in December 1950 airlifted over nine hundred Korean children to safety.[80] In the film's dramatic climax, Korean children with dirtied faces, torn clothing, and bare feet ran frantically and from every possible direction toward gigantic, rumbling planes, where US servicemen scooped them aboard and flew them to safety. The film's message about American servicemen who transformed war machines into vehicles of rescue for Korea's littlest victims earned it a 1959 Golden Globe Award for "Best Film Promoting International Understanding." The film itself was a transnational endeavor; scenes were shot in the United States and South Korea, filmmakers worked directly with the US military and the ROK government, and twenty-five Korean orphans from Orphans' Home in Korea were flown to Hollywood to play themselves in the film.

The movie tidily wrapped up the saga of the war, its refugees, and US power. On a macro level, the Korean children were a stand-in for Korea. US policy makers' patronizing view of Koreans, and Asians more generally, was a necessary component of political narratives that justified US guardianship of Asian nations.[81] Beyond this broader symbolism, the film communicated specific narratives about the children. It built from and melded existing scripts of Korean children that marked their transformation as a result of American aid. As well, the convergence of missionary and military man in the single character of Dean Hess, who was a pastor prior to joining the army, maximized the redemptive narrative. Hess's religious commitments likened him to contemporaneous figures like Bob Pierce of World Vision and Calvitt Clarke of the CCF. Together, their sensational rescue allowed these white, Christian men to take up the role of transnational hero, redeeming US military men for their violent participation in the Korean War, and helping to rewrite postwar American masculinity.

The US military saw the restorative potential of *Battle Hymn* and actively supported it from production to release. In 1955 the US Air Force sent several of its officers to act as consultants for the film, which it deemed "of primary concern to the National Military Establishment."[82] When filming began in Nogales, Arizona, the air force sent planes, men, and equipment from three bases in Arizona and Texas. The extent of US air force support, which was described as "more than the ordinary cooperation," was displayed in the film's opening.[83] Air force general Earle E. Partridge, who fought in Korea alongside Dean Hess, introduced the film. Wearing his uniform, with fighter planes in the background, Partridge described the film as "more than a dramatic demonstration of one man's capacity for good, [but also] an affirmation of the essential goodness of the human spirit."[84]

The ROK government, which felt that the film could boost images of a resilient Korea, also helped with its production. In 1956 the Korean Office of Public Information helped scout locations for filming.[85] President Rhee provided ample support to get the orphans, whom he referred to as "the young Korean ambassadors," to the United States for filming. He made arrangements with the US State Department and sent along a Korean cook, Lee Dai Wǒn, who also acted as a translator, two Korean nurses, and Wang On Soon, the director of Orphans' Home of Korea, which was founded by Blaisdell and Hess and located on the island of Cheju off the southernmost tip of the peninsula. When the children arrived in Arizona for filming, Governor Ernest MacFarland presented them with individual certificates of citizenship and remarked, "I trust this gesture of the state of Arizona toward these young living symbols of the independent strength of free Korea will help to strengthen the good-will between that country and the United States."[86] The international dimensions of the film and respective benefit to each country characterized the Hollywood production from start to finish, and echoed the goals of the transnationally produced Korean children's choirs.

Film reviewers did not hesitate to point out the overbearing message of "rescue by American open-heartedness."[87] *Newsweek* made room for the director's good intentions when it described the film as "perhaps unavoidably, hastily preachy now and then."[88] A *Time* magazine reviewer was less forgiving, noting that "Hudson spends most of his time exercising the vocabulary of uplift ('Your good deeds are your purest prayers'). . . . By the time the lights finally go up, the sugar count of this picture is so dangerously high that theater managers might be well advised to offer insulin shots in the lobby."[89] Some reviewers lamented the poor execution of a fantastic story and chalked up the film's deficits to shallow performances and "wooden" direction.[90] The one thing critics could agree upon was that the "disarmingly cute" children saved the film.[91]

According to one critic, the children brought audiences to "the heart of war, to where it hurts most."[92] While the children who played "starving orphans" in the film were "remarkably neat and plump," no filmgoer could leave the theater without acknowledging their desperate situation. In the film's final scene, Hess returns to the Korean orphanage with his wife, Mary, and children file out of the pristine countryside orphanage to greet them. Chu, the Korean orphan who grew particularly fond of Hess throughout the film, breaks past his Korean female caretakers and runs up to the colonel, who lovingly gathers the small boy up in his arms. In earlier versions of the screenplay, Mary and Colonel Hess visit the orphanage and bring their own son. The choice to remove their child from the final version of the film made room for the final shot to rest on the international family with Mary and Dean as parents to the Korean Chu.

The camera pauses on the US-Korean family as Mary smiles and remarks, "It's wonderful to see them so healthy. Darling, you look as happy as the children." To which Hess firmly replies, "It's always been the children." The camera then pans to hundreds of smiling Korean children, who sing "The Battle Hymn of the Republic." Standing in rows, the children form a veritable choir in the countryside, mirroring the contemporaneous Korean Orphan Choir. The words "Dedicated . . .

To those we could not save. Dean E. Hess, Colonel U.S.A." flash up as the children sing in the background. Just as the film began with documentary appeal, it ends the same way with the explanation that "The children from The Orphans' Home of Korea portrayed themselves in this motion picture." The film left no room for confusion. The children were innocent victims who needed homes and familial love, and viewers were asked to pick up where Hess left off. It also helped American audiences imagine how the frail waifs pictured in fundraising campaigns could be transformed into healthy, clean, and Christian children when placed under the institutionalized care of American-run orphanages in South Korea.

By this time, viewers knew what actions to take in order to help Korean children. According to the film production notes, the "entire population of Nogales was so inspired by the presence of the youngsters that American children near the location, aided by their parents, made a penny-nickel-dime-quarter collection, totally unsolicited by studio personnel, and presented $168.10 to Mrs. Whang for the orphanage."[93] Over a hundred requests to adopt the children seen in the movie kept the studio busy explaining that the orphans could not be adopted while they were in the United States.[94] Regulations governing their visit made it so that anyone interested in doing so would need to go through the regular channels. Still, the *New York Times* predicted that "judging from the number of requests, some of the visitors may be eating hamburgers steadily before long."[95]

Two of the children from the film, including Jung Kyoo Pyo, who played Chu, were in fact adopted. Those who worked with Jung on set described him as a "natural clown with a considerable smattering of the ham about him."[96] Nicknamed "Sam," he stole the heart of Rock Hudson, and while filming in Los Angeles he caught the attention of a "childless American couple." *Life* told of the completed adoption in 1957, offering pictures of the round-faced child playfully mugging for the camera. Like other adoptee narratives, the article described how Sam quickly adjusted to life with his new family and like a typical American boy "loved comic books and ice cream."[97] The article also noted that Sam taught his American parents how to eat Korean seaweed—a staple Korean food described as an "old Korean delicacy." The exchange of culture and familial love as reported by *Life* fused Cold War international understanding with domestic racial harmony, scripts imagined with the choristers and realized in the figure of the Korean adoptee.

The suggestion that Korean children would only benefit from American aid and thrive if brought to the United States encouraged Americans to take part in their rescue. Whether postwar narratives came in the form of waif appeals or choir tours, Americans were figured as the natural and primary caretakers of the children. Through US aid campaigns, Americans learned that they could play a direct and active role in the transformation of Korean waifs into modern citizens. The appeals taught Americans that they were well suited to this task; they could win these children to democracy by simply loving them. In particular, constructions of choir children, the "after" to waif campaigns' "before," figuratively cleared the way for actual adoptions. The singing children advertised both their need and model qualities, which could be resolved and realized, respectively, under the care of Americans in the United States. These postwar scripts of rescue were also scripts of transformation through which Americans could expand the ways that they imagined kin.

PART II

International Cold War Families

While state actors, including the US military and the Department of Defense, and state-supporting organizations like the American-Korean Foundation produced imagined family frames that figured Americans as caretakers of Korean children, US missionaries worked on a parallel project with vastly different outcomes. American missionaries were in Korea well before the war. Presbyterian and Methodist missionaries set roots in Korea beginning in 1884, when the Korean embassy was first established. Having learned from other foreign missions that direct proselytizing was an outmoded tactic, they focused instead on healing the sick, providing education, and offering social services to gain the trust of local populations.[1] This approach worked well in Korea, where there was no comprehensive social welfare program and citizens largely relied upon extended family for assistance. By focusing on providing aid, US missionaries opened a clear path for their proselytizing efforts in Korea.

Missionaries promptly established institutional roots in Korea. In 1885 Horace N. Allen of the US Presbyterian Church opened and ran the Korean Government Hospital. The Methodist Episcopal Church sent Henry Appenzeller to Korea to start the first Western-style school, Pai Chai Hak Dang. In 1886 Horace Grant Underwood established the first school of the Presbyterian Mission and organized a church one year later. The rapid Christianization of South Korea is often traced to these three figures, especially Horace Underwood, who was the first of multiple generations of Underwoods to proselytize in Korea. During Japanese colonization from 1910 to 1945, the colonial government persecuted foreign missionaries, severely limiting their operations. Yet the number of Christian converts steadily grew. By 1934, there were an estimated 340,000 Korean Christians and more than seven hundred Korean Presbyterian ministers.[2] By the mid-1940s, US missionaries nicknamed Korea "the most Christian land in the Orient," claiming that their work surpassed that of the largest and most prestigious foreign missions in China.[3]

Beginning in 1945 with US occupation of South Korea, US church and state worked in tandem, each directly benefitting the other while furthering its own projects. The arrival of the US occupying government gave US missionaries unfettered access to Koreans. As millions of Koreans flooded south of the newly made 38th parallel, the welfare needs of South Korea spiked.[4] Korea's Ministry of Social Welfare and US occupation forces scrambled to administer vaccination and food aid programs, but it was US missionaries with their well-established infrastructure who took the lead in addressing civilian needs.[5] US officials also turned to missionaries for help assembling its occupation administration. The state hired Korean Christians who had learned English through their US missionary education and could communicate effectively with the American Occupation Army. Six of the eleven Korean administrative advisors appointed by the US military in 1945 were converted Christians; three of them were ministers. In 1948 many Korean leaders of the newly formed Republic of Korea government had received their education either in the United States or in American missionary institutions in South Korea.[6]

US missionaries also benefitted from the US occupation of South Korea. They were able to solidify their place in the peninsula by aligning foreign mission goals with the state rhetoric of democracy and anticommunism. In 1951 Horace H. Underwood expounded, "The Christian group in Korea must survive. Christians are the most ardently democratic of Koreans and so oppose totalitarian domination."[7] He and other missionaries claimed that Christianity constituted the moral fiber of democratic thought and action, and that God and the nation backed missionary endeavors. The synergy between church and state fostered a cooperation that transformed US missionaries into unofficial state actors with special benefits. At the start of US occupation, government administrators privileged missionaries when distributing land confiscated from Japan.[8] Throughout the occupation period, AFAK provided materials and manpower to construct churches, as well as missionary-run orphanages and schools.[9] During the war, the US military continued to help build makeshift orphanages administered by US missionaries. The level of cooperation between missionaries and government administrators across multiple institutions established a firm foundation for US power in South Korea.

This brief history of US missionaries in Korea demonstrates how nongovernmental actors became indispensable to the inner workings of American empire by the mid-twentieth century. While the relationship between missionaries and the US government was symbiotic in many ways, their practices diverged after the war. The chapters in this section show how US missionaries responded to the war crisis in ways that far exceeded the US government's vision for humanitarian assistance. US missionaries' proselytizing tactics, which centered upon providing aid, followed tried-and-true foreign mission techniques. However, the extent of Korea's wartime crisis warranted new approaches that turned the foreign mission into a project that physically tethered Koreans and Americans across the Pacific. Missionaries, and missionary figures like Harry Holt, brought their work full circle when they implored Christians in America to enact the ultimate form of rescue by adopting Korean children. Their religious call dovetailed with US Cold War internationalist needs, which gave their efforts political relevance and, given the vast publicity surrounding their actions, required a US government response. Transpacific families of war were born in this political context that forced the hand of the state to put into practice its claims to internationalism. The resulting advent of Korean adoptions altered the trajectory of US empire. It created a new transnational network that included US missionaries, American women, social workers, state welfare agencies, and the Immigration and Naturalization Service, as well as Korean Christians, newly trained welfare practitioners, doctors, police officers, and government officials, including President Rhee himself, who all had a stake in a project of rescue that within a few years of the war became a matter of migration.

3

Missionary Rescue and the Transnational Making of Family

The proliferation of news about Korean children from wartime images of mascots to postwar visions of singing choristers made it nearly impossible for Americans not to know something about Korean children. In the early 1950s, Korean children were on American minds, and soon they had another kind of Korean child to add to their existing knowledge. On October 14, 1955, at the Portland International Airport, amidst the popping bulbs and flashing lights of fifty photographers and spirited questions from microphone-toting journalists hailing from as far as New York City, American and Korean attendants carried children dressed in colorful Korean hanboks from a plane (figure 3.1). The children on this flight were markedly different from the ones Americans had come to know—all of them were mixed-race. Harry Holt, a sawmill owner, orchestrated the dramatic event. Weeks after seeing a World Vision documentary about Korea's mixed-race children, Holt had a dream of a little girl with "almond-shaped eyes," a message from God, he determined, to save the children.[1] With this purpose, he flew to Korea and returned with twelve "GI babies"; eight would become part of his own family and the remaining four would be placed in other American homes. Richard Neuberger, the Oregon senator who pushed the special private adoption bills through Congress to grant them entry, was on hand to carry one of the infants off the plane and pause for photographers, whose pictures enabled the rest of America to bear witness to the internationalist spectacle.

At the press conference held at the airport, Harry Holt sat next to Bob Pierce of World Vision, who had helped finance the transpacific trip. With the only Korean-African American child from the flight sitting on his lap, Holt spoke passionately about the desperate plight of GI babies. Holt evenly remarked that "in Korea, parents have a right to kill them," to which the interviewer gasped, "Good heavens! I never knew that."[2] This exchange marked a significant shift in US-South

Figure 3.1. Harry Holt arrives in the United States with mixed-race adoptees in his inaugural "babylift." "Rancher and 12 Korean Orphans Arrive in the US," *Chicago Daily Tribune*, October 15, 1955, 2.

Korea relations, a permanent turn in the American project of rescue already well underway. A number of ideas unfolded on that day, ones that built upon existing conceptions and set the stage for new ones. Here, Holt took his place alongside other white male heroes, like Calvitt Clarke of the CCF and James Van Fleet of the AKF, who figured as saviors to Korean tots. But Holt differed from his contemporaries, whose campaigns centered on fundraising for children in South Korea; according to Holt, the rescue of GI babies required removing the children from Korea, a place where their situation was so dire that their own parents had the "right to kill them."

Americans were already familiar with the Korean waif, but news about the plight of mixed-race children added new dimensions to existing understandings about impoverished, war-torn Korea. This press conference revealed Korean discrimination against which Americans could claim racial liberalism; failed Korean mothers (who might even commit infanticide) against secure white motherhood; and heathen barbarism against the magnanimous love of American Christians. There was another message conveyed by Holt's decision to have a Korean-African American child sit on his lap for photographers to capture and news reporters to see. The visibility of the half-African American child as one worthy of American rescue highlighted the shortcomings of a United States that remained segregated by law and social custom, and was in the midst of a highly public civil rights struggle for racial equality that had garnered the attention of the world. In this context, Harry Holt positioned himself and others who might adopt from Korea as Christians whose love knew no bounds, and who saw only pitiable lives worth saving, not race.

Holt's actions were decidedly internationalist. He did what the US government promoted, but did not necessarily want. By rescuing "Amerasian" children, Holt acted as a benevolent humanitarian reaching across the Pacific to aid helpless Asian neighbors. Visions of interracial transnational adoptions that intimately bound white Americans to mixed-race and Korean children displayed exactly the kind of Cold War internationalism that could further US claims to racial democracy. Yet, in addition to spotlighting the domestic failures of racial integration, Holt also exposed the problems inherent within the figure of the GI baby, a child with a Korean mother and an American serviceman father who, in his estimation, was abandoned by both. Neither government wanted to take responsibility for these children, but Holt and soon other Americans who learned of their struggle made mixed-race children of the war an unavoidable issue for each.

For the United States, what Holt effectively proposed with this inaugural "babylift" was Asian immigration during a time of restriction and interracial families in a still segregated United States.[3] This chapter traces the processes behind the first large-scale transnational and transracial adoptions. It focuses on the role of US missionaries in fomenting transnational adoptions, a practice that since the war has resulted in the immigration of over 150,000 Korean adoptees to the United States and over 50,000 to European countries and Australia. The adoption of mixed-race and Korean children required more than altering existing restrictive immigration laws, it demanded a shift in the American mindset. It was no small gesture to bring Asian and, in the case of GI babies, interracial children into white American family homes in the 1950s. Christianity alone could not explain the fervor with which thousands of predominantly white Americans sought to adopt children from South Korea. In this exchange, Americans had to come to see themselves as more than internationalist participants, but as the actual makers of transpacific families. This process was rooted in US missionary work in Korea that connected Americans to the faraway land and its people. Behind the public work of figures like Harry Holt were the white female missionaries in South Korea and their Korean assistants who administered the more mundane daily tasks of childcare, Bible study, and eventually adoptions. On the other side of their rescue operation were prospective adoptive parents, in particular white American women, who came to envision themselves as the most critical part of this international mission. In the end, those celebrated for being "un-ugly" Americans were the same ones who forced openings in existing US gatekeeping policies, permitting nonwhite others to not only enter the United States, but also breach one of its most staunchly protected spaces: the white family home.[4]

Publicizing the Plight of GI Babies

Adoptions from Korea began on a limited scale during the war. A number of US servicemen, who were able to get through the red tape, brought Korean and mixed-race children home. In 1953 Seventh-day Adventists placed a small number of children in American homes. In 1955 Catholic Relief Services under the auspices of the National Catholic Welfare Council matched Korean children with Catholic families. The Christian Children's Fund, Church World Service, Foster Parents Plan, and World Vision also placed children during and immediately following the war. Yet it would not be until Harry Holt and his wife, Bertha, started the Holt Adoption Program in 1956 that Korean adoptions gained momentum. News of Holt's inaugural babylift reached Americans nationwide.[5] Harry Holt's daughter, Molly Holt, recalled the postman dragging bags overflowing with letters to the front door every day for weeks following the arrival of her Korean siblings. While some were curious about their race mixture and wanted to see the children, most of the letters in this "avalanche of mail" sought information about adopting a child from Korea.[6]

The Holt Adoption Program (HAP) became the most well-known agency due in no small part to Holt's own publicity efforts.[7] With flourish, Holt consistently flew planeloads of children to the United States, and was always certain to have media on hand to capture the arrival of his "stork planes." Molly recalled her father asking his children to tolerate the press. For one of his babylifts in 1958, Holt invited approximately two hundred people, including adoptive couples from Arizona, Colorado, Michigan, Tennessee, Texas, and several western states, newspaper reporters, Koreans in their "native dress," and numerous onlookers, to greet the children at the tarmac.[8] Local newspapers published photographs of mixed-race children as they were carried off the plane or grouped together in the moments before leaving with their respective adoptive parents.[9] Through US media, Holt not only publicized the supposed availability of Korean and especially mixed-race children, but also advertised to viewers that they, too, could adopt a Korean child.

The response was overwhelming. According to the *Christian Science Monitor*, by April 1956, the Holts received over a thousand requests for mixed-race Korean children from families across forty-six states.[10] By mid-1957, 7,500 Americans wrote to the Holts to inquire about Korean adoptions.[11] With no permanent legal paths to transnational adoptions at this time and restrictions to immigration from Asia still in place, HAP circumvented existing laws by using proxy adoptions. Though US adoptive couples still needed special congressional approval to bring Korean children into their homes, Holt found a way for couples to adopt them sight unseen. Proxy adoptions made it possible for Holt to act by power of attorney to procure fifty to a hundred children at a time. The primary criterion for those wishing to adopt through HAP was a demonstration of devout Christianity. In a two-page form letter sent to prospective adoptive parents, Holt emphasized, "*First and foremost*, we wish to place the children in born-again Christian homes. The name 'Christian' is used so carelessly nowadays that we wish to express our definition of the word . . . *we would rather that you did not fill out this card until you are assured that you are a saved person.*"[12] The cost of intercountry adoptions at this time was around $1,000.[13] In comparison, the Holts charged adoptive couples $343 to cover the adoption process, visa, transportation costs, and a "home study" conducted by private investigators that checked on the suitability of the couple as parents and verified that they were true Christians.[14] For those who could not afford the fee, Holt used a sliding pay scale to make adoptions available to them. Beyond a demonstration of Christianity, which Holt ascertained via a questionnaire that tested the couple's knowledge of the scripture or a statement of "personal faith," couples that went through the Holt agency had to prove little else.[15] Holt believed that Christianity could overcome financial or other possible shortcomings of the adoptive home; many couples previously denied by local welfare agencies found that they had a second chance through his agency. In addition to those with financial limitations, single adoptive parents and those considered too old for intercountry adoptions by accredited state welfare agencies could usually procure a child through Holt.[16] Holt adoptions became so popular in Christian circles that parents formed clubs, like the Christian Adoptive Parents of Eurasian Children of Orange County, that gathered families and their adopted children from Korea for picnics and other activities.[17]

US welfare professionals feared that Holt adoptions dangerously cut corners and were detrimental to the children. In 1957 an adoptive mother killed a twenty-two-month-old Korean child by "[striking] her on the head." Though the Holts, who had placed the child, came to the adoptive mother's defense, saying that the child was frail upon arrival, Wendy Kay Ott was charged with second-degree murder.[18] In 1958 a Korean infant too sick to endure the transpacific flight died on one of Holt's planes. These highly publicized incidents, coupled with numerous agency reports of Holt placements where children were abused, readopted, or ended up in foster care, alarmed social welfare professionals. The US Children's Bureau and the Child Welfare League of America accused Holt of masterminding a global mail-order baby racket, while hiding behind humanitarian rhetoric.[19] Others criticized his use of proxy adoptions for transplanting children "from one bad situation to another."[20]

Holt countered growing public criticism by insisting that Christian duty drove him to save Korea's mixed-race children from tragedy, even if that meant cutting corners. In 1957 *Time* reported that Holt searched orphanages and "disease-ridden huts and gutters" for the "babies fathered by American GIs and abandoned by their mothers," a story that helped to justify Holt's operations.[21] Numerous accounts constructed Holt as an adventurer and savior of the rejected mixed-race children of South Korea. World Vision's Bob Pierce, who worked closely with Holt, agreed with critics that potential adoptive families would not be properly studied and that "some would be unsound." However, Pierce still supported Holt's methods since he believed that the "only prospect for these children [was] to get them out of Korea," where mixed-race children "would never be accepted."[22] While not in agreement with Holt's practices, the International Social Service, a global social welfare organization with headquarters in Geneva, Switzerland, and branches around the world, concurred that children of mixed parentage carried upon their "innocent shoulders the burdens of being unwanted, resented and unclaimed."[23]

Mixed-race children in South Korea did face numerous challenges. Not only did they suffer from the same poverty, hunger, and illness of other Korean War survivors, reports suggested that they were "doomed to a life of discrimination in their country."[24] Korean cultural emphasis on family bloodlines and disapproval of illegitimate births, regardless of whether or not a woman was raped by a UN soldier, made the visibly mixed child a highly problematic figure. In 1953 President Rhee ordered a directive to remove mixed-race children from South Korea. Though the discrimination against mixed-race children in South Korea was real, US missionaries and adoption proponents sensationalized and homogenized the accounts in an effort to garner maximum sympathy and support from their constituents. Well-known internationalist Pearl S. Buck also weighed in on the issue. The daughter of US missionaries who grew up in China and mother of transnationally adopted and biracial children, Buck opened the Welcome House in 1958 to facilitate adoptions from Asia.[25] She wrote publicly and often about the plight of mixed-race children in magazines like *Good Housekeeping, Ladies' Home Journal, Women's Home Companion, Reader's Digest,* and *Ebony.* In 1959 the *New York Times* quoted Buck saying that the "children of American servicemen" were "dying like flies in Korean orphanages." She continued that President Rhee wanted the children removed from Korea "even if [they had] to drop them in the Pacific Ocean." While her comments were likely aimed at inciting Americans to act, her statements corroborated existing Orientalist conceptions that constructed Koreans as backwards and inhumane. Buck's report deeply offended the ROK government. Korean ambassadors wrote to Buck and the *New York Times*, which had published the piece, asking for a retraction of the "slanderous statements" and a formal apology. Though Buck wrote letters of apology to the ROK government claiming that US journalists had twisted her words, the damage was already done, and Americans had evidence to add to their existing understandings about Koreans and their mistreatment of mixed-race children.[26]

Sensationalized missionary accounts converged with US reports that often exaggerated the number of mixed-race Korean children, heightening the perceived level of crisis. While it was difficult to get an accurate count because the ROK government did not keep an official tally and Korean mothers often hid their mixed-race children from the public, US reports still erred on the side of overestimation. Buck placed the number at fifty thousand.[27] In 1965 *Time* estimated that there were twenty thousand mixed-race children in South Korea, with five to six hundred more born annually.[28] In comparison, the Korean newspaper *Chosŏn Ilbo* put the number of mixed-race children born between 1950 and 1965 at around 12,280, of which half had already been sent to the United States for adoption.[29]

Between 1957 and 1966, Pearl Buck's Welcome House received over four hundred referrals for Korean, Korean-black, and Korean-white children.[30] In comparison, by 1966, the Holt agency alone placed 3,576 children, the majority of them mixed-race, in the United States. The Holt Adoption Program surpassed the number of children adopted through all other agencies combined, making up 56 percent of the total 6,290 Korean and mixed-race adoptions to the United States between 1955 and 1966.[31] Publicity about the plight of GI babies spurred by figures like Holt and Buck resonated with American audiences already familiar with Korea's children. In the trajectory of existing missionary and aid campaigns that circulated around children, Holt's babylifts helped to make transnational adoptions the logical next step in an ongoing project of rescue.

US Foreign Missions and Women's Work in Korea

Given the existing infrastructure and established presence of American missionaries, it came as little surprise that they took the lead in South Korea's welfare needs during and after the war, though the scale of their involvement was less expected. In 1952 Western organizations, the majority of them missionary-run, operated 295 of 317 orphanages.[32] Their role only increased in the wake of the war, which left millions in need. With US and ROK administrators focused on infrastructural and economic rebuilding, the government came to rely on the work of US missionaries to aid its civilians.[33] After the war, US missionaries became synonymous with child welfare, and in 1955 the Korean Ministry of Social Affairs made it official. The ministry would grant licenses only to institutions that showed proof of property and missionary support.[34] This opened the door even wider to US missionaries, who by 1957 sponsored the majority of the 482 institutions that housed over 48,594 children.[35]

The war crisis along with US and ROK government support of missionary-led welfare efforts enabled them to dominate South Korea's care industry in the 1950s and beyond. For US missionaries, providing aid was supposed to be a means to a proselytizing end. Yet, like US servicemen, missionaries seemed to have lost their hearts to Korean children, which detracted from proselytizing aims. In a 1962 Presbyterian Mission advisory study, board members had to remind missionaries in Korea that their main purpose lay in spiritual work: "Humanitarian service is an integral aspect, but not the foremost aim, of Christian medical work. Through hospital work there should be a ministry to men's souls as well as to their bodies."[36] In another section, the board critiqued the language used in a previous advisory study on Korea by offering this corrective: "The unfortunate use of pronouns here seems to imply that the saving of the lost is not our primary objective in mission; whereas this *is* our primary aim. The political and social aspects of life are all a part of this central task, but they are not central in themselves."[37] The board did not mince words when reminding missionaries that whatever the path—be it by "twist[ing] their tongues" to learn the native language or through schools, orphanages, or hospitals—conversion remained the undisputed goal and the reason why missionaries were in South Korea in the first place.[38] Coming nearly a decade after the war, their recommendations stood as a direct response to postwar efforts that appeared to have shifted to prioritize aid over proselytization.

The advisory board's concerns were likely intensified by US missionaries who supported Korean overseas adoptions. Historically, US foreign missionary efforts faced outwards with the goal to convert the world, not bring converted Christians permanently into the United States.[39] Though in 1902 Horace Allen, US minister to Korea, helped send Korean Protestant Christians to Hawai'i at the request of sugar plantation owners who sought Asian laborers, and US missionaries continued to support converted subjects traveling to the United States to further their Christian education, the project of bringing children into the United States was uncharted territory.[40] When it came to postwar Korea, the advent of transnational adoptions and the place of Christianity at its center complicated the relationships between missionaries and the US government, as well as between missionaries in the field and the boards that tried to manage them.

Women were at the forefront of these shifting dynamics. Behind the highly publicized heroism of white male missionary adventurers, like Harry Holt, were the hundreds of white missionary women who carried out the day-to-day operations. Women had been integral to the work of foreign missions for over a century. As early as 1860, 60 percent of the US foreign mission board were married and single women. The board encouraged them to leave home for places like China to reform the world. Women seized the opportunity for travel, taking on "women's work" in international sites in the fields of medicine, education, and women's rights, such as the anti-foot-binding campaign of 1895 in China.[41] Their work catapulted them to the forefront of foreign missions, at times threatening to upstage the leadership of missionary men.[42]

After World War II, when women who had found independence working to meet wartime needs were asked to return home to care for husbands and children, missionary work offered women a way back into the public sphere.[43] The Korean War became the catalyst for their involvement in international politics, whether they participated from home or abroad. Cultural productions of Korean children during and after the war instructed white American women that it was their Cold War duty, as well as their innate right, to nurture Korean children. The war crisis allowed white women to expand their reach and influence while still staying within the acceptable bounds of the domestic sphere. At home, women spearheaded fundraising programs and food drives for Korea's children.[44] In South Korea, missionary women arrived to administer to the daily needs of children in orphanages, nurseries, and day care centers.[45] They joined the boards of the Woman's Christian Temperance Union and the Young Women's Christian Association to help keep liquor stores away from schools and set up homes for wayward Korean teens.[46] In the mid-1950s, with the advent of overseas adoptions, they expanded their maternal duties of feeding, bathing, and sheltering the children to include conducting child studies, corresponding with potential adoptive parents in the United States, and teaching Koreans how to mirror these Western practices. Their daily labor, like women's work in the home, went largely unseen, but the practices that they established gave them newfound global legitimacy and power during the Cold War.[47]

Missionary women in Korea made themselves the arbiters of morality. By embracing and touting their gendered ability to heal and nurture, they turned American motherhood into a tool of Cold War internationalism. They arrived in South Korea armed with lessons in care, hygiene, and the Bible. As children poured into US missionary-sponsored orphanages, American women found that they could make a true difference and eagerly taught Korean volunteers and administrators lessons in Western welfare. Molly Holt came to South Korea in 1956 after completing nursing school in Oregon. She volunteered at Song Haewon orphanage, where she recalled that of the ten children who entered every month, all ten would die within weeks. The children were so malnourished and the food supply so meager that they could not maintain life. She described how, with her help, the number of deaths dwindled to about one a month. Holt taught Korean caretakers how to prepare powdered milk and prevent the spread of disease by bathing the children separately and using different towels for each.[48] Like Molly, other American female missionaries came to Korea armed with Western lessons on childcare. Similar to US military officials who formed, trained, and disciplined the ROK army, white American missionaries told Koreans how to administer welfare practices that mirrored US systems.[49] Since South Koreans did not have a comprehensive social welfare system, the work of US missionaries filled this void almost entirely. They came to dominate the care industry during and just after the war, effectively foreclosing the possibility for Koreans to produce their own solutions to the pressing needs of their compatriots.[50]

In addition to teaching Koreans welfare practices, American missionaries imparted disciplinary strategies. They instituted schedules that routinized hygiene and prayer into the daily activities of children under their care. For instance, at the US Presbyterian Korean Crippled Children's Center (CCC), established in Seoul in 1959, the missionary women employed timetables to structure the children's days and get them into good habits. They were to start each morning with washing, brushing teeth, and making beds. The children attended "physio-therapy" sessions where nurses helped them utilize US-donated equipment to heal their various ailments; the children brought their own translated copies of the Bible to daily Bible study. Between lessons, the children were given thirty minutes of free time. After dinner the children had their second teeth brushing, and at 8:30 p.m., it was "prayers and lights out."[51] Missionaries used similar timetables, with much of the day dedicated to rehearsals for Korean children during the World Vision Orphan Choir tours to keep them on track while traveling abroad.[52] The schedules mirrored strategies used in US boarding schools, like Carlisle and the Hampton Institute, during the nineteenth and early twentieth centuries, techniques employed to discipline and turn into useful American subjects the nonwhite children under their care. These practices aimed to transform potential charges of the state into good subjects. Missionaries trained the children to carry out hygienic routines and lead their own prayers, structures that helped shape them into proper, self-governing subjects.[53]

Women missionaries also did the work of connecting Americans at home with projects underway in Korea. They sent letters to American constituents to thank them for their charitable donations. They also wrote newsletters that included updates and photographs to provide proof that US contributions positively impacted the lives of Korean children. In the US Presbyterian *Korea Calling* newsletter, missionaries at the CCC included a photograph of Korean children with their heads bowed in prayer with the following caption in all caps, "SPIRITUAL NEEDS MUST BE CARED FOR TO HAVE A WELL ROUNDED PROGRAM FOR DEVELOPING MINDS AND BODIES."[54] The children at the CCC were destined to stay in South Korea because their physical disabilities made them ineligible for US immigration. Thus, the money and supplies that Americans sent to the center went toward healing the faraway children, body and soul.

Making good Korean subjects was critical to the project of American empire, and missionaries in Korea and their supporters in the United States helped to further these aims. Whether the children would stay in South Korea or come to the United States, future democracy depended upon American subjecthood. The work of white women missionaries across South Korean welfare institutions contributed to this broader project. They passed on lessons of self-discipline, hygiene, and Christianity to Korean women who first acted as "helpers," but would later go on to administer South Korea's social welfare programs in the style of their American teachers.[55]

Like US military officials who argued that they could not leave South Korea at the end of the occupation period in 1948 because the ROK army was not yet self-sufficient, American women stayed on in South Korea well after the war, claiming that Korean administrators and nurses were not fully competent.[56] The advent of large-scale transnational adoptions in 1955 further justified their need to stay. White missionary women readily expanded their missionary work to include the administration of overseas adoptions. They completed the assessments, reports, and correspondence needed to carry out adoptions, further solidifying their place in South Korea.

Christian aims converged with America's Cold War agenda, adding relevance to the religious work of women and giving them greater access to and influence in South Korea. It was through their purported acts of healing that American missionary women defined themselves and could be seen by others as integral to a transnational Cold War project; and it was the advent of adoptions from South Korea to the United States that allowed thousands of white Christian women to participate in the same project, only this time from the comfort of their own homes.

White Imperial Motherhood

In the early 1950s, with McCarthyism in full swing, career women who politicized for equality in the workplace became targets of the House

Un-American Activities Committee. Accusing them of being "bad mothers" and "un-American" because of pursuits that led them outside the home, the Red Scare constrained the activities of equality-seeking women as it did African American civil rights advocates.[57] These were the Cold War boundaries that framed American women's involvement in helping Korean children of the war. Through donations and adoptions, women could participate in global politics without invoking criticism that they were overstepping domestic bounds. Indeed, their gender and their expected place at the center of the home made them especially well suited to exhibit and enact this kind of internationalism.

During the early Cold War, the prescribed formation of the nuclear family—a heterosexual married couple, children, and a middle-class suburban home—carried rhetorical and legislative power, becoming a necessary condition for the survival of democracy.[58] Adoption and the socially engineered family made it possible for those who were childless to participate in this national project. Stranger adoptions in the United States gained increased acceptance in the 1950s. By 1957 the US Children's Bureau estimated that there were approximately 91,000 stranger adoptions, compared to 16,000 in 1937.[59] This decade also saw the number of couples seeking to adopt far exceeding the number of children available domestically at a ratio of ten to one. Much of the interest came from the estimated four and a half million childless couples.[60]

By the 1950s, fewer domestic children were being relinquished for adoption, prospective adoptive couples faced long wait periods, and cases where birth mothers sought out their adopted children stoked concern.[61] These factors made the option of overseas adoptions an appealing alternative. With the child's parent(s) either deceased or living in a faraway land, the chances that a child would be reclaimed significantly decreased.[62] Intercountry adoptions were also more affordable and usually cut the average wait time of two to three years (for the domestic adoption of a white child) to just months (if adopting from South Korea through the Holt Adoption Program).

Logistically, the benefits of foreign adoptions made sense, but socially, this form of adoption required a radical reimagining of the American family. Throughout the 1940s and 1950s, biological likeness between children and adoptive parents dictated the majority of adoptee placements. Social welfare professionals believed that physical resemblance eased the transition for adoptive families and protected children from outside scrutiny. In this framework and to enable transnational adoptions, Korean and mixed-race children had to be made model adoptees. Circulating images of and understandings about Korean children made them honorary whites in a Cold War context. Politically billed as survivors of war and loyal children of democracy, and culturally manufactured to be resilient, Christian, and rapidly Americanizing, as described in the following chapter, Korean adoptees figured as safe additions to the white nuclear family. A critical part of this script relied upon the adoptive mother put in charge of raising the Korean child. For those who adopted from Korea, to the domestic value of white motherhood were added cosmopolitanism and internationalism. Adoptive mothers often understood their actions in these Cold War terms, a project inherently tied to an imperial right to mother.

Americans came to understand Korean adoptions as a First World responsibility. Countless postwar appeals on behalf of Korea's children affirmed for many the power and strength of America over a broken Korea. In a 1954 letter, a woman asked Congress to create a permanent adoption bill to allow for the admittance of Korean children. She explained, "My own little daughter is sleeping soundly in her crib, a full tummy, a nice warm bath, and an adoring Momie [sic] and Daddy. Yet, our happiness is blighted by the knowledge of these unfortunate children throughout the world."[63] The juxtaposition of First World and Third World made some feel guilty for all that they had and could potentially offer a Korean child. This "One World" logic served as the foundation upon which white women felt that they could accept an Asiatic baby.[64]

Convinced that Korean children would unquestionably lead better lives in the United States, women began demanding children and claiming ownership of them from afar. In one case, a woman tore a page out of a *McCall's* magazine and circled the face of the mixed-race child that she "wanted." Sending the page, as if an order form, along with a letter to President Rhee, she requested that he locate and send her this "unfortunate little girl."[65] The woman's presumption that she could enlist the direct help of South Korea's president and simply select a child reflected Americans' self-perceived right over and above Korea.

In another case involving a "full-blooded" Korean child, a white American woman had begun the process of adopting a girl whose parents were believed to have died in the war. After months of searching, the child's biological father discovered his child in an orphanage; they were among the thousands of families that had been separated while escaping bombs during the war. Overjoyed at being reunited with his daughter, the father, unsurprisingly, refused to sign the relinquishment forms. The potential adoptive American mother was incensed that she could no longer receive the child. In one of many letters to Korean consul general Young Han Choo, she argued, "I can't help feeling [that the child's] father would be unselfish enough to sign [her] release so that she might enjoy the benefits of life in America. She would have both a mother and father also, and we do love her very dearly. In fact we do not see how we can give her up."[66] That the woman already felt the child was hers, and that she along with her husband would make better parents than the child's own father highlighted her sense of First World superiority. Empowered by the firm belief that she could, without question, offer more to a Korean child in the United States than a Korean parent in South Korea, justified her assumed right to break the existing family apart. In a follow-up letter, the woman asked incredulously, "How will the persons who deprived her of a home here in America feel when they fully realize what they have done?"[67] The question made it clear that in her view, not only did she deserve to have the Korean child, but also, if the Korean father failed to relinquish her, he would be directly responsible for the deprivations that the child would presumably face in South Korea.

These stories show the extent to which average Americans had learned the lessons conveyed through postwar waif appeals that positioned them as the intended and ideal rescuers. By adopting from Korea, white women believed that they could complete the arc of humanity that transcended both nation and blood; they could enact the ultimate Cold War duty as only an American mother could. They also built on existing Orientalist ideas about an impoverished, backwards Korea, but now added a solution for that destitution. In the above examples, *being* American followed an imperialist mindset that excused white adoptive mothers from seeing the unevenness of these adoptions. The US government's economic and military involvement in South Korea and the desperation of the postwar situation granted American women a significant amount of power and rewarded their demands. In the first of the two examples above, President

Rhee enlisted the help of Child Placement Service (CPS), established in 1954 and South Korea's only welfare agency at this time, to contact the orphanage in Pusan to find the child described by the woman. After going through the adoption process, the woman received the child whom she had requested. In the second case, the child in question remained with her biological father, but only after a drawn-out confrontation between the potential adoptive American mother and the Korean father, who had to prove his paternity in order to keep his daughter.[68] Though the American woman's incessant efforts to take the child away from her Korean father raised red flags, CPS sent a "UN bab[y]" in her place.[69] In the end, the unequal relationship between nations shaped the unyielding presumption of adoptive American parents that Korean children would unequivocally lead better, happier lives under the care of white adoptive parents in the United States.

Tied into discourses about American adoptions benefitting Korean children were accompanying narratives about how the children benefitted white adoptive women. During the Cold War, when motherhood was considered to be a front line of defense against communism at home and a married woman's inability to reproduce was considered to be a symptom of hidden reservations about motherhood, Korean and Korean-white adoptees helped women access normative citizenry.[70] The hand-drawn image in figure 3.2 illustrates how the adoption of two Korean-white children did just this for one woman. The adoptive mother draws her house nestled in a wooded grove, but a small portion of the larger plot of land owned by her and her husband. Descriptions neatly line the length of the picture, detailing that they have two cars, a four-bedroom, two-bath home, chickens, a garden, a tool shed, and a bomb shelter, the latter a sign of wealth and Cold War preparedness. The arrival of the children, as mapped by the dots, shows that they were placed directly into the home, thus forming the family pictured in the upper left corner. "Papa," "Mama," "Son," and "Daughter" make up the new nuclear family, which completes her proverbial middle-class checklist.

Like the narrative fictions proliferating in the media, the woman's drawing conveniently leaves out certain details. Storks deliver the adopted children from "Korea to America," erasing the existence of the children's birth mother in Korea and birth father in the United States. The fairytale metaphor was commonly used to describe the arrival of

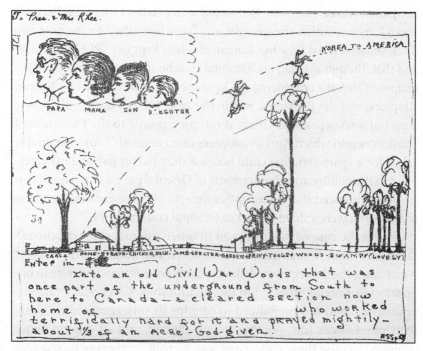

Figure 3.2. Drawing by an adoptive mother of two Korean-white children from South Korea. Mrs. S. to Syngman Rhee and Francesca Donner, March 16, 1958, reel P-2, section 18, 1390/1485.4, Koa kukŭi ibyang [Foreign Overseas Adoptions] 1956–60, MoFA. Courtesy of Ministry of Foreign Affairs, Korea.

children from Korea.[71] The illustration also described American racial discrimination as a problem of the past. In the text at the bottom of the image, the adoptive mother wrote that her land was in fact an "old Civil War Woods" that was part of the "underground from [the] South to . . . Canada." The land itself signified a safe passage that ushered slaves to freedom, and, symbolically, mixed-race children from Korean oppression to US acceptance. That she understood her actions as an expression of racial liberalism underscored the extent to which Korean adoption proponents framed transnational adoptions in these terms.

While she clearly saw herself as part of a broader democratic project that envisioned the United States as a racial democracy, she could not avoid seeing her adopted children in racialized terms. In another letter to Madame Rhee, she wrote that added to her "latest Oriental collection" was a kimono, which she thought was "very beautiful." In the next two lines, she described how her Korean children kept her "PLENTY busy" and that, though she had an "Oriental cookbook," she had yet to try the recipes.[72] That she considered the Japanese dress, the mixed-race Korean adoptees, and the cookbook within the same literary breath, all loosely a part of a smorgasbord Oriental category, points to the Orientalized constructs into which Korean adoptees often entered.[73] Another couple asked for a "part-Oriental child because they [were] particularly interested in the culture and characteristic of Oriental peoples," a request that further evidenced the consumptive aspects of these exchanges, where the children were valued in part as Oriental commodities.[74]

As was the case of binaries used in other colonial contexts, though the stories about Korea's mixed-race children said nothing directly about Americans, the descriptions defined exactly who Americans were in opposition to Korean others.[75] In this relationship, Korea was weak, impoverished, and too prejudiced to care for its miscegenated children; the United States was wealthy, racially diverse, and all-around better equipped to raise these children of war. Korean mothers of mixed-race children were assumed to be prostitutes and hence deemed unfit, undeserving mothers; white Christian adoptive mothers were their foil, women who were innately qualified to raise proper democratic citizens, even if the children were not biological kin.[76]

The legal and social unpreparedness of the US government to receive these children revealed the extent to which it did not expect the mobilization of thousands of Americans on both sides of the Pacific around this cause. Throughout the 1950s, Americans navigated through and around existing legislation to bring Korean and mixed-race children to the United States. The GI baby campaign publicized by figures like Holt and Buck and backed by the work of white American women turned a missionary crusade to save Korea's children into a nationwide movement aimed at forging permanent paths to transnational adoptions.[77]

Legal Makings of the Transnational Adoptee

In 1951 *Life* magazine celebrated the "one-family UN" created by Christian adoptive parents Helen and Carl Doss, who adopted children from around the globe.[78] In a 1952 *Saturday Review* article, Pearl Buck noted that intercountry adoptions that resulted in mixed-race, Asian and American families could improve political relations between the United States and Asia.[79] Buck and other adoption advocates framed the formation of US-Korean families as furthering US Cold War aims. Christina Klein has demonstrated how the "hybrid, multiracial, multinational family" that became a regular feature of postwar middlebrow culture during the Cold War encouraged Americans to think of integration in terms of voluntary affiliation rather than as a goal achieved by force.[80] Positioned in these ways, international familial ties could help assuage global accusations of US imperialism and promote visions of domestic racial harmony, just as a refusal to address Third World children-in-need could damage the United States' ever-important and vulnerable Cold War reputation.

Holt and others who publicized the plight of GI babies often pointed an accusatory finger at their American fathers and the US government. Americans who were deeply moved by these stories started to criticize the US government for its inaction. One woman wrote to the US Senate Foreign Relations Committee asking what they were doing to help the "babies left by our soldiers," who rove the streets "eating out of garbage pails, and even eating the bark off of trees."[81] A male repair shop employee from South Carolina wrote to a member of the House of Representatives directly blaming the US military for the "particularly awful" situation faced by GI babies. He asked what the government was doing to "relieve the terrible suffering and deprivation of the thousands of illegitimate children who were left in Korea by the US soldiers after the war in Korea."[82] In March 1954, Mrs. William Burns of the International Social Service was invited to speak at the Saturday Morning Club of New Haven, Connecticut. She criticized the government for barring legal marriage between US servicemen and "native" women abroad, because this led to the birth of thousands of illegitimate children. Shouldn't the US military and American fathers, she wondered, carry some of the burden?[83] Private citizens' critiques that highlighted the shortcomings of their government and military made administrators woefully aware of building public scrutiny and of the need to address the GI baby situation. A 1959 government report stated that "mixed children" were a "favorite subject of the Communist press," and that the US government scrambled to curtail the "hysteria" whipped up by popular US media.[84]

After the Korean War, US adoption agencies, including HAP, Welcome House, International Social Service (ISS), World Vision, and Catholic Committee for Refugees, together with American citizens wishing to adopt, submitted an increasing number of private adoption bills to Congress, pressuring the government to provide legislation for Korean children. Though some provisions existed for "eligible orphans" from war-torn countries after World War II, these measures did not apply to Korean children.[85] Existing immigration restrictions further complicated the process for Korean and other Asian children. The McCarran-Walter Act of 1952, which allowed one hundred Koreans to enter annually, counted "half-American" children as Korean. The categorization denied them nonquota status, thus requiring individual congressional bills for entry into the United States.[86] This process had been in place since World War II, when Americans began adopting "half-Japanese" children. The lengthy process for Japanese adoptions took anywhere from four months to two years, and screening for emigration eligibility could take up to twelve years.[87]

On March 19, 1953, Congressman Francis Walter introduced House Joint Resolution 228 in response to US military men who wished to adopt from Europe and Korea. The resolution permitted five hundred children under the age of six to enter from any country if a US citizen who was either serving abroad in the armed forces or employed by the US government adopted the child.[88] Later that same year, the Refugee Relief Act (RRA) allotted four thousand special nonquota visas, a thousand each for children from Greece, Hong Kong, South Korea, and Japan.[89] The largest number of children to come to the United States via the RRA came from Japan, Italy, Greece, Korea, Australia, and Germany, in that order.[90] Of the 2,418 Asian children who came under the first phase of the RRA, two-thirds were Japanese.[91] Although the wait list for Korean children in the United States reached well over 1,000, with 454 couples from California alone, war-torn South Korea could not easily meet the demand.[92]

The recent war in Korea and the complete devastation left in its wake made it difficult to process the children. At this point, adoption law in

Korea had been governed by customs, not statutory laws. US requirements that built upon already established immigration and domestic adoption laws were much more involved, making it difficult for Korean officials to gather the necessary documents.[93] As of July 1954, the Korean consul general in San Francisco reported that while Japan had filed several hundred applications, Korea had not yet filed any. He explained that they would need to begin immediately if they planned to send children before the RRA expired in December 1956.[94] With hundreds of thousands of displaced children and no legislation to govern overseas adoptions, the Korean Ministry of Social Affairs and the Ministry of Foreign Affairs scrambled to set up some kind of protocol. In accordance with the existing Korean Civil Act, Korean officials required a signed statement from the relatives of the child or director of the orphanage if the child was institutionalized or the parents were deceased or missing, the endorsement of two witnesses, the names, ages, and addresses of the adoptive couples, and a certificate by the Korean ambassador or from the government of the adoptive parents' country that guaranteed that the child would be granted citizenship in their adoptive country.[95] These forms were especially difficult to obtain for homeless children because it could not be easily determined whether the parents were deceased or alive and unable to find their children.[96] Complicating matters, the war and the rampant spread of disease that followed caused many children to fail US health inspections.

Madeline Hsu describes how the number of visas allocated to Asians through the RRA was but a "drop in the bucket" of the 1.5 million refugees in Hong Kong alone.[97] What was supposed to be a token gesture of US humanitarian concern soon exceeded the intentions of legislators when American citizens pushed them to do more to help Asian children. An "enormous volume of mail" from families across the country and those stationed overseas pleaded for a renewal of the RRA, all pressuring Congress to act.[98] The Department of Defense (DoD) assessed the situation and concluded that the RRA's expiration would not curtail the search for adoptable children abroad because intercountry adoption had become "so much a part of our 'folkways'" that people would find ways to adopt even without permissive legislation. The DoD determined that the government could not ignore the "remarkable mobilization of voluntary child welfare agencies and departments of public welfare in relation to intercountry adoption planning."[99]

Though it did not state names, the DoD was likely referring to the Holts when describing how intercountry adoption proponents had become "increasingly vocal and succeeded in using the press to foster the impression that short-cut methods were fully justified in view of the desperate needs of children abroad."[100] Indeed, the Holts were always on hand to offer their opinions about Korean adoptions. In July 1957, Bertha Holt complained to newspaper reporters that while Congress was quibbling over the law, children were dying. She explained that Korean birth mothers brought mixed-race children on their backs to orphanages in South Korea to sign adoption releases. According to Holt, the Korean mothers knew that the children had "no future in Korea and that if they [came] to America they would be loved and cared for."[101]

Pushed by adoption proponents and citizens, the DoD recommended that Congress pass the Orphan Bill of 1957 to replace the Refugee Relief Act of 1953. Lawmakers considered the bill necessary after extensively analyzing the several hundred private immigration bills that accumulated after the RRA expired. Wishing to reduce the number of private bills from a "flood to a trickle" and in an effort to halt the "quickie" adoptions that bordered on "black market" practice that multiplied after the RRA, Congress enacted a new bill that did not cap the number of visas that could be issued and increased the age limit of eligible adoptees from ten to fourteen years old.[102]

When the Orphan Bill expired on June 30, 1959, the lapse in adoption legislation again brought about a surge of pressure from intercountry adoption proponents and prospective parents. In September 1961, international adoption was finally given a permanent place in US law. As an amendment to the Immigration and Nationality Act, the 1961 clause required that adoptive couples meet the pre-adoption requirements of their state of residence to assure that the internationally adopted child would have the same protections as that granted to a child adopted domestically.[103] The biggest change brought about by the 1961 law was an end to proxy adoptions. The new law stipulated that adoptive parents see and observe the child prior to or during adoption abroad, and that the child would need to come to the United States for subsequent adoption.[104] There remained a loophole that made it possible for proxy adoptions to continue. Likely in response to pressure from Holt and his growing constituency, proxy adoptions were still permitted as long as the child was readopted once he or she arrived in the United States. Yet despite the loophole, the new law significantly curtailed Holt's operations, decreasing the number of HAP placements of mixed-race children by 40 percent.[105]

The battle for permanent adoption legislation was waged by a mix of missionaries, adoption advocates, and average Americans, many of whom had learned about the plight of GI babies from missionary accounts. Armed with this knowledge, they took the US government to task for not providing for the children. US missionary campaigns exposed the damage wrought by US military servicemen upon thousands of Korean women and children. In particular, Harry Holt's alarmist news about GI babies and sensational stork plane rescues furthered his mission to bring these children into Christian American homes, but also simultaneously aired the failures of the US government, forcing the latter to react. What Holt, Buck, and others who spoke publicly about children abandoned by American fathers effectively did was criticize American empire. Like other cultural internationalists, American transnational adoption proponents pushed their government to have a more open door policy when it came to immigration.[106] Further and indirectly, their advocacy for Korean adoptions called attention to the ongoing domestic problem of racial segregation and discrimination. While the primary reason for adoption advocates to lobby for legislation was to establish permanent paths to transnational adoptions, they leveraged the Cold War needs of the US government to reach their goals. Similar to civil rights activists who used the international realm to bring attention to US racial discrimination to win civil rights legislation, Americans publicized the plight of abandoned children of US empire and forced the government to make changes in restrictive immigration laws to remedy the problems that it was responsible for causing.[107]

From Mission to Movement to Erasure

Between 1955 and 1966, approximately 6,050 US families adopted children from Korea; 2,750 of these children were Korean-white, and roughly 800 were Korean-black.[108] Behind these numbers were the American missionaries who worked to disseminate news of Korea's GI babies, administer orphanages in South Korea, initiate overseas adoptions, and mobilize thousands of American women to respond to the transnational call for motherhood. It is remarkable to see how the work of private American citizens altered the course of American empire in material ways. The short amount of time it took to make transnational and transracial adoptions appealing to Americans, especially amidst the racial tensions of the 1950s and in the face of restrictive Asian immigration laws, reveals the collective power of average Americans who answered their nation's call to internationalism. The US government may have initially supported the humanitarian work of missionaries, but it could not stop the fervor of those same missionaries who pushed for transnational adoptions or the desire of American women who wanted to bring Korean children home. The practice had grown so rapidly that by the late 1950s, it was argued that children had become Korea's largest export.[109]

The flurry of activity surrounding the making of transpacific Cold War families began with the making and management of the mixed-race child. It is revealing, but perhaps not surprising given the imperial context, how these processes excised the very subjects at its center. From missionary caretakers in South Korea to Harry Holt and others who exposed the children in order to garner support for them to the women in America who imagined that these children always already belonged to them, those who sought to save the children constructed lofty conceptions of self, while erasing the children themselves. Decisions were hastily made in their "best interest" without a full consideration of what the children, who had survived the war but lost their family along the way, wanted. While the presumption that children were too young to be a part of the decision-making process surrounding them seems logical, especially when it came to those under the age of one or two, it is revealing to see how multiple identities were created over and above the Korean child—the adoptive American mother, the benevolent missionary, the magnanimous US government—while thousands of individual children were forced to inhabit a single identity—a helpless child in need of rescue.

In the 1950s, self-perceptions of what adoptive couples, and especially mothers, believed they were doing to help Korea's children, to carry out the work of God and support Cold War internationalism, prevented many from questioning the true extent of their liberalism or their complicity in participating in American empire. The assumption that Korea's children and especially its mixed-race children were unarguably "better off" in the United States reflected an imperialist mindset blinded to the perspectives of the Korean children themselves. Jane Jeong Trenka, who was adopted from Korea by a white couple from Minnesota in 1972, explains that the situation was more fraught than most could have imagined:

> Would I rather have not been adopted? *I don't know.* The question demands that I calculate unquantifiables. How can I weigh the loss of my language and culture against the freedom that America has to offer, the opportunity to have the same rights as a man? How can a person exiled as a child, without a choice, possibly fathom how he would have "turned out" had he stayed in Korea? How many educational opportunities must I mark on my tally sheet before I can say it was worth losing my mother? How can an adoptee weigh her terrible loss against the burden of gratitude she feels for her adoptive country and parents?[110]

Trenka asks questions that lay at the heart of transnational adoptions past and present, ones that were further supplanted when the children arrived in the United States and were swallowed whole by assimilation narratives that made them acceptable immigrants at the expense of seeing the trauma that they carried with them as they stepped off the plane and into America.

4

Producing Model Korean Adoptees

The arrival of the Korean adoptee to the United States beginning in the mid-1950s completed the full arc of the Korean child narrative. From images of wartime mascots and waifs to the modern Korean choirs performing in the United States to the now all-American child thriving in his or her new home, the journey and transformation of the Korean child as told by the press was remarkable. Seemingly overnight, Korean children became American. In the context of 1950s America, Korean adoptees should have signaled a litany of problems—nonwhite immigration, interracial families, and the corporeal return of American empire. Yet US media, adoption proponents, and even the US government, which had recently tried to block their entry, made it appear as though the children were destined to be in America. Of course, it was not simply fate that brought them permanently to the United States; rather, politics had made Korean children essential to US efforts to negate accusations of imperialism abroad, and, once they arrived in the United States, racism at home. Korean adoptees living in America, despite their unintended arrival, remedied the shortcomings of US democracy, a process that needed US media outlets to script their arrivals just so.

With children made legal members of American families, the ambiguity and distance of the imagined child far away in Korea or even temporarily in the United States, as in the case of the choir children, collapsed into the identity of the Korean adoptee. Like carefully crafted wartime stories about GIs caring for mascots, narratives about Korean adoptees were meticulously conceived. That mainstream media framed this story primarily around "full-blooded" Korean children, typically during their first day in America, spoke volumes about the problems that lay just below the surface. These narratives supplanted mixed-race children, who made up nearly 70 percent of Korean adoptions in the 1950s, and the concomitant problems of the GI baby, which included miscegenation, interracial sex, out-of-wedlock birth, abandonment by

US serviceman, and the existence of Korean birth mothers. They also helped to correct the failures of the war and suggest a future transpacific kinship in democracy. For Korean adoptees to work for US Cold War aims, the children had to become indisputably American. In popular magazines, the Korean face of the child was the only remaining trace of the unpopular war and America's continued militarism in South Korea. When placed in Western clothing and surrounded by American things from television sets to carousels to toy pistols, the transformation of the children subsumed their Koreanness—an assimilative quality essential to emerging visions of Asian model minorities. Despite what the media reported, this process did not happen overnight and it was not as natural as it was made to appear. It was a transnational process that began in South Korea in US-sponsored institutions, continued with the Immigration and Naturalization Service (INS), which screened immigrants across the Pacific, was managed by social workers on the US side, and was finally remade through popular media to fit the Cold War and civil rights needs of 1950s America.

Gatekeeping and Placement

Though on the surface, the adoption laws described in the previous chapter promoted US liberalism, resistance to making those laws permanent and built-in assurances to manage who could enter more accurately reflected the continued tepidness of the US government when it came to admitting foreign, and especially nonwhite, immigrants.[1] Adoption proponents and potential adoptive parents may have been successful at prying openings in immigration laws, but the INS was quick to add restrictions. To illuminate how international imperatives of the Cold War improved the acceptance of certain kinds of Asian immigrants, Madeline Hsu considers immigration as both a restrictive and selective process. Hsu describes how screening immigrants for educational attainment and economic potential opened the gates to some Chinese refugees in the 1950s, while keeping the gates closed to those deemed likely to become public charges.[2] Similar structures were put in place for non-laboring Korean migrants. When it came to Korea, built-in assurances that the children—and, in the case of brides, women—were of upstanding moral character and would not become charges of the state dictated who could enter and who could not, and served as reminders of the limits of Cold War liberalism.

Given the gatekeeping habits of US policy makers when it came to immigration, even the admittance of small, seemingly apolitical children triggered fears about how their entry might negatively affect the health of the nation. Lawmakers worried about the potential bad influence that refugee migrants might have upon their American peers.[3] Some fretted that the children would become national security threats or drain US resources. In an effort to prevent such outcomes, the INS established and enforced a set of rules. The INS issued visas only to those with irrevocable releases signed by the child's parent or guardian that guaranteed the severance of all ties to the child's country of origin. Only married couples, of which at least one was a US citizen, could adopt no more than two children (except in cases when limiting the number would result in the separation of siblings). The INS made it explicit that the adoptive family would be responsible for the schooling and proper upbringing of the child so that he or she would not "require aid at public expense for essential food, clothing, shelter or for medical treatment."[4] By placing the onus of responsibility upon the adoptive parents to assure that their child would never become a charge of the state, the US government abdicated its responsibility for the child before the child ever arrived.

Still, the question of who could enter and where the child should be placed remained. State and local welfare agencies facilitated the placements, but it was ultimately the INS that took charge of what, in its perspective, was first and foremost an immigration issue. Under the Refugee Relief Act, visa issuance depended upon the recommendation of a recognized US child welfare agency; however, the amended 1957 Refugee Relief Act made these studies supplementary to the INS's own investigations.[5] Child welfare professionals criticized the policy, arguing that INS staff was not adequately trained to make such assessments. This was likely true, but the decision reflected the prioritizing of national concerns over and above child welfare interests. A branch of the US Department of Justice, the INS was primarily concerned with assessing the suitability of immigrants. As such, INS officers "personally preexamine[d] adopted children." They scrutinized two things in particular: communist affiliations and the moral, mental, and physical fitness of the child, any of which if unsatisfactory would be grounds for visa denial.[6] That a child under the age of five, as was the case for most Korean adoptees at this time, could have communist affiliations seemed absurd, yet the provision was part of the law. Child reports from South Korea often included a line confirming that the child was indeed not a communist.[7]

In accordance with the 1957 amendment, the INS denied the entry of criminals, prostitutes, former prostitutes, or procurers unless they were entering as a spouse or child of a US citizen who would face "extreme hardship" if the "alien" was denied entry.[8] The assumption here was that the family unit (the husband in the case of a military bride or the parents of an adopted child) would be responsible for transforming the morally questionable immigrant into a respectable member of American society. Finally, INS officials inspected the child's medical examinations, also a new requirement as of 1957. Similar to the rules in place for Korean brides seeking entry to the United States, INS rules required officials to deny children with communicable diseases, like active cases of tuberculosis, or those who were physically or mentally impaired. By having the legislative power to pre-screen applicants, the INS effectively weeded out those determined to be unfit for American citizenry. As put by Pearl Buck, only those not "defective in mind or body," but rather "strong and intelligent" could gain entry into the United States.[9] To the extent that it could, the INS curated Korean immigration, screening those deemed Americanizable and barring any outliers.

When it came to transnational adoptions, the INS did what it was created to do—act as gatekeepers to suit the needs of the nation. In the case of Korean adoptions, the INS designed rules to benefit the United States, but left few assurances for Korea or the children themselves. Historically, Korean family registries mapped patrilineal genealogy based on a sequence of male heads of the household, leaving Korean women without legal recognition independent of their fathers or husbands. Bloodlines and lineage governed social belonging and cultural acceptance. Children slated for adoption were removed from existing Korean family registries if they had one; mixed-race children who were born out of wedlock did not have registries to begin with. Prospective adoptees had new family registries drawn up in Korea that made the child the head of his or her own single-person household, a document produced to guarantee that all ties to Korea would be fully severed. This step, intended to prevent future chain migration, stripped the child of citizenship from either country.[10] Given these circumstances, it was unsurprising that the Korean government sought additional assurances for their overseas adoptees.

On September 30, 1961, South Korea established the Orphan Adoption Special Law, the country's first modern adoption law. It followed this with the Child Welfare Act in an attempt to use intercountry adoption to resolve the problem of child institutionalization that emerged with the arrival of US missionaries in South Korea. Though the laws were hastily put together to coincide with the 1961 US adoption law, Korean welfare professionals and policy makers attempted to include added protections for the children, seeing that the United States prioritized its immigration needs over the well-being of Korean children. First, Korean lawmakers suggested that there be an immediate change of citizenship, from Korean to US, once the child was adopted. The advisory committee of the International Social Service and the INS rejected the idea, explaining that it would be difficult to send notice of US citizenship to the Korean government since US law required a residency period of two years prior to naturalization.[11] Second, the Korean committee asked that a child be officially adopted prior to leaving South Korea. The ISS felt that the request was "a bit of an international insult" since other countries did not doubt that the United States would follow through with the formal adoptions once the children arrived.[12]

Korean lawmakers conceded on these two points, but remained firm on their commitment to find relatives of a child before declaring her or him eligible for adoption. Korean advertisements seeking living relatives of children slated for adoption were posted in local newspapers and on court bulletin boards for a period of forty days.[13] This sought to prevent the accidental placement of children who had been separated from parents during the chaos of war, a problem that occurred with unfortunate frequency. The 1961 Korean law also established a Korean Civil Code that declared that adoptive parents should be "well conducted morally and ethically [and] not a malignant couple," that they would not "trade" or use the child for "hard work, drudgery, and kinds of work which tramples upon human rights," and that they would sign a pledge to recognize the child's "freedom of religion and provide education and protection."[14] Though difficult to enforce, the code reflected the Korean government's concern for the proper treatment of its young nationals. Yet when the child left Korea, while the guidelines remained in place, the ROK government's responsibility for and connection to the children ended. Once the child made it through the INS screening and was placed in an American home, so too did the US government's responsibility for the child end; the burden transferred from both states directly to the private adoptive family.

While mixed-race children hardly fit the INS's conception of the ideal immigrant, the public advocacy of adoption proponents made denying Korean and mixed-race children a liability. As much as the INS attempted to control exactly who and how many could enter, its disciplinary strategies were limited. Inserting Korean children into already existing American homes and managing them once they arrived extended beyond the purview of the INS. In an attempt to remedy the government's inability to manage the immigrant adoptees, the INS and the Department of State officially placed the International Social Service in charge of overseeing the actual placements.[15] Since the children would be entirely under the protection of their adoptive parents and peripherally by the child welfare agency assigned to them, the INS relied upon private and state agencies to pick up where it left off in an effort to ensure that those who entered would become the right kind of citizen without too radically disrupting the existing racial status quo.[16]

The US Department of Defense chose to work with and fund the ISS to oversee transnational adoptions beginning with the RRA in 1953. The DoD appreciated the organization's "positive role in substituting service for hysteria, in a professional approach to this sensitive subject [of 'mixed children']."[17] In operation since 1921, the ISS assisted individuals who as a consequence of "voluntary or forced migration or other social problems of an international character" needed a solution that required the coordinated action of several countries.[18] Over the years, the ISS worked with agencies like Church World Service, UNESCO, UNICEF, the World Council of Churches, and the International Refugee Organization, gaining the respect of social welfare workers and governments worldwide.[19] The ISS Korea branch opened in 1956 in response to the problem of mixed-race children. Working in conjunction with the ISS American branch and World Adoption International Fund (with the unmistakable acronym WAIF), a "Hollywood group" led by actress and adoptive mother of a Korean child, Jane Russell, ISS Korea used its best practices to match Korean and mixed-race children with American families.[20]

Official US government backing and funding helped professionalize the ISS and the state social welfare agencies with whom the ISS worked. Social welfare practitioners had spent a good part of the twentieth century struggling to establish the legitimacy of the field; the advent of the Cold War called attention to the growing significance and importance of social work. Though college-educated women first ventured into public welfare charity work in the 1880s and 1890s, the profession of social welfare gained momentum after the establishment of the US Children's Bureau in 1912, and its counterpart in the private sector, the Child Welfare League of America, in 1921. The number of social workers and child welfare reformers rose during the first two decades of the twentieth century. Professionalization remained a challenge that social workers tried to solve by increasing their programmatic presence in colleges and universities. Some remained skeptical of the field because practitioners based much of their research on their own personal experience, making their conclusions about effective techniques appear biased and unscientific. However, by midcentury, the profession had gained a permanent place in the United States, especially in the realm of domestic and international adoptions.[21]

Sara Fieldston charts professionalization through the globalization of US social welfare practices in the post–World War II era. She notes that between 1945 and 1949, over two hundred new private voluntary organizations worked overseas to help the vulnerable and "reshape the postwar world in the image of the United States."[22] The ways in which social workers implemented US child-rearing practices in their aid efforts abroad demonstrate the extent to which the field aligned itself with the Cold War needs of the state. As described in the previous chapter, US missionaries, though not formally trained (except for those who were also nurses, as was the case for Molly Holt), similarly brought Western modes of childcare to South Korea. While missionaries' efforts were intended to further proselytizing goals, social welfare workers sought professionalization of the field and, more specifically, women's professionalization through social welfare.

Fieldston shows that it was in large part the work of American welfare workers that placed children at the center of US efforts to contain communism, impressing freedom upon malleable children who would grow up embracing American democracy. The ISS was at the forefront of these practices and this form of child-centered global outreach. One of the main principles of the ISS American branch was to be "truly international, with its members and units in various countries working together on an equal footing, no one seeking to dominate or superimpose its ways on another."[23] While the work of US missionaries and the ISS ideologically converged and at times merged in material ways, there were significant differences. Missionaries, while adopting the Cold War language of internationalism, focused on their goal to save the children to Christianity. While this was actualized through the process of adoption, it was firmly bound to proselytizing efforts from the missionary-run orphanages in Korea to the Christian adoptive homes in America. The ISS aligned itself more squarely in the global politics of the postwar era, describing its work as an anti-imperialist approach to global influence, an alternative to US military power. It was in this context that the ISS embraced the liberal potential of transnational adoptions and understood the importance of sound placements upon the credibility of its field.

To assure the success of ISS placements, the organization's trained social workers were involved in the intercountry adoption process nearly every step of the way. ISS workers acted as liaisons between the INS, local welfare agencies, and Korea's only national welfare agency, Child Placement Service (CPS). The ISS reviewed the home studies conducted by accredited local state welfare agencies to determine the fitness of the prospective adoptive couple based on the following criteria: financial stability (was the family middle-class?), racial tolerance (could they love a Korean or mixed-race child who did not look like biological kin?), and cognizance of obstacles faced by multiracial families (would their neighbors, school, and church accept their nonwhite child?).[24] Meanwhile in South Korea, members of the ISS Korea branch worked with the child's existing parents or relatives, if any were known, and orphanage directors and guardians to assure that the child was available for adoption. The ISS also procured child history reports from CPS that detailed the child's mental and physical development.

Once the studies were complete, the ISS orchestrated the exchange. The potential adoptive couple received CPS's reports along with photographs of the child. Korean orphanage directors and CPS social workers reviewed the home studies. Once both sides approved, the adoptive couple completed the "Petition to Classify Alien as an Eligible Orphan" form and submitted it to the INS along with their birth certificates, marriage certificate, employment statement or income tax return, bank statements, and fingerprint cards. The ISS would then provide the INS with an abstract of the child, a signed release from the parent or guardian, proof of death or disappearance of parent(s), and the child's birth certificate or excerpt from a family registry. From here, the INS forwarded its recommendations to the appropriate consular offices and notified the ISS of its decision. Finally, a US consular official made his own examination and investigation of the child's eligibility for a nonquota visa, which included the child's health exam and a full review of documents, at which point a visa was either granted or denied.[25] The adoptive couple would then pay the ISS the visa, passport, and transportation fees, at which point the child's flight would be arranged. This lengthy process took a year on average (and usually longer), but was considered by the ISS and the INS to be the best protocol, and was the only one officially condoned by the US government for overseas adoptions from Korea.[26]

Despite the INS's intention to have the ISS be the single agency in charge of overseeing intercountry adoptions, the government could not control the activities of Harry Holt, whose expedited process of proxy adoptions drew thousands of Americans to his agency. In addition to the Holt Adoption Program, the National Catholic Welfare Service, the Seventh-day Adventist Church, Welcome House, and American Soul Clinic conducted their own operations independent of and sometimes in competition with the ISS.[27] Throughout the 1950s and into the 1960s, the ISS and Holt Adoption Program had a particularly contentious relationship. The ISS believed that Holt's hasty proxy adoptions resulted in increased adoption breakdowns. The ISS kept a running tally of Holt cases in which children were abused, had unstable parents, or were reassigned to another home.[28] Meanwhile, Holt criticized the ISS for its drawn-out process and purported obsession with race-matching practices, insisting that the situation of "mixed bloods" in Korea required much quicker and less stringent action.[29] Despite ISS attempts to coordinate with Holt, his agency refused to work with the ISS, which continued to lobby against proxy adoptions.

Complicating matters, an increasing number of potential adoptive parents readily chose HAP over the ISS because adopting through Holt was faster, as well as the only option for those previously denied by accredited agencies due to old age, single status, or financial instability.[30] As a result of these combined factors, Holt brought in the largest number of Korean adoptees in the 1950s. According to the Korean Ministry of Health and Social Affairs, between January 1955 and September 1960, the Holt Adoption Program placed 1,822 Korean children, or around 53 percent of all Korean adoptions during this period, whereas the ISS placed 180 children, or 5 percent of the total. While the Holt agency focused solely on South Korean adoptions at this time, the ISS served children from Austria, the British West Indies, British Guiana, Chile, Cyprus, Denmark, Finland, France, Germany, Great Britain, Greece, Hong Kong, Iran, Ireland, Israel, Italy, Korea, the Philippines, Portugal, Spain, Switzerland, and Yugoslavia.[31] Though the ISS was spread thin, the INS instructed all state social welfare agencies to conduct overseas adoptions through the ISS. Meanwhile, the Holt Adoption Program sent letters directly to its constituents, offering to carry out Korean adoptions expeditiously and without the hassle of state welfare agencies. In the end, HAP and the ISS worked autonomously, utilizing different methods to bring Korean children stateside.

Though the 1961 adoption law curbed Holt's use of proxy adoptions, the INS could not fully curtail that organization's operations. In choosing to partner with the ISS, which handled a much smaller caseload, the INS showed that it valued the extra assurances provided by the ISS. The ISS firmly believed that the right kind of adoptive family—namely, middle-class, heteronormative, homeowning American couples with a breadwinning male head of the household and stay-at-home mother—was the best bet for Korean adoptees; the INS believed that these were the conditions that could assure that the child would not become a charge of the state. The INS was not solely interested in the ISS's ability to select suitable homes for Korean children; it was also intently invested in how the ISS and the state welfare agencies with whom it worked approached the issue of race. The interracial and international aspects of Korean adoptions were groundbreaking for this time. From 1930 to 1960, US social workers aimed for biological likeness when matching children to adoptive parents. Welfare professionals believed that looking related helped children adjust to the family and made it easier for adoptive parents to accept the children as their own.[32] This social policy also assured the actual separation of races in domestic adoptions by preventing the creation of interracial families.

Korean adoptions pushed the boundaries of existing US adoption practices. A long history of restrictive immigration made for a small population of Koreans in America. For cultural reasons, few Koreans in Korea or the United States adopted children who did not share the same bloodlines. The number of Asian American couples interested in adoptions was also considerably low. These factors combined made it necessary for social workers to cross racial boundaries on a large scale for the first time.[33] Circulating cultural productions of Korean children from the cosmopolitan choir children to desperate GI babies helped white Americans interested in adoptions to broaden the scope of acceptable kinship to include interracial, transnational families. From the outset, white couples dominated the requests for Korean and Korean-white children, making it easier for social workers to find homes for Korean children.[34]

The ISS and local welfare agency home visits conveyed the success of these adoptions. According to post-placement visits, white parents who adopted Korean children typically demonstrated their capacity to love the children as if they were biological kin. Assessments concluded that Korean and Korean-white children adjusted particularly well to American life.[35] Some social workers and adoptive parents believed that the pronounced Caucasian features of Korean-white children eased the adjustment. Several social workers commented that Korean-white children even resembled their adoptive white mothers. One US serviceman described the two mixed-race Korean girls whom he wanted to adopt as "entirely Caucasian in appearance." He was certain that their whiteness coupled with their good behavior would guarantee them a "normal American childhood."[36] In the words of another adoptive couple, Korean-white children were "usually very lovely and . . . not always as dark as the Korean children."[37] Some considered the race mixture of Asian and white to be particularly exotic.

Frequent descriptions of "almond shape eyes" and the general good looks of Korean-white children made it into social worker assessments in South Korea and the United States.[38]

In the context of race-matching practices, that social workers and adoptive parents *saw* whiteness and felt it worthy of comment was tied into preconceived notions about acceptable forms of kinship. Historically in the United States, cultural imaginings of mixed-race families represented taboo interracial crossings, and this did not suddenly change in the 1950s to suit Cold War needs. Though some states began to dismantle antimiscegenation laws in the late 1940s, others still upheld the practice, if not legally, then socially.[39] The nation's perspective on mixed marriages reflected its views on interracial intimacies more broadly. According to a 1958 Gallup poll, nearly as many northern and western whites as southerners disapproved of interracial marriages, 92 and 99 percent, respectively.[40]

Long-standing and ongoing efforts to protect the fiction of white racial purity should have made Americans particularly wary of mixed-race children. That many Americans instead viewed Korean-white children as ideal adoptees was surprising. By culturally producing Korean-white children as "half-American" and similar to white Americans in appearance and behavior, those who adopted could embrace integrationist aims without disrupting the racial status quo. Korean-white adoptees did not dismantle the more rigid boundaries between white and black during the 1950s, and, as a result, their race mixture was less threatening. Further, the fact that the interracial sex that resulted in the mixed-race child happened outside of the United States in faraway Korea figured GI babies as not part of the domestic history of race mixture and its concomitant fears. The innocence of the child bound up in the cultural production of the GI baby helped assuage the problem of the child's miscegenation. These factors, coupled with the prevailing assumption that "full" Korean adoptees quickly assimilated, helped push Koreanness into the background, instead foregrounding desired whiteness in the behavior *and* appearance of Korean-white adoptees.

The carefully navigated construction of Korean and Korean-white adoptees achieved three state goals: it eased the nation's acceptance of interracial families formed as a result of the Korean War; it mollified Orientalist fears by showing that Koreans could be like Americans; and

it supplanted the underlying realities of interracial sex and child abandonment. This is not to say that Koreanness entirely disappeared. In
fact, Koreanness remained critical for the Cold War narrative to adhere. The visual trace of Koreanness in full-Korean and Korean-white
children evidenced US racial democracy. These particular versions of
transnational adoptions suggested that Americans accepted nonwhite
foreigners not only as members of the nation, but also as members of
their own families, but these were not the only kinds of children coming from Korea.

Upholding the Black-White Color Line

When it came to "Negro-Korean" children, as they were often referred
to in administrative documents, Cold War internationalism found
its limits. While social workers and Holt himself felt that Korean and
Korean-white children belonged with white American families, they felt
that "Negro-Korean" children belonged with African American couples.
When it came to overseas adoptions, the effort to maintain the black-
white color line reflected domestic adoption policies. In South Carolina,
for example, it was a crime to give colored persons custody of white
children. In Amityville, New York, the courts rejected a white couple's
plea to adopt a black child. In Cincinnati, two children of a white, female
divorcee were placed in an orphanage shortly before her marriage to an
African American man.[41] Legal barriers to black-white adoptions came
to include mixed-race children from Korea for whom any amount of
black blood constituted a black racial identity in the United States.[42]

Korean-black adoptees were socially, legally, and culturally categorized as African American. Unlike Korean-white children, whose sus-
pect Asianness was redeemed by white blood, "Negro-Korean" children
could not be saved by their model Korean half and instead confronted
the same racial prejudice as African Americans in the United States. In
segregated neighborhoods, Korean-black children could not live with
white families.[43] In a case of mistaken racial identity, a Korean adoptee
who according to records from the Holt agency was part Native American turned out to be "definitely actually part Negro." Upon making the
discovery, the neighborhood forced the adoptive family to move, warn-
ing that the child would never be accepted should the family try to stay.[44]

Instead of pushing for adoptions that crossed black-white boundaries, a practice that might have helped normalize integration, agencies and welfare workers upheld these existing racial boundaries in their practices. Specifically, the INS turned to the ISS to do what it itself could not without harming America's Cold War image—to place mixed-race Korean children along black-white racial lines. The resulting logic, which was liberal on the one hand and racially discriminatory on the other, characterized the US government's dilemma in enacting racial liberalism, upholding centuries-old domestic conceptions of white supremacy, and tending to its political objectives in South Korea all at once. When it came to mixed-race Korean adoptees who arrived in the United States already mixed, the only way to uphold the racial status quo was to determine their placement along the black-white color line.

Private citizens bolstered and socially policed existing racial boundaries independent of state or federal law. A white mother of two wrote to her local child welfare agency, "We have no prejudices toward dark coloring, however a too dark skin (for example a Negro GI-Korean mixture) would cause comment as our two [biological children] are fair."[45] Cases like these made social workers hesitant to place a child in certain homes due to the fear of community antagonism based "on the grounds that negroes [were] not apparently accepted."[46] Thus, whether the objection came from white neighbors or was the adoptive couple's racial preference, average American citizens played an active role in preventing the formation of adoptive black and white families.

In June 1958, Pearl Buck wrote an article titled "Should White Parents Adopt Brown Babies?" for *Ebony* magazine. Buck told the largely black readership of *Ebony* how they could adopt a child, and explained how by doing so they would also help combat US and South Korean racial prejudice toward the mixed-race youngsters.[47] Despite efforts like these, Pearl Buck and US social welfare professionals concluded that there existed an apparent dearth of African American couples interested in adoption.[48] Domestically, by the mid-1950s, 96,000 "non-white" children were born out of wedlock in the United States and were in need of adoptive homes. In 1951 only 4 percent of adoption petitions filed involved African American children.[49] Not only was it the perceived fault of presumably poor, single black women for having children, thus creating a strain on government resources, white policy makers also blamed the

African American community for not doing its part to resolve the problem through adoptions.

Social workers complained that it was difficult to place African American children because of adoptive couples' focus on coloration matching. According to welfare workers, African American couples requested children with fair or dark complexions that resembled their own, a matching process that stymied the number of placements. Between 1953 and 1961, the nonpartisan civil rights organization National Urban League (NUL) sponsored a "cultural study" called the Adoption Program. Though the NUL worked to help African American families and urged social welfare agencies to do the same, it also criticized African American adopters, reporting that there was "too much emphasis on color and a negative approach on the part of prospective parents on the way a child [would] turn out in terms of coloration and hair texture."[50] It was also believed that African Americans were culturally opposed to adopting children who were not related by blood. Regardless of the validity of these claims, the very idea that the difficulty of placing black children was the fault of African Americans was a red herring. It was what happened behind the scenes that acted as the greatest barrier to finding adoptive homes for African American and, after the Korean War, "Negro-Korean" children.

Most state adoption laws stipulated that adoptive couples be married, middle-class homeowners with a separate bedroom for the child, a stay-at-home mother, and financial stability. With African Americans being denied bank loans, receiving unequal pay, and not being able to buy homes in segregated neighborhoods where affordable homes were mass produced, many couples interested in adopting could not meet the minimum state requirements. The problem was so pronounced that the ISS found that it needed to bend the rules when placing Korean-black children. In one ISS case, an African American woman who wanted to adopt a mixed-race child from Korea was allowed to keep her job because her family needed the additional income.[51] Given that 40 percent of black women with small children worked outside the home, and that married black women were five times more likely to work for wages than married white women, social workers had to make concessions if they wanted to place African American or Korean-black children.[52] Kori Graves importantly notes that when African American couples were successful in adopting Afro-Korean children, they exposed placement agencies to family patterns practiced in black communities, and, as demonstrated in the above example where a working mother successfully adopted a child from Korea, came to alter existing conceptions of what constituted a good adoptive home.[53]

Local agencies with whom the ISS worked also resisted facilitating overseas adoptions of Korean-black children. State welfare agencies consistently tried to place local African American children first. Some did not want to admit more black children into the nation for fear that they too would eventually become charges of the state, an opinion tied to racialized assumptions that linked African Americans with state welfare. To avoid the issue, some agencies simply did not respond to couples wishing to adopt Korean-black children. In 1957, for instance, when the ISS sent profiles of available children to different state agencies asking that they try to find African American adoptive parents in their area, hardly any wrote back.[54]

In other cases, the ISS reported that "Negro applicants [hesitated] pressing their interest" because they did not feel comfortable with the local agency. A National Urban League survey found that agencies often alienated, discouraged, or offended African American prospective adopters, while some states rejected them outright. Time and again, African American women who sought adoption services were turned away.[55] Sweeping prejudice against African Americans more generally and African American women in particular, the latter deemed "unfit" mothers, no doubt triggered the denials.[56] If white adoptive mothers took their position as the primary rescuers of Korea's children, an action for which they were praised, the opportunity for African American women to do the same was foreclosed by the discriminatory practices that prevented them from adopting in the first place. In the public making of US-Korean families, then, heroism was racially reserved for whites only.

In the 1940s and 1950s, federal and state officials maintained that African American women were "reproductively unnatural." Women were accused of having babies so that they could get welfare, not for the purpose of making a family or out of maternal feeling.[57] When slotted into a black-white binary, racialized assumptions about black motherhood acted as a foil to white motherhood. Whereas white women purportedly desired children and accordingly gave birth to and reared them within nuclear families, thus exercising proper citizenship, black women were accused of having children out of wedlock in order to receive state assistance at the expense of white taxpayers, thus weakening the nation. Figured as outside the possibility of respectable motherhood, African American women were made to be unfit for any kind of family, biological or adoptive.

Racial discrimination had palpable consequences. Susan Pettiss, assistant director of the ISS, reported that though the organization had received about eighty letters of inquiry from African American families between September 1956 and April 1957, not more than a handful would materialize. In 1956, only four of the one hundred individually referred cases involving Korean-black children were approved for adoption.[58] To make matters worse, the series of obstacles blocking the placement of Korean-black children only increased the number of children institutionalized in Korea—an outcome that perpetuated the stereotype that Korean-black children were the "unwanted" or "undesirable" ones who would be reliant upon state welfare whether in the United States or South Korea.

The following Ohio case typified the barriers faced by African American couples wishing to adopt. To begin, the process usually took much longer than adoptions involving Korean or Korean-white children. The ISS opened the case in January 1955, and it remained active until August 1959, at which point Mr. and Mrs. S. finally adopted a "Japanese-Negro" girl and a "Korean-Negro" boy. To coordinate the adoption, the ISS worked with the director of Children's Protective Services of the Ohio Humane Society, which not only initially refused to help with the placements, but also actively worked against them. The director tried to convince Mrs. S. and Susan Pettiss of the ISS that they were wrong to "even think of adopting a child from the Far East" and that he would only assist in securing a "local child" as a substitute for a "foreign child." He reasoned that his agency was responsible to the local taxpayers who would have to pay for the child in the event that "both [adoptive parents] were killed in an accident before the child became 21."[59] The absurdity of this fictional scenario was a racialized code that reflected the director's belief that African American children because of their race were more prone to becoming charges of the state. Though clearly not a proponent of overseas adoptions more generally, the agency director demonstrated that at the heart of the matter was his belief that admitting foreign black children would increase the number of domestic children already reliant upon the state. It was only after Susan Pettiss wrote to his superiors at the Child Welfare Services of the Division of Social Administration and the State Department of Public Welfare to see whether his position could be "clarified" that the director hesitatingly changed his tune, indicating that he would assist in the placement of the foreign children in question.[60]

While home visits and interviews were required of prospective parents regardless of race, African American couples had to go above and beyond in their performance of citizenship in order to meet the minimum requirements for adoption. The social worker who visited the home of Mr. and Mrs. S. noted that they were a "good, clean, respectable couple, who [were] unusually ambitious and intelligent in relation to their background."[61] The caseworker continued that Mrs. S. "appeared" to be an "intelligent woman, cultured, well-educated" and a proper stay-at-home mother. A special note was made that she quit her job because her husband "wanted a wife, not a school teacher." Included in this couple's file were reference letters from their Methodist minister, insurance agent, and a construction business owner who had known the couple for two years and vouched that "their parental duties, cultural, physical, spiritual, moral, and finance [would] be carried on in the tradition of the average American home."[62] The standard measure, of course, was white and middle-class. Thus, "average" meant that the couple was similar to whites despite their "dark coloring." The report concluded that the couple had their priorities straight and that Mrs. S. demonstrated her fitness for motherhood. Like other prospective African American adoptive parents, the couple was judged for their proximity to whiteness in character, class, and intelligence, and, by default, their distance from blackness and its perceived negative traits.

Though photographs were not required of white adoptive couples, photographs of African American prospective adoptive parents were used to judge their "suitability" to raise a child. In a different case involving a Japanese-black child, the US secretary of the American Joint Commission for Japanese Orphans, who worked in Tokyo, wrote to the ISS that he was concerned upon receiving photographs of the potential parents. He claimed that some photographs revealed them to be "bright and normal," but others made them appear to be "poorly adjusted and sub-normal." According to psychological studies conducted on the child in question, her intelligence was "judged to be slightly above normal," and the secretary wanted to make sure that the African American couple was of "matching intelligence."[63] Though it was customary protocol for the child welfare agency in the states to send a photograph of the potential adoptive parents to the orphanage so as to acquaint the child with his or her future parents, rarely were such images used to assess the intelligence of the couple, as if intelligence were a visually identifiable trait in the first place.

For all the claims to liberalism surrounding overseas adoptions, the efforts made to keep Korean-black children out of white families and out of the United States altogether reified the deep and unwavering boundaries of race. In fact, the extent to which some agencies, social workers, and average Americans slotted Korean-black children into and as part of the existing domestic "Negro problem" before the children ever stepped foot in America reflected the disturbing ability of US racism to travel across national borders and take root in transnational processes. While Holt, who did not work directly with state welfare agencies, could more readily cross the black-white color line, he never strayed from his commitment to place children in Christian homes. In these ways, whether by race or religion, the purported liberalism of transnational adoptions from Korea were limited by the normalizing structures put in place to manage their arrival.

In the end, by adhering to the black-white color line, administrators avoided becoming the focus of ongoing integration debates. Maintaining black-white boundaries muted the potentially radical liberalism of mixed-race placements. It tamped down the latent controversy surrounding mixed-race adoptees from Korea and contributed to their erasure once they were physically in the United States, an elision made complete by the accompanying media fanfare surrounding their counterpart, the "full-blooded" Korean adoptee.

Making the Model Korean Adoptee

Although mixed-race adoptees outnumbered Korean children five to three during the 1950s, the most well-known adoptees were "full-blooded" Korean children. Media outlets gravitated to the less complicated story of the Korean child purportedly orphaned by the war, not abandoned by the American GI father and unable to be cared for by the Korean mother. Alongside news of the Korean children's choirs, popular magazines, including *Life*, the *Saturday Evening Post*, *Look*, and *McCall's*, and newspapers regularly published stories about Korean adoptees. One of the first widely publicized Korean adoptions was that of Lee Kyung Soo, whom we met at the start of this book. The renamed James Lee Paladino went on to become one of the most recognizable Korean adoptees, making appearances at fundraising events and documentary screenings where Americans could continue to witness his successful Americanization.

The adoption of Kang Koo Rhee followed a similar trajectory. *Life* chronicled his arrival in 1956 and reminded readers that the adopted child was the same boy who had appeared in war relief posters just a few years earlier.[64] *Life* first introduced Kang in a July 1951 article titled "The Little Boy Who Wouldn't Smile" (figure 4.1). His "small face drawn by hunger," skinny frame lost amidst too-large clothes, and downturned mouth represented Korea's luckless postwar children.[65] The institutional setting surrounding him—the paltry tray of food before him and the empty tables and chairs behind him—reminded viewers that Kang had no family and no home. Americans were familiar with the photograph of Kang, and thousands had made donations to support children like him. Five years later, the once frail Kang appeared healthy and happy in the United States, where he now lived with his adoptive mother, a white American widow (figure 4.2). The 1956 article juxtaposed the wartime photograph of Kang next to an image of the healthy and smiling ten-year-old adoptee, Korea's "before" to America's "after." Kang's complete transition from waif to all-American boy appeared to be immediate, effortless, and natural.

In addition to the physical and emotional transformation of Korean adoptees, the media aligned them with the United States politically. A photograph of adoptee Kathy Kim aptly demonstrated the prescribed

THE LITTLE BOY WHO WOULDN'T SMILE

Figure 4.1. War orphan Kang Koo Rhee in a Korean orphanage. Image used for Korean War relief posters. "The Little Boy Who Wouldn't Smile," *Life*, July 23, 1951, 91. Photograph by Michael Rougier. Getty Images.

path to proper citizenship for America's nonwhite minorities. According to the caption, the picture of John Kennedy Jr. that appeared on the front page of the *Chicago Tribune* on January 5, 1964, inspired the adoptee to "strike a similar pose."[66] The iconic photograph of little Kennedy Jr. at his father's funeral resonated deeply with American viewers, for whom the memory remained fresh. Kathy had climbed atop a dining room chair so that she could reach the photograph hanging on the wall and stand side-by-side with the young Kennedy in a salute for his father. The girl, newly arrived through the Holt Adoption Program, grieved alongside other Americans who lost a beloved leader. By likening Kim to Kennedy Jr., the photo positioned her and other Korean children like her as true democratic citizens whose heartfelt connections to the nation were immediate and sincere. The docile and quiet vision of Kim, wearing a dress with one hand delicately placed on the back of the chair for balance and the other in a shy salute, suggested a noncombative path to American citizenship. The photo revealed information about her adoptive parents, as well. They framed and hung the image of Kennedy Jr. in their home, a memorial that displayed their patriotism and possible alignment with the civil rights views of the assassinated president, each a marker of their fitness to raise a foreign child as a democracy-loving American.

Productions of Korean adoptees merged with domestic constructions of Asian American model minorities.[67] The postwar years saw legal, social, and economic changes as demonstrated by the removal of racial barriers against Asian Americans in some areas of the labor market and the ability of Asian American World War II veterans to buy homes (sometimes in integrated towns) and attend college. While some of these shifts were more symbolic than sweeping, they reflected positive views

Figure 4.2. Adopted Kang Koo Rhee rides a carousel in Los Angeles. "Wearing new American clothes, smiling Kang enjoys Los Angeles Carousel ride on first day in US." "A Famous Orphan Finds a Happy Home," *Life*, May 14, 1956, 129.

of Asian Americans during the early Cold War. Media touted the model qualities of Japanese Americans who after years of wrongful imprisonment had "pulled themselves up by their bootstraps" and integrated back into American society, purportedly without uttering a complaint, and of Chinese Americans whose adherence to nuclear family norms brought them into domestic respectability.[68] In the context of civil rights, the accommodating path exhibited by Asians in America was the administration's preferred mode of integration, as opposed to the public and legal approach to equal rights pursued by African Americans.

Korean adoptees arrived in the midst of this shifting domestic racial landscape and in some ways became the super model minority. They shared the model qualities of Asian Americans by being compliant and also, given their age, too young to have a political voice. Yet the circumstances of their adoption increased their potential to become even closer to whiteness. Social workers believed that the young age of the adoptees figured centrally in their path to assimilation.[69] For those too young to remember Korea, they were clean slates upon which American ideals, values, and behaviors could be readily imprinted. For those who were old enough to remember, Americans presumed that the children would be forever indebted to the United States for saving them from communism and grateful to their adoptive parents for the chance to grow up American.[70] Either way, Korean adoptees symbolized a silenced path to inclusion, demonstrating that nonwhite and even foreign others could receive the love and acceptance of white America if they obediently adhered to white norms.

Geographic considerations in the placement of adoptees also quite literally brought them closer to whiteness. Two social welfare professionals from Washington Children's Home Society found that "Oriental" adoptees adjusted particularly well when fully immersed in white American settings. Contrary to what one might have expected, Helen Jamison and Lucille Kane indicated that adoptees were better accepted in communities where there were "few Orientals, particularly when adopted by a family of good standing." The women explained that for those adopted into a community like Seattle, where Asians were segregated, the stigma and "old prejudices" tended to be passed on to the children.[71] In their assessment, assimilation into a predominantly white community made Korean adoptees more acceptable, whereas their presence in a community with other Asians where they would be negatively associated with that ethnic minority would result in racial discrimination. In their professional opinion, assimilation to whiteness rather than identification with Asianness proved the best path for Korean adoptees. Decisions like these geographically and socially denied adoptees the option of identifying with ethnic Asian communities, and left them few paths other than assimilation to whiteness.

Stories that appeared in the popular press almost always captured adoptees on their first day in the United States, and from what they wore to what they did, they seemed to be ready-made for life in America. Photos showed adoptees suited up as cowboys with toy pistols, talking on the telephone, eating ice cream cones, and watching television.[72] Adoptive parents spoke publicly and often about their well-behaved little charges. One bachelor father who adopted a mixed-race child said that "all Korean children are very well behaved. They are a lot less trouble than American children. They obey without question."[73] Public displays of the Korean waif transformed into a happy American child supported Cold War scripts that highlighted the opportunities available in a US democracy, and did more. These narratives imbued average Americans with the confidence that they could radically change the lives of destitute Third World children with very little effort. By now, Americans had learned from the media that the differences between life in the United States and life in South Korea were so vast that a Korean child would be exponentially better off just by being in the United States. The assumption that an American adoptive parent, even if single or elderly, would only benefit the child, further bolstered scripts of American greatness in the postwar era.

Social workers reinforced these cultural scripts. The ISS brochure "Practical Hints about Your Korean Child," sent to adoptive parents, included the "Morning prayer" and "Meal prayer" for parents to continue to use with their child, who had already learned these lessons in South Korea.[74] In addition to expected Christianity, Margaret A. Valk, ISS senior case consultant, explained in a matter-of-fact tone that "none of these [adoptive] families have tried very hard to learn any of the Korean words because the children have so quickly learned English words." Valk goes on to indicate that many of the children use the table manners taught to them when they were in Korea, and "all of them sing and keep the families entertained."[75] Valk's description was representative of the home studies that reported how Korean children quickly learned their ABCs and loved American food.[76]

Cultural constructions and welfare reports together demonstrated the extent to which the children had started on this path to Americanization before ever leaving South Korea. The transnational making of family included regular reports from orphanage administrators in South Korea, who corresponded with prospective adoptive parents, offering updates that detailed how the children were being prepared for life in America. Some reports included photographs of the children already dressed in the American clothing sent them by the adoptive couple or other American donors. They included descriptions of the children's temperament and often charted their improvement while under the care of Americans, or Koreans trained by Americans, in Korea.

The behavioral, model qualities of potential adoptees fell along gendered lines in accordance with US norms. One ISS report described how a boy who lost his parents and sisters in a bombing raid had turned to thievery to "satisfy the pangs of hunger, stay warm and find places to sleep." But under the care of the US military outfit that took him in, he become "honest and pure." The family that wished to adopt him wrote him weekly and received letters in return that detailed how the child had already assumed the American name that they gave him and became "very angry if referred to by his Korean name."[77] Typical of reports about boys, the emphasis was on behavior. To allay fears of a rebellious child, the reports noted whether he got "along fine with the other children," "obeys the teacher well," and whether or not he was generally a "good boy."[78] One orphanage administrator wrote, "[The child] likes to ask me when he would be taken to America and I answer him that he would when he has done a lot of nice good things and behaved well. And then he tries to be very nice."[79] Another report about the same child describes him as a "model boy and very good in every way."[80] The condition of adoption for boys relied upon their behavior and ability to listen to adult caretakers, and an absence of any signs of delinquency.

For girls, reports centered primarily upon their ability to nurture and clean. In the welfare reports of girl subjects, it was common to see notes like she "willingly takes care of younger children in the Home, and helps house-keeping too" or "she does kitchen works [sic] or cleaning rooms."[81] Many reports indicated that the girls were shy or quiet or liked to read. Gendered scripts of what made a "good boy" and a "good girl" revealed the extent to which the making of transnational families went beyond race to include US gendered expectations. From these reports, many of which were written in Korean and then translated to English to be sent to prospective adoptive couples, the ways in which US expectations were imposed upon everyone from the children themselves to the Korean administrators who were asked to report on these characteristics revealed the intimate workings of empire that, in the case of adoptees, served to make Koreans good American subjects prior to entering the United States.

These transnational processes converged to produce the US-Korean Cold War family. While US missionaries, social workers, nurses, volunteers, and government officials had their own goals in South Korea, their work intersected with and contributed to the making of the model Korean adoptee, a project that started in South Korea and ended in the United States. The upbeat tone of reports coming from Korea, correspondence intended to paint the children in a positive light to make them attractive to potential adoptive parents, set up unrealistic expectations for adoptive parents, some of whom grew impatient with their newly arrived children. One mother grew frustrated with her Korean child, who "could speak no English," and spanked her "severely" when the child grew "troublesome."[82] For welfare professionals and the couples that expected Korean adoptees to arrive already assimilated or at least well on their way to assimilation, the concept of preserving any bit of Korean culture fell out of their purview. Deemed a hindrance to the child's ability to belong, social workers and adoptive parents alike focused nearly all of their energy toward transforming the child into an American as swiftly as possible.[83]

Public narratives and private practices merged to produce particular visions of international democracy at the very same time that they suppressed the day-to-day realities of children's lives in Korea and the United States. Reports of a child who could not stop "chanting 'I want to go home' in Korean" did not make it into the mainstream press.[84] In these ways, media representations produced Cold War stories at the very same time that they eclipsed Korean ones. Scripts of extreme

assimilation left adoptees few options outside of complete Americanization. Further, the assimilation of Korean adoptees was total, and different from assimilative narratives applied to immigrants who came to the
United States by choice. For adoptees, national inclusion was predicated
upon an erasure of ties to South Korea, past and present, and a disavowal of the trauma that they had experienced there and continued to
experience in the United States.

The new American name given to adoptees, a process that often
began the moment a prospective adoptive couple saw a picture of the
child whom they would someday adopt, marked the violence inherent
in assimilating projects. One adoptive couple named their mixed-race
child from Korea Elizabeth and called her Libbie for short. They found
it endearing that the child could not pronounce her own name, saying
"Bibbie" instead.[85] In another case, a social worker identified potential
problems faced by an adoptee who "dislike[d] only rice" and rejected
Korean culture, but did not suggest ways to remedy his angst.[86] Rather
than reflect on the possible causes of these symptoms, such as a fear of
being rejected by his new American family or because he did not want
to be reminded of a home that he missed, American parents and social
workers were eager to view these behaviors as the hiccups on the way to
adjustment, not signs of trauma. A California social worker described
a Korean adoptee as "anxious to please," viewing this as a positive trait
rather than a potentially troubling expression of stress or fear.[87] Regardless of whether or not the noted behavior exhibited model qualities or
a lessening of non-model behaviors—such as not wetting the bed or
crying less frequently—the children were placed on a singular path to
Americanization that left little to no room for any lingering traces of
Korea or the trauma of war and separation.

Another key factor in making Korean adoptions acceptable and desirable was the fiction of eternal youth and childhood. Few publicly
discussed what would happen when these adoptees grew up into labor-
ing and sexualized adults. But in the private correspondence between
welfare workers, the limitations of US racial liberalism within transnational adoptions emerged. For example, in 1954, during a home study of
a white couple who wished to adopt a Korean girl, a social worker found
that the parents would not want the adopted child's Korean friends to
interact with their biological white children. Mrs. H. told a social worker

that "of course [the adopted child] could not marry a white person and would have to look for marriage amongst her own people." When the social worker suggested that, given the racial demographics of the neighborhood and surrounding area, the adoptee might not have the opportunity to meet "people of the child's own race," Mr. H. quickly said that he would still "insist upon her marrying into her own race." At one point during the interview, Mr. H. showed a bit more flexibility. Stating that while he would "definitely want [his adopted Korean daughter] to marry a man of her own race, . . . [he] would not object to her marrying a white boy if she fell in love with one." But after this he "spoke bitterly" about the marriages of American GIs with "Oriental women" and how people discriminated against the women once they arrived in the United States. When asked by the social worker how he reconciled this statement with the previous one, he simply answered, "She is a child and they are adults."[88] For Mr. and Mrs. H., the child's Koreanness did not pose a problem when she was young, but would certainly be a problem when she was an adult. Though positioned as protecting the child, Mr. H.'s comments ultimately demonstrated the fear of continued intermixture, not to mention the heteronormative expectations that he would place upon his adopted daughter.

Judging from the topics discussed amongst welfare professionals, it seemed that many shared Mr. H.'s views on intermarriage. In 1959 at a symposium sponsored by the ISS, a Yale psychology professor predicted that the largest obstacles for Asian adoptees in white families would come when the adoptee was of marriageable age. In her example of Chinese adoptions by white American couples, the psychologist explained that Americans viewed Chinese people, and thus the Oriental child, to be "secretive and clannish," "mysterious," and "perfidious."[89] A year later, US anthropologists, a Chinese American psychologist, a social psychiatrist, and a geneticist at a child welfare symposium explored the key question, "How should a family's ability to accept the child be judged if they believe that the child should marry only an Oriental?"[90] The question itself signaled the frequency with which this issue arose when placing Asian adoptees. An attendee expressed pessimism about interracial marriage, which, despite its increase, remained a "real problem in this country." He concluded with the poignant rhetorical question, "So, even if the child learns to compensate for his foreign background and physical distinction by competitive striving—what about intermarriage?"[91] *Ebony* magazine referred to the issue as the "puberty argument" to explain adoptive couples' anxieties about the marriage partners of the children in their interracial household.[92] Understanding the tenor of the nation, the media steered clear of discussing the long-term effects of Korean adoptions or what would happen when they were old enough to date and marry.

Importantly, Mr. H.'s contradictory opinions about race reflected his inability to reconcile conflicting attitudes about race in light of his seemingly internationalist action of trying to adopt from Korea. His personal dilemma of considering the young, innocent adoptee as separate from the sexualized adult version of that same person reflected the problem at the heart of Korean and mixed-race adoptions in the 1950s—being an internationalist, Christian American by adopting from South Korea did not supplant the existing Orientalist and racial logic also characteristic of being American at this time.

Seeing Korean Children

Photographs were central to communicating narratives of the model adoptee; and they were essential to the management of them. Collectively, they told a story of proper American citizenry, and offered a path for nonwhite and even foreign subjects to become American. Kandice Chuh notes the inherent problem with celebrating citizenship as tantamount to achieved equality. She warns that the model minority could be co-opted in the perpetuation of injustice.[93] Narratives that celebrated white American couples who adopted Korean children visually transformed Koreans into US citizens. Their model minority status served multiple functions: to mitigate the violence of war, to soften the excesses of ongoing US militarization in South Korea, and to provide a political context for US-South Korea relations through the familiar and nonthreatening framework of family, all while leaving the racial status quo in the United States largely intact. Korean adoptees became the vehicles through which the United States could claim exceptionalism. The publicness of their arrival allowed the liberatory potential of US racial democracy to linger, while obscuring the less favorable aspects of their difference. Their Koreanness furthered state needs by solving domestic and international shortcomings of US democracy, but their absorption into the private family home simultaneously capped the possibilities. Since racial integration was relegated to the space of the home, Korean adoptees disappeared almost in the very same moment that they were made visible by US media. They were shown to indicate that they exist, that this was happening, but then shuffled safely out of sight under the tutelage of white adoptive parents who would presumably continue the assimilating project under their own roof.

Public photographs could not always contain the fissures of these narratives. The strains surfaced in the expression of the child whose photograph, though carefully staged and selected from among sometimes hundreds of shots, could not fully temper the sadness. The perspectives of children were most clear in the private photographs used for administrative purposes. The one-and-a-half-inch headshots of children that appeared in South Korean wartime orphanage registries show the children with eyes puffy from crying and unsmiling with their lips pursed. They were told to sit still and look at the camera, an apparatus that most had probably never seen before. These photos identified the children, and the handwritten notes around the images provided additional information about whether the child had a "lighter color than this picture" or was "not so clever." Also recorded was the date they had "gone to America," yet these children looked nothing like the adoptees pictured in the United States.[94]

These ruptures of representation reveal the extent to which adoptee narratives were managed and produced for US and global consumption. Attempts to wipe away the perspectives of children traumatized by loss and separation are made hauntingly clear in the private photographs of wartime orphanages and welfare agencies. In order for narratives of rescue and benevolence to hold, everything had to be spun into a positive—Americans saved children, they provided bright futures for Korean children in a powerful country, Korean children who had been awaiting adoption were rapidly assimilating and happy to be in America. There was no room for the sadness, confusion, and pain experienced by the children. The registry photographs serve as a stark reminder that the public stories told to Americans about what was being done in the "best interest of the child" was more a reflection of who that child needed to be for the benefit of Americans. There were entire experiences and lives lived outside the frame in South Korea and the United States, stories that were markedly different from the ones Americans had grown so fond of seeing.

PART III

Erasing Empire

In 1952 US Staff Sergeant Norval E. Packwood published comic strips
that he drew while serving in the First Marine Division during the war.
In one cartoon, American GIs round up a group of Korean women (figure P.1). The scenario referenced the North Korean guerrilla tactic of
hiding weapons under women's clothes. Here, it was the captain's "task"
to search the women, who wore dresses resembling Korean hanboks save
for the snug fit of the tops and bold patterns of the skirts. The women,
with identical facial features, at once coy and inviting, suggestively
awaited the captain's search. Their lips painted and pursed together, the
women stood mute, in contrast to the open-mouthed soldier who yelled
at the men to keep them at bay.

The hypersexualized visage of Korean women so early on in the war,
seen here and in other cartoons that appeared in the military newspaper
Pacific Stars and Stripes, reflected the firm place of prostitution in US military operations.[1] Beginning at the turn of the twentieth century, prostitution was employed near US military bases in the Philippines, Guam,
and Hawai'i, and later appeared in Okinawa, South Korea, Vietnam, and
Thailand.[2] The portable imperialist practice merged and supported gendered US Orientalism that justified unfettered access to Asia and Asian
women, conceptions that made Asia perpetually ready for the taking. In
South Korea, US racialization of Korean women also intersected with
and continued the violence of the previous Japanese colonial military.[3] As
early as 1904, Japanese colonial authorities established public prostitution
that catered to Japanese soldiers stationed in Korea. The Japanese forced
200,000 women, most of them Korean and some as young as eleven, to
work in brothels during Japan's 1937 expansionist war in China. "Comfort
women" were kidnapped and some sold into sexual servitude by human
traffickers.[4] These overlapping imperial geographies were mapped upon
the bodies of Korean women.

Figure P.1. Cartoon of Asian women awaiting a US military search (detail). The soldier holding the rifle announces, "Awright, you guys stand back! The captain says *he'll* search this group of civilians for concealed weapons hisself . . ." Norval E. Packwood Jr., *Leatherhead in Korea* (Quantico, VA: Marine Corps Gazette, 1952), 26–27.

The first camptown or "GI town" was formed within months of the US occupation of South Korea in 1945.[5] The US Army Military Government (USAMG) condemned prostitution and attempted to outlaw it in 1946, while at the same time imposing inspections of women who served American GIs. Authorities permitted the practice to continue, stipulating that it was illegal only if a woman engaged in sexual intercourse with a member of the occupying forces while suffering from a sexually transmitted disease in an infectious stage.[6] Prostitution grew exponentially during the war. US military commanders tolerated the women so long as they provided services that the military did not want to supply itself, and did not slow down the troops as they moved from battle to battle. Many of the women began as camp followers, serving military needs as cooks, laundresses, and nurses.[7] The women came primarily from poor families in Korea's countryside. Some had been forced into sexual servitude during the Japanese colonial period.[8] Some were kidnapped and many were tricked into answering job placement advertisements only to be raped, beaten, and forced into indentured sexual slavery. War widows and orphans turned to prostitution in order to support themselves and their families.[9] By 1953, one government report estimated that there were 350,000 prostitutes in Korea, with 60 percent working around US military bases throughout the 1950s and 1960s.[10]

During and after the war, the US and South Korean governments sanctioned prostitution. The US military argued that its men stationed abroad needed sexual outlets to keep morale high and prevent them from deserting. Like other countries forced to contend with US occupying forces, the South Korean government felt that camptowns were far from ideal, but necessary to protect Korea's "virtuous" women from becoming victims of rape.[11] Though the US and South Korean governments did not systematically regulate camptowns until the 1970s, when they became profitable and permanent fixtures near established US bases, both actively tried to manage the women in an effort to mitigate sexually transmitted diseases.[12]

According to a 1952 UN Civil Affairs activities report, of the over thirty thousand prostitutes examined during the month of November, 30 percent showed infection of one or more diseases. The ratio of syphilis to gonorrhea was one to three. The city of Seoul's estimates put the infection rate of registered prostitutes at 22 percent and unregistered at 50 percent.[13] The very existence of "registered" and "unregistered" women evidenced institutionalized regulation that began with the war. The US military used this information to assure that infected women would not come in contact with its servicemen. In 1956, for example, US commanding generals in the Taegu area used hand-drawn maps to indicate which houses of prostitution reported high numbers of venereal disease. They hung "off limits" signs on these buildings and warned servicemen to stay away from establishments that were "detrimental to the health, welfare and morals of UN personnel."[14] The Korean police also regularly patrolled the brothels. For Koreans, the rising number of STD cases signaled the need to stop prostitution altogether.[15] Yet even these reports placed the blame upon Korean women for "sell[ing] their bodies for money" rather than directing attention to the root cause of prostitution.[16] These early monitoring practices imposed by both governments bound Korean women to US militarization, an association that lumped them together, summarily dismissing the women's needs and rights as individuals. The authorities were aware that for the estimated 335,000 war widows, there were few alternatives but to "shack up" with American soldiers as a "means of survival" for themselves and their children, but little was done to provide them aid.[17]

After the hostilities ceased, an estimated seventy thousand US combat support troops remained stationed in South Korea.[18] A decade later the number hovered around sixty-three thousand US servicemen.[19] Mounting reports of violence revealed the systemic and long-term effects of the US military upon Korean women.[20] In November 1956, a US serviceman was charged with life imprisonment for raping a Korean woman.[21] In June 1958, Korean witnesses stated that a US soldier raped, killed, and set fire to a Korean woman.[22] That same year, Specialist William G. Tefft strangled Woo Son Yi to death and set fire to her home. While originally charged with premeditated murder, Tefft received a much lighter sentence for involuntary manslaughter, signaling the kinds of protections that US servicemen received while stationed in South Korea.[23] In January 1960, American sergeants shaved the heads of two Korean women in the barracks. The incident was widely reported in South Korea and the United States. Korean senator Jung urged Korean women not to go near US military bases to prevent further "unfortunate happenings," while Kee Kang Hak, the national police director, declared that South Korea would demand punishment of the responsible American soldiers.[24] By the mid-1950s, Koreans openly and regularly criticized the US military. Korean civilians grew fearful of US soldiers who attacked locals.[25] A 1962 *Dong-A Ilbo* article reported that just outside the barbed-wire fences of US military bases, American servicemen attacked and raped innocent women, and stole from homes.[26] For Koreans, the article reified what many had witnessed firsthand—the problems brought by the US military were ongoing and affected a broad swath of the Korean public, particularly women.

For all of these reasons, it was best for the US government to elide the figure of the Korean woman. After the war, the publicity surrounding GI babies made her erasure even more pressing. Her omission became imperative to sustain the visions of US internationalism so carefully crafted around the figure of the Korean War adoptee. The final part of this book centers upon those who remained always outside of possible Cold War family frames. Korean prostitutes, birth mothers, and brides, as well as the children of GIs who remained in South Korea, required active removal for how they exposed US violence. In South Korea, abject women and children were hidden in institutions from camptowns to segregated schools to orphanages. In the United States, Korean military brides had to be obscured while in plain sight. Parts 1 and 2 of this book traced how the United States navigated its post–World War II power by transforming American servicemen into benevolent saviors of children and utilizing the unintended US-Korean families of war to evidence American racial democracy. Part 3 tells the other side of these narratives, the concomitant erasures necessary to support these productive scripts of empire. The Korean women and children in the following chapters are the untenable subjects of America's intimate empire, those hidden for fear of the truth that they could reveal.

5

Mixed-Race Children and Their Korean Mothers

In April 1956, the wife of a US serviceman stationed in South Korea wrote to President Rhee. In the letter, she explained that her husband met a "little girl of mixed heritage" in a Korean hospital. The child was around the same age as their own daughter who had died. The woman went on to explain that the child's Korean "mother was willing to give [her up] for adoption." However, just before she was to sign the release forms, the mother ran away, leaving her child behind. The serviceman and the national police searched for the Korean mother but could not find her.[1]

This story was incomplete. The statement that the Korean mother was "willing" to give up her daughter for adoption played into existing US scripts that supported the American couple's desire and right to adopt from Korea, in this case to presumably fill the void left by the loss of their own child. Yet when viewed from the perspective of the Korean mother who ran away, the story shifts. Bound up in her actions are the strains of caring for a mixed-race child rendered stateless by Korean law and made an outcast by society. Did the mother run away because she could not bear to sign the document that would permanently separate her from her daughter? Was it because she could not endure saying goodbye? Did she hope that if she disappeared, her child might find a fate different from the one decided at her hand should she sign that form? What became of the mother? Where could she have gone? Was there anyone who could have helped her? Did the child ultimately go to the United States like so many before her? Or did she remain institutionalized in South Korea?

Korean mothers and their mixed-race children flashed up in letters, adoption correspondence, and welfare reports *because* they were the objects of concern. The extent to which mixed-race children appear across state archives was disproportionate. Since they constituted but a small fraction of the South Korean population, the sweeping efforts made to track them signaled the problem that they posed for both governments. The documents that reveal colonial attempts to tally and manage mixed-race children made up what Ann Laura Stoler has called "blueprints of distress," responses to an increase in undesirable (poor, mixed-race) charges. Management of these subjects in European colonial contexts show how administrators scrambled to control the unwanted outcomes of occupation.[2] Their efforts were aimed at resolving current problems and staving off future ones—to contain who mixed-race children were feared to be and to prevent who they might become.

That the above letter was housed in the administrative archives at the Korean Ministry of Foreign Affairs exposes the South Korean government's active involvement in removing mixed-race children from Korea, and raises innumerable questions about the uneven dynamics that framed these processes. The United States was implicated too. Not only was the "plight of GI babies" a direct outcome of US military presence in the peninsula, the ongoing Cold War needs of the United States demanded that some Korean children and all Korean women remain unseen. Internationalist scripts of Korean adoptions *relied* upon the public erasure of Korean mothers and their mixed-race children who had to remain in South Korea in order for the fiction of US racial harmony to hold.[3] For Korean mothers and their mixed-race children, their lives were made to unfold in the shadows of the faraway peninsula, out of sight and over there.

Removing GI Babies from South Korea

Koreans could not easily deny the aid of US missionaries even if some objected to their methods of proselytizing, institutionalization, and, after the war, overseas adoptions.[4] Once the immediate crisis of war subsided, Koreans began vocalizing the need to keep Koreans at home. Some argued that not being able to care for orphans domestically was a sign of national weakness. Others felt that, with the war's death toll reaching close to four million by Korean estimates, repopulation efforts depended upon the retention of Korean natives. In the words of a concerned Korean citizen who wrote to his government in 1955, it had become "cliché" and a "fad" for Koreans to believe that the emigration of children was a good solution to the war crisis. In his opinion, Korea needed to keep "right-minded and able-bodied" citizens in South Korea to help rebuild the country.[5]

Koreans tried to find local solutions for its children. In 1956 police chiefs in Seoul called upon wealthy Korean residents to each adopt one Korean child.[6] Thousands of Koreans gathered in Seoul City Theater to adopt a total of 1,911 orphans between the ages of five and ten. The media celebrated those who demonstrated their nationalism by adopting children not related by blood.[7] The event was unprecedented and also singular, leaving thousands of children still in need. Transnational adoptions to the United States far outpaced domestic efforts, and by the late 1950s it was rumored that Americans sold Korea's children on the black market.[8] Koreans feared that Americans were smuggling valuable young nationals into the United States and made additional efforts to increase domestic adoptions. In 1963 Korean orphanages held open houses for childless couples to visit and select a child to take home.[9] However, local efforts remained ineffective due to the cultural emphasis on bloodlines, limited support from the ROK government, and the available option to send children overseas.

The other side of the national goal to keep "pure" Koreans in South Korea was the pressure to remove all "mixed bloods." For a racially homogenous country, mixed-race children hampered Korean claims to independence and were troubling reminders of American empire. Previous colonization by China and Japan led to interethnic mixture, a problem that was less pressing since this population could "pass" as Korean.[10] Part-American children could not escape discrimination due to the visibility of their race mixture. Social stigma was backed by legal erasure. Born "out of wedlock" with assumed prostitute mothers and American GI fathers, mixed-race children were not assigned to a legal registry, the latter required for Korean citizenship. Mixed-race children were rendered stateless, a status that denied them basic human rights into adulthood.[11]

Visibly mixed-race GI babies ran counter to an emerging Korean modernity that had sovereignty as its end goal. In 1953 South Korean president Syngman Rhee made this clear by ordering a directive that mixed-race children be sent to "the country of their father's" birth. Rhee suggested that the "half-American" children were America's responsibility and hence belonged in the United States, where they would have

greater opportunities.[12] Madame Rhee, the Ministry of Health and Social Affairs, and the Welfare Committee of the Korea National Assembly
agreed with the president that "beggar and unwanted children" might
fare better in another country, and together declared that the number
one welfare project in South Korea was to send mixed-race children
to the United States.[13] The president and his administration's choice of
words revealed a desire to hold Americans accountable as much as it
reflected Korean prejudice against mixed-race children. US extraterritorial rights made it increasingly difficult for the ROK government to hold
American servicemen responsible for their actions. Widespread abandonment of children occurred alongside ongoing US military offenses
against Koreans, including skirmishes with locals and regular assaults
on women.[14] In this context and somewhat unexpectedly, the work of
US missionaries gave the Korean government a way to hold the United
States accountable for its servicemen's indiscretions.

On January 20, 1954, Rhee created Child Placement Service (CPS)
to administer overseas adoptions for Korea's mixed-race children.[15]
In the beginning, CPS had only a single employee, but the organization soon found much-needed assistance from and an eager partner in
Harry Holt.[16] The Ministry of Foreign Affairs instructed CPS to grant
Holt and his agency, the Holt Adoption Program (HAP), all cooperation
and assistance to "spiritually and physically . . . get as many [mixed-
race] children as possible to the United States."[17] CPS referred mixed-
race children who were brought to the agency or found near US military
bases directly to the Holts for placement.[18] As early as February 1956,
just months after Holt personally adopted eight children, CPS helped
him place forty more children in American homes. Within its first year
of operation, HAP in cooperation with Korea's CPS placed approximately 250 predominantly mixed-race Korean children in the United
States.[19] By 1966, HAP alone had placed 3,576 children in the United
States, handily surpassing the number of children adopted through all
other agencies combined.[20]

As described in chapter 3, it was Holt's use of the press and proxy
adoptions that made him the "go-to" agency for Korean adoptions in the
United States; similarly, South Korean publicity surrounding Holt made
him the most well-known agency when it came to sending mixed-race
children to the United States. President Rhee presented Holt with one

of its highest awards for assisting Korea's mixed-race children.[21] It was rumored that the ROK government "would do almost anything [Holt] asked." For example, it changed a law that no building could be constructed near a gunpowder factory (for fear of an explosion that would result in the "loss of life") in order to accommodate the Holts, who planned to build an orphanage next to an existing plant.[22]

Korean newspapers, which were largely censored arms of the South Korean state, shared their government's enthusiasm about Holt.[23] In 1958 *Chosŏn Ilbo* printed an article that chronicled the successful placement of a mixed-race adoptee named Paulina. The journalist wrote that Paulina was abandoned by her parents, subsequently adopted by an American family, and now lived in California. At the age of four, she returned to Angel's Haven Orphanage in Seoul with her adoptive mother, who wanted to see where her daughter lived before coming to the States. Paulina's previous caretakers were overjoyed upon seeing the child's vibrant health and happiness. The article described her fine red dress and took note of the fact that Paulina warmly called Mrs. Daver "mom," indicators of prosperity and familial love that mixed-race children like Paulina would not find in Korea.[24] Paulina's fairy tale, which began with destitution and discrimination in Korea and ended with her thriving in an American home located in Hollywood, no less, affirmed the work of Holt. Her physical, emotional, and social transformation served as an advertisement for Holt's adoption services. Here, the taboo figure of the mixed-race child was conjured for the express purpose of promoting his or her removal. If US media constructions of the Korean adoptee at this time focused on the making of interracial Cold War families, South Korea's story was one of resolving the issues of fractured families, a way to promote overseas adoptions for mixed-race children without guilt.

Missing from US and South Korean public constructions of Korean adoptees were details about exactly *how* children like Paulina came to the United States. In the months before their "happily ever after" in America, mixed-race children underwent a series of procedures in South Korea that were kept out of public view. Behind the scenes in camptowns, orphanages, and welfare institutions, the children experienced lives wholly different from the ones seen by the South Korean or American public. While the circumstance of their arrival at welfare institutions varied, as described later in this chapter, once they found themselves there, they were monitored and diagnosed for the primary purpose of adoption to the United States. While orphanage administrators bathed, fed, and clothed the children, the orphanage was not a home. It was an institutionalized space in which doctors, nurses, administrators, missionaries, and social workers were free to enter to inspect the children, ask them questions, and take photographs without their consent. The children's placement inside orphanages rendered them subjects open to disciplinary practices and, for those who were mixed-race, additional levels of examination.

The ROK government's push to remove "as many as possible" of the mixed-race children to the "land of their fathers" opened South Korea to US racialized practices. As described in the previous chapter, US state welfare agencies stringently upheld black-white racial lines when it came to placing mixed-race Korean children. This required that the racial paternity of mixed-race children first be identified in South Korea. Though not always working together, US missionaries, social workers, and aides each contributed to bringing US race-identifying techniques to South Korea.

Americans taught Korean volunteers, welfare workers, and administrators how to identify whiteness and blackness for US race-matching purposes. American missionaries and social workers arrived in Korea already well-versed in US pseudo-scientific methods of race analysis, processes that were embedded socially and structurally. For instance, in response to the difficulty of identifying with certainty the "Negro heredity" of a Korean mixed-race child slated for US adoption, the director of child welfare at the Iowa Department of Social Welfare called upon the director of the Dwight Institute for Human Genetics at the University of Minnesota, Sheldon Reed, for advice. After describing the "mechanism of heredity of Negroid traits," Reed offered to personally help the agency identify black ancestry among their adoptable children. Reed wrote, "If you would like to collect some of the babies with alleged colored blood together on some one day in January or February I would be glad to give a short talk to examine them, pointing out the diagnostic characteristics which are useful."[25] Reed's willingness to identify for the purpose of teaching the "diagnostic characteristics" of blackness carried the weight of US racism dating back to slavery and the eugenics movement, and continuing through policies that used skin color and blood to uphold projects of white supremacy.[26] When Americans imparted similar lessons upon Koreans, they bound South Korea's social welfare state to a US domestic race politics that still lent credence to Jim Crow.

While US racism initially made itself known through occupying forces in 1945, when Koreans saw firsthand the mistreatment and segregation of African American servicemen, systemized processes used to identify race were not employed until the advent of transnational adoptions.[27] When it came to mixed-race children, the child's exact racial paternity may have mattered less to Koreans than the fact of miscegenation itself, the latter a visible marker of non-Korean blood. Thus, while Koreans saw and perhaps assigned difference to whiteness and blackness, it was not until US adoption needs required racial identification that South Koreans instituted processes to determine that difference. By 1954, US missionary-sponsored welfare agencies were using fill-in-the-blank forms to more efficiently identify the race mixture of children, indicating how quickly Western practices surrounding race were institutionalized and routinized in South Korea.[28] On one standardized form, directly underneath the section for the name and birth date of the child, administrators could quickly note whether the child's skin color was "light," "medium," "medium-dark," or "dark," and whether the child's hair was "straight" or "curly," "fine" or "coarse" by simply checking one of the provided boxes.[29] The upper right corner of the form was reserved for a snapshot of the child. Lines supplied next to the photograph gave administrators space to write whether the child appeared "lighter than this picture" or "darker in person."[30] Even dental records had a spot for the child's photograph and a designated space for the examiner to describe the child's "complexion" or "face color"—racial identification that had nothing to do with dental health.[31] In being told how to look for these racial markers, Koreans effectively learned how to *see* race like an American.

These processes exposed Korean children to invasive examinations. In unclear cases, of which there were many, administrators would turn to physical inspections in search of "negro traits." Americans taught Koreans how to examine the color of nail beds to assess the child's true coloring. They told them to examine the skin tone of genitals, especially scrotums, to predict the skin color babies would develop as they grew older.[32] Americans also asked Korean administrators to make special note of mixed-race children's bodily functions—about their sleeping patterns, whether or not they could "control elimination," and whether they cried more than the "average" amount.[33] These were notes that were combined with racial identification to determine whether the child was "good adoption material" and where the child belonged in the United States, with either a white or black family.[34]

US racializing processes did more than give a name to racial difference; it presented Koreans with ways to pathologize mixed-race children. In his 1955 appeal to US Congress for the admittance of six GI babies, Harry Holt explained,

> I am sure that Congress would be more than willing to help these little children of American fathers if they knew the facts. These little ones do not thrive well here [in Korea] because they do not have the resistance to parasites and disease that full-blooded Koreans have. Also, the [sic] seem to need a different diet than Korean children get along on, and do not thrive too well in Korean orphanages. There are several hundreds of these mixed-blood children here, many of them black.[35]

The ease with which Holt utilized social scientific and biomedical explanations to explain the additional challenges faced by mixed-race children evidenced how eugenic logic, even after it had lost favor in the wake of World War II, was used to justify and, in this case, demand US intervention. Holt's assessment tied a biological degeneracy to all mixed-race children, but especially to those who were part-black. This kind of racial logic served as the foundation upon which other US racial logics transferred to South Korea.

In 1955 CPS estimated that the proportion of "white to negro" was four to six.[36] Koreans came to understand this ratio in which a greater number of Korean-black children were left unadopted in US terms. According to Youn Taek Tahk, the president of CPS in 1965, the reason Americans did not adopt Korean-black children was that "Negro families [were] generally poor and unable to cover expenses to adopt a child; Negro families tend[ed] to have more children and [were] able to locate a child for adoption in the US," and that the "US government seemed not to be in favor of adoptions of Negroid children from other countries."[37] Tahk's generalized conclusions mirrored contemporaneous

US constructions of blackness that marked African Americans as impoverished without addressing the structural barriers that denied equal access.

In these ways, US-administered welfare institutions in South Korea served as locations for a transnational biopolitics. For mixed-race children, institutions were diagnostic centers, an in-between place where the details of their transition to the United States were worked out. The identifying and disciplinary practices imposed upon the children by both states were means to different ends. For South Korea, corralling mixed-race children into these institutions to then remove them to the United States was a way to eliminate those who lay permanently outside of Korean citizenry. The institutions disciplined and removed from society the "wrong kind" of reproduction; they managed mixed-race populations that visibly disrupted conceptions of a "pure" Korean identity at the heart of Korean modernizing projects. For the United States, since the government could no longer deny the entry of mixed-race Korean children due to the public outcry of American adoption proponents, the processes instituted in South Korea racially managed, to the extent that they could, the incoming population of mixed-race children. With US military fathers, the mixed-race adoptee could not convey the less complicated Cold War message of the Korean orphan, making the placement of GI babies along black-white racial lines all the more important.

These needs collapsed upon the bodies of mixed-race children, who were closely inspected—their hair touched, bodies examined, photographs taken and then scrutinized. These were the processes endured by babies too young to remember and young children who could recall, by those who found themselves away from their mothers and in an institution where they had little to no understanding of what might come next. It was here, in the welfare institution, that US race-matching needs converged with South Korean nationalist goals of removal, the latter a fate that would forever alter the lives not only of these children, but also the mothers who tried to raise them.

Erasing Korean Mothers

Public narratives about Korean mixed-race children in the United States and South Korea typically began and ended with their adoption. US adoption advocates repeatedly told a singular story about GI babies discovered on the doorsteps of Korean police stations, train depots, and orphanages.[38] They described the children as destitute with US serviceman fathers and Korean mothers who abandoned them; they said that GI babies were abundant, unwanted in South Korea, and awaiting adoption to the United States. These accounts eclipsed the experiences of the children and their birth mothers, who, like the children, experienced entire lives in South Korea that the public rarely saw. Yet unlike mixed-race children, who were made hypervisible to administrators for the purpose of their removal, Korean mothers were excised entirely, and at times by force. The adoptee narrative did not work with the mother as a visible part of the story. Telling about a child wrested from his or her mother could not support US scripts of benevolent rescue, nor could it foster South Korean narratives that insisted that mixed-race children were "better off" in America. The Korean mother was an impossible figure for both the United States and South Korea, a position that rendered her a liminal subject with the barest of rights.

While eclipsed from view, Korean mothers were at the center of the GI baby story. Records make it clear that contrary to public accounts, mixed-race children did not suddenly appear, unaccompanied and ready for adoption. Many were found under the care of their mothers. Increasing US demand for Korean children, especially children "mixed with white," coupled with South Korean efforts to remove them, set in motion processes that *made* children available for adoption. With President Rhee's 1953 directive to remove mixed-race children, South Korean government agents and adoption proponents began to advertise overseas adoptions as an option that was not only viable, but also ideal for mothers and their children.[39] It was common practice for Korea's Child Placement Service to show photographs of happily placed mixed-race Korean children with their adoptive American families to prove to wavering mothers the benefits of US adoption.[40] They inaccurately billed the United States as fully accepting of racially mixed children, leading many women who had witnessed discrimination against their children in Korea to view intercountry adoption as a possible solution.

A wide range of South Korean agents participated in the national project to send mixed-race children overseas. South Korea's first lady, Francesca Donner, avidly supported these efforts. An Austrian woman interracially married to Syngman Rhee with no biological children but who later adopted two Korean boys, Francesca Donner was able to skirt around the interracial details of her own family to support her husband's directive.[41] She vowed to help in "every way possible" to find American homes for Korea's GI babies.[42] In 1957 she informed Pearl Buck that the number of available mixed-race children recently "increased sharply" because mothers learned of Holt and other adoption programs and wanted their children to "lead a normal, happy life" in the United States.[43] As the target audience for advertisements about overseas adoptions, Korean mothers knew which agencies to approach if they wanted help sending their child to the United States. In one 1956 case, a mother brought her two-year-old child to the World Vision orphanage because the child's American father abandoned them and her family forbade her to keep the child. She explained that her Korean boyfriend was willing to make her "respectable" through marriage, but would do so only if she relinquished the child. World Vision could not accept the toddler at that time due to overcrowding. At five the next morning, orphanage staff found the child on the steps "half frozen," and subsequently took the child in.[44] Given the pressures placed upon her by Korean society, her boyfriend, and her family, it would have been impossible for the woman to have made a decision that was entirely her own.

The option presented to Korean mothers—that adoption was a chance for them to start anew and for their children to live in better circumstances—mirrored concurrent practices in the United States to "solve" the problem of unwed teen pregnancy. In the 1950s, American missionaries often removed unwed pregnant teenagers from their families and placed them in maternity homes or other remote locations where they could convince the girls to relinquish their babies.[45] While these processes were put in place to purportedly rescue the girl by giving her a chance for respectable marriage and her child by placing him or her in a family with two parents rather than a "broken" home with no father, such placements did not take into account the desires of the girls or their children. In both the United States and South Korea, there was little to no concern about what happened to the woman or her child once the adoption was complete; nor were the fathers of the children included anywhere in this process. In the case of Korean mothers, they were rendered even more inconsequential since they remained physically far away in South Korea, with an ocean separating them from their children. Also dismissed was the fact that Korean mothers who tried to hold on to their children as long as they could, like the woman described above, were relinquishing children, not babies. Having raised and watched sons and daughters grow, the mothers in these cases found separation all the more difficult.[46]

Rather than address the individual needs or concerns of mothers, the South Korean government was quick to speak on their behalf. In 1959 the minister of health and social affairs, Chang Whan Sohn, remarked that most mothers of "mixed blood" children chose "to offer their children for adoption by American homes where they realize that background and environment [would] help erase the accident of birth."[47] According to his statement, US voluntary agencies merely carried out the wishes of birth mothers who, in his estimation, viewed their children as "accidents." It suggested that mothers had a choice, when in reality the ROK government made it nearly impossible for them to raise their mixed-race children in South Korea. In the years following the war, legal and social rejection of mixed-race children left few options outside of adoption for many Korean women.

To meet the demands of both states, American and Korean administrators used aggressive tactics to procure mixed-race children for adoption to the United States. HAP employees went to local orphanages daily to see whether there were any available mixed-race children.[48] Cho Kyu Hwan recalled that Holt administrators would visit Angel's Haven regularly to pick up any mixed-race children under their care. US commanders of the army supplied the whereabouts of mixed-race children to the Office of Government Services so that it could begin processing the children for overseas adoptions.[49] The chief of women's police in Pusan regularly checked local orphanages to obtain updated lists of mixed-blood children.[50] According to the ISS American branch associate director, efforts to find racially mixed children in South Korea remained competitive as late as 1968.[51] The wide range of individuals— from missionaries to US military officers to ROK administrators— reflected that while positioned as a humanitarian effort, the drive to remove mixed-race children supported a dual state project. The US military was happy to aid HAP and other agencies that relieved it from having to take responsibility for the children of its military men; and the South Korean government assisted anyone who could remove mixed-race children from South Korea.

In an effort to meet growing US demand and Christian goals, some HAP administrators used coercive means to convince Korean mothers to relinquish their children. One American couple employed by the Holts boasted that they went out in jeeps and "collected over one thousand children of mixed blood for adoption." In addition to asking orphanage directors to give them all of the interracial children under their care, the couple went to camptowns in search for more. Once they spotted a mixed-race child, they followed him or her home so that they could talk to the "prostitute" mother. If the women rejected the missionary couple's offer to take the "unwanted" children, Holt employees would return with a translator to convince the women that their children would have greater opportunities in a more racially diverse and tolerant United States.[52] The repeat visits often worked; women who had wavered were persuaded to sign relinquishment papers.[53]

The Holts were not alone in using coercive tactics to secure mixed-race children. Mrs. Baumgartner of the ISS and her "Korean helper" went out two days a week looking for children. Baumgartner explained that "rarely [did] the mothers want to release [their children]" but that "if [the ISS could] just wait a little longer . . . [they would] have more children to offer." The statement suggested that it was only a matter of time before Baumgartner and her Korean translator could convince the mothers to relinquish their children.[54] Doctors who worked with the camptown women would tell the ISS which women were pregnant and who was expected to deliver soon.[55] The ISS discovered that some organizations even bribed women, giving them money in exchange for the right to care for their mixed-race children, at which point, unbeknownst to the mother until it was too late, agencies sent the children to the United States for adoption.[56]

Instances of physical violence were also reported. A concerned Korean doctor told the ISS that he witnessed three occasions where Korean women were physically forced to give up their mixed-race children. In one such case, a Korean woman accused Molly Holt and her boyfriend of striking her when the mother told them that she no longer wanted to relinquish custody of her child.[57] The aggressive schemes raised red flags for members of the International Social Service. Margaret A. Valk of the

ISS wrote that "nobody wants, of course, to have the girls being forced to release their children [handwritten in the margins: 'like Mr. Holt's cases!'] if they have any way of caring for them."[58] The ISS wanted to assure that its employees did not forcibly take children away from their birth mothers, and that Korean women understood that their signature on relinquishment forms meant that they forfeited their rights to the child "forever."[59] The ISS wrote it into its administration best practices that employees should conduct lengthy casework for mothers who were uncertain about releasing their children for foreign adoption. Despite these efforts, the ISS did not ultimately have the capacity to address Korean women's needs. With limited staff and casework from other countries, including Germany, Greece, Hong Kong, and Japan, the ISS was spread too thin to provide individualized assurances for them.[60]

Unprotected and exposed to US and Korean state and non-state pressures, Korean mothers who relinquished their children whether by choice, coercion, or force reflected the unevenness of the processes that left Korean women without rights and with few options. Symptomatic of these power structures, when birth mothers did sign relinquishment forms, they had to "unconditionally" and "one hundred percent" give up rights to their child. The binding document benefitted American adoptive parents and the South Korean government, not the women or children. It permitted what adoption administrators referred to as a "clean break" from the child's pre-adoption past, an agreement that severed all legal ties between the birth mother and her child.[61] By signing the document, the Korean mother could not make legal claims to the child or try to contact him or her.

Most importantly for the INS, the contract also denied the future immigration of birth mothers, a condition intended to prevent chain migration through adopted children. This provision countered the liberal optics of Korean adoption legislation that pried openings in existing restrictive immigration laws. When it came to mixed-race adoptees, their admittance, which was framed in the context of creating a new family, was concomitant upon the dissolution of an existing one, an institutional disenfranchisement of Korean women that legally substituted white women in their place. When situated in the broader trajectory of US immigration law, Korean adoptees hovered somewhere between exclusion and inclusion. As a preview to the more sweeping changes of the 1965 law, which contained a clause for family reunification, the 1961 legislation that permitted the entry of adopted children did the opposite by breaking Korean families apart.

The ISS feared that Korean mothers did not fully understand the binding terms of relinquishment. Margaret Valk asked Oak Soon Hong, the director of CPS, regarding a 1955 adoption case, "What [the ISS is] most anxious to know . . . is whether the mother of [child's name] really understand [sic] that she is giving her child up forever and that she will not be able to hear about her from the adoptive parents in the US? Can you tell us whether you discussed this point with [her] and whether she understands it?"[62] Valk's concern signaled that this was a known problem in mixed-race adoption placements. Administrators at CPS and Holt were not always communicative with Korean mothers and sometimes cut them out of the process entirely. The Holt Adoption Program's "Foreign Country Adoption Immigration Permit" revealed this point. It was written in Korean and translated to read:

> The named "orphan" had been cared for by the following orphanage director, who has fed and taught this homeless child. The Director believes that foreign country adoption is the best option for this child and from this point forward, relinquishes unconditionally and 100% all rights to this child who is being given to your organization, which will arrange the adoption.

At the bottom of the document was a line for the director's signature and a witness, as well as a space for the address of the orphanage and the director's job title.[63] There was no signature line for a living parent or relative. Since HAP employees regularly went to orphanages to find mixed-race children, this document permitted the director to transfer children to Holt without the mother's consent; HAP could then arrange for the adoption of that child. While a mother's signature was needed to remove a child from under her direct care, once a child entered an orphanage, he or she was placed under the guardianship of the director. Even in the cases where the mother of the child was known to the orphanage, the director's signature was the only one needed to remove the child from the orphanage and into the custody of HAP. The fact that the director's signature was legal and binding made it possible to send children to the United States for adoption without involving or even notifying the birth mother.[64]

In the end, Korean governmental and US private care industry efforts to send mixed-race children to the United States, the Korean stigma against racially mixed children, the absence of support for Korean birth mothers, and the at times coercive tactics used to convince women to release their children led to the mass removal of 2,348 mixed-race children in the 1950s, roughly 65 percent of the mixed-race child population in South Korea.[65] Overseas adoptions of mixed-race children foreclosed the possibility of family for Korean mothers and their children in South Korea. In these ways, the production of the transnational Cold War family in the United States was concomitant upon the breaking apart of South Korean ones. From South Korean law that rendered the child stateless to relinquishment documents that permanently denied the mother all rights to her child, Korean mothers and their mixed-race children were not given the right to be part of a family in South Korea.

While the ISS believed that life in the United States would be better for most mixed-race children, it also felt it important that the children have "their mother's love and care." ISS staff noted that mother-child relationships were often close, making it unclear whether or not adoption was the best answer.[66] What one social worker described as "a mother's sorrow" reflects the longing of birth mothers who wished to know how their children fared in the United States.[67] In the 1950s, an estimated 35 percent of mixed-race children (numbering roughly 1,200) remained in South Korea. By 1960, Korea's Children's Survey Committee estimated that the number had grown to 1,518 mixed-race children, of which 205 had African American fathers.[68]

While it is unclear how many mixed-race children were in orphanages, there is evidence that many Korean women raised their children against all odds. Ostracized by relatives and friends, they often lived near military bases in poverty. Some women who had been raped turned to prostitution in order to raise their mixed-race children. Others moved far from their families so as not to bring disgrace upon them.[69] Mothers disguised their mixed-race children by dyeing their hair in order to protect them from people's jeers or from being stoned.[70] They knew to hide their children when social workers or missionaries came to camptowns in search of mixed-race children.[71] These defenses and daily tactics of survival demonstrate the extent to which women struggled and had to persevere in order to hold on to their children.

With the establishment of US and South Korean permanent adoption laws in 1961 that banned proxy adoptions, the percentage of mixed-race children sent abroad dropped to around 10 percent of all Korean adoptions.[72] According to Susan Pettiss, assistant director of the ISS American branch, by 1960 fewer than a thousand mixed-race children remained in South Korea, and few if any were available for adoption because they were living with their mothers. With continued US military presence in South Korea, more mixed-race children were born. In 1963 one US social worker estimated that two to three thousand mixed-race children were under the direct care of their Korean mothers. She predicted that most of these women would be forced to "give them up eventually" due to "intense prejudice."[73] Yet records show that Korean women were increasingly finding ways to stay with their children. By 1965, the ISS found that a growing number of children were leaving Korea with both parents.[74] The Ministry of Health and Social Affairs estimated that as of 1966, 6,293 mixed-race children had been sent primarily to the United States and 1,541 remained in Korea.[75] Other reports estimated that five hundred mixed-race children were now of middle school age, suggesting that they were being raised by their mothers, who placed them in schools.[76] The thousands of women who raised their mixed-race children in the face of seemingly insurmountable pressures by adoption agencies and ongoing discrimination took their place alongside the hundreds of women who found ways to keep their biracial children during the war. Left without resources or support, Korean women worked vigorously and daily to make a home for themselves and their children, a life that they navigated in the shadows of empire.

Mixed-Race Children in South Korea

In 1961 US and Korean social welfare professionals, psychologists, doctors, and judges came together to assess and provide solutions for Korea's most destitute children. The joint US-South Korean *Handicapped Children's Survey Report Korea* involved the work of twenty-six thousand trained officials at all levels of the ROK government who distributed surveys and interviewed seventy-eight thousand disabled children under the age of eighteen, the majority of whom were affected by the war or suffered as a result of postwar poverty and illness. The culminating 257-page study took over a year to assemble, and was by far the most comprehensive Korean child welfare study to date.[77]

Survey administrators made their goals clear. The study was intended to "fill [a] gap in the development of [South Korean] social welfare services" by making up for the "extremely meager statistical information available on the nation's children." US and South Korean professionals used a "scientific approach" to "introduce facts" in order to develop much-needed services. The end goal was to help disabled children achieve their "maximum degree of function or usefulness of the total person" so that they could move away from a state of dependency toward one of "self-support" that would "benefit the child, the family and society as a whole."[78] The goal of the project was to first identify and then transform impaired children into productive citizen-subjects and normative members of South Korean society.

Though it was a joint study, the methods and goals replicated US practices and ideas.[79] To begin, the mantra of self-sufficiency, improvement, uplift, and the production of useful citizens mirrored US standards for proper citizenship and, in the case of the subjects of this study, proper imperial subjecthood. Since US immigration law denied the entry of children who were "feebleminded" or physically or mentally handicapped, those who were the focus of the study were destined to stay in South Korea. Lucile L. Chamberlin, chief of the Social Welfare Section of United States Operations Mission to Korea, wrote in the survey report that "[m]any of these pitiful children, now hidden away in disgrace, permanent charges for support and care upon family, government and others, if given the opportunity, could learn to be self supporting adults contributing to the well-being of society."[80] With improved (Westernized) systems of care, Chamberlin predicted, disabled Korean children could be disciplined into becoming independent and productive citizens. The message of uplift was inherently tied to American imperialist values past and present. It also reflected the broader aims of American empire to stabilize Korea's population, a first step in solidifying a US democracy that could serve as an example to its Asian neighbors.

To achieve these goals, Americans taught Koreans how to gather statistics, information that could then be used to monitor and discipline their subjects.[81] The ability to identify, locate, and count was crucial to managing a population, and, in the case of disabled children, to find patients and administer care. The study used three distinct sections with clear subcategories. The first section, for "physical handicaps," included references to amputees, "hunchbacks," "club foot," "severe harelip," and "cleft palate"—categories that most survey conductors would be able to visually identify. The second section, "mentally handicapped," required the more subjective assessment of the interviewer. Americans equipped Koreans with information about how to identify symptoms of "psychotic," "epileptic," or "feeble-minded" individuals. The third and final section of the survey was reserved for the "socially handicapped," the "children of racially different parents" or "mixed blood children." Unlike the other handicaps listed in the study, the "symptoms" of race mixture were not easy to categorize.

To help survey administrators, this section came with detailed instructions about how to assess "social handicaps" and clarified what information to record. First, children who were ethnically mixed with Chinese or Japanese ancestry and/or born of "legitimate" marriages were not to be counted. Ethnic mixtures could pass as Korean and, therefore, did not face the challenges of racially mixed children, the survey administrators concluded.[82] This section was expressly for children with "UN fathers" who were "born after '45." With over 90 percent of wartime UN forces from the United States, and the US military still stationed in South Korea, the fathers of these children were American. The second section asked administrators to mark one of three "skin color" choices— "white," "black," or "other"—and to ascertain the father's "nationality" or race.[83]

Similar to the forms used in orphanages just after the war, the survey's effort to identify the whiteness or blackness of Korean children created what Keith Wailoo has called a "patient identity"—a diagnosis and labeling that opened the path to surveillance, discipline, and control.[84] Once a child was marked as visibly mixed, an array of social problems was attached to him or her. The survey located the problem within the children rather than the forces that created and ostracized them. As diagnosed patients, mixed-race children were exposed to the assessments of various professionals. According to Anne M. Davison, a US social worker of the ISS branch in Seoul and contributor to the study, mixed-race children shared the "insecurity that their parent's [sic] . . . made for them." The low class status of their mothers (many of whom turned to prostitution because of a lack of other options in war-torn Korea, as noted in more nuanced descriptions written by Korean authors in the same report) coupled with a "foreign" father who abandoned them made for a future of criminality fueled by feelings of resentment should no one step in and intervene, Davison warned.[85]

Judge Soon Yung Kwon, director of the Seoul Juvenile Court, agreed with Davison's assessment, remarking that "children born out of wedlock including mixed racial children may be emotionally insecure and tense. Also, they may be impulsive and nervous with a defensive mechanism which makes it hard for them to win friends." Judge Kwon concluded that they are inclined to delinquency and an animosity that could lead to "aggressiveness" or perhaps even "murder, arson, or illicit love affairs."[86] The issue of juvenile delinquency, a major concern in the United States at this time, likely contributed to the attention given to this subject in the joint survey. The US and Korean professionals who wrote about mixed-race male delinquency, in particular, concluded that social welfare intervention at a young age would help restrain the impending recklessness of the mixed-race teenager. This assessment reflected a dual state concern about the importance of creating good subjects to fulfill the needs of Korean nationalism *and* American empire. The fact that a judge weighed in on this issue mirrored US practices that viewed criminal justice and welfare as two modes of public policy that informed and supported one another. The potential delinquency of the mixed-race child might be curbed by child welfare efforts, but if it failed, the criminal justice system would be there to retrieve the child and keep him removed from society, where he might harm or negatively influence others.[87]

At once, the conclusions reached by US and Korean professionals made race mixture an identifiable and definable pathological condition that required social welfare intervention. The study concluded that unlike the physically handicapped children in the report, there was no cure for the social ailments faced by South Korea's mixed-race children. By and large, US and Korean professionals felt that intercountry adoption was still the best option, since there was no treatment to remedy the circumstances of their birth. Even though Davison herself admitted that adoptions were only a partial solution to the ongoing problem of race mixture, she and several other survey contributors felt that severe discrimination in South Korea warranted the children's continued removal. Nak Choong Kim, director of the Korea Child Welfare Research Center, described in the study how visibly mixed-race children faced "problems of social isolation and adjustment." Kim detailed the case of a child who had an African American serviceman father whom she had never met. The child was ridiculed at school because of her "curly hair and dark skin." An American family that "loved her like their own daughter" adopted her, dramatically improving her chances in life.[88] Amidst passing suggestions by survey administrators to provide education for mixed-race children in South Korea, make provisions for legal birth registrations, and establish some kind of "socio-legal policy and framework together with treatment facilities" to assist these "unfortunate children," the by then well-established practice of overseas adoptions trumped other options and remained the overwhelmingly preferred solution.[89]

The final page of the report asked surveyors to describe the "protector's desire for the child." Three of the eight choices clearly demonstrated the permanence of US practices that were first introduced after the war. "Adoption," "institutionalization," and "vocational training" did not exist prior to US arrival in 1945; they made up the structural afterlives of US imperialism in South Korea and the primary solutions for mixed-race children at this time. In the end, the survey placed the problem of miscegenation firmly upon the bodies of mixed-race children. Though administrators made it clear that it was not the fault of the child, all recommendations pointed to what needed to be done to that child. Rather than approach the US military to take responsibility for the practice of militarized prostitution and the birth of GI babies or address South Korean societal and legal discrimination against them, the survey solidified the place of the mixed-race child as a problem that needed to be solved.

Some suggested boarding schools. In the mid-1960s, the Holts created an institute in Ilsan, just outside Seoul, where they housed approximately a hundred mixed-race children, 55 percent of whom were "Negroid," between the ages of ten and thirteen.[90] The older age of the children and, for many, their black ancestry made them doubly difficult to place in the United States. Though the Holts did not consider institutionalization to be the best solution, they shared the conclusions of the 1961 survey that this population's social handicap left few alternatives given the prejudice of Korean society. At the residential boarding school located at the Ilsan Holt Center, children could grow into adulthood and gain vocational skills aimed at making them productive members of society. Efforts like these carried forth the recommendations of the *Survey* but foreclosed possibilities for the acceptance of mixed-race people in South Korea.[91] Kept out of mainstream society for much of their lives, residents learned to cook, clean, and take care of themselves into adulthood. Some who left the institution found jobs or got married, but many returned after encountering obstacles and finding that they had nowhere else to turn.[92]

The Korean Association of Voluntary Agencies (KAVA), an organization that came together in 1952 and was made up of representatives from churches and other voluntary groups from the United States and South Korea, sought Korean solutions for Korean problems and felt that integration, not segregation, was the best solution for Korea's mixed-race children. In 1964 KAVA only supported US programs that encouraged the integration of mixed-race children. KAVA and many Korean citizens argued that separation policies only exacerbated the problem of intolerance in Korean society. A newspaper reporter reminded readers that current Korean laws stress equality and that separate schools for mixed-race children was a legal violation. He urged Koreans not to be provincial about the issue and to think deeply about mixed-race children, whose ability to grow up as contributing members of society relied upon the public's ability to accept and nurture them.[93]

Korean assimilation proponents argued that schools like Seoul's Yŏnghwagungmin hakyo (English National Elementary School) for mixed-race children, which enrolled approximately fifty students in 1962, only temporarily sheltered the children from the harassment and ostracism that they would face when mainstreamed into middle schools or when having to find jobs as adults.[94] Programs like the Eurasian Children Living as Indigenous Residents (ECLAIR), a program funded by the United Presbyterian Mission of the United States, United World Mission, Foster Parents Plan, and Church World Service, aimed to fully integrate mixed-race children into Korean society.[95] Set up in the early 1960s by George P. Whitener of the US Presbyterian Mission and endorsed by the Korean Ministry of Health and Social Affairs, ECLAIR worked to incorporate mixed-race children into South Korean Christian middle schools. In a letter to US donors, Whitener reported that a handful of mixed-race children, now in their teens, were enrolled in a mainstream school and their integration "turned out in reality to be no problem at all." However, he recognized that much work remained. Whitener lamented that the project to "export these social rejects" made it nearly impossible for Koreans to make room for the soon-to-be adults who remained in Korea. He proclaimed, "An opportunity must either be made for them now or a whole generation of social outcasts will plague the Korean Society in the next ten years. They will either have a great deal or nothing to offer their native land."[96]

In 1964 Child Placement Service and the Pearl S. Buck Foundation teamed up with ECLAIR to open the first integrated school in the Yong Dong Po area of Seoul.[97] In July 1965, CPS took full control of the program and its 112 enrolled students. The mixed-race children attended school with Korean children and lived with their mothers, who were being concurrently "rehabilitated" from prostitution. Like similar US projects, the program instituted in South Korea aimed to "fix" the women rather than the system of militarized prostitution responsible for their circumstances. The program appeared to be successful, but it was a single school that could accommodate only a small percentage of the population. The stigma surrounding mixed-race children made it nearly impossible to remedy the problem, which Korean social workers described as extending "beyond [their] abilities." According to a 1973 report to the ISS from Korea's Social Welfare Society (formerly CPS), mixed-race children continued to fall into "isolated lives" and faced many "social entanglements."[98] Jane Yeon-hee, who was born in 1964, describes the alienation and racism she experienced growing up mixed-race in South Korea. She was bullied and called names at school; her half-brother, who was also Korean-white, dropped out of middle school, no longer able to handle the discrimination, and went to work at a factory. Kang Hwa-sim, whose father was an African American soldier, recalled being verbally abused and spat on for her appearance for the first nineteen years of her life growing up in Korea.[99]

Even in integrationist programs, administrators brought with them preconceived ideas about the presumed inferiority of mixed-race children. Teachers at one of the integrated campuses determined that the mixed-race children were generally a little slower than Korean children, but believed that continued integration would help them catch up.[100] In 1967 South Korean social workers conducted IQ tests to compare the intelligence of mixed-race children to that of full-blooded Korean children. The study showed that the mean IQ of mixed-blood children was "quite similar to pure Korean children," leading administrators to conclude that the "eugenic theory that mixed-blood children are clear-headed [or dim] seems to be inapplicable to those in Korea."[101] As in the United States, these assessments were then used to justify intervention. US instruments of racialization that were first administered and employed by US missionaries in South Korea were later passed on to Korean administrators. By the 1960s, the importation of US racialization found a permanent place in the processes applied to the mixed-race children of American GIs, practices that continue to have palpable effects on the daily lives of these children.

Choices for Korea's mixed-race population in the decades following the war could not shake the legacies of mass removal, what one mixed-race adoptee activist has likened to "ethnic cleansing."[102] The director of the Korean National Red Cross described it this way: "By pursuing inter-country adoption as a goal for racially-mixed children we are depleting that particular group of exactly those members who might in the future help to alter their image on the society and to mitigate against prejudicial attitudes towards them."[103] According to the director and other "responsible and enlightened Koreans," the confluence of South Korean and US efforts to place mixed-race children in American homes ultimately allowed the Korean public and government to dismiss their very existence, a practice that foreclosed the possibility of their acceptance in Korea.[104] The ways in which mixed-race children were made legible produced subjects that could then be dismissed as outside of proper Korean subjecthood, a group that could be identified and then denied state resources.[105] In the end, where the child lived had a direct bearing on his or her identity, and geography mattered a great deal in these processes. The very same mixed-race child who represented racial liberalism in the United States was identified as socially disabled in South Korea, a split embodiment born from America's intimate empire.

Missing Military Men

This chapter outlined how American empire shaped the lives of mixed-race children and Korean women who stayed in South Korea. Not all Korean women and children directly affected by the US military experienced the postwar years in the same way. There were other scenarios. Some American men brought their Korean wives and children to the United States. Some remained in South Korea and found ways to stay together. While no single story could describe the totality of their experiences, the practices and structures responsible for their circumstances supported the needs of the United States over the lives of Korean women and children.

This was made particularly transparent by the fact that the US military man went missing in these machinations. This was no mistake, for he was made to disappear. There was no culpability except in the public accusations of adoption advocates.[106] More troubling was the US military's soft suggestions about what its men should do with their free time; suggesting wholesome pursuits and establishing structures to adjudicate that behavior were two different things.[107] The US military could not tell its men to stop consorting with Korean women when it permitted and regulated prostitution. It was telling that the primary "solutions" for GI babies and Korean mothers in South Korea did not involve US military men, who were just as much at the center, if not the very root cause, of these transnational dilemmas. The man's ability to be absolved came courtesy of gender, and of the US military's active role in excusing his actions and then his inactions. Cynthia Enloe reminds us of this unseemly pattern, which follows the US military in its exploits around the globe, a gendered militarization that has affected countless women with little to no ramifications for military men.[108] When we see what mixed-race children and their Korean mothers have endured and continue to endure, we understand more accurately that contrary to public reports of women abandoning their children, it was often the American man who first abandoned the mother and child. When family frames were so central to US citizenship and Cold War strategy, this irresponsibility of the American man was not only unacceptable, but also un-American. In this context, it becomes clear *why* military men had to be excised from the situation that they produced and, moreover, why they had to appear in public accounts saving Korean children who were orphaned by bombs rather than saving their own flesh and blood.

While the absence of US military fathers was purposeful and functioned to preserve empire, the absence of Korean mothers and their mixed-race children resulted from the Americans and Koreans who disavowed them. These women and children occupied a liminal space somewhere between South Korea and the United States. Regardless of where they lived, they were a phantom presence, an excess of American empire and Korean nationalism that threatened both if made too visible.

6

Managing Korean War Brides

Lee Yong Soon married Johnie Morgan on Valentine's Day in 1951. As their ship pulled into the Seattle harbor, a band struck up "Here Comes the Bride" and "crowds cheered excitedly, whistles tooted." Nicknamed "Blue" for the color of the sweater that she wore when working as a communications supervisor for the US Army, Lee was one of eleven Korean war brides to come to the United States that year.[1] In the November 5, 1951, issue of *Life*, readers saw photographs of Blue's parents, who lived on a farm in Seoul, alongside pictures of her new American in-laws, who wore the hanboks that Blue's parents sent them. Johnie's parents posed for pictures with their son and daughter-in-law in the kitchen, domestic images that solidified the international bonds of this new family. The article closed with Johnie's mother teaching Blue how to cook his favorite Carolina-style gravy (figure 6.1). The parting image left Americans to imagine Blue's assimilation as an American housewife, a process that would presumably continue well after *Life* photographers packed up for the day.

Similar to adoptee narratives, Blue's story was less about her and more about the internationalist spirit of exchange, a triumphant Cold War parable about American democracy. However, unlike adoptee narratives that came to dominate news of Korea by the mid-1950s, Blue's was one of only a handful of stories that highlighted the arrival of Korean military brides. This was due in part to the small number of Korean women entering the United States during the war: 1 in 1950, 11 in 1951, 101 in 1952, and 96 in 1953.[2] Yet even as the numbers grew, reaching 13,904 by 1970, a number that far exceeded that of Korean adoptees at this time, public news of Korean brides remained scarce.[3]

The narrative of interracial love and hope communicated through Blue's story at the outset of war could not be sustained as the war progressed, when it became increasingly clear that the United States might not win. After the war, the tens of thousands of US servicemen who

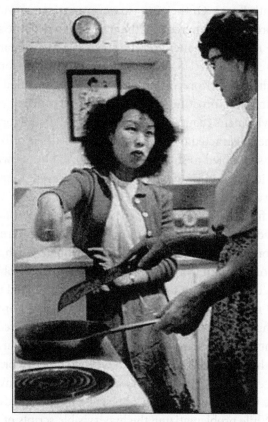

Figure 6.1. Korean bride makes gravy for her US military husband. "A War Bride Named 'Blue' Comes Home," *Life*, November 5, 1951, 41.

stayed on in South Korea signaled the continuation of military marriages. What began as the anomaly of the Korean war bride soon became a steady and constant stream of nonwhite immigrants. In the 1970s, four thousand Korean women entered annually as the brides of US servicemen.[4]

This chapter begins in South Korea with the US military's efforts to stop its men from marrying Korean women and ends in the United States with representations of the Korean war bride. It considers how the identity of the Korean military bride became fused with that of the prostitute, an association tied to the practice of US militarized prostitution in South Korea. Of the over 350,000 American servicemen who fought in Korea, only 38 percent of them were married; the sheer number of single men, not to mention those who had extramarital affairs, made it difficult for the US military to prevent them from developing relationships with Korean women beyond the intended purpose of military-sanctioned prostitution.[5] According to military administrators, like servicemen's requests to adopt children, their efforts to marry Korean women distracted the men from fulfilling their primary duties. The military scrambled to stop what it had started by allowing its men to consort with Korean women, but could not prevent them from trying to marry and bring home their new brides.

While at first the Korean bride may have been viewed alongside the celebrated Korean adoptee, her adult sexuality and presumed ties to prostitution made her an unviable figure through which to promote US internationalism. In fact, she was made even more problematic *because* of concurrent adoption scripts. The highly publicized plight of GI babies could not simultaneously support the arrival of Korean women who might figure as their biological mothers. When paired alongside US servicemen, the women disrupted existing adoptee narratives that relied upon the fiction that the children were all orphans or, in the case of mixed-race adoptees, had mothers who were unable, unwilling, and unfit to raise them. The bride's very presence fractured tidy Cold War narratives. While problematizing the hypervisible scripts of rescue surrounding adoptees, she also brought attention to the hidden—though well-known—practice of US militarized prostitution in South Korea.

Preventing the Korean War Bride

During World War II, US politicians and military officials discouraged servicemen romances with local women. Claiming that they would "degrade duty performance and draw resources from the defense mission," the US Army imposed restrictions to curb marriage requests. Despite the efforts, American GIs found ways to marry British wives as early as 1942 and other European women in the years that followed.[6] Unable to stop the unions, President Truman signed the War Brides Act in 1945 to allow the nearly sixteen million American servicemen mobilized in fifty-seven countries during World War II to bring home brides. Between 1946 and 1948, over ninety thousand women entered the United States from Europe, Australia, and New Zealand.[7]

While the military did not condone any marriages with foreign women, it was particularly adamant about denying interracial marriages with women from Asia. The original War Brides Act did not apply to Asian women because it required that spouses be racially eligible for citizenship, which at the end of World War II Asians were not.[8] And until 1967, when the Supreme Court declared barring interracial marriages unconstitutional, multiple states upheld antimiscegenation laws. It was only with growing requests from US servicemen stationed in Japan that the War Brides Act was amended in 1947 to allow the entry of Asian brides. With legal paths opened, the US Eighth Army Command in Korea strategized its own ways to prevent marriages. A 1951 memorandum laid out the lengthy process intended to dissuade its men from pursuing marriage, a procedure that added to the protocol already used in neighboring Japan.[9] The Korean process took anywhere from four months to two years.[10] Couples had to appear together in the office of the American vice consul with the following documents in hand: original or certified copies of birth certificates, the woman's official and complete Family Census Register, the authorized approval of one of the five US Army commanders, written permission of the woman's parents (if living) and the head of household if she was under the age of twenty-five, an affidavit of eligibility for marriage prepared by the Office of the American Consular Service, and an oath signed by the prospective bride and groom in the presence of the American vice consul.[11] Once all of these documents were procured, a Report and Certificate of Marriage was prepared, which the couple would then bring to the city mayor to legalize the marriage. The documents were returned to the consul, who certified the authenticity of the mayor's signature, at which point the vice consul issued the Certificate of Witness to Marriage.[12] Within five days, the couple would have to apply for a US visa and undergo health evaluations, acquire passports, and arrange for transportation to the United States.[13]

The involved process was made more difficult by the fact that it was challenging to procure the required Korean documents. Many of the papers were destroyed during the war. Women who were orphans did not have a family registry or birth certificate. Ji-Yeon Yuh interviewed a Korean woman who came to the United States via Japan in 1951. Having fled the war, she was missing key documents, but was able to obtain her visa and passport because the consul at the Korean embassy turned out to be an old acquaintance from when she worked at a US military base.[14] Most couples did not have such luck and failed to meet the many required steps. To complicate matters, by the time of the Korean War, when the number of marriage requests increased, the 1947 amendment had already expired. It would not be until 1952 with the McCarran-Walter Act that Asian wives of US citizens could enter the United States again.[15] The 1952 act eliminated racial exclusion for spouses and children of European descent, but Asian fiancées and adoptees were still counted toward the limited annual quota of one hundred persons per year for South Korean immigrants.[16] By the mid-1950s, servicemen had to return to Korea or Japan to marry, since visas from both countries were oversubscribed.[17] While the McCarran-Walter Act made an opening for some Korean women, the US military and the INS created additional hurdles to stymie their efforts.

In 1956 the US military altered its practices for fear that the existing ones were "too lax [in] both policy and procedures."[18] Though the military streamlined some of the American Consular Service steps, it added new requirements. The serviceman now had to submit an application to his unit commander at least 160 days prior to the end of his tour of duty. If the soldier was under twenty-one years old, he would need the written consent of his parents before moving forward with the application process. Many would not get the support that they needed. The parents of one serviceman asked the military to deny their son the tour extension that he had requested because they did not want him to marry a Korean national, a request that stopped the application process before it could even begin.[19]

All couples seeking marriage had to first undergo an interview with an army chaplain. Army commanders instructed chaplains to warn couples about the discrimination that they would face in the future and inform them that interracial marriage was forbidden in some states. Officers sent letters to applicants that outlined the antimiscegenation laws of the serviceman's state of residence.[20] If the couple still expressed interest, the chaplain would sign a statement either approving or disapproving the union. Chaplain Dreford J. Devoto wrote in 1956, "[The

American serviceman] is determined to marry this non-national at all costs. I have pointed out to him every pitfall of the road ahead and from years of experience in dealing with these situations I have advised him strongly that the odds of a successful marriage are not in his favor."[21] The chaplain approved this union, but did so "reluctantly and unwillingly." According to chaplain journals, marriage "interviews" where they told the couple of the many challenges that they would face as an interracial couple in the United States were part of a "routine day in Seoul," and by the mid- to late 1950s it was common for chaplains to conduct five to ten such interviews monthly in each unit.[22]

If the chaplain's approval was granted, the commanding officer would then request an investigation of the "prospective alien spouse," a process that took about three months. Potential brides had to secure character references from friends, family, and employers, as well as a background investigation conducted by the local chief of police. Family members and neighbors wrote statements in Korean that were then translated into English. The letters contained information similar to this one written in November 1955: "I hereby reference the thought of the above person is sound and moderate, also a woman of virtue, well behaved, and in high sense of responsibility."[23] Assurances that the woman was "of virtue" (thus not a prostitute) and "well behaved" made her an ideal immigrant and wife. English translations that used the word "model" to describe the women further positioned them as exceedingly suited for entry. Given the shared phrases that appeared across these statements, those writing the character assessments seemed to have a template to help them cover the points most important to the INS. Letters and police reports from Japan and Korea listed in bullet points that the woman was of virtuous character, was never convicted of a felony "or misdemeanor involving moral turpitude," and did not have communist sympathies but rather "a good belief in democracy."[24] Since US immigration officials used these statements as evidence that the women were neither prostitutes nor communists, requirements stipulated by US immigration law, the letters were produced toward these ends.[25] Some statements may have been knowingly fictionalized. Bok-Lim C. Kim believed that many Korean parents willingly approved of and assisted in such marriages because it was the only way out of a life of poverty and prostitution for their daughters.[26]

Health reports rounded out the assessments to assure that the women were sound in body and mind. The INS was most concerned that the women were disease-free. Korean doctors at local hospitals conducted physical exams, chest x-rays, and laboratory tests to report whether or not the woman in question was "free from mental illness, infectious venereal disease, active tuberculosis and other major communicable diseases."[27] The health reports were used to help determine whether or not she was a prostitute. Clinical evaluation forms asked examiners to inspect all parts of her body, including her nose, scalp, pupils, feet, sinuses, and skin.[28] The remaining steps of the application, which included securing a visa and arranging for transportation, had to be timed perfectly before the health exams expired.[29] Only after application approval and marriage could the serviceman make provisions with the American embassy to secure a nonquota visa for his spouse, a process that took approximately six to eight weeks.[30] If this last step exceeded sixty days, the invasive health exams would have to be repeated.

These added assurances benefitted only the receiving country and did little to protect the women. They also drew out the process, which the Department of the Army hoped would lead couples to abandon the quest. US servicemen were well aware that though it was their legal right to marry Korean women, the military could thwart their efforts to do so. Many men complained to their commanders, but others sought outside help, much to the dismay of the US military. In 1956 a US major general wrote to his Illinois state senator that the army discouraged Korean marriages. He explained that he loved a Korean woman "with all of [his] heart" and that she was "a girl that anyone could be proud of." He expounded that he had fought in Korea for one of America's "most cherished freedoms: The Pursuit of Happiness" and that he intended to exercise this freedom. A self-proclaimed career man in the army, he threatened to change his mind because of the "lack of cooperation from the Army, and all of the Red Tape and the wall that [he ran] into when [he brought] up the subject of marriage."[31] Congress urged US military officials to investigate this case. The US military complied and determined that the woman was sound physically and mentally, and that the major general had "excellent . . . character and efficiency."[32] The language used in marriage applications reflected the extent to which couples had to debunk preexisting assumptions that Korean women were prostitutes. Before even entering into the application process, Korean women were marked as already guilty of immorality, and the documents that followed had to prove otherwise.

This case and others like it prompted the Department of the Army to send out a memorandum to its five commanding officers, the only ones who could authorize marriages. The memo outlined that though the army "does not encourage marriage," commanders should not try to prevent them when the parties involved have met all of the requirements. In 1956 Colonel and Adjutant General Robert H. Shell warned that "any additional restrictions placed on marriage could be expected to arouse increased congressional interest" and could be interpreted by the ROK government as being "discriminatory against its people." Yet Shell closed his memo with a handy list of approved reasons for denial: length of courtship, the financial capability of soldiers, and chaplain or commanding officer disapproval based on "cogent reasons."[33] Shell reminded the commanders that women could not request passports and visas until after they were officially married, a three- to four-month process during which time a commander could "properly disapprove a marriage based upon brief courtship." Ultimately, commanders were left to determine their own "cogent reasons" to reject the requests. Given the numerous paths to denial, one can assume that for the number of marriages that were approved, there were many more that were not.

To further assure that the men would run out of time, Colonel George McGee declared that military personnel who processed "alien dependents," brides or children, for entry into the United States should not be granted an extension. When their tours of duty ended before passports and visas could be issued, the men would have to return to Korea at a later point if they wanted to bring their wives and children home, a scenario that proved infeasible for most. McGee explained that this rule was "coordinated informally" with Far East Headquarters expressly to prevent marriages from going through. Exceptions were made only when "compassionate reasons exist[ed] which would warrant approval"; as an example, McGee attached an approved appeal from a serviceman whose Korean bride was pregnant with his child.[34]

With the start of the Korean War, an increasing number of Americans stationed abroad contacted the International Social Service for help with "problems related to marriage . . . with nationals of other countries." By

December 1955, the number of requests grew, prompting the ISS to seek official cooperation with the US Department of Defense.[35] While it is unclear whether or not the DoD signed the memorandum, subsequent correspondence indicates that the line of communication between the two organizations was open and regular. In 1957 the ISS worked with representatives of the US Air Force Personal Affairs Branch to determine the best course of action when the ISS received requests from its men. The air force lieutenants told the ISS to send the men back to the officials on their base, but only after telling them that "although he may think 'no one cares', that [the ISS knows] that the Air Force does have a concern for individuals" and that military administrators can help them "within the limits of the immigration laws and current Air Force regulations." Referencing a recent case where an airman wrote the ISS a second time indicating that he "met serious obstacles" and was denied permission to marry a Korean woman "for what the Air Force considers good reasons," the lieutenants suggested that the ISS ask the airman to forward all copies of letters related to his request, at which point they suspected that "there would be no further answer." Finally, if an airman were to appeal to the ISS a third time to indicate that there was a clear breakdown in procedures as a result of "carelessness, prejudice, or lack of insight on the part of someone in the 'chain of command,'" the lieutenant asked that the ISS send the documentation directly to him, at which point "one in nine or ten cases might need to be explored by their office," though he hoped that "the proportion [would not be] as high as that."[36] The protocol revealed the extra obstacles put in place to fatigue even the most persistent of servicemen. What the lieutenant suggested was to give the men the runaround and send them back to the very entity that denied them in the first place, thus rendering the third party, in this case the ISS, unable to help the men in any substantive way.

For the couples that got past the military red tape in Korea, the INS served as the final hurdle. The amended War Brides Act of 1947 required servicemen to submit sworn statements that they would pay any fees related to the entry of their wives.[37] These statements often made the women prime beneficiaries in case of serviceman death or included assurances that the bride in question was fully capable of finding work in the United States; such statements assured that she would not become a charge of the state.[38] Some files included letters of support from relatives of the servicemen. In one such letter, a serviceman's sister stated that she would take care of her future sister-in-law if her brother was disabled or became a casualty of war.[39] The content of these declarations demonstrated the extent to which applicants seeking the permanent entry of Korean wives understood the conditions of that immigration—the wife entered as the husband's charge, and he assumed full responsibility for her. The legal and social parameters of bride immigration, then, further solidified the place of Korean and other foreign brides as dependents under the stewardship of their military husbands. The domestic arrangements embedded Korean women into the private American home, placing them out of sight in America.

Supplanting the Korean War Bride

Adding to existing perceptions of war brides from World War II that pegged the women as opportunists who preyed upon homesick American boys, women from Korea were also assumed to be prostitutes who chose their own path to immorality.[40] Contrary to public perception, not all military brides from Korea were prostitutes. Since 1945, the United States employed Korean nationals as dishwashers, cooks, waitresses, receptionists, secretaries, and cashiers at the PX or commissary on US bases. In the 1940s and 1950s, women who came to US bases looking for jobs found that they needed some knowledge of English or a personal contact.[41] Regardless of the jobs that these women held while or prior to dating an American, they were automatically viewed with suspicion afterwards. It was not uncommon for other GIs to proposition any woman dating a US soldier, assuming that she was a prostitute.[42] The presumption that all marriages stemmed from prostitution was symptomatic of how military relationships dictated the social construction of Korean women. It also signaled the ubiquity of the practice in foreign US military outposts.

When it came to Korea, Americans seemed exceedingly aware of the existence of prostitution near US military bases. This was in large part due to the publicity surrounding the plight of GI babies, through which Americans learned about US servicemen fathers who abandoned Korean mothers and their children. Knowledge of Korean prostitution was so widespread that it made its way into popular culture. The 1962 cult classic *The Manchurian Candidate* opens in a Korean brothel filled with American servicemen. Sergeant Raymond Shaw cuts the late-night carousing short, leading one of the men to quip, "I'm afraid our Sergeant Raymond, he don't approve." The uptight and unpopular sergeant signals the danger of queer masculinity in a militarized context where boys *should* be boys, the latter a gendered construction that normalized and excused the place of prostitution in South Korea. Further, since Shaw falls prey to a communist brainwashing scheme, he is the presumed weak link whose difference from other military men makes him a security threat.[43] Public awareness of prostitution near US bases during and after the war problematized Korean women, thus rendering Korean military marriages a less than ideal location to showcase integrationist aims. Instead, during the 1950s, the Japanese war bride emerged in their place.

While the geopolitics of US-South Korea relations made Korean brides problematic, Japanese brides figured differently at this time, due in large part to Japan's political stability. Since World War II, Japan had become a stronghold of democracy in Asia, unlike Korea, which some feared was on the brink of another war. This in addition to the rapid increase in the number of Japanese brides entering the United States, totaling several hundred in the early 1950s but reaching 55,456 by 1970, garnered greater attention.[44] Caroline Chung Simpson argues that the figure of the Japanese war bride helped the US government redeem democracy in light of the recent incarceration of over 120,000 Japanese Americans and the deployment of atomic bombs in Hiroshima and Nagasaki. As outsiders unchained to the history of internment, Japanese war brides settling into domestic American lives with their white servicemen husbands conveyed a cultural pluralism that countered Soviet criticism. Simpson continues that the figure of the Japanese war bride addressed the issue of racial integration without acknowledging the continued inequalities faced by African Americans.[45]

Cultural representations of Japanese brides in the late 1940s and 1950s helped Americans make sense of the entry of both Japanese and Korean brides. Melani McAlister and Christina Klein have shown that popular culture helped Americans understand its new global commitments, framing emerging international relations through popular representation.[46] In the 1950s, films about Japanese brides did important work by helping to culturally resolve the problem of Japanese brides (through production) and Korean brides (through erasure). Japanese women became a proxy for Korean women, a homogenizing fiction that contained the threat of each. Films like *Japanese War Bride* (1952) and *Sayonara* (1957) safely paired Japanese women with white men.[47] Though each told of Japanese-American romance, both significantly opened in Korea. In the beginning sequence of *Japanese War Bride*, the camera scans a dark Korean battlefield where US serviceman Jim Sterling is injured. After this short scene, Sterling awakens in a bright antiseptic hospital in Japan, where he meets the Japanese nurse who becomes his wife, Tae Shimizu. In *Sayonara*, the film begins in 1951 with Major Gruver (played by the popular Marlon Brando) as a fighter pilot in Korea. Within seconds, his character is whisked away to Japan for the duration of the film because his future father-in-law, General Webster, wants to keep him safe from the war. While stationed in Kobe, Gruver falls out of love with his white American fiancée, Eileen Webster, and falls head-over-heels for the Japanese theater actress Hana-ogi.

In both films, the male protagonists' ties to Korea allude to US-South Korea relations and Korean military brides without having to deal with either directly. Because of the recentness of the unpopular Korean War and continued US military presence in a politically unstable South Korea, both of these films managed to make Japan a stand-in for the less politically tenable Korea.[48] In particular, *Japanese War Bride* was released in the middle of the Korean War, when the outcome was yet unknown. And when *Sayonara* hit theaters, it was still too close to the tragic war to make it viable for filmmakers to tell a story about Korea.

In addition to shoring up the geopolitical challenges in Asia, the films solved the domestic crisis of masculinity by making Japanese women traditional in contrast to increasingly independent white American women. In the altered landscape of postwar America, where assertive women ruled the domestic sphere, men looked to reassert their dominance.[49] In both films, Japanese women acted as a corrective to threatened gender norms. The Japanese women who lovingly doted upon their male partners modeled for white American female viewers how they *should* behave. In *Japanese War Bride*, Tae is humble, quiet, and eager to learn American ways. At every turn, Tae bends to meet the needs of her white American husband almost to a fault. In one scene, Jim chastises

Tae for her "Japanese ways" when she grows silent, unable to articulate her feelings. Focusing instead on her Japanese dolls that she brought from Japan, Tae is infantilized in stark contrast to Jim's masculinity. As her husband, teacher, and parent, Jim reclaims white masculinity in the process of disciplining (in the guise of helping) a naïve, foreign, and childlike Tae. Jim's relationship to Tae suggests that white men could shape Asian brides to become the kind of American and the kind of wife that they wanted them to be.[50]

Japanese War Bride also offers a corrective for the white women who threatened white masculinity. Tae's foil is the wily, manipulative Fran. Married to Jim's brother, Art, but still in love with Jim, her former flame, Fran causes problems for Tae throughout the film. In scene after scene, Fran appears in smart, fashion-forward ensembles straight from the pages of *Vogue*. Her materialism and her overt sexuality, which render the men around her impotent, are in stark contrast to Tae's innocence and loyalty, which empower her husband. Jim repeatedly rejects Fran's untoward advances, finally pushing her to become the film's spiteful villainess when she writes an anonymous letter suggesting that the father of Tae's son was the Japanese American farmer Shiro. The scandalous accusation, if true, would destroy the Sterling family's chances of heading the farmers' association. To save them from disgrace, Tae takes her son and runs away. Jim eventually finds her standing on the craggy cliffs high above the Pacific Ocean, seemingly about to commit suicide. Acting as her hero, Jim once again shores up white masculinity by saving the damsel in distress. Meanwhile, back at home, Art punishes Fran for her indiscretions with a sharp slap across the face. Disciplining her for her obvious wrongdoings as well as her less obvious but equally dangerous overt sexuality and cosmopolitan ways, Art drags Fran back into the house, where she belongs.

The white American female lead in *Sayonara* is similarly regulated by that film's narrative. Eileen Webster is Gruver's feisty fiancée. In asking Gruver whether he ever just wants to "grab [her] and haul [her] off to a shack somewhere," Eileen embodies the independent and sexually aware postwar woman. Gruver is made feeble by her forward advances and finds solace in the mysterious woman of few broken-English words, Hana-ogi. In the end, he chooses the elegant, noncombative Japanese woman over his expressive, assertive white fiancée. In both *Sayonara*

Figure 6.2. "In a Japanese tea garden, Charles Kapitzky watches his wife eat an *aisu kuriimu* cone." Chester Morrison, "East Meets West . . . ," *Look*, October 29, 1957, 73. Photograph by Bob Lerner.

and *Japanese War Bride*, the Japanese women are celebrated for their perceived ability to fulfill traditional gender roles as wives committed to the happiness of their husbands. The backlash to an emerging feminism tempered the more radical storyline of interracial, international love in each of the films.

The gendered appeal of fictive Japanese brides in these two popular films crossed over into media conceptions of real-life Asian women. In the October 29, 1957, issue of *Look* magazine, a film review of *Sayonara* immediately followed an article about a white sailor and his Asian bride, a pairing that blurred the line between Hollywood fiction and lived reality.[51] In "East Meets West . . . ," Charles Edward Kapitzky II looks on as his wife, Kaneko, eats an "aisu kuriimu" cone (figure 6.2). Kapitzky gazes adoringly at his Asian bride, who enjoys her frozen treat with childlike relish. His navy uniform and her kimono signal the already familiar story of the Japanese war bride. Countering naysayers, Kapitzky explains, "Anyone who has known the delicacy and intelligence of Oriental womanhood will understand how such marriages as mine can come about." In life as on the big screen, the Asian bride embodied a gendered, exoticized Orientalist fantasy.

Kapitzky and his wife lived near a US base in Japan, but Kaneko was actually of Chinese descent. These two details hardly mattered, because her Asian face and kimono easily slotted her into the culturally constructed narrative of the Japanese bride. The film review of *Sayonara* that followed further drew the connections. The one-page review included four stills from the film, including one of Katsumi (Miyoshi Umeki) giving Joe Kelly (Red Buttons) a bath and another of Hana-ogi (Miiko Taka) and Gruver passionately kissing with Hani-ogi's line from the film, "I will never fall in love again, but I will love you if that is your desire." Hana-ogi's words solidified the unwavering commitment of Japanese brides to their white American husbands, while Katsumi bathing Joe fictionalized the so-called good life that men could lead if they too married an Oriental woman.

The ostensible parallels between fiction and reality did not stop there. In *Newsweek*, the reviewer for *Japanese War Bride* wrote that Hollywood backers dubbed Shirley Yamaguchi, who played Tae, the "Betty Grable of the Orient." Much like her on-screen persona, Yamaguchi was "a quietly eloquent little charmer who ha[d] about her the fabled grace and dignity of well-bred Japanese womanhood."[52] In just a few sentences, the reviewer blurred the line between the film character Tae and the actress Yamaguchi. The review also suggested that neither Yamaguchi nor the character she played was a prostitute, thus allaying fears of Asian prostitution most clearly associated with Korean women at this time. The US military newspaper *Pacific Stars and Stripes* also took great interest in the supposed Japanese characteristics of the actress. In an interview, Yamaguchi explained that she had been "trained from childhood to please the man." She continued, "[Japanese women] want to make a man as comfortable as possible. . . . When a man returns to the house I don't like to see him move around. I want to do things for him. It makes me uncomfortable to have men do things for me." Though the article stated that Japanese women now vote and divorce more easily, Yamaguchi assured the interviewer that they still considered "pleasing the males their prime duty in life."[53] In life as on the big screen, Yamaguchi fulfilled illusions of the modern-day lotus blossom wife.

Adding to their purported amenableness and subservience were stories that celebrated their rapid assimilation. A 1954 article that appeared in the *Saturday Evening Post* remarked that Japanese brides had become so entirely American that "they've just disappeared."[54] Successfully integrated into American family life and sheltered within the suburbs, Japanese brides slipped quietly and rather unremarkably into the private realm of family. Under the stewardship of military husbands, Japanese brides were contained by domesticity where, like their on-screen personas, they would presumably spend their time doting on their husbands in the private space of the home.

Media reports did not discuss the transnational dimensions of producing model Japanese brides. In 1948 the Christian Women's Association (CWA) in Tokyo opened the first brides school. American wives of US Army officials volunteered to teach English language, "civics," and cooking classes for a small group of Japanese women. In 1951, after Public Law 717 allowed Japanese women to immigrate, the US Department of State requested that the CWA open another brides school. The American Red Cross (ARC) soon took over and, at the request of the US Army, expanded to army, navy, and air force bases throughout Japan. By 1957, 2,474 American women had volunteered at 102 brides schools, which graduated as many as 3,979 Japanese women.[55] ARC schools that taught Japanese women how to baste a turkey, bake a pie, wear a girdle, and apply makeup were in operation as late as 1963.[56] The ARC even created a standard textbook in the late 1950s covering information about visas, passports, transportation, legal rights of dependents, customs, culture, manners, grooming, and housekeeping. To help debunk glamorized visions of America perpetuated by US magazines and films and to prepare them for the farming communities in poorer sections of the United States where many were headed, ARC women taught them how to budget and sew sensible patterns from Sears Roebuck rather than *Vogue*. The schools became a model for others in Okinawa, the Philippines, and even in the United States, where the ARC opened a brides school in 1957 for foreign wives of US servicemen.[57]

In these ways, US journalists who marveled over Japanese brides' adjustment to life in the States gave all the credit to American democracy rather than the transnational acculturation projects of US imperialism well underway in Asia. What the brides schools signaled was the private sector's attempt to transform the women who would soon be coming to America—a stopgap measure to discipline gendered Asian bodies via

US lessons in religion, hygiene, and culture. US missionary-run orphanages functioned in similar ways when it came to making good Korean subjects *prior* to entering the United States as adoptees. Yet not all were eligible to become model. Unlike Korean adoptees, Korean women remained outside of the possibility of rescue, while their presumed cultural, geopolitical, and social baggage made them unable to be taught like their Japanese counterparts.

Korea was not Japan, and the Far East Command frequently measured the differences. The threat of another war in Korea required a larger deployment of US servicemen in the peninsula than in Japan, and along with it the growing permanence of prostitution. In 1965, one out of every forty American servicemen posted in Korea the previous year had married a local woman. An army spokesman explained that men were marrying girls they had "met in bars" and contended that prostitution could be constructive as long as it could be contained in its proper place. Susan Zeiger asserts that the blurring of "military prostitute" with "military bride" contributed to the erosion of military-sponsored programming and assistance for Korean brides. The conflation of the two in South Korea prompted the ARC and the Far East Command to explicitly exclude Korea from brides school programs.[58]

In 1968, in response to the growing number of Korean military brides, the United Service Organizations (USO) took on the task of opening brides schools to fill the existing void. A privately funded nonprofit organization in operation since 1941, the USO was best known for its camp shows that brought American performers to the warfront to boost the morale of soldiers. In Korea, the USO continued to host the shows but expanded to institute a variety of programs, all under the supervision of the Department of Defense.[59]

That the USO opened brides schools so soon after the Far East Command deemed them ineffective in Korea shows once again the extent to which the US government relied upon private organizations to mitigate the intimate outcomes of US militarization. Private organizations like the ARC and the USO took on the excesses of empire, shoring up the US military's failed attempts to prevent marriages. A 1968 USO flyer announced the opening of a brides school in Seoul, explaining, in English and Korean, that it offered an "excellent opportunity for wives and fiancées of American Servicemen in Korea to learn . . . from outstanding instructors" about "American Stateside Customs and Dress, proper American etiquette and manners," legal rights and responsibilities, education, religion, public health, personal and feminine hygiene, passport and visa requirements, how to cook American meals, and how to apply makeup. They promised refreshments, door prizes, and field trips to the commissary.[60] Much like the ARC brides schools in Japan and the Philippines, the USO trained the women in American ways to help ease their transition into the United States, but also to mold them into proper gendered American citizenship prior to their arrival.

During the 1970s and 1980s, the USO expanded to bases outside of Seoul, and an estimated three hundred women enrolled annually. The numbers dwindled to around seventy by the 1990s, but the fact that the schools were still running reflects the success of and perceived need for the program.[61] Early 1970s photographs from the Taegu USO brides school show that the gatherings were often held in a home. In one photograph, titled "Thanksgiving Buffet," seven Korean women sit on one side of a large coffee table with dishes placed before them.[62] They turn their heads to look at the Korean woman speaking while the instructor, a white American woman who sits in a chair across from the others, leans forward to hear her. The image displays the kinds of American cultural and gastronomy lessons that the women received.

What seems less clear is the extent to which the Korean women understood the information. In another photograph, titled "Bride's School," two white American teachers, one male and one female, gesticulate with their hands, mouths open mid-speech as they actively convey their lessons. The Korean women listen intently, some with their heads tilted toward the teachers and one with a hand raised to her forehead as she concentrates on what they are saying.[63] The photograph reveals the strains of communication. Beyond conversational phrases, English language lessons went largely missing from the USO schools in South Korea. The Taegu monthly calendar from 1972 shows that classes met twice a week, a frequency sufficient for cultural lessons and immigration information, but not for effectively teaching a new language. It could be argued that speaking English would be the most useful skill for someone new to the country, and while the demanding logistics of learning a language might explain why the USO did not offer such lessons, it also suggests that the schools privileged the teaching of appearances and behaviors over the ability to communicate verbally. Elisions like these connected the schools to US nation-building projects that sought to mitigate the potential dangers of nonwhite immigrants by turning them into American subjects, not engaged citizens. The Taegu calendar with its twice-weekly brides schools, Friday orphan nights, and weekend Korean cultural and shopping tours was but a microcosm of a larger project aimed at cultivating American postwar power, curating the behavior of Americans and locals, and ameliorating the long-term effects of the interpersonal relationships that formed when US servicemen were stationed abroad.

While connected to state efforts, USO schools were also beneficial to the women who attended. The Taegu photographs show the intimacy of the gatherings and suggest that it was through the schools that Korean women could foster a community that was otherwise not available to them. In the space of the brides school, there was a closeness between the women who were made outcasts in Korean society and viewed as problems by the US military. The classes physically brought women together, making them visible to themselves and one another in possibly affirming ways. Outside of the USO, women began to organize support groups in South Korea to protect their interests. These autonomous groups were often co-opted by pimps and the local police, but evidence the extent to which the women valued the need to come together.[64] Unfortunately, connections made in South Korea were broken by distance and a lack of programs for military brides once they came to the United States.[65] From a collective identity for which there was a named school and a gathering of like individuals in South Korea to an isolated existence in the United States, Korean military brides moved through American empire as subjects on the periphery. Their needs were largely supplanted by efforts made to make them safe for arrival in the United States, a transnational project that began with brides schools in Korea and continued through US cultural projects aimed at rewriting Korean women to make them acceptable to American audiences.

Rescripting the Korean War Bride

In December 1957, the Republic of Korea sent to the United States 187 art pieces from the National Museum of Korea, Duksoo Palace Museum of Fine Arts, and the Christian Museum in Seoul. Over the next two years, the *Masterpieces of Korean Art* exhibit traveled to eight premier museums across the United States. The American-Korean Foundation organized the Metropolitan Museum's opening gala in New York. The three-hour celebration, held on February 6, 1958, broke previous attendance records with over five thousand visitors. While the AKF chose young Korean choristers to headline its 1954 fundraising campaign, for the Korean art exhibit the AKF arranged for seven "really beautiful . . . Korean girl singers" and twenty more Korean hostesses, all in "native dress," to circulate through the galleries. Patricia Culler of the AKF's program division explained that when the women played and sang Korean folk songs, "the interest and pleasure of the crowd was so great that it was necessary to move the [Korean performers] from gallery to gallery throughout the evening to keep the people moving."[66] At the World House Gallery opening, also in New York, the AKF similarly arranged for "native color—with Korean music, singers, and hostesses in their native dress, which again delighted all present."[67] The Korean women must have been a rather unforgettable sight to behold. Dressed in colorful hanboks that billowed to the floor, playing double-sided drums and singing enchanting songs in a foreign tongue, the women were exotic feasts for American eyes and ears.

The AKF spokesperson described how audiences "oh'ed and ah'ed" over the women.[68] Like the artwork in the gallery, they were to be viewed, not touched. Here the Korean women entertainers were tamed by their museum surroundings, a setting that elevated Korean women by association. While the AKF's opening soirees showcased an Orientalist and timeless version of Korean women that likened them to the ancient art of that faraway country, it was only the well-heeled museum attendees in New York who benefitted from these cultural lessons. It would not be until 1959 that the rest of the nation would meet Korean women who would help rescript existing conceptions of Korean military brides.

During the war, sisters Sook-ja and Ai-ja Kim and their cousin Myoung-ja Kim sang for US troops in Korea. Sook-ja and Ai-ja, age twelve and ten, lost their father in the war and performed with their mother and cousin Myoung-ja, age eleven, to provide for the family. Since they could not speak English, the young girls phonetically learned popular American rock and roll songs, to the delight of homesick troops. In 1958 American agent Tom Ball saw them and booked the trio for a four-week residency at the Thunderbird in Las Vegas. For showbiz purposes and to help get a passport for Myoung-ja, the girls became the "Kim Sisters." The women were the closing act of Ball's *China Doll Review*, which boasted "the most beautiful Oriental Show Girls in the World." Ralph Pearl, who reviewed the show in 1959, remarked that the Kim Sisters "tore down the house with their versatile and charming ways" and were as good as "top sister harmony teams" like the McGuires, Boswells, Andrews, and Fontanes. Their popularity won them another gig at the Stardust, and from there they skyrocketed to fame. They were featured in *Life*, *Newsweek*, and numerous other magazines, and performed over twenty-five times on *The Ed Sullivan Show*, making them among the top ten most frequent acts in the history of the program, which aired from 1948 to 1971.[69] Louis Armstrong, Frank Sinatra, and Peggy Lee were members of their fan club.[70] In interviews, the women remember rehearsing and performing nearly every day and describe both the exhilaration and the exhaustion of it all.

In marketing the trio, their manager had the Sisters play into the Orientalist expectations of their American audiences. Their first album used an Orientalized script and displayed the women dressed in Chinese cheongsams holding splayed fans, a cultural trifecta intended to sell albums precisely for their commodifiable Oriental appeal (figure 6.3). The Asian identity of the Kim Sisters merged with existing Orientalist scripts that made them legible to US audiences. For example, their performance of "Fan Tan Fanny" and "I Enjoy Being a Girl," popular numbers from the Rodgers and Hammerstein musical about a Chinese American family, *Flower Drum Song*, situated the Sisters in existing gendered Orientalist and model minority scripts. Here and in other performances, the Asian-faced singers regaled a stunning range of songs in English with the trace of a Korean accent. *Life* described how Americans found the Sisters' "Oriental touch on US tunes a highly refreshing one."[71] Christina Klein describes the value of "Asian" appearances in Cold War America that both conveyed their role as cultural ambassadors and reified a pluralist embodiment of American democracy.[72] The Kim Sisters communicated this blend of East meets West. Like other cultural productions of model minority Asian Americans at this time, the Kim Sisters allowed viewers to enact pluralism from a safe distance, to consume their performance as a passive demonstration of racial tolerance.

Figure 6.3. Album cover, *The Kim Sisters: Their First Album*. 1959. Monument Records, MLP 8022.

Yet, in the context of the recent war and ongoing US commitments in the peninsula, their distinction as Korean also mattered. While the generic Orientalism into which they were slotted helped make them legible in a US context, their Koreanness carried additional cultural relevance. The women made great efforts to highlight their Korean identities. In nearly all of their performances, they incorporated Korean lyrics. Sookja was surprised to find that Americans did not know the difference between the Japanese kimono, the Chinese cheongsam, and the Korean hanbok. She actively corrected those who remarked upon her "beautiful kimono," explaining to them that what she wore was a Korean dress. When she realized that "nobody knew where Korea was at the time," she recognized her role as a "Korean Ambassador" and set out to teach her audiences through her performances.[73]

South Koreans also viewed the Kim Sisters as cultural ambassadors who could promote Korean modernity and cosmopolitanism. Much like the Korean Orphan Choir, which toured concurrently, the Kim Sisters were a cultural export, the veritable beginnings of modern day K-Pop and the pride of South Korea.[74] The newspaper *Kyŏnghyang sinmun* heralded the Sisters' appeal to global audiences, praising their talent for blending Korean and other cultures, which made them beloved by both Eastern and Western worlds.[75] When they returned to visit Korea after entertaining in the United States for nine years, Myoung-ja, who went by Mia, said that Korea's welcome was "like a house on fire."[76] In 1967 the South Korean government awarded them medals of honor for promoting Korean culture and improving Korea's reputation in the Western world.[77] And the Korean embassy in the United States gave them Plaques of Merit and Gratitude for improving US-Korea relations.[78]

Recognized for their internationalist work both in the United States and South Korea, the Kim Sisters were cultural brokers who helped explain the complex and shifting relationship between South Korea and the United States. During their acts, they performed a variety of instruments, dances, and songs. For example, when they appeared on *Hollywood Palace* in the 1960s, they performed a bossa nova number that opened with "Annyŏnghashimnikka, this is Korean Bossa Nova. . . . Now catch the mood and say 'ah-so.' [They bow, with fans splayed.] Caramba!" They then broke into spirited dance before walking over to play the marimba.[79] Starting with the formal "hello" in Korean and moving into Brazilian song and dance, the women embodied internationalism in cultural form. In a 1963 *Ed Sullivan Show* performance, their mother, Lee Nan-young, joined them onstage to sing "Hallelujah," replacing several English verses with Korean lyrics. The vision of a Korean family singing a religious hymn melded Koreans and Christianity much like the World Vision Korean Orphan Choirs. Given the popularity of both singing troupes at this time, American audiences could draw parallels between both sets of performers as survivors of the Korean War who were won to democracy. The Kim Sisters further modernized these scripts. Their ability to play twenty instruments, including Scottish bagpipes, also displayed Cold War internationalism at its pop cultural best,

American democracy's embrace of global diversity choreographed into a stage show.[80]

Connections between the Kim Sisters and Korean War orphans were actively made in other ways. On October 14, 1962, the women appeared on NBC's *Ensign O'Tool*, a show that starred Dean Jones as a US Navy officer aboard the fictional USS *Appleby*, which anchored around the Pacific.[81] In this episode, titled "Operation Benefit," the navy hosted a variety show to raise money for Korean orphans. The Kim Sisters were the headlining act and opened with a performance of the Korean folksong "Arirang" wearing hanboks and playing Korean instruments. The next shot shows the seamen becoming visibly excited; one naval officer drops his mouth open in surprise before settling into a broad smile. The camera cuts to the girls to show what the men were reacting to: the Kim Sisters were removing their loose-fitting hanboks to reveal the curve-hugging cheongsams that they wore underneath. The women who just moments ago played Korean kayagums were now dancing and singing, swinging their hips and strumming banjos. The men erupted in applause.[82] The episode ends with Dean Jones visiting the orphanage to tell the Sisters that they raised $2,000 for the children. Flanked on either side by smiling orphans, the Sisters, now dressed in modest, all-white hanboks, bow with gratitude. In "Operation Benefit," sentimentalism surrounding the by then well-known story of Korean orphans reined in the threatening sexuality of the Kim Sisters. Pictured amidst the children and positioned as their caretakers, the youth and innocence of the sisters supplanted their earlier performance that was intended to appeal to US servicemen, but only to garner donations for the children. The sexuality displayed at the start of the episode was sanitized and contained by their pure intentions by the show's end.

The duality of the Kim Sisters as innocent war survivors and exotic Oriental lotus blossoms was captured in photographs, as well. On February 22, 1960, *Life* spent a day with the Kim Sisters on a farm that belonged to their manager's mother in Illinois. The article closed with images of the girls watching television and riding a sleigh. The captions described how "in pony-tails" the girls watched *Queen for a Day* and "were surprised to learn the show's winner ruled nothing" (figure 6.4). The visual juxtaposition of young Koreans watching television was by then a familiar trope of the Korean adoptee—an image that signaled both the

Figure 6.4. The Kim Sisters watch television, "in pony-tails." "Three Korean Kims and Their Kayagums," *Life*, February 22, 1960. Getty Images.

modern-day benefits of American capitalism and the Korean youngsters' embrace of American ways. Yet the full-page photograph that opened the article showed the girls made-up and striking suggestive poses fitting for adults, not children (figure 6.5). Mia, to the far left, winks with her mouth wide open; Ai-ja, in the middle, is feigning surprise; and Sook-ja (or Sue), to the right, makes a comic, overly strained smile. The women are exaggerating their onstage personas for the camera with acute self-awareness. Mia remembers that *Life* photographers took 2,500 shots that day but selected only six images for print. The pictures that the editors chose captured the duality of the Kim Sisters as innocent children akin to

Korean orphans/adoptees and sexualized adults that evoked connections to Korean prostitutes/brides.

Their 1967 performance on *The Dean Martin Show* displayed these tensions. Martin introduces the sisters with a joke: "Oh, you're gonna love the Kim Sisters. There are three of 'em! I know because when I look at them I see six of 'em!" While the joke referenced the fact that the host was tipsy (he enters the show carrying a martini), there are other possible associations. The audience laughs, familiar with and perhaps made a bit uncomfortable by the weight of his humor, which played upon tropes of plentiful and available Korean women, and the supposed indistinguishableness of Asians. He goes on to say that they were born in Korea, where they entertained troops, and emphasizes that they have made it all the way to "Ameree-ca, here in the United States. . . . That's where America is,

Figure 6.5. The Kim Sisters pose in hanboks with their Korean instruments. "Three Korean Kims and Their Kayagums," *Life*, February 22, 1960. Getty Images.

right here in the United States!" Dressed in bubble-gum pink sequined cheongsams, the women emerge singing. For their second number, Martin saunters over to join them. He tells them that he knows them because they are famous, but that he does not know their names, to which they reply, nice and slow so he can understand, "I'm Sue, I'm Ai-ja, I'm Mia," to which Martin, whose arms are wrapped around the waists of Sue and Mia, replies with a raised brow, "And I'm Frank." The audience erupts in laughter again at the handsome Martin, a reputed womanizer on his second marriage, who changes his name to permit his flirtation with the girls. Huddled close and swaying together on stage, the four of them begin singing "Getting to Know You" from the musical *The King and I*. Midway through the song about internationalist exchange there is an interlude where the women ask Martin what he knows about them. He starts with, "Well, uh, you were born in Japan." The girls shake their heads and Mia explains in a teacherly way, "No, in Korea." He comes back more confidently with "Well, you sing and dance," to which they nod and Sue leans in smiling to say, "Whatever you like."

As the song wraps, audience members are left with a conundrum. The women fit existing constructs of the demure Asian lotus blossom, innocent and there to please, as well as that of a sexualized woman, which placed the Sisters in association with the figure of the Korean prostitute and war bride. The slits in their snug and sparkly dresses, their makeup, and the coquettish exchange with Dean Martin fit with coeval representations of Korean prostitutes. Yet their youth, high ponytails, and sisterly connection helped to curb their sexuality. In interviews and articles about the Sisters, they were commonly portrayed as virgins. *Life* made special note of the fact that they were "faithful to a Korean tradition that a girl should not go out alone until she [was] 23." The writer went on to explain how the oldest, Sook-ja, solved the "stage-door Johnny" problem by telling the men who asked her out after the shows that her younger sisters had to tag along.[83] At a party at the Playboy mansion to which their manager forced them to go for advertising purposes, they hid in the bathroom after seeing naked women swimming inside a huge water tank.[84] Their innocence allowed the contradictory juxtaposition to hold—they were pure and seemingly unaware of their adult sexuality, an invitation for audiences to ogle without guilt. Thus, while the "split-sheathed singers" sold their sex appeal on stage, it was made public that they were not available, an important distinction that brought them closer to concurrent constructions of Korean children than Korean women.

In these ways and throughout the first decade of their popular US performances, the Kim Sisters did not disrupt the status quo as much as they carried forth ideas of global cultural exchange and US cosmopolitanism. At the height of their popularity in the late 1950s and through much of the 1960s, the Sisters gave Americans an alternative lens through which to remake Korean brides as pure and innocent in their desirability. Yet in 1967, when all three of the women married white men, the fantasy collapsed. Once married, they could no longer serve as the palatable, safe, sexualized but not sexual bridge that intimately connected the United States to South Korea. Nor could they convey the innocence that they did as virginal performers who were still foreign enough to register as a wholesome example of internationalism. Even though Mia married an Austrian and none of their spouses were servicemen, their marriage to white men brought them into closer association with Korean war brides than Korean orphans. The racial pairing of white men to Korean women was enough to conjure these less appealing associations of GIs and prostitutes, US servicemen and Korean brides. No longer the visage of a charming family act, the women became an uncomfortable reflection of intimate interracial realities.

Sook-ja and Ai-ja both explain that the reasons the Kim Sisters broke up had to do with personal conflicts as well as the challenges of touring once married.[85] Mia concurred, explaining that marriage, and later children, made it increasingly difficult to travel for shows. Adding to the problems brought about by their marriages, the Vietnam War in the late 1960s introduced other Asian women to the gendered Orientalist mix—the Vietnamese prostitute and Viet Cong guerrilla fighter—figures that further complicated the pairing of Asian women to white American men. While numerous factors possibly contributed to the decline in popularity of the Kim Sisters, their coupling with white men altered their appeal. Mia left the group, and Ai-ja and Sook-ja continued to perform through the 1970s, but this time with the "Kim Brothers."[86] The family act did not achieve the same popularity, and by the mid-1970s, the Kim Sisters slipped out of view.

Hidden in Plain Sight

In the mid-twentieth century, US militarized prostitution became the starting point from which multiple identities of Korean women emerged. Whether figured as prostitutes, brides, entertainers, or mothers of GI babies, Korean women were forced to navigate unequal relations of power as a result of American empire. Even the Kim Sisters, who found fame and opportunity in the United States, had to contend with the uneven structures. Tom Ball demanded that they not cut their hair so that they could wear their signature ponytails, and insisted that they wear tight cheongsams because the hanboks were too billowing and made them look pregnant.[87] In 1963, after years of being taken financial advantage of by their manager, Bob McMackin (who "scared" the Sisters, according to Sook-ja), they were finally able to fire him, but not before having to pay him $45,000.[88] Indeed, multiple American actors, from for-profit agents to entities like the US military, produced and then tried to remake the Korean woman. Yet in the context of empire, she was a figure who could not be easily resolved. The lengths taken to obscure, hide, or reconfigure the Korean woman revealed the high stakes; her very existence threatened to unravel US nation-building efforts. Just by being, she challenged US claims of anti-imperialism and benevolence. This explains in part why Korean women had to be erased, their experiences and perspectives overwritten, even in the moments when they were made to appear.

Amidst these erasures were flashes in which the Korean woman could not be contained. In 1951, when two African American soldiers wrote home that they had married Korean girls, Toki Schalk Johnson, columnist for the *Pittsburgh Courier*, entertained the possibility that the "new influx of brown-skinned people into the United States" might force prejudices to "vacate certain minds." Yet in the end she predicted much heartache for the Korean women, whose "tanned complexions will force them into a category they won't like. That of being second class citizens."[89] Knowing full well the ongoing failures of racial integration and the deep-rooted domestic problem of racial inequality, Johnson was remarking upon the discrimination faced by nonwhite peoples in the United States, whether American- or foreign-born.

In 1956 the *New York Times* relayed news of a Korean bride who was hospitalized after becoming despondent in the absence of her air force husband. Neighbors reported that she had been weeping uncontrollably in her apartment in the months before she was admitted. Her husband left his tour of duty early to be with his wife, and things were "looking up" since his return.[90] The article made it appear as though the Korean woman simply missed her husband. There were other possible reasons for her angst, including isolation, trauma, and loss.[91] She married her GI husband in 1952 in the midst of war, and entered the United States shortly thereafter, where she had to navigate a community that did not look kindly upon Korean brides; she also had to raise two biracial children in this environment.[92] That she "had been in that state virtually since the birth of her second child" and that she did not leave her apartment for months was telling, for where would she go, and was there anyone there who could help her?

Even in death, discrimination followed Korean women. In a 1961 case, the Hillcrest Park Cemetery in Springfield, Massachusetts, initially refused "to bury a Korean war bride because she was not white."[93] These brief encounters offer a glimpse into the private lives of Korean women, ones that laid bare the afterlives of empire that began in South Korea, but lived on through the bodies of those moved by war and US militarization. These stories told of experiences wholly different from the cultural productions of Japanese brides and the Kim Sisters. Popular representations circulating in the 1950s and 1960s helped to deny their very existence. Viewers were invited to imagine women who resembled Korean brides without needing to engage or address the real Koreans living amongst them, who were left to navigate the outcomes of America's intimate empire on their own.

Conclusion

Broken Family Frames

In 1956 an African American veteran living in Michigan approached the ISS for help adopting his Korean mixed-race child. His wife, while unhappy about his infidelity, understood the choices that he had made amidst the pressures of war and agreed to the adoption. The serviceman asked a friend still stationed in South Korea to keep tabs on the boy. The friend wrote that the child was well cared for, and that the men on base bought him winter clothes and fed him in the camp mess hall daily. He described the growing child as a "little joker" and soon-to-be "heart-breaker."[1] An ISS caseworker was also in contact with the child. She described an incident when two Korean boys taunted him, but how he "just held his head in the air" and walked along as if he were the only one on the street. The child seemed strong, but the caseworker still feared that he would soon need to support himself and that he'd likely become "hardened and shifty."[2] The GI father regularly sent money to the child's Korean foster mother, whom he referred to as "mama-san." Mama-san frequently removed the child from the orphanage, disappearing with him for months at a time. At various points, she demanded more money from the father, while he continually implored her to send the boy to America so that he could live in a family setting.[3]

In November 1958, the ISS found the Korean birth mother and learned that the child was born in May 1953.[4] The mother visited the ISS office in Seoul several times seeking clarification about what was going to happen to her son. She could not remember the father's name and asked for a picture so that she would feel "more easy about the whole plan [to send him to the United States for adoption]."[5] The ISS assured the father that requests like these were common as the "girls [were] usually scared that if they release[d] their children they [would] not go to the person to whom they [thought]." The caseworker explained that this has "happened many times in the past," adding that "natural mothers are often very attached to their children, and do care very much about their future happiness, even though they themselves cannot provide for them."[6] In the end, the ISS denied the serviceman's request for adoption because he was deemed financially unstable. The man's wife also changed her mind and decided that she no longer wanted to adopt the boy. The ISS searched for other potential American homes, but closed the case in 1961, concluding that there were no "suitable Negro PAPs [potential adoptive parents] at the present time to offer."

This story was a casting call of empire, one that included roles played by Americans and parts that Koreans were forced to fill. It started with the military father, who was part of the same battalion as his friend still stationed in South Korea. Despite President Truman's 1948 order to integrate the military, it is probable that they were part of the same all-black battalion, since the army remained segregated throughout much of the Korean War.[7] His friend, who had married a Korean national, met his wife on base or in a nearby camptown and would bring her to the States when his tour of duty was over. "Mama-san," a slang term used to describe a woman in charge of a camptown bar, was both a benefactor and a victim.[8] The letters show that she knew the serviceman father and his GI friend, and other African American soldiers as well, since camptown bars often doubled as brothels that served segregated clientele.[9] While she moved freely between the US military base and the GI town, these spaces contained her. Outside of militarized geographies, she was a fallen woman, and even within them she was positioned by race, gender, and profession as always below the men she served.

The birth mother was also excluded from the Korean polity. Once she learned that the ISS was trying to send her child to the United States, she intervened to the extent that she could to advocate for her son. However, her request to send the child to his father was overwritten. When the ISS determined him ineligible and began to search for another African American couple, it was following its "best practices" even though this went against the mother's wishes. The ISS's inability to find a "suitable" family reflected US structural barriers facing African Americans in the United States, while the segregation that they faced when serving in the US Army evidenced the discrimination that followed them overseas. Finally, there was the child, who at five years old when the case opened and eight when it closed, was old enough to recognize the vacillations in his life, the rotating cast of caretakers and the multiple institutions that served as home.

As for what happened to the child and his mother, photographs are the only traces that remain. Tucked into the case study file were three snapshots. Two were of the boy standing next to a US jeep, smiling broadly. The other showed him with his mother seated for a studio photograph. In this image, he sits awkwardly on her lap in front of a backdrop of painted flowers. They wear their best clothes; the mother in a hanbok and the boy in a sweater and coveralls. She stares directly at the camera and he looks off to the side; neither smile. The studio setting suggests that this marked some kind of an occasion, but the deep concern on both of their faces intimate that it was not a happy one. Did this photo mark the last time that they would see one another? Was this photo taken as a keepsake for the mother to remember him by? The photograph could not contain the weight of the circumstances that surrounded them. From the absent father to the non-home setting to the quiet stillness to the deep sadness, the picture was missing all of the expected markers of a family photograph. It was a broken family frame.

The fragmented story of this mother and her son reveals the overlapping tensions of America's intimate empire—the US structures that shaped it, the relationships born from it, the excesses that it could not contain, and the lives that it forever changed. These accounts haunt public productions of the Cold War family that asked everyone to look at what was captured in the frame so that they would not have to see the many things left outside it. In this book, I have attempted to understand how US militarization created the war orphan, adoptee, GI baby, birth mother, prostitute, and bride; and how American empire both produced and required the management of these populations, processes that ultimately resulted in their erasure.

Korea was not a singular episode of US empire. Like imperial encounters that came before, it was through the realm of intimacy that US administrators and an array of imperial actors extended their reach to foreign populations. Yet when it came to Korea, the war and America's role in it reconfigured the boundaries and outcomes of empire. So too did the geopolitics of a post–World War II era that witnessed global decolonization and required a democratic vigilance to meet the growing pressures of the Cold War. Representation became key to helping the United States navigate the altered terrain of power under the scrutiny of the world; it was in this context that intimate narratives of care and kin emerged to allay ample evidence of US imperialism in Asia.

What ensued was a mix of US governmental and nongovernmental efforts to further state and private goals, respectively, through Korea's children and women. It was in the global constructions of family, both real and imagined, where the goals of US empire came undone. In particular, representations of Korean children that helped soften the look of American power also came with scripts that invited broad American participation in Cold War projects of rescue. To add to the hundreds who went to South Korea to head up postwar recovery efforts were the hundreds of thousands of Americans who heeded the call from home through donations, and for some, through adoptions. It was this outpouring of support from average Americans, on a scale not seen before, especially in the assistance of Asian others, that made it impossible for the US government to keep its imperial intentions confined to the faraway peninsula. Sentiment grew through the war and beyond it to bind Americans together with Koreans as kin, a transnational making of family that forced the United States to figuratively and literally open its borders to make room for the returns of US empire.

Processes that began with the Korean War continue to affect Koreans on both sides of the Pacific. To date, there are well over 150,000 Korean adoptees living in the United States, and an estimated 50,000 living in European countries and Australia. Their arrival in Western nations is a result of the wartime processes that were established to facilitate their departure. Ch'oe Wŏn-gyu argues that prolonged US aid beginning with the war gave the Korean government little time (or incentive) to come up with its own comprehensive social policy. Criticizing the Korean government for evading major welfare responsibilities, Ch'oe describes how the overwhelming task was left to the private sector, which by the 1960s had been largely shaped by US missionaries and welfare workers.[10] In 1961 the ROK government handled only five orphanages, which housed 954 children, while private, mostly US organizations administered the remaining 542 orphanages and nurseries.[11] In 1965 Americans still financed 75 percent of Korean orphanages and welfare centers.[12] Complicating matters, many American missionaries and social workers found reasons to stay in South Korea. Time and again, in ISS, US missionary, and voluntary organization correspondence, Americans lamented the shortcomings of Korean staff who followed procedures based on "intuition and pragmatism."[13] Americans considered Koreans to be eager learners, but always insufficient, an Orientalist construction also used by the US military to justify its need to remain in South Korea.[14] Americans may have been blinded by their own quest for religious conversion (in the case of missionaries) and professionalization (in the case of social workers), and thus not able to see the extent to which foreign incompetence was a necessary precondition for their projects to take root and grow. Neither did they acknowledge how, far more than "helpers," Koreans were active agents who administered care for children with and without American guidance.

By the 1960s, institutionalization and transnational adoption had become established solutions for a range of welfare needs stemming from political upheaval. On April 19, 1960, a student uprising brought an end to President Rhee's increasingly autocratic rule. Park Chung Hee's military coup ushered in a dictatorial regime that brought with it rapid industrialization and its concomitant ills. Between 1963 and 1985, the female workforce increased nearly seven and a half times; workplace assaults became common and contributed to the growing number of children born out of wedlock.[15] The number of abandoned children rose dramatically, from 715 in 1955 to 11,319 in 1964. In 1968 the Ministry of Health and Social Affairs reported that many poor families looked to orphanages to provide food and shelter for their children.[16] Transnational adoptions remained the other primary solution for Korea's welfare problems, which now stemmed from industrialization instead of war. Transnational adoptions reached their peak during the regimes of Park Chung Hee (1963–1979) and Chun Doo Hwan (1981–1987), when 75 percent of all Korean placements took place.[17] This would shift in 1988, when Seoul hosted the Olympics and North Korea seized the opportunity to publicly accuse South Korea of exporting babies. The ROK government responded by trying to curb transnational adoptions. The numbers have since steadily declined to fewer than 2,500 children per year in the 1990s, and to around a thousand per year by the late 2000s. Recently, the numbers have dropped into the hundreds annually.[18] For decades, the Korean government did not acknowledge Korean adoptees, who were both reminders of a painful war and embodiments of national shame for a country that was unable to care for its own.

By 1959, when the immediate war crisis had subsided, full-Korean children took the place of mixed-race children as the primary focus of overseas adoptions.[19] While mixed-race children no longer constitute the bulk of transnational adoptions, the birth of mixed-race children as well as the discrimination that they face through adulthood continues as a result of ongoing US military presence in South Korea.[20] The *Korean Herald* estimates that forty thousand mixed-race children, the majority of them with American GI fathers, were born between 1955 and 1969. Government efforts to remove mixed-race children, which began with President Rhee's 1953 directive, have since taken on a variety of forms. From training programs aimed at sending mixed-raced people overseas for employment in the 1970s to exempting mixed-race people from military conscription (mandatory for all Korean males between the ages of eighteen and twenty-six for an average service of two years) so that they could leave the country before they were eighteen, the government has continued in less obvious ways to try and remove mixed-race individuals. Efforts like these have contributed to the ongoing societal rejection of Korea's mixed-race population, pushing many out of Korea and making it inhospitable to those who have stayed.[21]

While the Korean government has begun to recognize Korean adoptees by offering cultural return tours and producing popular reunion shows that bring adoptees together with their Korean mothers, these efforts often privilege Korean nationalism over the individual needs of adoptees. Today, adoptees from the United States, Europe, and Australia are actively forging their own paths. Artists, filmmakers, and writers are foregrounding a conversation about their lives and daily experiences, and are together cultivating a global network on their own terms that redefines rote notions of kinship and nation.[22]

As for Korean women, US empire that began with occupation in 1945 continues to directly affect them. To date, over 100,000 Korean military brides have come to the United States. An estimated 40 to 50 percent of the approximately 850,000 Korean immigrants who entered between 1965 and 2002 gained admittance because of kinship ties to Korean military brides.[23] Since the war, more than one million Korean women have worked as sex providers for the US military.[24] They have come together in the face of continued discrimination to advocate for themselves. In the 1950s, the Mugunghwa ch'inmokhoe (Rose of Sharon Friendship Society), the K'ŭlobŏhoe (Clover Society), Saessakhoe (Sprout Society), and Paengnyŏnhoe (White Lotus Society) formed to assist women. In 1960, fifty women in Pusan protested against their exploitative pimp, who they claimed treated them like slaves, and sex workers in private brothels distributed thousands of flyers demanding equality. Today, Du Rae Bang (My Sister's Place), Ae Ran Won (Planting Love), and Saeumto offer counseling, education, shelter, and alternative employment for women working in camptowns.[25] These organizations aim to empower women by promoting self-reliance and encouraging them to make demands on Korean and US governments to recognize and improve their situations. They also look to educate the wider society to unravel the myth of the *yanggonju*, or Yankee princess, by making transparent US and South Korean state pressures upon Korean women.[26] In 2017, 120 Korean women brought charges against the South Korean government for illegally detaining them and forcing them to undergo STD treatment. While they did not win a formal apology from the government, 57 women received a settlement of just $4,240 each to compensate for physical and psychological damage.[27] Though not a definitive victory, the case brought attention to the ongoing issue and forced the Korean government to acknowledge its role in the abuse of women who, during and after the war, were told that they were "patriots" for their duty.[28] A year later, in 2018, 117 Korean women sued the Republic of Korea government for justifying and encouraging prostitution in US military camptowns. In February 2018, the court concluded that the state "violated its obligation to respect human rights" by using the women's "sexuality as a means of achieving state goals."[29] That the women in both of these cases, still deeply ostracized in Korean society, held signs and picketed, drawing attention to the cause by first drawing attention to themselves, shows their bravery in the face of power. It is important to remember that a well-protected US military has yet to be censured for being the root cause of the circumstances endured by these and millions of other women across the US-militarized Pacific.

In South Korea, prostitution near US bases, the institutionalization of Korean children, and the ongoing practices of transnational adoptions and military marriages are all direct legacies of the Korean War. Together they evidence that extricating oneself from empire is no easy task. Indeed, when it came to Korean adoptees and military brides in the 1950s and 1960s, US imposition followed them from one side of the Pacific to the other. From their subjecthood in South Korea to their arrival in the United States, Korean adoptees and brides were bound to transnational projects that sought to make them good, or at least unproblematic, US subjects.[30] Today, however, they are redirecting the trajectory of empire by foregrounding their own experiences and collectively speaking against power.

This story of US intimate empire is not over; as Jodi Kim explains, it has a protracted afterlife that extends well beyond the Cold War and across the globe.[31] To begin, the Korean War was the crisis that occasioned the radical buildup of America's military-industrial complex and a quadrupling of America's defense spending. The resulting growth of the US military has contributed to the current post–World War II condition that Mary Dudziak terms "war time" to indicate that conflict is no longer the exception, but the norm.[32] The ways the United States built and then utilized the South Korean army have shifted the militarized terrain of the Pacific. At the height of the Vietnam War, the United States deployed fifty thousand South Korean soldiers and marines annually to fight its war, a function of what Simeon Man describes as American empire's transnational security state.[33] Today, there are still an estimated twenty-eight thousand US servicemen and women stationed in South Korea, and the US military maintains primary control of the ROK army. The reach of the US military extends far beyond South Korea; in 2007, more than 737 bases or military installations could be found outside the United States.[34]

Alongside an expanding US global militarism, the Korean War structured permanent shifts in the interpersonal practices of US foreign operations through the second half of the twentieth century and to the present.[35] When we consider operation babylifts during the Vietnam War, see news footage of children playing soccer with US servicemen in Kabul, and hear a US soldier recount that he spent more time delivering crayons to schools than in combat during his 2009 tour in Afghanistan, it bears remembering Korea.[36] The humanitarian framework that placed Korean children at its center found politicized meaning and new structures to support it, bringing children firmly into the orbit of future US military operations abroad, and providing familiar paths to understanding across difference for Americans watching from afar.

Beyond the Frame

In this book, I have attempted to piece together what happened to Korean children and women as a result of US contact. While there are copious materials that identify Koreans as subjects, there are scant wartime and immediate postwar documents produced by the children and women themselves. This trouble with the archives is not unique, given the uneven parameters of imperial rule and the records created to administer it.[37] Yet, while they did not pen the materials, Korean children and women are present across the archive in military memorandums, missionary records, caseworker files, and public and private photographs. They are, to borrow from Avery Gordon, ghostly matters that weigh down each word written about and photograph taken of them. Their "seething presence" ruptures the very documents intended to contain them, and punctures the simplified narratives created to serve others with evidence of the many things lost along the way.[38] These fissures lay bare the strained fictions needed to support US power and Korean state needs, and the attending violences resulting from these efforts.

This book opened with the story of the Korean War adoptee Lee Kyung Soo. In 1955, two years after the initial coverage of his arrival in the United States in *Life* magazine, the *Los Angeles Times* caught up with the then six-year-old Lee in an article titled "Korean Waif Becomes Real American Boy."[39] Photographs of Lee in suspenders, a white button-down shirt, and a tie, sharing a book with a white classmate demonstrated his transformation into proper US citizenry. Not only had his name since changed to James Lee Paladino, his whole person, behavior, and appearance made him American, no longer Korean. The article corroborated these points. After living in the United States for a year, James's "sad memories" of Korea were "blotted out." He stopped calling his father "abuji" and started addressing him as "Dad." Vincent Paladino confirmed that the boy's "Americanization [had] almost completely wiped out memories of less happy times in his native Korea." The article served as a farewell to the Korean Lee and allowed viewers to witness how he had simply become American.

Most who came to know Lee through these reports likely did not see the short column buried deep in the *New York Times* on January 21, 1958. Here it was reported that Vincent Paladino's new wife felt that nine-year-old Lee caused "friction" in the home.[40] Paladino relinquished custody of the child, who, after eleven "unhappy" months in foster care, was taken in by Paladino's parents. By this point, Lee had become a figurehead for orphaned children around the world, making appearances at the Korean Children's Choir performances and the opening of *That All May Know You Are Their Brother*, a documentary about rescuing children from Africa.[41] Publicizing his re-adoption would have troubled existing narratives surrounding his arrival in the United States. It would have negated the ability of the American family to anchor US claims to democracy. As well, broad knowledge of what happened to Lee would have exposed the tenuousness of US-Korean ties and the faulty foundations of that relationship. This explains in part why the press did not widely report on the unwelcome twist, allowing most who had come to "know" Lee to continue the fantasy first laid out for them in the pages of *Life*.

Like other images of Korean adoptees, photographs of Lee that appeared in the popular press were carefully staged. Lee's poses were choreographed by photographers and held by the child. When we consider these processes, far from organic moments, it was more likely that Lee's broad smile required effort. As in the cowboy photographs taken of him when he first arrived in the United States (figure I.2), Lee was asked to fill a role, to tote toy pistols and play a part in the drama of American empire. The strains of that performance seeped through. Weighing heavily in all of these photographs were the things that were harder to see—the loss and trauma that he carried with him as he maneuvered through life in a country that was far from the home he knew.

Whether through assimilation or disavowal, Korean children and women have become the forgotten population of a forgotten war. Yet as they themselves have not been allowed to forget, neither should we. This book has tried to reveal the processes that framed their experiences. From how and under what circumstances to where and with whom they lived—and from whom they were kept apart—Korean children and women of the war did not get to choose the events that changed their lives, but found ways to navigate the fallout every day. Empire changed them, but they also changed empire. Korean children and women altered the boundaries of US rule by bringing Americans intimately and permanently together with Koreans in ways neither intended by nor conducive to empire. Korean children and women drove Americans to put internationalism into practice. Through their labor, donations, and adoptions, Americans pried openings in US borders of race, family, and nation. In these ways, Korean children and women embodied the excess of empire, a population born from US militarization that could be managed but never fully contained.

Since the war, Koreans have been telling their stories, and it is imperative that we listen.[42] They remind us that the war and America's role in it made Korea unlivable. As a result of US militarization, countless Korean women and their mixed-race children have been pushed to the fringes of Korean society. Adoptees and military brides in the United States and other parts of the world have lived within and between nations. Thus, though they may have had little to no choice, Korean children and women did choose to struggle.[43] Lee's story serves as an important reminder of that struggle. Behind mediated portrayals and public directives were a multitude of stories not meant for public consumption. These moments left outside of the frame belonged to Lee. As for those times when he and fellow Koreans were put on display, it is incumbent upon the viewer to look for the experiences of children and women before and after that moment frozen in time to see the unseen events that constitute America's intimate empire.

While we cannot undo over half a century of US military, political, and social imposition, we must force a remembering in order to see how empire violates on national and intimate scales. It was in Korea that violence and humanitarianism came to support one another: the war created victims in need of rescue and US aid provided cover for ongoing intervention. Making these structures transparent is a first step to reimagining and generating different futures. Korean children and women have moved within and outside of US dominance, showing us that though ever present, power is neither fixed nor total. They expose how it was that violence and care became partners in US rule, and challenge us to unravel that union so that empire has nowhere to hide.

ACKNOWLEDGMENTS

One of the many things that I've learned while writing this book is that it's hard to let go. To those who have cheered me on, thank you for your steadfast support year after year. And then thank you for prying this manuscript out of my hands so that it could exist outside of my laptop.

The seeds for this book were first planted at UCLA, where the Asian American Studies Department makes a home for countless students, and I was one of its lucky residents. My thesis committee made me fall in love with school, so much so that I never wanted to leave. Valerie Matsumoto, whose patience and careful edits pushed me to be better, remains my model for how to be a scholar and mentor. I have Henry Yu to thank for life-reordering conversations, and for knowing (when I had no idea) that American studies would make a happy intellectual home for me. Don Nakanishi, whose smile, even when offering critiques, always buoyed me with hope, you will forever be the heart of that department. For bringing Korean American studies and communities front and center, thank you to K. W. Lee, Kyeyoung Park, Edward T. Chang, and Edward Park. Movers and shakers at the University of Hawai'i at Manoa, Erin Kahunawai Wright, Roderick Labrador, and Christine Quemuel; community makers at the Asian American Studies Center, Sefa Aina, Dennis Arguelles, Judy Soo Hoo, Mary Kao, Marjorie Lee, Russell Leong, Irene Suico Soriano, Meg Thornton, and Min Zhou; and fellow MA students Jih-Fei Cheng, Sang Chi, Jessica Kim, Daehwan Lee, S. Heijin Lee, Stephen Lee, Masako Nakamura, Gladys Nubla, Dean Itsuji Saranillio, Brandy Lien Worrall-Soriano, and Anthony Yuen, filled the halls with laughter and fostered a place where we could all belong together.

The American Studies Department at Yale University pushed me in directions I never thought possible. Matthew Frye Jacobson with his signature enthusiasm and good cheer encouraged this project from beginning to end. Laura Wexler urged me to think deeply about everything from my methodology to what was at stake in the act of writing. I am indebted to Mary Lui for her insightful and careful comments on nearly everything I wrote as a grad student, as well as professional advice at various stages; her mentorship has been a gift. Jean-Christoph Agnew, John Mack Faragher, Seth Fein, Glenda Gilmore, Paul Gilroy, Margaret Homans, and Sanda Mayzaw Lwin expanded, and oftentimes exploded, what I thought I knew. Grad school is hard and there were many who helped me make it through. Alicia Schmidt Camacho and Stephen Pitti were there for me the moment that I stepped on campus. Liza Cariaga-Lo and Pat Cabral at the Office of Diversity and Equal Opportunity were mentors who calmed me when I was overwhelmed. Vicki Shepard vanquished my homesickness. Megan Glick and Laura Grappo, together with whom I stressed, laughed, and ate, motivated me every day. I frequently found myself sitting next to Emmanuel Raymundo on the last train out of Manhattan, happy to have a friend who made grad school way more fun than it should be. Wendy Fu, my neighbor and shopping/yoga/conference companion, could brighten even the dreariest of New Haven days. Thank you to Amina El-Annan, Mike Amezcua, Adam Arenson, Aisha Bastiaans, Kimberly J. Brown, Geraldo Cadava, Amanda Ciaphone, Deborah Dinner, John Duncan, Melissa Garcia, Francoise Hamlin, Sarah Haley, Gretchen Heefner, Tisha Hooks, Amanda Izzo, Leah Khaghani, Simeon Man, Uri McMillan, Christina Moon, Monica Muñoz Martinez, Dara Orenstein, A. Naomi Paik, Shana Redmond, and Elizabeth Son, whose generosity and bright intellect made me feel lucky to be in grad school with them. I will forever be grateful for the collective good will of those who made up this remarkable community.

As an American Council of Learned Societies (ACLS) New Faculty Fellow in the Department of American Studies and Ethnicity (ASE) at the University of Southern California, I met a dream team of supporters. My mentor extraordinaire, Viet Than Nguyen, went above and beyond, finding time to read my manuscript, offer tips on teaching, and prep me for the job market. Nayan Shah offered much-needed pep talks during and after my time at USC. For welcoming me into the ASE community and offering friendship, as well as professional support, I'd like to thank Crystal Baik, Jih-Fei Cheng, Jack Halberstam, Hillary Jenks, Lon Kurashige, Kitty Lai, Jujuana Preston, Nic John Ramos, John Carlos Rowe, and George Sanchez. For welcoming me wholeheartedly into USC's Korean Studies Institute, I'd like to thank David Kang, who also hosted and brought in two of my academic heroes, Elaine Tyler May and Ji-Yeon Yuh, for a manuscript review. Their incisive feedback, along with that of Emily Hobson, Crystal Baik, Sandra Fahy, and So-Young Kim, helped me see the project in a new light.

Several foundations supported this project through its many stages. The Mellon Foundation and the Council on Library and Information Resources funded my research in the United States and South Korea; and the Yale Center for International and Area Studies, the Council on East Asian Studies, and the John F. Enders Travel Research Grant extended my time in Seoul. The Woodrow Wilson Foundation's Charlotte W. Newcombe Fellowship and the ACLS gave me the time needed to write. Research and summer writing grants from California State University, Fullerton, and a Nancy Weiss Malkiel Scholars Award supported by the Mellon Foundation made it possible for me to bring the manuscript across the finish line.

This book would never have come together without the boundless knowledge of archivists. In the United States, Sonya Lee and Rod Katz at the Library of Congress, Eric Van Slander at the National Archives, and Linnea Anderson and David Klaassen at the Social Welfare History Archives were my guides who enthusiastically helped me find materials and always knew where else I should be looking. In Korea, Kim Yŏng Chu at the National Assembly Library; Pak Un Kyŏng at Ewha Library; Pak Chun Hyŏng at the Yonsei Severance Hospital Museum; Chung Yŏn Sŏn at the Korean Military Academy; and Chong T'ae Yŏn at the US embassy in Seoul helped me navigate Korean databases and pointed me in the right direction when I was admittedly lost. At Ewha Women's University, Jung-Hwa Oh, Jin-Sook Park, and Min-Jung Kim welcomed me into their campus community. To directors and employees of wartime adoption agencies, Cho Kyu Hwan, Im Yong Ok, Jung Ae Ri, Kang Ji Yŏng, Kim Don Yŏng, Molly Holt, No Wŏl Ae, Park Jun Hyŏng, Shin Dong Han, Shin Hye Sŭk, Sŏng Kyŏ Hŭi, and Yŭ Mi Yŏng, thank you for granting me interviews and access to private collections that transformed my project. While in Seoul, I had the great fortune of meeting Jane Jeong Trenka and Sa-jin Kwok, whom I thank for sharing their perspectives and for inspiring me with their activism and courage.

This book has benefitted greatly from the comments of attendees at the annual meetings of the American Studies Association, the Asian

American Studies Association, the Alliance for the Study of Adoption and Culture, and the American Historical Association. To Catherine Ceniza Choy, Laura Briggs, Lene Myong Petersen, Karen Balcom, Eleana Kim, Hosu Kim, Kimberly McKee, Kim Park Nelson, SooJin Pate, and Sarah Park Dahlen, who are at the forefront of critical adoption studies, thank you for the conversations and for inspiring me with your work.

This book, like Humpty Dumpty, has been repeatedly broken apart. For helping to put it back together again, the following people deserve credit for the things that work (and excused from its faults, which remain my own). The Asian American Women's History writing group—Constance Chen, Kelly Fong, Dorothy Fujita-Rony, Jane Hong, Adria Imada, Karen Leong, Valerie Matsumoto, Isabela Seong Leong Quintana, and Judy Tzu-Chun Wu—read some to all of the chapters, locating the problems and then helping me to see the possibilities of each. I am so grateful to share meals and ideas with you, and deeply value your exemplary scholarship and friendship. For bringing together the Asian American and Pacific Islander Working Group at the Huntington Library, a special thanks to Constance Chen, Lon Kurashige, and David Yoo, and to Mariam Lam and Judy Tzu-Chun Wu, who prepared comments for one of my chapters. Their insights along with those of workshop attendees—Alfred Flores, Mana Hayakawa, Michelle Magalong, Chichi Peng, Brandon Reilly, Kirisitina Sailiata, Christen Sasaki, Rosanne Sia, and Paul Spickard—sharpened my arguments, while their positivity fueled me with energy. Emily Hobson has read multiple versions of each chapter, offering astute suggestions and careful edits, always when I needed them the most. Thank you for your friendship and for gifting us with your groundbreaking scholarship.

At New York University Press, thank you to Eric Zinner, who supported this project through its many stages. I am so grateful to him and the anonymous reviewers whose insights helped strengthen the book. Thank you to Rosalie Morales Kearns for her keen editorial eye. Ciara McLaughlin helped in its early stages, and Dolma Ombadykow, Alexia Traganas, and the press production team have worked patiently and always cheerfully to turn my dream into a reality.

In this book, I have thought about family frames that are both made and given. The American Studies Department at California State University, Fullerton, is my newest family. To my students who hold full-time jobs, support their families, and come to class grateful for the chance to learn something new, you remain my inspiration and give me hope for good things to come. Karla Arellano, Aissa Burgarin, and Sandra Medina, thank you for the countless things that you do for the department and our students. Daniel Kwag, Cheryl Wuo, and Drew Bahna were the best student researchers, each with an enthusiasm that matched their attention to detail. To Craig Loftin and Sharon Sekhon, thank you for the classroom collaborations and for modeling the importance of public scholarship. To Allan Axelrad, Dustin Abnet, Erica Ball, Jesse Battan, Sara Fingal, Adam Golub, John Ibson, Alison Kanosky, Karen Lystra, Carrie Lane, Elaine Lewinnek, Terri Snyder, Michael Steiner, Pamela Steinle, and Leila Zenderland, who demonstrate daily that intellectual rigor, teaching, and mentorship go hand in hand, you are among my favorite people to be around.

There have been many who were with me well before I ever imagined writing a book, and then stuck by me every (grueling) step of the way. Tracy Tong, for whom I have my coffee maker to thank for bringing us together our freshman year, has been my rock and is at the center of my happiest memories. Elisa Babigian's positivity and good humor have been rays of sunshine. Claudia Chiovare, Rachel Lilburn, Kathleen Romeiro, and Lauren Toubes have brought me side-splitting laughter and near run-ins with the law, the best distractions anyone could ever wish for. To the McNeill family, with whom I grew up, thank you for celebrating whatever Kimmi and I did (including our Thompson Twins dances, which, I'm certain, were as fabulous as you said they were); and to Grace Huang, who has had my back since we were fifteen, thank you for being a cheerleader in everything that I've ever tried to do. To Kelly and Noel Morrison and Chaghig and Trey Walker, you made San Francisco home for me; the world is better because you and your children are in it.

These past few years, people have circulated through our home, providing support in their own special ways. Bill Gong came bearing cupcakes, pies, and wine to help sustain many late nights. Andrew Nagata and David Yun arrived with sass and skill for our billiards showdowns, giving me much-needed breaks (Dave, I think we're ahead, yes?). And to Casandra Joseph, who has cared for and kept my children happily entertained while I stared at my computer, you are like a daughter to me. I'm thankful for the love that you share with my family and proud of what you will continue to do for others as you embark upon your nursing career.

To the Laras, thank you for wholeheartedly welcoming me into your family. Juan Francisco Lara, a loving father-in-law and grandfather, heartily celebrated every milestone big and small. He is deeply missed, and lives on in what we do as parents, educators, and members of a community that is always, as he taught us, much bigger than ourselves. To Joanne Lara, whose generosity is boundless—from letting us live in her home when we returned to Los Angeles to caring for our children when we needed to work—thank you for your unflagging love and support. Kiela, Andrew, Leotei, and Eisling Conway have cheered me on with their cards, treats, and hugs. I could not have done this without them.

This book is dedicated to my parents, Do Keun Woo and Moon Sook Oh, whose sacrifice for me and my sister is something that I think about every day. I never would have had the option to pursue academia or write this book, both huge privileges, had it not been for them. I'm so proud to be your daughter, and hope that I can give my children the kind of unconditional love and support that you've given us. To my sister, Peggy, who raised me while our parents worked, you made every day an adventure with creative games, disco choreography, and Wonder Woman costuming. I learned how to be in this world from you, how to see the beautiful in everything and the good in everyone. Thank you for bringing Claude Meyers into our lives and for bringing Sig and Alex into this world—they are amazing like you.

Finally, to my family who had no choice but to inhabit this book and bear with me as I sat at my desk still in my pajamas, still writing. To Kalyx, my first son. You were six months old when I finished the first draft of this manuscript. When you were older and able to write (because, yes, this took that many years), you made me charts with prizes to celebrate each chapter and brought me stuffed animals to keep me company. To Tsela and then Mylo, who as newborns slept on my lap while I typed, thank you for sleeping as much as you did. You helped me keep everything in perspective, and when I couldn't put a sentence together, reminded me that I was good at UNO and baking brownies. You three are my everything. And, finally, to Ankarino Lara, who changed the direction of my life the moment that he stepped aboard the Maya Mobile. You have shown me how important it is to find the joy in every day. From taking red-eyes to New Haven to cooking all of my meals (because, as you say, cereal is not dinner) to whisking the kids out of the house for "appa days" (and toward the end, "appa weekends") to reading and making better countless versions of this book, you have been my biggest supporter. I am so lucky to share this life with you.

NOTES

PREFACE

1 Yuh, "Moved by War," 281. Also see Liem, "History, Trauma, and Identity."
2 Chungmoo Choi, "Politics of War Memories," 395.

INTRODUCTION

1 Jon Brenneis, "A New American Comes 'Home,'" *Life*, November 30, 1953, 25–29. News of Paladino's adoption of the "chunky, cheerful four-year-old in a miniature chief's uniform" also appeared in *Time* magazine. "The Chief's Son," *Time*, November 21, 1953.
2 The armistice suspended hostilities, but did not technically end the war. Statistics from Halliday and Cumings, *Korea: The Unknown War*, 200–201; and Rhem, "Korean War Death Stats." The US Army reports 33,686 battle deaths and 103,284 wounded. It places the number of enemy deaths at 1.5 million, of which 900,000 were Chinese. "Fact Sheet," US Army Center of Military History.
3 In the 1950s and 1960s, "intercountry" or "overseas" were the terms used to describe the adoption of children from countries outside the United States. In this book, I use these terms along with the now more commonly used "transnational" to highlight the dynamics of adoptions that take place between nation-states.
4 In 1948 *Life* magazine had three times the circulation of Henry R. Luce's other flagship publication, *Time*. *Life* had a circulation of 5.45 million in 1948 and was "passed along" to multiple individuals, more than any other periodical. Baughman, "Who Read *Life*?," 42, 44.
5 Gibson and Jung, "Historical Census Statistics." For pre-1965 Korean immigration to the United States, see Patterson, *The Ilse*; Min, "Korean Americans"; and Hing, *Making and Remaking Asian America*, 65–67.
6 The McCarran-Walter Act continued the national origins quota system at a rate of one-sixth of 1 percent of each nationality's population in the United States in 1920. While this favored those of northern and western European lineage, it limited the immigration of those from Asia. "Immigration and Nationality Act of 1952," US Department of State Office of the Historian. For seminal studies on race and immigration law in the United States, see Ngai, *Impossible Subjects*; and Erika Lee, *At America's Gates*.
7 Statistics culled from various sources, as exact figures remain unknown. US Department of Justice, "Korean Immigration to the United States, 1903–1996,"

reprinted in Hurh, *Korean Americans*, 33; Korean Ministry of Health and Social Affairs, reprinted in Youn Taek Tahk, "Measures for the Welfare of Mixed-Blood Children in Korea" (hereafter "Welfare of Mixed-Blood Children"), August 8, 1967, pp. 3, 4, 7, Box 35, Folder 6, SW109, Social Welfare History Archives, University of Minnesota (hereafter SWHA); US Commissioner of Immigration and Naturalization, *Annual Reports, 1947–75*, table 6, reprinted in Bok-Lim C. Kim, "Asian Wives of US Servicemen," 99.

In addition to adoptees and military brides, an estimated six thousand Korean students came to the United States during this period. Yoo and Chung, "Introduction," 4. The US government sponsored an extensive Korean exchange program to train students and return them to South Korea. US and South Korean administrators grew concerned when a large number of students illegally stayed in the United States. Dillon, confidential memorandum from US Department of State, June 18, 1960, Record Group (hereafter RG) 59, Box 1082, Folder "Decimal 511.945/1–1461," Department of State Files, National Archives, College Park, MD (hereafter NA); Huntington Damon, memorandum, August 16, 1960, RG 59, Box 1082, Folder "Decimal 511.95B3/8–1660," Department of State Files, NA; Young Han Choo, "Weekly Report of the Korean Consulate General," March 28, 1951, File 543, Syngman Rhee Papers, Yonsei University, Seoul, Korea (hereafter Rhee Papers).

8 This study focuses primarily on the period from the start of the war in 1950 to the end of Rhee's presidency in 1960, but also considers the years of US occupation (1945–1948) and ongoing US intervention in South Korea through the 1960s.

9 Ian Hacking's conception of ontologies as "what comes into existence with the historical dynamics of naming" and his discussion of "looping effects," where social scientists classify "human kinds" that change the people who are categorized, guide my examination of identities produced by and managed through US empire. Hacking, *Historical Ontology*, 26; and Hacking, "Looping Effect of Human Kinds."

During World War I, it was believed that "GI" stood for "government issue" or "general infantry," but it was used more broadly to refer to anything military-related. The term was popularized during World War II with the creation of the 1942 cartoon "GI Joe" and President Roosevelt's "GI Bill" for returning veterans in 1944. By the Korean War, "GI" was commonly used by soldiers and the general public to refer to any enlisted person in the US armed forces. Patricia T. O'Conner and Stewart Kellerman, *Origins of the Specious: Myths and Misconceptions of the English Language* (New York: Random House, 2009), 72–73.

In the 1950s, Americans commonly used the term "GI baby" to describe the children of US servicemen and international women. After World War II, the term was typically used to denote a dilemma resulting from US servicemen stationed abroad. The label connected the children to American GIs, while eliding the presence of foreign, in this case Korean, mothers. Koreans often referred to these children as *honhyŏl* (mixed-race). In this book, I use "GI baby" when considering how Americans used the term to construct particular narratives or describe specific agendas, such as overseas adoptions. Otherwise, I use the descriptors "mixed-race," "Korean-white," or "Korean-black" to help clarify how racial processes determined the ways children were constructed, categorized, and managed in the United States and South Korea.

The term "war bride" was common parlance after World War II in the United States. Ji-Yeon Yuh notes how this term tied the women to American men and the war, connections that failed to recognize how Korean women arrived in the United States not just during the war, but also before and after it, given US military presence in the peninsula from 1945 to the present. For this reason, Yuh uses the term "military bride," which I have also adopted for this book. Yuh, *Beyond the Shadow of Camptown*, 1–3. As in my use of the term "GI baby," I use "war bride" when referencing how Americans utilized the term to describe the newly arrived women.

10 Byrd, *Transit of Empire*.
11 For masculinity and US imperialism, see Bederman, *Manliness and Civilization*; and Hoganson, *Fighting for American Manhood*.
12 Matthew Frye Jacobson, *Barbarian Virtues*, 229. Representative Francis Newlands of Nevada warned that Filipinos would arrive in "swarms" if Congress ratified annexation. Baldoz, *Third Asiatic Invasion*, 29.
13 Matthew Frye Jacobson, *Barbarian Virtues*, 177.
14 Kaplan, *Anarchy of Empire*, 10; Iriye, *Pacific Estrangement*, 26–28. For US colonialism in the Philippines, see Rafael, *White Love*; Go and Foster, *American Colonial State in the Philippines*; and Stuart Creighton Miller, *"Benevolent Assimilation."* For US colonialism in Hawai'i, see Kauanui, *Hawaiian Blood*; Silva, *Aloha Betrayed*; Imada, *Aloha America*; and Saranillio, *Unsustainable Empire*. For US militarism in Guam see, Camacho and Monnig, "Uncomfortable Fatigues."
15 Wexler, *Tender Violence*, 108–13.
16 For race and Chinese labor in the nineteenth century, see Jung, *Coolies and Cane*. For Filipino migration and labor in the context of US empire, see Baldoz, *Third Asiatic Invasion*, 45–69; Fujita-Rony, *American Workers, Colonial Power*; Quinsaat, *Letters in Exile*; Lasker, *Filipino Immigration*; and Choy, *Empire of Care*. For race, state power, and the making of "foreign" and "domestic" spaces in the decades surrounding the US-Philippines War, see Jung, "Seditious Subjects"; and Kramer, *Blood of Government*.
17 Cumings, *Korea's Place in the Sun*, 185–87.
18 Skirmishes erupted along the 38th parallel in the year leading up to the outbreak of war. Ibid., 255–67.
19 Chester Bowles to Harry S. Truman, April 14, 1952, Truman Files, Part II, Reel 3, p. 96, Manuscript Division, Library of Congress, Washington, DC. Michael H. Hunt and Steven I. Levine describe America's four wars in Asia beginning with the Philippines in 1899 as part of an ongoing imperial project aimed at regional dominance. Hunt and Levine, *Arc of Empire*.

20 Jelly-Schapiro, *Security and Terror*, 33.

21 Geoffrey Barraclough, *An Introduction to Contemporary History* (Baltimore: Penguin, 1967), 153, quoted in McMahon, *Colonialism and Cold War*, 11.

22 This total included 32,557 tons of napalm. In comparison, 503,000 tons of bombs were dropped in the entire Pacific theater of World War II. Armstrong, "Destruction and Reconstruction." For personal accounts that describe the destruction of these bombs, see *Memory of Forgotten War*, DVD, directed by Deann Borshay Liem and Ramsey Liem.

23 This mirrored how Washington tried to reconcile its "liberation" of the Philippines, Puerto Rico, Cuba, and Guam from Spanish tyranny, while exercising dominion over them. Baldoz, *Third Asiatic Invasion*, 21–27.

24 Stephens, "'Cultural Fallout.'"

25 For discussions of children and nation building, see Banet-Weiser, "Elián González"; Briggs, "Mother, Child, Race, Nation"; and Wexler, *Tender Violence*, 94–208.

26 May, *Homeward Bound*, 10–29. For family, consensus, and containment policy, see Coontz, *Way We Never Were*; Kozol, *Life's America*; and Stephens, "Nationalism, Nuclear Policy and Children."

27 Klein, *Cold War Orientalism*, 147–52. Also see Simpson, *Absent Presence*, 113–48.

28 Serlin, *Replaceable You*, 105.

29 Hirsch, *Family Frames*, 48, 53.

30 Laura Briggs describes how photographs of suffering children in war-torn Europe and Asia in the late 1930s called upon the reading public to demand US entrance into the war. Briggs, "Mother, Child, Race, Nation," 185.

31 Conceptions of the Republican mother date back to the post-Revolutionary period, when women were charged with the national responsibility to raise good citizens. Kerber, "Republican Mother." At the turn of the twentieth century, women harnessed the politicized power of motherhood to expand their role to spheres outside the home. Victorian women applied their "women's values" and moral judgments to their work in rescue homes, where they found authority in a society that largely dismissed them. Pascoe, *Relations of Rescue*, xv. For discussions of motherhood and nation building, see Davis, "Moral, Purposeful, and Healthful"; Davin, "Imperialism and Motherhood"; Ragoné and Twine, *Ideologies and Technologies of Motherhood*; Margaret D. Jacobs, *White Mother to a Dark Race*; and Linda Gordon, *Great Arizona Orphan Abduction*.

32 Untitled list of US couples interested in adoption, February 1954, File 553, Rhee Papers.

33 "A Washington View of Intercountry Adoption Legislation," February 1959, Box 23, Folder 21, SW109, SWHA (hereafter "Washington View," SWHA).

34 For Orientalism in a Europe/Middle East context, see Said, *Orientalism*. For US Orientalism, see Robert G. Lee, *Orientals*; Okihiro, *Margins and Mainstreams*; Yu, *Thinking Orientals*; and Sueyoshi, *Discriminating Sex*.

35 "How to Tell Japs from the Chinese," *Life*, December 22, 1941, 81–82.

36 See Shibusawa, *America's Geisha Ally*; and Dower, *Embracing Defeat*.

37 Simpson, *Absent Presence*, 152–64; Matsumoto, *Farming the Home Place*; and *History and Memory*, DVD, directed by Rea Tajiri.

38 Shah, *Contagious Divides*, 242–50. Cultural representations of Chinese American families did not translate to equal access to housing. Cheng, *Citizens of Asian America*, 71–84. For how Chinese Americans secured a place for themselves in the United States during World War II, see Wong, *Americans First*.

39 Borstelmann, *Cold War and the Color Line*; Dudziak, *Cold War, Civil Rights*; Von Eschen, *Race against Empire*. Also, see Lentz and Gower, *Opinions of Mankind*.

40 For US pluralism in the postwar era, see Nikhil Pal Singh, "Culture/Wars"; Gerstle, "Protean Character of American Liberalism"; and HoSang, *Racial Propositions*.

41 Promoting internationalism was also a US administration tactic to counter what it believed was Japan's appeals for nonwhite peoples to collectively resist white imperialism in Asia. See Iriye, *Power and Culture*, 34–35. For Afro-Asian solidarity see Onishi, *Transpacific Antiracism*.

42 For the conditional boundaries of liberal empire claims, see Mimi Nguyen, *Gift of Freedom*, 12–15.

43 Bok-Lim C. Kim, "Asian Wives of US Servicemen," 99; Jung Ha Kim, "Cartography of Korean American Protestant Faith Communities," 193.

44 Oak Soon Hong, director, Child Placement Service, Seoul, to Bessie C. Irvin, supervisor, Bureau of Adoption, Department of Social Welfare, California, April 20, 1955, p. 2, Box 10, Folder 37, SW109, SWHA.

45 Höhn and Moon, "Introduction," 11. In 1963, 62,000 US soldiers were in Korea; in the 1970s, an estimated 42,000 were stationed there. Lie, "Transformation of Sexual Work," 316. There are still over 28,000 US servicemen in South Korea today.

46 Laura Briggs cautions against using the term "neocolonialism" because US power after 1945 was not new, but rather a carryover from British colonial practices with much the same outcome. Briggs, *Reproducing Empire*, 33. Anne McClintock warns that to use the temporal axis of colonial/postcolonial masks the "*continuities* in international imbalances of imperial power," thus making imperialism appear less damaging and harder to theorize. Italics in original. McClintock, *Imperial Leather*, 13. Julian Go examines how US "liberal exceptionalism" emerged and developed in the colonies through a comparative analysis of the Philippines, Guam, and Samoa. Go shows how the United States used tactics like tutelage and sought native collaborators to exact rule. Go, "Provinciality of American Empire."

47 Nkrumah, *Neo-Colonialism*, ix–xvi. Also see Rifkin, "Debt and the Transnationalization of Hawai'i."

48 See Bailkin, *Afterlife of Empire*; Stoler, "Tense and Tender Ties," 831; Hurtado, *Intimate Frontiers*; and Van Kirk, *Many Tender Ties*.

49 Stoler, *Race and the Education of Desire*, 2.

50 Briggs, *Reproducing Empire*; Vaughan, *Curing Their Ills*; Warwick Anderson, *Colonial Pathologies*.

51 Gonzalez, *Securing Paradise*, 6, 13–15.

52 For the colonial management of private and public spaces, see Stoler, *Carnal Knowledge and Imperial Power*; and Stoler, *Race and the Education of Desire*.

53 The Korean Association of Voluntary Agencies, made up of US and South Korean representatives, pushed to remove US aid, which had become ubiquitous after the war. The Ministry of Foreign Affairs tried to find domestic solutions for Korea's problems but found it difficult to deny US aid. "Kŭmnyŏn manse ibyang doelkŏshida" [This year 10,000 will be adopted], *Chosŏn Ilbo*, February 23, 1962, 3. For US influence upon Korean social welfare, see Ch'oe, "Oeguk min'gan wŏnjo danch'e" [Activities of Foreign Voluntary Agencies]; Suh and Williamson, "Impact of Adjustment and Stabilization Policies"; and Arissa Oh, *To Save the Children*, 194–202.

54 Cultural ambassadors did not always cooperate with the US State Department. Louis Armstrong, one of the United States Information Agency's most popular jazz ambassadors, publicly denounced the Little Rock incident, accusing Arkansas Governor Faubus of racism and President Eisenhower of inaction. Von Eschen, *Satchmo Blows Up the World*, 63–64. The US State Department also censored figures, like Paul Robeson, Josephine Baker, and Pearl Buck, who publicly decried US racial discrimination. Beeching, "Paul Robeson and the Black Press."

55 Arendt, *Origins of Totalitarianism*, xx. Anne McClintock adds that this was particularly true of "US imperialism-without-colonies" after 1945, when America's global reach operated in concealed and half-concealed ways. McClintock, *Imperial Leather*, 13.

56 For national memory and memorialization, see Trouillot, *Silencing the Past*; Blight, *Race and Reunion*; Young, *Texture of Memory*; Yoneyama, *Hiroshima Traces*; Yamashita, *Letters to Memory*; Viet Thanh Nguyen, *Nothing Ever Dies*; and Sturken, *Tangled Memories*. For discussions about representation and US national identity through the Vietnam War, see Appy, *American Reckoning*; Sylvia Chong, *Oriental Obscene*; Denise Chong, *Girl in the Picture*; and Bradley, *Imagining Vietnam and America*. For how the Korean War became forgotten, see, Liem, "History, Trauma, and Identity"; and McCann, "Our Forgotten War."

57 Katherine H. S. Moon, *Sex among Allies*; Moon, "South Korean Movements"; Yuh, *Beyond the Shadow of Camptown*; Cho, *Haunting the Korean Diaspora*; Seungsook Moon, "Regulating Desire." Also see Glenn, *Issei, Nisei, War Bride*; Soh, *Comfort Women*; and Chungmoo Choi, "Politics of War Memories."

58 Cynthia Enloe's seminal works on militarized prostitution include *Does Khaki Become You?*; *Bananas, Beaches and Bases*; and *Maneuvers*.

59 The figure for Korean military brides does not include women who came to Hawai'i between 1947 and 1950, who were not counted by the Immigration and Naturalization Service. Bok-Lim C. Kim, "Asian Wives of US Servicemen," 99; and Kim, "Casework with Japanese and Korean Wives." Some estimate that the numbers of Asian military brides has been inflated over the years as studies include all foreign women married to US citizens. Saenz, Hwang, and Aguirre, "In Search of Asian War Brides."

60 Hübinette, *Comforting an Orphaned Nation*; Arissa Oh, *To Save the Children*; Catherine Ceniza Choy, *Global Families*; Catherine Ceniza Choy and Gregory Paul Choy, "Transformative Terrains"; Pate, *From Orphan to Adoptee*. The field of critical adoption studies has grown significantly in the past few decades. For example, see Eng, "Transnational Adoption and Queer Diasporas"; Volkman, *Cultures of Transnational Adoption*; Dorow, *Transnational Adoption*; Trenka, Oparah, and Shin, *Outsiders Within*; Bergquist et al., *International Korean Adoption*; Marre and Briggs, *International Adoption*; Yngvesson, *Belonging in an Adopted World*; Dubinsky, *Babies without Borders*; Jerng, *Claiming Others*; Bongsoo Park, "Intimate Encounters, Racial Frontiers"; Balcom, *Traffic in Babies*; Briggs, *Somebody's Children*; Varzally, *Children of Reunion*; and McKee, *Disrupting Kinship*.

61 Eleana Kim, *Adopted Territory*; Park Nelson, *Invisible Asians*.

62 Prébin, *Meeting Once More*; Hosu Kim, *Birth Mothers and Transnational Adoption*; Hosu Kim, "Mothers without Mothering"; and Hosu Kim and Grace M. Cho, "Kinship of Violence."

63 Trenka, *Language of Blood*; and *First Person Plural*, DVD, directed by Deann Borshay Liem. For memoirs and autobiographies of Korean adoptees, also see Nicole Chung, *All You Can Ever Know*; Clement, *Unforgotten War*; Arnold, *Litany for the Long Moment*; Cox, *Voices from Another Place*; Elizabeth Kim, *Ten Thousand Sorrows*; and Robinson, *A Single Square Picture*.

64 Espiritu, *Body Counts*; and Espiritu, "We-Win-Even-When-We-Lose." Jana Lipman offers another dimension by considering the Vietnamese who chose repatriation over resettlement. Lipman, "'Give Us a Ship.'"

65 Tang, *Unsettled*, 5, 14.

66 Mimi Nguyen, *Gift of Freedom*. In official South Korean narratives, liberation from Japan was described as a gift of the Allied forces, especially the United States. Chungmoo Choi, "Discourse of Decolonization," 80.

67 Eiichiro Azuma's examination of heterogeneous transnational Japanese American identities illuminates what it means to be "in between," while Kwame Anthony Appiah imagines how one could be of the world through his conception of "global citizenship." Azuma, *Between Two Empires*; and Appiah, "Global Citizenship."

68 Stoler describes "non-events," the unrealizable plans and failed projects that tried to manage those who "occupied the racial corridors," as revealing of the anxieties of empire. Stoler, *Along the Archival Grain*, 4, 105–7. Also see Benjamin, "Thesis on the Philosophy of History."

69 Anne M. Davison, headquarters representative, ISS Korea branch, to Margaret A. Valk, senior case consultant, ISS American branch, November 6, 1960, Box 167, Case 37317, SW109.2 ISS, SWHA; Kimi Tamura, Japan-American Joint Committee for the Assistance of Orphans, Tokyo, to Margaret A. Valk, July 16, 1956, Box 167, Case 37163, SW109.2, SWHA.

70 Pratt, *Imperial Eyes*, 7.

71 Kaplan, *Anarchy of Empire*, 14.

72 LaKisha Michelle Simmons utilizes Jane Flax's poststructuralist and feminist reinterpretations of subjectivity to consider black girls' experiences with the emotional and physical violence of Jim Crow. Megan Grant and Amanda Rubens, "Interview with Jane Flax," *Melbourne Journal of Politics* 24 (1997): 2, quoted in Simmons, *Crescent City Girls*, 5.

73 Hirsch, *Family Frames*, 8. For examinations of the family, photograph, and memory, see Hirsch, *Familial Gaze*.

74 "Welfare of Mixed-Blood Children," tables 1 and 2, pp. 4, 6, SWHA.

PART I. IMAGINED FAMILY FRAMES

1 George Kennan, "The Korean People," *Outlook*, October 21, 1905, 409–10, quoted in George L. Paik, *History of Protestant Missions*, 11. Theodore Roosevelt commented that he "liked very much" another of Kennan's articles, titled "Korea: A Degenerate State," which appeared in *Outlook* on October 7, 1905, demonstrating the broad reach of Orientalist ideas. Wilz, "United States Policy Vis-a-vis Korea."

George Trumble Ladd, Yale professor of philosophy, similarly described Koreans as "undoubtedly fond of their ease and even slothful," likening them to "lazy animal[s]." George Trumble Ladd, *In Korea with Marquis Ito* (New York: Scribner's Sons, 1908), 290.

2 Homer B. Hulbert, *The Passing of Korea* (Seoul: Yonsei University Press, 1969), quoted in George L. Paik, *History of Protestant Missions*, 12.

3 Oliver, *50 Facts*, #1. Missionaries made similar claims. A 1937 Presbyterian missionary pamphlet likened Koreans to "Middle European Peoples," with mixed-race heritage from Mongolia to the north and a "Caucasic element" from India. Board of Foreign Missions of the Presbyterian Church in the U.S.A., *Chosen Mission*, p. 3, HR 1391, Box 6, Folder 43, Records of the Presbyterian Church, Foreign Missions 1834–1962, Yale University Divinity Archives (hereafter YDA).

4 Underwood, *Tragedy and Faith in Korea*, 9.

5 "America's War," US Department of Veterans Affairs; "Korean War Fast Facts," CNN Library.

6 Halliday and Cumings, *Korea: The Unknown War*, 115, 118.

7 Oh Moon Sook, interview by author, Los Angeles, CA, June 2016.

8 Cho Kyu Hwan, interview by author; Keck, "How American Air Power Destroyed North Korea," *The National Interest*, August 12, 2017.

CHAPTER 1. GIS AND THE KIDS OF KOREA

1 Mauldin, *Bill Mauldin in Korea*, 10.

2 Advisors told Truman to not be "alarmist" about the "pint-sized" incident. Quoted in Casey, *Selling the Korean War*, 20.

3 Cumings, *Korea's Place in the Sun*, 271–72.

4 George Barrett, "Navy Fliers Blast Dam at Army's Bid," *New York Times*, May 2, 1951, 3; Cumings, *Korea's Place in the Sun*, 269.

5 Hanley, *Bridge at No Gun Ri*.

6 Belkin, *Bring Me Men*, 6; and Renda, *Taking Haiti*, 15.

7 SCAP monthly reports 1945, RG 331, Box 261, p. 1, Summation of Non-Military Activities September 1945 to October 1946, NA.

8 "Report of the Agent General of the UNKRA: Immigration and Emigration," 1952, p. 4, Folder "Social Welfare," UNKRA 1950–1960, United Nations Archives, New York (hereafter UN).

9 Brazinsky, *Nation Building in South Korea*, 71–78.

10 Nitz and Drew, *NSC-68*, 25.

11 Lay, "Report to the National Security Council." For histories of the Cold War, see LaFeber, *America, Russia, and the Cold War*; Leffler, *Preponderance of Power*; and Williams, *Tragedy of American Diplomacy*.

12 Belmonte, *Selling the American Way*, 44–45. For the implementation of NSC-68 policies during the Korean War see, Gaddis, *Strategies of Containment*, 87–124.

13 Cumings, *Korea's Place in the Sun*, 265; Charles J. V. Murphy, "What Ike Faces in Korea," *Life*, December 1, 1952, 51–52. For histories of the Korean War, see Cumings, *Origins of the Korean War*; Halliday and Cumings, *Korea: The Unknown War*; and Stueck, *Rethinking the Korean War*.

14 Casey, *Selling the Korean War*, 35–36, 206. At the start of the Korean War, Americans felt that the US military should push north of the 38th parallel if it wanted to defeat the communists. MacArthur's successful landing at Inch'ŏn fueled this initial optimism, but once China entered the war, public support for the war declined. Masuda, *Cold War Crucible*, 91, 95, 104–6.

15 Gallup, *Gallup Poll*, 961.

16 While journalists were asked to omit reporting that could jeopardize US security or diminish the administration, there was no formal censorship program at that time. Casey, *Selling the Korean War*, 8; Huebner, "Kilroy Is Back," 106. Reports coming from Korea exposed the violence. See, for example, "The Savage, Secret War in Korea," *Life*, December 1, 1952, 25–35; Carl Mydans, "Refugees Get in Way," *Life*, August 21, 1950, 22; David Douglas Duncan, "The Durable ROKs," *Life*, September 11, 1950, 52–55; Walter Sullivan, "GI View of Koreans as 'Gooks' Believed Doing Political Damage," *New York Times*, July 26, 1950, 5; Choe Sang-Hun, "Korean War's Lost Chapter: South Korea Says US Killed Hundreds of Civilians," *New York Times*, August 31, 2008.

    David Roediger traces the origins the American term "Gook" to the early twentieth century, when it was used to denote foreignness. The term became inseparably tied to Asians during the Korean and Vietnam wars. Roediger, "Gook: The Short History of an Americanism."

17 George Barrett, "Radio Hams in US Discuss Girls, So Shelling of Seoul Is Held Up," *New York Times*, February 9, 1951, 3.

18 Cumings, *Origins of the Korean War*, 289–94.

19 Murphy, "What Ike Faces in Korea," 51–52.

20 Truman, *Questions about the Battle in Korea*, 10. Truman's strategic language demonstrates the extent to which the US military's role in the Korean War made

it challenging to uphold the ideals of the "American Century" set forth by Henry Luce a decade earlier. Luce, *American Century*.

21 Eckert et al., *Korea Old and New*, 337. Soviet administrators allowed the work of the Korean People's Republic and its people's committees to continue, and kept a close eye on government affairs at P'yongyang without officially setting up a formal occupation government. Koreans responded more positively to Soviet occupation, carrying out imposed land and labor reforms without revolt, as opposed to those in the South who actively protested US occupation. SCAP monthly reports 1945, RG 331, Box 261, p. 1, Summation of Non-Military Activities September 1945 to October 1946, NA.

22 Charles Grutzner, "A Few GIs Abuse Koreans in Seoul," *New York Times*, December 20, 1950, 4. Also see "GI Held in 2 Korean Slayings," *New York Times*, May 29, 1953, 2.

23 Eighth US Army, G-5 Civil Affairs Administration General Correspondence Files, 1956, RG 338, Box 643, Folder "Korean National Employees, Prostitution, Marriage," NA. The Korean press regularly reported on assaults committed by US servicemen. For example, "Hŭginpyŏngsaga sarin" [Black soldier kills Korean man], *Dong-A Ilbo*, December 19, 1952, 2.

24 "Idaet'ongnyŏng Haengboksan goawŏn shich'al" [President Rhee visits Happy Mountain Orphanage], *Dong-A Ilbo*, August 15, 1951, 2.

25 August 15 remains a national holiday when Koreans observe the end of Japanese rule. Independence day is often accompanied by protests against US-South Korean military cooperation and is tinged with a recognition that freedom from Japan did not lead to unity, but as one Korean remembers, "exploded and split the people." Susan Chira, "Koreans Remember the Day Japanese Yoke Was Lifted," *New York Times*, August 16, 1985. For a discussion of "liberation day" in light of US empire, see Diaz, "Deliberating 'Liberation Day.'"

26 "Chŏnjaeng goa 10-man" [100,000 war orphans], *Kyŏnghyang sinmun*, February 17, 1952.

27 "Koa shisŏrhwakch'ung ganghwa 19-ch'ŏnmyŏng suyongk'iro" [Expansion of orphanage facilities for 19,000 children], *Kyŏnghyang sinmun*, March 1, 1952, 2.

28 "Migunch'ŏlsujungjihara" [Stop US military from leaving], *Kyŏnghyang sinmun*, August 20, 1954, 1; "Migunŭi Nal Kyŏngch'uk Idaet'ongnyŏng metseji balp'yo" [Rhee's announcement on US Soldier's Day], *Dong-A Ilbo*, May 23, 1955, 1.

29 Letters from Kim Soo Whan, February 19, 1951, and Park Yung Hae, February 20, 1951, Office of Public Information, ROK, *Letters to Tall Soldiers*, 11, 6.

30 "Korean War Fast Facts." A total of 1,789,000 US servicemen served in the Korean theater of war. "America's War."

31 Letter from Ahn Jung Ai, February 19, 1951, Office of Public Information, ROK, *Letters to Tall Soldiers*, 13.

32 Shibusawa, *America's Geisha Ally*, 15–16, 28–34.

33 "Chaplain Robert Sherry's Report," January 15, 1951, pp. 2–6, RG 338, Box 1784, Folder "Chaplains/Entry A1 234," NA. Similar activities are listed in "Report of

Chaplain Frederick E. Morse" and "Daily Journal Entries of Chaplain Coffey," December 1951, pp. 1–6, RG 338, Box 1888, Folder "AG to Chaplains," NA.

34 UN Civil Affairs Activities in Korea monthly summaries, June to November 1952, RG 550, Box 75, Folder "USAFF-Statistical Data 1952 to 'Fight Cold War,'" NA.

35 Fred W. Baars, "GI Buddies," *Pacific Stars and Stripes*, June 30, 1951, 2.

36 Koreans started *Dong-A Ilbo* and *Chosŏn Ilbo* while under Japanese rule; the imperial government often stepped in to control both. Under President Rhee, leftist newspapers were outlawed and the administration heavily monitored newspapers to promote the official line. During the Korean War, military censorship was imposed upon Korean newspapers and continued well after the fighting stopped. Since Rhee needed the support of the US military, stories that highlighted the good deeds of American GIs circulated regularly in the press. Youm, "Press Freedom under Constraints," 869–70.

37 "Chŏnjaeng goa gujeganghwa sahoesaŏpkadaehoesŏksang Ch'oejang gwanŏnmyŏng" [Minister Ch'oe reinforces the need to strengthen support for war orphans], *Dong-A Ilbo*, February 16, 1952, 2; "Sŏure sonyŏnŭi kŏri" [Boy's street in Seoul], *Dong-A Ilbo*, July 22, 1952, 2; "Expansion of orphanage," *Kyŏnghyang sinmun*. For discussions about GI humanitarianism, see Arissa Oh, *To Save the Children*; and Pate, *From Orphan to Adoptee*.

38 "Chŏnjaeng goa Mi'guge ibyang! Kyŏlshilhanmigunin'gwaŭi ŭiyŏn" [War orphan adopted to America! US soldier finds a way], *Kyŏnghyang sinmun*, April 17, 1953, 2.

39 Casey, *Selling the Korean War*, 8–9.

40 Ibid., 7.

41 Pate, *From Orphan to Adoptee*, 35–36; "Catalog of *The Big Picture*," Army Pictorial Center: Single Corps Photographic Center.

42 Universal Newsreels, Release 451, April 26, 1951.

43 In 1953 alone, US Army personnel hosted 481 parties for Korean children. Pate, *From Orphan to Adoptee*, 36.

44 Eighth US Army, "Korea Command Reports 1950–1952," March 1951, RG 338, Box 1811, Folder "Chaplains/Entry A1 234," NA; and film footage of the IX Corps Orphanage Christmas Party in Kinsal, Korea, December 24, 1953, RG 111, Department of Defense, Department of the Army, Office of the Deputy Chief of Staff for Operations, US Army Audiovisual Center, moving pictures, NA (hereafter US Army Audiovisual Center, NA).

45 "Christmas Party for Orphans at YongDongPo," December 24, 1953, film reel, RG 111, LC-34684, US Army Audiovisual Center, NA.

46 For discussions on the politics of making visible another's pain, see Scarry, *Body in Pain*; and Sontag, *Regarding the Pain*.

47 Cho Kyu Hwan, interview by author.

48 "Korean Shipyard at Chinhae, Korea: South Korea Orphans," May 18, 1951, film reel, RG 111, ADC-8931, US Army Audiovisual Center, NA.

49 "Navy Mascot," *Pacific Stars and Stripes*, June 30, 1951, 3. Also see Pate, *From Orphan to Adoptee*, 54–56.

50 Allen, "A Note from the Author," *Keen Teens*.

51 *Miami News*, April 21, 1950; Barbara Sue Cohen and Paul Nielsen, "Keen Teens Cartoonist Says Roundup 'Best Ever,'" *Miami News*, March 31, 1950.

52 Peter Linden, "Chocoletto: A Korean War Orphan Joins the Marines," *Reporter*, April 14, 1953, 28.

53 Houseboys did more formal domestic work than mascots. Arissa Oh, *To Save the Children*, 31–35.

54 Robert H. Mosier, "The GI and the Kids of Korea," *National Geographic*, May 1953, 635–64, quotes from 635, 637.

55 The same Roy Rogers photograph was printed in a 1953 US Department of the Army publication. John Miller, *Korea, 1951–53*, 169. For examples of cowboy imagery, see Brenneis, "New American Comes 'Home'"; Robert L. Brown, "Orphan, 7, Leaves Korea for New Home in Texas," *Stars and Stripes*, June 15, 1954; and Karl Kohrs, "An Orphan Boy Comes 'Home' to America," *Parade*, April 27, 1958, 10–11. In the Kohrs article, an American couple first saw pictures of their adoptive Korean boy with "two six-shooters in holsters slung about his waist."

56 "Young Marine Adopts South Korean Orphan Who Refuses Rice after Tasting GI Food," *New York Times*, August 22, 1950, 5; Linden, "Chocoletto," 28.

57 Michael A. Lipton, "Baby on Board," *People Weekly*, December 8, 1997, 137–38.

58 Pardue, *Korean Adventure*, 63–64; "Report of Frederick Morse, Chaplain," December 1951, pp. 1–6, RG 338, Box 1888, Folder "AG to Chaplains," NA; "GIs' Exodus Hits Orphans in Korea," *Los Angeles Times*, December 17, 1954, A3. One air force captain spent twenty-seven months as a prisoner of war in Korea and gave his accumulated pay while a prisoner to a Korean orphanage. "A Promise Fulfilled: Flier Gives PW Pay to Orphans," *Pacific Stars and Stripes* (Korea edition), January 18, 1955, 11.

59 "Expansion of orphanage," *Kyŏnghyang sinmun*.

60 Sergeant G. to Susan Pettiss, assistant director, ISS American branch, September 24, 1954, p. 1, Box 166, Case 36618, SW109.2, SWHA.

61 Sŏng Kyŏ Hŭi, interview by author. Stories of US servicemen providing money and manpower to build orphanages appeared in *Pacific Stars and Stripes*. For example, "Kids Take Over Seoul Home by Sgt. Charles P. Taylor," *Pacific Stars and Stripes* (Korea edition), May 22, 1955, 11; and "KMAG AFAK Orphanages," *Pacific Stars and Stripes*, February 20, 1955, 12–13.

62 "Young Marine Adopts South Korean Orphan," *New York Times*; Linden, "Chocoletto," 28. For postwar consumer culture, see Lizbeth Cohen, *Consumers' Republic*.

63 Mrs. T., Idaho voter, to Gracie Pfost, Idaho congresswoman, March 11, 1954, Box 18, Folder 126/2/01 "Child Welfare," UNKRA 1950–1960, UN.

64 "Clothing Sent to Korea," *New York Times*, June 6, 1951, 33.

65 Mosier, "GI and the Kids"; Linden, "Chocoletto"; and Shin, "Senator Paull Shin's Speech," Korean American Community Foundation.

66 A photograph of Marine Master Sergeant Harold Harris and his houseboy, Bae Dae Soon, shows the boy receiving treatment for tuberculosis. Official US

Marine Corps photograph, "Houseboy Gives Thanks," August 25, 1952, Military Photographic Collection, Schomburg Center for Research in Black Culture, New York Public Library.

67 Shah, *Contagious Divides*, 89–97.

68 Red Cross, pamphlet, Box 173, Case 40378, March 1956, SW109.2, SWHA.

69 For postwar trials against Japanese Americans, see Shibusawa, *America's Geisha Ally*, 140–75; and Simpson, *Absent Presence*, 76–112.

70 For military masculinity, see Belkin, *Bring Me Men*.

71 Margaret A. Valk to Julius A. Graber, executive director, Oklahoma City Jewish Community Council, October 30, 1959, Box 34, Folder 14, SW109, SWHA. Social workers often agreed that mascots did not make good adoptees.

72 Steve Roper comic strip, *Pacific Stars and Stripes*, May 7, 1955, 8, and May 9, 1955, 8.

73 Nora Waln, "Our Softhearted Warriors in Korea," *Saturday Evening Post*, December 23, 1950, 67.

74 Letter to Commanding General Eighth United States Army in Korea (EUSAK), Frank W. Pew, William L. Carroll Jr., "Adoption of Korean Orphans," August 6, 1951, RG 338, Box 491, Folder 290, NA.

75 Military authorities openly warned their soldiers not to become too attached to unofficially adopted children in Korea. Hübinette, "Korean Adoption History," 4.

76 Waln, "Our Softhearted Warriors in Korea," 67; Brown, "Orphan, 7, Leaves Korea"; Dan Lutz, "Waif Eyes Boys Town Life," *Pacific Stars and Stripes*, June 7, 1953.

77 Herman, *Kinship by Design*, 218. Also see Lovelock, "Intercountry Adoption."

78 "Adopted Children's Report," c. 1955, RG 338, Box 45, Folder 292, NA.

79 US servicemen notified the Eighth Army commanding general if they were completing the adoption process (some of the men adopted more than one Korean child). P.S., memorandum, October 10, 1956; J.H., memorandum, May 21, 1956; H.F., memorandum, May 8, 1956; J.E., memorandum, May 16, 1956; A.B., memorandum, May 17, 1956; C.W., memorandum, May 17, 1956; F.B., memorandum, May 10, 1956; J.W., memorandum, May 11, 1956; J.C., memorandum, May 18, 1956; RG 338, Box 645, Folder 292, NA. Some children were sent to the United States temporarily for schooling. "P'alcha nŭrŏjin goa" [A fortunate orphan], *Kyŏnghyang sinmun*, March 30, 1952, 2.

80 Records for the month of May 1956, for example, total approximately twenty-five children, but there was no follow-up to indicate whether any of the adoptions were completed. RG 338, Box 645, Folder 292, NA.

81 "Lee Dia Koon's Winning Smile," *Pacific Stars and Stripes*, December 14, 1953.

82 Mildred Zeis, caseworker, St. Louis County Child Welfare Services, Missouri, to Lorena Scherer, supervisor, Department of Public Health and Welfare, Missouri, Adoptive Study, September 16, 1954, p. 5, Box 16, Case 36568, SW109.2, SWHA.

83 Strom, US Department of State, "Summary Narrative Report," December 21, 1955, RG 469, Box 49, Korean subject files, 1953–1949, NA; Grace H. Rue, Seoul Sani-

tarium and Hospital Orphanage, to Bessie C. Irvin, n.d., Box 35, Folder "Korea Correspondence," vol. 1, ISS records, SWHA. Also see Graves, "Domesticating Foreign Affairs," 33–34.

84 K. to Miss Richmond, July 28, 1955, file 553, Rhee Papers.

85 *Pacific Stars and Stripes*, July 14, 1952.

86 "War Orphan Adopted to America!," *Kyŏnghyang sinmun*.

87 *Pacific Stars and Stripes*, October 19, 1953.

88 *Pacific Stars and Stripes*, December 9, 1953.

89 Brown, "Orphan, 7, Leaves Korea."

90 Shin, "Senator Paull Shin's Speech"; Kang, "Shin Named Honorary President," *Korea Times*, May 23, 2010. Other completed military adoptions appear in ISS case files, including one in 1955 where a young serviceman had his parents adopt a boy whom he met while stationed in Korea. Box 168, Case 37708, June 21, 1955, SW109.2, SWHA.

91 Statistic from the Korean Ministry of Health and Welfare, 1999, quoted in Hübinette, "Korean Adoption History," 5.

92 This story was later turned into a television movie, *A Thousand Men and a Baby*; Lipton, "Baby on Board."

93 Universal Newsreels, Release 469, May 28, 1953.

CHAPTER 2. US AID CAMPAIGNS AND THE KOREAN CHILDREN'S CHOIR

1 UNKRA defined "refugees" as persons displaced from their homes, "war sufferers" as those who had undergone a material loss or whose means of support was disrupted by the war, and the 4.3 million "locally destitute" as those who, regardless of the war, were impoverished. United Nations Civil Assistance Command Korea, "Immigration and Emigration: Migration," internal memorandum, 1952, p. 22, Folder "Social Welfare," UNKRA 1950–1960, UN.

2 Cho Kyu Hwan, interview by author.

3 Im Yong Ok, interview by author.

4 "Working Group on Long-Range Activities for Children 1951–1952," p. 71, Box 9, Folder 18/02, UNKRA 1950–1960, UN; UNCACK and UNKRA acknowledged the extent to which voluntary agencies helped to provide humanitarian services for groups "not receiving attention from elsewhere." Report of the Agent General of the UNKRA, 1952, p. 2, Folder "Relief and Social Services," UNKRA 1950–1960, UN. Also see, Klein, *Cold War Orientalism*, 54.

5 Go, "Provinciality of American Empire," 86. Scholars from the Massachusetts Institute of Technology's Center for International Studies (CIS) urged President Eisenhower to continue the previous administration's foreign economic aid policy, which started with the Truman Doctrine in 1947 as an anti-communist measure. The CIS suggested that aid to countries like Korea should arrive "unlinked," or without political strings attached, to maximize the effectiveness of the policy. Gilman, *Mandarins of the Future*, 174–82.

6   US military statistics in Höhn and Moon, "Introduction," 11; US appropriations figures from Brazinsky, *Nation Building in South Korea*, 33.

7   Howard A. Rusk, "More Than Bullets Needed to Win the Battle of Korea," *New York Times*, March 29, 1953, 9.

8   "Report of the Rusk Mission to Korea 1953," pp. 2–3, Box 46, Folder 10.6-1, UN-KRA 1950–1960, UN.

9   Howard A. Rusk, "Voice from Korea," *Life*, June 7, 1954, 187.

10   Leonard W. Mayo, "2,000,000 Reasons to Help South Korea," *New York Times*, August 2, 1953.

11   "Report of the US Army Human Factors and Operations Research Unit," RG 550, Box 75, Folder "USAFF-Statistical Data 1952 to 'Fight Cold War,'" NA.

12   "Korea's Children," n.d., p. 2, Folder 20 "Orphanages, Part II," UNKRA 1950–1960, UN.

13   "Warmth for the Orphans of Korea," *McCall's*, October 1953, 16–17, photograph on 16.

14   A series of these letters can be found in the Syngman Rhee Papers at Yonsei University; for example, letter from Mrs. O. to Young Han Choo, October 21, 1953, File 547, Folder "February 1954," Part I, Rhee Papers.

15   Photographs emphasized the smallness and isolation of children. For example, in one photograph a boy is dwarfed by the truck behind him as well as the US servicemen wearing large puffy coats in the foreground with the caption "The Kid Who Walks Alone: War's Little Old Man Ascends the Ramp to a Rescue Plane," and another shows a young boy carrying a forty-pound load on his back. Both appeared in Mosier, "GI and the Kids," 638, 643.

16   Briggs, "Mother, Child, Race, Nation," 185–186.

17   In discussing the ethics of photography, Nicolas Peterson explains that children offer a way into normally inaccessible, private spaces. Peterson, "Changing Photographic Contract," 139.

18   Laura Briggs argues that the tragic consequences of war as imaged in photographs existed almost separately from the structural, political, military, and economic causes. Briggs, "Mother, Child, Race, Nation," 180.

19   Scarry, *Body in Pain*, 9.

20   Ibid., 61.

21   Rusk, "More Than Bullets Needed"; "Report of the Rusk Mission."

22   Howard A. Rusk, "Gifts in Christmas Spirit," *New York Times*, December 20, 1962, 6.

23   American Federation of Labor, "Some Reasons for Chinese Exclusion: Meat vs. Rice. American Manhood against Asiatic Coolieism. Which Shall Survive?," pamphlet entered into the congressional debate about extending the 1882 Chinese Exclusion Act, 57th Cong., 1st sess., 1902.

24   Agamben describes the political dimensions of what happens when the biological needs of survival are given value over the quality of life lived. Agamben, *Homo Sacer*.

25   "Proposal and Suggestions to General Mills from the Meals for Millions Foundation," June 2, 1958, Box 7, Folder 2, Meals for Millions, University of California, Los Angeles Special Collections, (hereafter UCLA).

26 "Highlights of Meals for Millions Program," July 1960, Box 7, Folder 2, Meals for Millions, UCLA.

27 In 1951, when the CCF expanded to other Asian countries, it was renamed the Christian Children's Fund. Caldwell, *Children of Calamity*, 32–35.

28 By the mid-1960s, photographing suffering children became a familiar fundraising tactic. Photographs depicted Third World peoples as feeble and childlike, while positioning the West as the benevolent savior. Stanley Cohen, *States of Denial*, 178.

29 Klein, *Cold War Orientalism*, 154.

30 Tagg, *Burden of Representation*, 64. Also see Sekula, "Traffic in Photographs."

31 Caldwell, *Children of Calamity*, 36.

32 Ibid., 39.

33 Howard A. Rusk, "Treat for Children," *New York Times*, October 30, 1955, 45; Rusk, "Good Halloween Ghosts," *New York Times*, October 27, 1957, 58.

34 Reel P-2, Section 18, 1390/1485.4, Koa kukŭi ibyang [Foreign overseas adoptions] 1956–60, Ministry of Foreign Affairs, Seoul, South Korea (hereafter Foreign Overseas Adoptions, MoFA).

35 Howard McKee, president, student council, Nitro High School, to C. J. Yu, secretary to President Rhee, February 27, 1957, Reel P-2, Section 18, 1390/1485.4, Foreign Overseas Adoptions, MoFA; C. J. Yu to Howard McKee, April 5, 1957, ibid.

36 CCF newsletters included letters written by Asian children thanking Americans for their donations. For example, Clarke quotes from a translated letter written by Ui Li Tong, an "adopted" orphan in China, who writes, "My kind friend, since you love like this, in the future I want to show the same love to other people." "The Adoption Plan," *China News* 3, no. 1 (Winter 1950–51): 4, China's Children Fund 1943–51, HR 1083, YDA. For the People-to-People program, see Klein, *Cold War Orientalism*, 49–56.

37 Klein, *Cold War Orientalism*, 13–14, 150–51.

38 South Korea sent the deputy prime minister, Hwang Woo Yea, and North Korea sent the president of the Presidium of the Supreme People's Assembly, Kim Yong Nam. Wondam Paik, "60th Anniversary of the Bandung Conference." Korean newspapers reported that half the world's population would convene at Bandung, the first global conference where Japan (its former colonizer) and China (its recent enemy in the war) would be fully and equally represented. "Imbakhan Bandung'hoeŭigwa kŭ chŏnmang" [Prospects of the upcoming Bandung Conference], *Kyŏnghyang sinmun*, April 15, 1955, 1; "Pit'aedŭngbulch'amshi ashia ap'urik'a hoeŭimimyo" [Concern about absences at the Asian-African conference], *Dong-A Ilbo*, January 8, 1955, 1.

39 The pictorial included sections on South Korean current events, landscapes, traditions, modern factories and industries, and art. Kelso, "Pictorial Korea."

40 Kyung Cho Chung, *Korea Tomorrow*, 293.

41 Chae Kyung Oh, *Handbook of Korea*, 1–2.

42 "Korea—A Nation Rebuilds," *New York Times*, August 11, 1957.

43 Syngman Rhee, "A Message from the President of Korea," *New York Times*, August 11, 1957.

44 In April 1957, the South Korean government paid close to $10,000 to US publisher L. E. McGivena to produce one of the first postwar tourism booklets, titled *Warm Welcome to Korea*. McGivena advised Koreans that they would need to undo negative wartime images if they planned to build a tourism industry. L. E. McGivena Co. to Young Chin Choi, April 9, 1957, File 540, no. 275–276, Folder "Korean Consulate General in New York, General Young Chin Choi, Consul General D. Y. Namkoong, January–December 1957," Rhee Papers.

45 According to McGivena, Americans were most interested in the "customs, habits and mores" of the Korean people. The publisher suggested that the booklet contents be "down-to-earth, practical, and informative, but with enough of the foreign color, interest, and character, to supply the attraction of the exotic." Ibid.

46 "Scenic Korea Invites Tourists," *New York Times*, August 11, 1957.

47 Chae Kyung Oh, *Handbook of Korea*, 1–2.

48 Lim, *Feeling of Belonging*, 184.

49 "Korean Children's Choir Tunes Up for US Tour," *New York Times*, April 16, 1954, 23; "Children's Choir Here from Korea," *New York Times*, April 13, 1954, 6.

50 The AKF had a positive relationship with the South Korean government since the war. "Chinjihan hwalyakhŭimang paekch'ongni hwanyŏngdamhwabalp'yo" [Minister Baik gives a hopeful welcome speech], *Dong-A Ilbo*, August 21, 1953, 1. The relationship between the organization and the ROK government remained strong after the tours ended. "Pakdaet'ongnyŏng yebang" [Dr. Rusk visits President Park], *Kyŏnghyang sinmun*, April 21, 1965, 1.

51 Korean papers reported regularly on the traveling choristers. "Han'guk Ŏrinihapch'angdae chŏt sŭtat'ŭ" [Korean Children's Choir starts], *Dong-A Ilbo*, May 3, 1954, 2; "Mi 50-kaedoshirŭl sunhoe Han'guk Ŏrinihapch'angdan gongyŏn'gaeshi" [Korean Children's Choir begins tours in 50 cities], *Dong-A Ilbo*, May 6, 1954, 2; "Paegakkwansŏ yŏnjuhoe 11-il Han'guk Ŏrinihapch'angdan" [Korean Children's Choir performs at the White House on the 11th], *Dong-A Ilbo*, May 8, 1954, 2.

52 "$10,000,000 Drive for Korea Opens," *New York Times*, April 27, 1954, 3.

53 "Children's Choir Here," *New York Times*.

54 "Philanthropy: People to People," *Time*, April 20, 1953.

55 "Korean Children Begin Choir Tour," *New York Times*, April 16, 1954, 23.

56 All quotes from "$10,000,000 Drive," *New York Times*.

57 "Korean Choir to Tour US," *New York Times*, April 8, 1954, 25.

58 Tchen, *New York before Chinatown*, 97–130. Also see Phalen, *Unmarked*, 10–11.

59 "First Lady Serenaded by 25 Korean Children," *New York Times*, May 12, 1954, 36; "Truman Hears Koreans," *New York Times*, June 6, 1954, 83.

60 Advertisement for Liberty Music Shops and Urania Records, *New York Times*, May 16, 1954, 1.

61 "Korean Children Begin Choir Tour," *New York Times*.

62 Klein, *Cold War Orientalism*, 146.
63 A photograph of the children with Ahn Byŏng Wŏn appeared in Korean newspapers. For example, "Korean Children's Choir performs at the White House," *Dong-A Ilbo*.
64 "25 Koreans Turn American for Day," *New York Times*, April 19, 1954, 25.
65 "On Television," *New York Times*, May 3, 1954, 32.
66 "Ŭmaksa chŏltan'gwiguk" [Music ambassadors return], *Kyŏnghyang sinmun*, July 8, 1954, 2.
67 "Kkomahapch'angdan hwanyŏngdaehoe sŏnghwang" [Welcoming event for the successful Korean Children's Choir], *Dong-A Ilbo*, July 11, 1954, 3.
68 Ellen Shulte, "From South Korea with Love," *Los Angeles Times*, December 15, 1965, 3; Pierce, *Korean Orphan Choir*.
   Under World Vision, the Korean Orphan Choir performed in countries around the world, including Germany, the Philippines, Hong Kong, New Zealand, and Australia. In 1964 the children sang for 450,000 people at 130 concerts in fourteen countries. The Korean choirs were renamed the Korean Children's Choir in the 1970s and continue to travel under the sponsorship of World Vision Korea, a regional branch of World Vision International. World Vision, Central Records, "Ministries 3rd Korean Choir World 1965–66," Folder 73, World Vision International Archives, Monrovia, CA (hereafter World Vision Archives).
   South Koreans were just as supportive of the World Vision choirs as they were the AKF's choir. "Ch'yŏugaesŏne hŭibigyoch'ak" [Cherished Korean Orphan Choir welcomed with tears], *Kyŏnghyang sinmun*, October 31, 1961, 1; "Mi k'anegihore tŭngjang, kamdongŭi togani koahapch'angdan" [Orphan Choir appears at Carnegie Hall], *Kyŏnghyang sinmun*, November 13, 1961, 3; "In'gijŏlchŏng uri koahapch'angdan" [Our popular Korean Orphan Choir], *Kyŏnghyang sinmun*, December 9, 1961, 3; "Noraehanŭn koashijŏl hŭibiro ŏlkhin yŏnjuyŏhaenggi" [Singing orphan ambassadors and their journey], *Kyŏnghyang sinmun*, February 4, 1962, 4; "Chogukŭl charanghago dorawa" [Returns after making our nation proud], *Dong-A Ilbo*, February 8, 1962, 4.
69 "Shoppers Ignore 14-Degree Cold," *New York Times*, December 17, 1961, 74.
70 "Billy Graham—Pittsburgh Crusade," *New York Times*, October 20, 1968, 73.
71 "Korean Orphans Arrive and Meet New Parents," *Los Angeles Times*, June 13, 1956, 1, 21.
72 World Vision, Central Records, "News Releases Korean Orphan Choir Tour #2 1962–3," World Vision Archives.
73 George Reasons, "1.5 Million Expected to See Rose Parade," *Los Angeles Times*, December 30, 1962; "Korean Orphan Choir," *New York Times*, December 24, 1962.
74 Alan Rich, "33 Korean Orphans Give Song Program," *New York Times*, December 7, 1962, 45.
75 Pierce, *Korean Orphan Choir*, 59.

76 Ibid., 54.

77 Rich, "33 Korean Orphans."

78 Shulte, "From South Korea," E1. In 1958 a Korean orphan band traveled to Hong Kong. Ernest Nash of the CCF remarked upon the capability of the children, who packed and unpacked their suitcases and learned modern and ancient Korean music and dance. Their modernity bridged "the two freedom-loving peoples of the Republic and the British Colony" together. Ernest T. Nash to Park Chan Il, March 31, 1958, Reel P-2, Section 18, Image 550, Foreign Overseas Adoptions, MoFA.

79 Shulte, "From South Korea," 3; Bob Pierce explains that none of the children spoke a language other than Korean, but learned English songs phonetically and were taught how to answer key questions in English. Pierce, *Korean Orphan Choir*, 40–41.

80 Army chaplain Russell Blaisdell organized Operation Kiddie Car, but the film depicted Colonel Dean Hess as the sole orchestrator of the mission. Eleana Kim, *Adopted Territory*, 78. Also see "Korean War Children's Memorial."

81 Jacobs, *America's Miracle Man*, 96.

82 Travel Authorization, Leonard C. Hicks to Gilbert Kurland, Folder 2 "Battle Hymn," Gil Kurland Collection, Margaret Herrick Library, Fairbanks Center for Motion Picture Study, Beverly Hills, CA (hereafter MHL).

83 "Air Force, Treasury Aid Film," *New York Herald Tribune*, June 3, 1956.

84 Hye Seung Chung, *Hollywood Asian*, 145; and for a full analysis of the film, 141–68.

85 "US Air Hero's Story Will Be Filmed in Korea," *Korean Republic*, September 15, 1955.

86 Production notes, Motion Picture Association of America, Production Code Administration Records, 6, MHL.

87 James Powers, *Reporter*, December 18, 1965, newspaper clippings, Motion Picture Association of America, *Battle Hymn*, Universal, 1955, MHL (hereafter newspaper clippings, MHL).

88 "War Is Not All Bad," *Newsweek*, February 25, 1957, newspaper clippings, MHL.

89 "The New Pictures: Battle Hymn," *Time*, March 11, 1957, 102.

90 "Battle Hymn," *Cue*, February 16, 1957; and Philip K. Scheuer, "'Battle Hymn' Stirring Saga of Hero Dean Hess," *Los Angeles Times*, February 21, 1957, newspaper clippings, MHL.

91 Powers, *Reporter*.

92 Scheuer, "'Battle Hymn' Stirring Saga."

93 Ibid.

94 Production notes, 26, MHL.

95 Douglas Robinson, "From Cheju Island to California," *New York Times*, May 6, 1956, X5.

96 Production notes, 27, MHL.

97 "A Saga of Sam and a Colonel," *Life*, February 25, 1957, 137.

PART II. INTERNATIONAL COLD WAR FAMILIES

1 Hugh Dinsmore to Thomas Francis Bayard, April 21, 1888, Letter no. 105 in Mc-
Cune and Harrison, *Korean-American Relations*, 206–7.

2 Board of Foreign Missions, *Chosen Mission*, p. 7, YDA; Board of Foreign Missions of the Presbyterian Church in the U.S.A., *Korea*, pamphlet, HR 1391, Box 5,
Folder 42, Records of the Presbyterian Church, Foreign Missions 1834–1962, YDA.

3 Oliver, *50 Facts*, #25.

4 In 1945 the population of the south was estimated to be a little over 16 million, but
it increased to over 20 million in 1949. Tai-Hwan Kwon, "Demographic Trends,"
21.

5 Chang, "Korea, South," 179.

6 Whanyung Kim, "Political Economy of Development," 103–4.

7 Underwood, *Tragedy and Faith in Korea*, 55.

8 Whanyung Kim, "Political Economy of Development," 104.

9 News of US servicemen providing money and manpower to build orphanages
appeared in Korean and US newspapers. See, for example, "Kids Take Over Seoul
Home by Sgt. Charles P. Taylor," *Pacific Stars and Stripes* (Korea edition), May
22, 1955, 11; and "Nambugaeyugwŏn chŏngch'osik kŏhaeng" [Opening of the
South-North Orphanage], *Dong-A Ilbo*, November 2, 1954, 2. This orphanage was
sponsored by AFAK and the CCF; with aid from the United States, the wartime
orphanage expanded to accommodate two hundred war orphans.

CHAPTER 3. MISSIONARY RESCUE AND THE TRANSNATIONAL MAKING OF FAMILY

1 Holt, *Bring My Sons*, 2–3.

2 Press conference video, October 14, 1955. Video viewed October 4, 2005, private
collection of Molly Holt.

3 While laws like the Magnuson Act of 1943 and the McCarran-Walter Act of 1952
allotted small numbers of visas for immigrants from Asian countries, immigration from Asia would remain largely restricted until the Immigration and Nationality Act of 1965. And though the US Supreme Court ruled in the 1954 *Brown
v. Board of Education* case that racial segregation in public schools violated the
Fourteenth Amendment, a decision that also rejected the 1896 *Plessy v. Ferguson*
"separate but equal" doctrine, schools and other public places remained largely
segregated in custom and social practice throughout the 1950s and beyond.

4 *The Ugly American* was a Cold War novel that emphasized for American readers
the importance of acting in benevolent and humanitarian ways when abroad.
Lederer and Burdick, *The Ugly American*.

5 Gene Kramer, "'Pied Piper' Corrals 12 Korean Babies, Flies Them to America for
Adoption," *Washington Post and Times Herald*, October 14, 1955, 71; "'Stork' Plane
Bring 12 Korean Foundlings," *Washington Post and Times Herald*, October 15,
1955, 26; "Tears and Kisses Greet Tiny Korean War Orphan," *Los Angeles Times*,
October 16, 1955, 27; Malcolm Bauer, "Oregon Family of Eight Adds Eight More,"

Christian Science Monitor, October 21, 1955, 3; "8 Korean Orphans in Oregon Family," *New York Times*, December 4, 1955, 36.

6 Molly Holt estimates that over four hundred letters arrived in that first week alone. Molly Holt, interview by author.

7 Social welfare professionals remarked that Holt's self-promotion led many Americans to request adoptions from Korea. "Report to the Subcommittee on Supply of Children to the Intercountry Adoption Committee," November 7, 1963, Box 3, Folder 2, SW109, SWHA. The 1964 television documentary *Korean Legacy* promoted the Holt Adoption Agency. Hamamoto, *Monitored Peril*, 100–101.

8 Arnold Lyslo, "A Few Impressions on Meeting the Harry Holt Plane, the 'Flying Tiger,'" December 27, 1958, Box 10, Folder 3, SW109, SWHA.

9 "Rancher and 12 Korean Orphans Arrive in the US," *Chicago Daily Tribune*, October 15, 1955, 2; "An Airlift for 89 Orphans Flies Korean Children 'Home' to the US," *New York Times*, December 18, 1956, 33.

10 Malcolm Bauer, "Korean Orphans Find US Homes," *Christian Science Monitor*, April 9, 1956, 3.

11 "Mrs. Holt Says Korea Tots Dying," *Daily Journal*, July 24, 1957, Box 10, Folder 30, SW109, SWHA. Dorothy M. Frost, executive director, American-Korean Foundation, memorandum, November 25, 1958, Box 10, Folder 31, SW109, SWHA; S. Talisman, associate director, ISS American branch, "Report on Visit to Korea, June 24–July 2, 1968," p. 5, Box 34, Folder 18, SW109, SWHA.

12 Underline from original modified to italics. Harry Holt, letter to adoptive parents, c. June 1956, private collection of Molly Holt. In Holt's home videos, markers of their Christian home can be seen in the family's use of prayer at dinnertime, and in signs that read "God bless our home" and "The way of the cross leads Home." Home videos viewed October 4, 2005, private collection of Molly Holt.

13 WAIF press kit, n.d., Box 17, Folder 29, SW109, SWHA.

14 "Children: New Faces," *Time*, December 23, 1957, 16. "Private business men" conducted HAP studies. Harry Holt, letter to prospective adoptive parents, December 14, 1955, Box 10, Folder 30, SW109, SWHA. Also see Arissa Oh, *To Save the Children*, 79–111.

15 Harry Holt, "Method of Adoption through Welfare and International Service v. Adoption by Proxy," n.d., Box 10, Folder 30, ISS, SWHA.

16 Oak Soon Hong to prospective adoptive parents, n.d., Box 10, Folder 38, SW109, SWHA. By 1975, the Holts were using a sliding pay scale, charging 4 percent of the family's adjusted gross income (not to exceed $1,000) for adoption services. John Adams, memorandum, September 11, 1975, Box 3, Folder 5, SW109, SWHA.

For those who were deemed "unsuitable" for overseas adoptions and went to the Holts for help, see Andrew F. Juras, director, Department of Social Welfare, Oregon, to Susan Pettiss and William T. Kirk, director, ISS, May 4, 1956, Box 10, Folder 30, SW109, SWHA. Additional letters describing this issue appear in Box 10, Folder 31, SW109, SWHA; and Box 165, Case 36167, SW109.2, SWHA.

17 "Unit Has 30 Members," *Los Angeles Times*, October 4, 1959, A24. Similar clubs
    existed in other parts of the country. "Korean Children Feted at Picnic," *New York
    Times*, July 9, 1961, 65.

18 Raymond W. Riese, director, Department of Social Welfare and State Public
    Welfare Commission, Oregon, to William T. Kirk, March 3, 1958, Box 10, Folder
    31, SW109, SWHA; "Holt Activity on Defensive," newspaper clippings, n.d., Box
    10, Folder 30, SW109, SWHA; "Indict Woman in Tot's Death," *New York Journal
    American*, July 2, 1957.

19 Walter A. Heath, director, Bureau of Adoptions, Department of Charities, Cali-
    fornia, to Ralph L. Goff, area director, Department of Social Welfare, California,
    November 7, 1956, Box 10, Folder 37, SW109, SWHA; Susan Pettiss to Lorena
    Scherer, January 8, 1957, Box 10, Folder 29, SW109, SWHA.

20 Keyes Beech, "South Korea 'Exports' Children," *Honolulu Star Bulletin*, February
    16, 1959, clipping, Reel P-2, Section 18, Foreign Overseas Adoptions, MoFA.

21 "Children: New Faces," *Time*.

22 "Report of Meeting with Dr. Pierce of World Vision," March 13, 1956, Box 10,
    Folder 29, SW109, SWHA.

23 World News ISS newsletter, February 1957, Box 4, Folder 6, SW109, SWHA.

24 Bauer, "Korean Orphans Find US Homes," 3; "Orphaned, Abandoned Children
    Report Subject," *Atlanta Daily World*, October 20, 1961, 3.

25 Leong, *China Mystique*, 12–68; Klein, *Cold War Orientalism*, 144; Briggs, *Some-
    body's Children*, 151–52; and Rochelle Girson, "Welcome House," *Saturday Review*,
    July 1952, 21. For more on Buck's life, see Conn, *Pearl S. Buck*. For more on Buck's
    role in transnational adoptions, see Graves, "Domesticating Foreign Affairs,"
    211–21.

26 Homer Bigart, "Pearl Buck Upholds Adoptions by Proxy for Waifs in Korea," *New
    York Times*, January 7, 1959, 14. Korean ambassador You Chan Yang stated that
    Buck's comments were "unfounded" and that there was not the "slightest shred
    of evidence that our great humanitarian, Christian President [Rhee] has ever
    deviated in any way from his strong position of devoting his mind and energies
    to protecting and helping all of the unfortunate orphan children of my country."
    You Chan Yang quoted in "Aiding Korean Waifs: General Lot of Orphans, Rhee's
    Attitude Defended," *New York Times*, January 27, 1959, 32. Chang Whan Sohn of
    the Korean Ministry of Health and Social Affairs wrote to the US government that
    there were few mixed-race children left in Korea and that Pearl Buck's statement
    about them "dropping like flies in Korean orphanages" was untrue. Chang Whan
    Sohn to US government, January 19, 1959, Reel P-1, 457/1486, Foreign Overseas
    Adoptions, MoFA.

    Pearl Buck wrote a letter of apology, explaining that reporters were un-
    reliable. Pearl Buck to Chon Baeoun, January 21, 1959, Reel P-2, Section 18,
    1390/1485.4, Foreign Overseas Adoptions, MoFA.

27 "Report on Activities of Pearl Buck Foundation," n.d., Box 17, Folder 2, SW109,
    SWHA.

28 "South Korea: Confucius' Outcasts," *Time*, December 10, 1965, 49. According to Gardner Munro, director, ISS Korea branch, the total number of mixed-race children was estimated to be 1,511 in South Korea, though he felt it was higher, at around 5,000; Gardner Munro to Edna Weber, December 11, 1965, Box 35, Folder 2, SW109, SWHA.

29 Statistics from the Republic of Korea's Ministry of Health and Social Affairs quoted in Hurh, "Marginal Children of War," 14–15. A September 1962 report indicated that 4,218 mixed-race children had gone to the United States and that roughly 800 remained in South Korea. "Han'guk chŏnjaeng koa" [Korean war orphans], *Chosŏn Ilbo*, September 7, 1962, 3.

30 Of this group, 98 requested Korean, 325 Korean-white, and 19 Korean-black children. Graves, "Domesticating Foreign Affairs," 220–21.

31 Statistics from administrative records at Holt Children's Services, Seoul, Korea, 2004. According to Korea's Ministry of Health and Social Affairs, Holt placed 3,469 predominantly mixed-race children in the United States between 1955 and 1965. Child Placement Center was the second largest placement agency, responsible for 1,537 international adoptions. The International Social Service was third, with 555 placements. "Welfare of Mixed-Blood Children," table 2, p. 6, SWHA.

32 "Relief and Social Services," UN.

33 "Korea—A Nation Rebuilds," *New York Times*, August 11, 1957. Also see Arissa Oh, *To Save the Children*, 55.

34 "Orphans in Korea," April 18, 1955, p. 1, Folder 20, UNKRA 1950–1960, UN. Korean newspapers wrote frequently about US-established orphanages. "Ŏrini kuhodanch'e" [Children aid organizations], *Dong-A Ilbo*, March 25, 1957, 4; "Nambugaeyugwŏn chŏngch'osik kŏhaeng" [Opening of the South-North Orphanage], *Dong-A Ilbo*, November 2, 1954, 2.

35 Chakerian, *From Rescue to Child Welfare*, 40–41. Chakerian based his study on the findings of a survey team sent to Korea by the Church World Service in 1961 and from his own visits between 1962 and 1967 as a Church World Service social welfare consultant. Ibid., 7. Also see Bowman, Gjenvick, and Harvey, *Children of Tragedy*; and Hallam C. Shorrock Jr., ed., *Is the Emergency Over? A Report about Korea and the Programs of Korea Church World Service during 1959* (Seoul: Korea Church World Service, 1960).

36 Korean Mission, *Evaluation*, 9. The same message was outlined in an earlier publication that stated, "Medical work [w]as an evangelizing agency. Public health work and sanitation as well. . . . However, our medical missionaries, both doctors and nurses, have not failed to recognize that the prime object of their lives and service was to bring men to a saving knowledge of Jesus Christ through their professional service and personal witness." Board of Foreign Missions, *Chosen Mission*, p. 15, YDA.

37 Underline from original modified to italics. Korean Mission, *Evaluation*, 17.

38 Underwood, *Tragedy and Faith in Korea*, 18.

39 The early work of the American Board of Commissioners for Foreign Missions, founded in 1810, assumed the cultural superiority of Anglo-Americans and their right to alter foreign cultures, an imperialist mindset that mirrored that of US governing powers. See Conroy-Krutz, *Christian Imperialism*, 11–13.

40 For Korean Christian immigration to Hawai'i between 1903 and 1905, see Yoo and Chung, "Introduction," 2–3; and Patterson, *The Ilse*, 8–9, 55–67.

41 At the turn of the century, female missionaries also found paths to domestic influence. Peggy Pascoe has described how women worked in rescue homes for Chinese immigrants, Mormon polygamous wives, and Native American women. Pascoe, *Relations of Rescue*.

42 By 1919, 13 percent of all missionary centers in China were entirely staffed by single women. Hunter, *Gospel of Gentility*, xiii, 12–14, 52. For American women missionaries in India, see Maina Chawla Singh, *Gender, Religion, and "Heathen Lands."*

43 Talcott Parsons, an influential US sociologist, explained that the "normal" family consisted of a man who specialized in the practical, individualistic activities needed for subsistence, and a woman who took care of the emotional needs of her husband and children. Coontz, *Marriage, A History*, 224–28, 242.

44 There were numerous drives across the country. For example, the Legion Auxiliary knit fourteen thousand sweaters in the winter of 1952 for the children of Korea. "Warmth for the Orphans of Korea," *McCall's*, 16–17.

45 Missionaries did the same in China. Single women were particularly valued in the foreign field because they did not need the medical attention required by missionary men and their families. Hunter, *Gospel of Gentility*, 52. Also see Varg, *Missionaries, Chinese, and Diplomats*.

46 Underwood, *Tragedy and Faith in Korea*, 40–43.

47 Choy, *Global Families*; Fieldston, *Raising the World*.

48 Molly Holt, interview by author.

49 For discussions of US military instruction of South Koreans, see Brazinsky, *Nation Building in South Korea*, 84–100; and Man, *Soldiering through Empire*, 41–44.

50 Ch'oe, "Activities of Foreign Voluntary Agencies."

51 Elizabeth Richelson, wife of US missionary Mark Richelson, and Miss Bournes introduced and implemented timetables at the CCC. Mrs. Mark Richelsen, "Crippled Children's Center 1964–1968 Newsletter," October 15, 1964, Group 11A, Box 180A, Folder 2549, YDA.

52 Pierce, *Korean Orphan Choir*, 38.

53 Foucault, "Governmentality"; Foucault, *Discipline and Punish*. For discussions of disciplining child subjects, see Margaret D. Jacobs, *White Mother to a Dark Race*, 237–42.

54 Capitals in original. Crippled Children's Center, brochure, Group 11A, Box 180A, Folder 2549, YDA.

55 Ch'oe, "Activities of Foreign Voluntary Agencies."
56 Reports of purported Korean incompetence appeared across ISS records. "ISS Report on Korea 1968," p. 4, SWHA; Marcia J. Williams, ISS Korea branch, to Susan Pettiss, April 22, 1958, Box 34, Folder 21, SW109, SWHA; Susan Pettiss to Reuben E. Carlson, caseworker, Board of Public Welfare, North Dakota, February 25, 1960, Box 10, Folder 14, SW109, SWHA; "Activity Report, ISS, Korea," May 22, 1963, p. 4, Box 34, Folder 24, SW109, SWHA; "Notes on ISS Korea," June 15, 1961, p. 5, Box 34, Folder 22, SW109, SWHA.
57 Masuda, Cold War Crucible, 212–16.
58 For a discussion of state intervention and the regulation of family, see Donzelot, Policing of Families.
59 Melosh, Strangers and Kin, 105; 1957 statistics from National Center for Health Statistics data, Bonham, "Who Adopts."
60 "Child Adoption Is Better Managed Than It Used to Be," Saturday Evening Post, August 24, 1957, 10. For US domestic adoption practices, see Berebitsky, Like Our Very Own; and Carp, Family Matters.
61 Mrs. John C. Carrington, Theodore M. Plowden, Dr. Samuel Karelitz, and Charles T. Akr, "Report to the Subcommittee on Supply of Children to the Intercountry Adoption Committee," November 7, 1963, Box 3, Folder 2, SW109, SWHA.
62 Melosh, Strangers and Kin, 192–93. Prospective adoptive parents stated in letters to agencies that they hoped to adopt from overseas precisely to avoid the problem of birth mothers reclaiming their children. Dorothy H. Sills, caseworker, ISS American branch, to Susan Pettiss, August 10, 1955, Box 10, Folder 3, SW109, SWHA.
63 Mrs. T. to Gracie Pfost, March 11, 1954, Box 18, Folder 126/2/01 "Child Welfare," UNKRA 1950–1960, UN.
64 Mr. W. and Mrs. K. to William T. Kirk and Susan Pettiss, January 12, 1955, Case 37220, January 19, 1955–April 4, 1956, Box 167, SW109.2, ISS, SWHA.
65 Mrs. O. to Young Han Choo, October 21, 1953, File 547, Folder "February 1954," Part I, Rhee Papers. For an examination of how photographs were used by adoption agencies to attract potential adoptive parents, and to diagnose and classify them for medical screening purposes, see Cartwright, "Photographs of 'Waiting Children.'"
66 Mrs. C. to Young Han Choo, October 23, 1954, File 550, Folder "February 1954," Part IV, Rhee Papers.
67 Mrs. C. to Young Han Choo, November 15, 1954, File 550, Folder "Korean Consulate in San Francisco, General Young Han Choo," Part IV, Rhee Papers.
68 Mrs. C., radiogram to Ministry of Communications, Republic of Korea, File 550, Folder "Korean Consulate in San Francisco, General Young Han Choo," Part IV, Rhee Papers.
69 Letter from C. J. Yu to Mrs. C., January 5, 1955, File 550, Folder "Korean Consulate in San Francisco, General Young Han Choo," Part IV, Rhee Papers.

70 May, *Barren in the Promised Land*, 127–29, 176–77; Marsh and Ronner, *Empty Cradle*, 196.

71 "'Stork' Plane Bring 12 Korean Foundlings," *Washington Post and Times Herald*.

72 Capitals in original. Mrs. S. to Mrs. Syngman Rhee, January 7, 1957, Reel 2/18/51–52, 1390/1485.4, Foreign Overseas Adoptions, MoFA.

73 Kristin Hoganson describes how around the turn of the twentieth century, white, middle-class women decorated their homes with evidence of international connections, particularly from Asia. Hoganson, *Consumers' Imperium*, 16–20. Also see Yoshihara, *Embracing the East*, 25–43.

74 "Summary of Home Study," January 1955, Box 167, Case 37317, SW109.2, ISS, SWHA.

75 For constructing the Orient in opposition to the West, see Said, *Orientalism*, 86–110.

76 Solinger, *Pregnancy and Power*, 140–41; May, *Barren in the Promised Land*, 131–34.

77 Rusk described the generosity of Americans who donated to Korean causes as a "movement." "$10,000,000 Drive," *New York Times*, April 27, 1954.

78 "*Life* Visits a One-Family UN," *Life*, November 12, 1951, 157–63; Herman, *Kinship by Design*, 212–15.

79 Klein, *Cold War Orientalism*, 144; Girson, "Welcome House."

80 Klein, *Cold War Orientalism*, 146.

81 Burnett P. Tiller to the US Senate Foreign Relations Committee, May 31, 1960, RG 59, Box 2909, Folder 8952.411/2-160, NA.

82 George V. Roberts Jr. to W. J. Bryan Dorn, house representative, Washington, DC, December 15, 1959, RG 59, Box 2909, Folder 895B.40/6-1261 "Adoption Inquiries, Pearl Buck, Mixed Race Legislation Discussion 1960–63," NA.

83 Mrs. William Burns, "Four Thousand Orphans," March 1954, Box 3, Folder 4 "Inter-Country Adoptions, Committee ISS Reports," SW109, SWHA. Public critiques of the US military also occurred after World War II, when thousands of children fathered by American GIs remained throughout Europe, as well as Japan and the Philippines. One journalist reported that "Uncle Sam has shown virtually no interest" in the problems faced by the mothers of these children, especially those with "half-Negro" children. "The Babies They Left behind Them," *Life*, August 23, 1948, 41–43.

84 "Washington View," SWHA.

85 In December 1945, President Truman ordered a directive that allowed for the entry of "eligible orphans" from war-torn countries. He followed with the Displaced Persons Act of 1948, which allowed for 205,000 displaced persons from countries in Europe, with 3,000 spots made available to children. During the two years before the act expired, 2,838 children under the age of sixteen from Germany, Italy, Greece, and other European countries entered as nonquota immigrants, becoming the United States' first intercountry adoptees. Federal Security Agency, Social Security Administration, and US Children's Bureau, "Standards for Care of Displaced Children Coming to the United States under the Displaced Persons Act

of 1948," March 1949, Box 12, Folder 4, SW109, SWHA (hereafter "Standards for Care," SWHA). Edith Lowenstein, editor, "An Information Service on Immigration, Naturalization and Related Problems," *Common Council for American Unity, Interpreter Releases* 34.37, September 17, 1957, Box 13, Folder 2, SW109, SWHA.

86 "Immigration and Nationality Act of 1952"; "Adopter of 8 Koreans Off to Get 200 More," *New York Times*, March 26, 1956, 31.

87 Koshiro, *Trans-Pacific Racisms*, 184. For example, in the month of October in 1951 alone, six separate bills allowed for the special entry of Japanese-American children as nonquota immigrants.

88 Ibid., 187.

89 Lovelock, "Intercountry Adoption," 912.

90 Laurin Hyde and Virginia P. Hyde, "A Study of Proxy Adoptions," June 1958, Box 3, Folder 4, SW109, SWHA.

91 Alstein and Simon, *Intercountry Adoption*, 3.

92 Untitled list of US couples interested in adoption, File 553, Folder "February 1954," Part I, Rhee Papers.

93 Syngman Rhee to Young Han Choo, December 3, 1953, File 547, Folder "February 1954," Part I, Rhee Papers.

94 Mr. M. to Young Han Choo, July 22, 1954, File 550, Rhee Papers. Korean media outlets shared news of the RRA to specifically encourage sending mixed-race children to the United States. "Adaet'ongnyŏngt'ŭkpyŏlchishi Han'guk honhyŏradong Mi'guk ibyang'ganŭng" [Eisenhower allows Korean mixed-race children adoption], *Dong-A Ilbo*, November 13, 1956, 3.

95 "Procedures for Adoption of Korean Child," July 6, 1953, Box 34, Folder 21, SW109 SWHA.

96 Augusta Mayerson to Helen Wilson, February 25, 1953, Box 18, Folder 126/2/01 "Child Welfare," UNKRA 1950–1960, UN.

97 Hsu, *Good Immigrants*, 19–20.

98 Miss Viser to the Korean Ministry of Foreign Affairs, memorandum, n.d., Reel P-2, Section 18, 1390/1485.4, Foreign Overseas Adoptions, MoFA. The ISS believed that Holt mobilized potential adopters to write to their congressmen to lobby for an extension of the RRA and proxy adoptions. Rollin Zane, executive director, Department of Children's Services, Connecticut, to Edwin H. May Jr., house representative, Connecticut, March 25, 1957, Box 10, Folder 37, SW109, SWHA.

99 "Washington View," SWHA.

100 Ibid.

101 "Mrs. Holt Says Korea Tots Dying," *Daily Journal.*

102 "Washington View," SWHA.

103 Hochfield, "Across National Boundaries," 4.

104 "Meeting of Child Welfare Experts: Intercountry Adoptions," January 31, 1963, Box 10, Folder 36, SW109, SWHA.

105 "Welfare of Mixed-Blood Children," table 1, p. 4, SWHA. For letters from potential adoptive parents pushing to keep proxy adoptions legal, see Box 10, Folder 26, SW109, SWHA.

106 Iriye, *Pacific Estrangement*, 122.

107 See Dudziak, *Cold War, Civil Rights*; and Borstelmann, *Cold War and the Color Line.*

108 US Department of Justice, "Korean Immigration to the United States, 1903–1996," reprinted in Hurh, *Korean Americans*, 33. According to a Korean newspaper, 2,670 mixed-race children entered the United States by 1959. "Mi'guk iminbub 1-nyŏn dŏ yŏnjangdoem" [US immigration law extended one more year], *Chosŏn Ilbo*, September 20, 1959, 3.

109 Beech, "South Korea 'Exports' Children."

110 Trenka, *Language of Blood*, 229.

CHAPTER 4. PRODUCING MODEL KOREAN ADOPTEES

1 For race and gatekeeping policies, see Ngai, *Impossible Subjects*; Erika Lee, *At America's Gates*; and Saxton, *Indispensable Enemy*.

2 Hsu, *Good Immigrants*, 4, 20, 134–35.

3 Lovelock, "Intercountry Adoption," 913.

4 "Standards for Care," SWHA.

5 Lovelock, "Intercountry Adoption," 914.

6 Paul Saylor, US army captain, memorandum, September 1956, RG 338, Box 645, Folder "Decimal 292," NA.

7 In cases involving children from North Korea, social workers described them as refugees fleeing communism. Helen Yepes, caseworker, ISS, to Lorena Scherer, October 8, 1954, Box 166, Case 36568, SW109.2, SWHA.

8 Edith Lowenstein, "An Information Service on Immigration, Naturalization and Related Problems," *Common Council for American Unity, Interpreter Releases* 34, no. 37, September 17, 1957, Box 13, Folder 2, SW109, SWHA.

9 Pearl Buck, "Should White Parents Adopt Brown Babies?," *Ebony*, June 1958, 26–31.

10 Eleana Kim describes how the child became "a person with the barest of social identities, and in the context of Korean cultural norms, she [lacked] the basic requirements of social personhood—namely, family lineage and genealogical history." Eleana Kim, "Our Adoptee," 521.

11 "Method of Adoption through Welfare and International Service v. Adoption by Proxy," c. 1955, Box 10, Folder 30, SW109, SWHA.

12 Anne M. Davison to Susan Pettiss and Florence Boester, representative, ISS Far East division, January 21, 1962, Box 34, Folder 24, SW109, SWHA.

13 Anne M. Davison, "ISS Korea Report for January 1–August 31, 1961," Box 34, Folder 21, SW109, SWHA. After the war, most of the children in Yŏngnak Orphanage had parents who had either died in the war or were missing. If the parents were alive, they would need to fingerprint and sign relinquishment forms.

If after six months no one claimed the child, then it was possible to adopt without these legal documents. Shin Dong Han, interview by author.

14 "Korea Adoption Law, draft confidential," Box 34, Folder 21, SW109, SWHA. In the legislative records at the National Assembly Library in Seoul, I found only one passing mention of the 1961 adoption bill in a handwritten note indicating that the law existed.

15 "Washington View," SWHA; Susan Pettiss to Eleanor Wright, supervisor, Department of Public Welfare, South Carolina, March 26, 1956, Box 10, Folder 3, SW109, SWHA; and minutes of meeting of the Board of Directors, ISS, September 23, 1954, Box 4, Folder 3, SW109, SWHA.

16 The Displaced Persons Act of 1948, which aimed to help children from war-torn Europe, outlined the responsibility of the adoptive family of "displaced orphans," and was a precursor to the RRA of 1953. "Standards for Care," SWHA.

17 "Washington View," SWHA. The ISS was partly funded by the US State Department. Ruth Larned, "International Social Service, A History 1921–1955," 1957, Box 3, Folder 18, SW109, SWHA.

18 "50 Years of International Social Service," c. 1955, p. 7, Box 3, Folder 18, SW109, SWHA.

19 Larned, "International Social Service."

20 Jane Russell's movie-star status helped raise money and bring public awareness to adoptions from Korea. Florence Boester, "ISS Delegation Korea Prepared for the International Council Meeting Geneva, May 31–June 1, 1957," May 6, 1957, Box 4, Folder 6, SW109, SWHA. President Eisenhower included his endorsement in WAIF's pamphlet. Untitled pamphlet, Box 17, Folder 29, SW109, SWHA. WAIF's relationship with the ISS was at times strained; there were periods when they operated independently of one another. Mrs. Morris Hadley, "History of International Services," Second WAIF Leadership Conference, Los Angeles, May 4, 1964, Box 17, Folder 29, SW109, SWHA; Bayard Forster, "Integrating Waif and ISS Operations," n.d., Box 17, Folder 29, SW109, SWHA.

21 For the professionalization of social welfare through the governance of adoptions, see Herman, *Kinship by Design*, 55–81; and Melosh, *Strangers and Kin*, 40, 109. For the history of US social welfare, see Axinn and Stern, *Social Welfare*.

22 Fieldston, *Raising the World*, 3–4.

23 "What Are the General Principles of ISS?," Box 3, Folder 20, SW109, SWHA.

24 Letter from ISS American branch to a woman requesting adoption of a foreign child, August 1956, Box 3, Folder 4, SW109, SWHA.

25 "Procedures for Processing Foreign Children for Immigration and Adoption by American Citizens," Box 3, Folder 15, SW109, SWHA.

26 "Korea Adoption Law, draft confidential," SWHA.

27 Though Buck went the route of proxy adoptions, a practice not condoned by the ISS, by the mid-1950s she tried to cooperate with the organization. World Vision also worked with the ISS and even contributed funds for its operations. Paul R. Cherney, general director, ISS, "General Directors Report for 1962," Box 3, Folder 2,

SW109, SWHA; Paul R. Cherney, "Request for Support from Church World Service," December 5, 1963, Box 3, Folder 2, SW109, SWHA.

28 "Breakdown with Holt Cases," 1955, Box 10, Folder 37, SW109, SWHA; "Report from WAIF-ISS," February 10, 1958, Box 10, Folder 38, SW109, SWHA.

29 Harry Holt to US Secretary of State, April 13, 1956, RG 469, Box 49, Folder "Agric-commodities," NA.

30 Andrew F. Juras to Susan Pettiss and William Kirk, May 4, 1956, Box 10, Folder 30, SW109, SWHA. Letters describing how couples denied by social welfare agencies went to Holt or World Vision can be found in Box 10, Folder 29, SW109, SWHA.

31 Gladys Weinberg, "In Foster Home Placement," n.p., paper presented at "The Alien Child: A Symposium," New York Committee on Immigration and Naturalization, New York, May 7, 1959 (reprinted in *Social Casework*, March 1960), Box 11, Folder 9, SW109, SWHA.

32 Social workers used race matching as a tool to craft a good "fit" between a child and family. The practice also served the larger social purpose of boundary maintenance. Herman, *Kinship by Design*, 50, 128–133; Melosh, *Strangers and Kin*, 102–4.

33 While US media reported on Japanese adoptions after World War II, the public work of Holt drew attention to Korean adoptions specifically. Peter Kalischer, "Madame Butterfly's Children," *Collier's*, September 20, 1952, 15–18.

34 Between November 1955 and March 1956, the ISS received 250 inquiries from families "wanting Asian mixed blood children." Susan Pettiss to Agnes Miller, executive director, Welcome House, February 13, 1957, Box 23, Folder 34, SW109, SWHA. In 1957 the ISS reported that there had "not been sufficient children to suggest to those families wanting American-Korean (Caucasian) children." "Intercountry Adoption Program for the Year 1958," Box 11, Folder 5, SW109, SWHA.

35 Letitia Di Virgilio, supervisor, WAIF adoption division, ISS American branch, "Adjustment of Foreign Children"; Thomas Maretski, Child Welfare League of America, remarks recorded at "Adoption of Oriental Children by American White Families: An Interdisciplinary Symposium," May 1, 1959," May 1960, Box 11, Folder 9, SW109, SWHA (hereafter "Adoption of Oriental Children by American White Families," SWHA).

36 Mr. G. to Susan Pettiss, September 24, 1954, Box 166, Case 36618, SW109.2, SWHA. In a follow-up visit, the social worker reported: "One little girl shows her Korean background more than the other who resembles Mrs. G." Boston Children's Services Association, "4 Year Later 1959 Follow Up on G. Family," ibid.

37 C. J. Yu to Mr. and Mrs. S., February 22, 1954, File 549, Folder "February 1954," Part III, Rhee Papers.

38 One caseworker described the Korean-white child as being "quite handsome" and "more Caucasian-appearing than Oriental." The adoptive mother explained that many people said that he resembled her. Lucille C. Evers, caseworker, Department of Social Welfare, California, to Susan Pettiss, April 25, 1956, redacted case files, SW109.2, SWHA. Another described a Korean-white child's appearance as "very

outstanding" and that he looked "attractive and intelligent." Oak Soon Hong, "Social History of B.," March 8, 1955, Box 21, Case 37220, SW109.2, SWHA.

39 In *Perez v. Sharp* (1948), the California Supreme Court ruled the unconstitutionality of antimiscegenation laws. Other states followed suit, culminating in the *Loving v. Virginia* decision on April 10, 1967, which repealed all state bans on interracial marriages. For more on antimiscegenation law, see Pascoe, *What Comes Naturally*; Botham, *Almighty God Created the Races*; and Orenstein, "Void for Vagueness."

40 Spickard, *Mixed Blood*, 292.

41 "Are Interracial Homes Bad for Children?," *Ebony*, March 1963, 131–34.

42 For the shifting dynamics of race, blood, and law in the United States, see Pascoe, *What Comes Naturally;* Wadlington, "*Loving* Case," 1201; and Woo, "When Blood Won't Tell."

43 Melosh, *Strangers and Kin*, 53. For a discussion of the racial triangulation of Asian Americans vis-à-vis whites and blacks, see Claire Jean Kim, "Racial Triangulation of Asian Americans."

44 "Breakdown Cases from Holt Agency: Case 4," Box 10, Folder 31, SW109, SWHA. Some white parents chose to keep their adopted children upon learning that they were part-black. "A Rare Lesson about Love," *Look*, April 30, 1957, 42–46. For transracial adoptions in the United States, see Patton, *BirthMarks*; Plummer, "Brown Babies"; Fehrenbach, *Race after Hitler*, 143–56; and Potter, *Everybody Else*.

45 Mrs. T. to Grace Krejce, caseworker, Department of Social Welfare, California, c. 1956, Box 167, Case 37182, SW109.2, SWHA.

46 January 1955, Box 167, Case 37164, SW109.2, SWHA.

47 Buck, "Should White Parents Adopt Brown Babies?" The black press reported on successful placements. "Korean, Adopted by Negro Couple, Arrives in US," *Jet*, February 19, 1953, 21.

48 The ISS reported that hardly any African American couples requested to adopt Korean-African American children. Susan Pettiss to Virginia Baumgartner, representative, ISS Korea branch, March 19, 1959, Box 34, Folder 26, SW109, SWHA. The State Public Welfare Commission agreed. Jeanne Jewett and Lois McCarthy to William T. Kirk, June 7, 1957, Box 10, Folder 39, SW109, SWHA. As did the American Council of Voluntary Agencies for Foreign Services, "Notes from Meeting Held on December 3, 1958," Box 10, Folder 36, SW109, SWHA.

49 Melosh, *Strangers and Kin*, 108.

50 National Urban League Conference Report, "A Suggested Community Organization Program in Child Welfare," September 8, 1953, Box 19, File 1 "National Urban League Records, Group I, Series II, 1953–61," Library of Congress Manuscript Collection, quoted in Melosh, *Strangers and Kin*, 101. Graves describes NUL efforts to help African American adopters. Graves, "Domesticating Foreign Affairs," 110–56.

51 December 1954 to August 1957, Box 19, Case 37013, SW109.2, SWHA.

52 Michael Harrington, *The Other America: Poverty in the United States* (New York: Macmillan, 1962), 53, quoted in Coontz, *The Way We Never Were*, 30.

However, other organizations, like the Children's Bureau Department, forced women to quit their jobs before even granting a home visit. The CBD held fast to the conviction that motherhood was a full-time job and the most important one a woman could hold. Melosh, *Strangers and Kin*, 114.

53 Graves, "Domesticating Foreign Affairs," 3.

54 "Notes from Intercountry Adoption Committee Meeting," December 13, 1957, p. 3, Box 4, Folder 6, SW109, SWHA.

55 Melosh, *Strangers and Kin*, 108, 172.

56 For more on producing the stigma against black motherhood during the 1940s and 1950s, see Solinger, *Pregnancy and Power*, 144–53; Feldstein, *Motherhood in Black and White*, 69–70; Feldstein, "'I Wanted the Whole World to See'"; Solinger, *Wake Up Little Susie*; and Ortiz and Briggs, "Culture of Poverty." Gunnar Myrdal's influential study argued that racial inequality contributed to family "disorganization" among African Americans, which became grounds for withholding state welfare. Myrdal, *American Dilemma*.

57 Solinger, *Pregnancy and Power*, 148; and Feldstein, *Motherhood in Black and White*, 62–73.

58 Susan Pettiss to Marcia Speers, staff member, ISS Korea branch, January 9, 1958, Box 34, Folder 21, SW109, SWHA. This excludes those adopted via proxy without the involvement of the ISS.

59 Mrs. S. to Susan Pettiss, September 22, 1955, Box 167, Summary 36901–37500, SW109.2, SWHA.

60 Margaret A. Valk to Mr. and Mrs. S., September 26, 1955, Box 167, Summary 36901–37500, SW109.2, SWHA.

61 Margaret Mary Kelly, caseworker, Department of Social Welfare, Ohio, "Adoptive Study," September 16, 1954, Box 167, Summary 36901–37500, SW109.2, SWHA.

62 "Home Study Report," February 2, 1955, pp. 2, 5–6, Box 19, Case 37013, SW109.2, SWHA.

63 Lloyd B. Graham, secretary, American Joint Committee for Assisting Japanese American Orphans, Tokyo, to Margaret A. Valk, March 31, 1955, Box 167, Summary 36901–37500, SW109.2, SWHA.

64 "A Famous Orphan Finds a Happy Home," *Life*, May 14, 1956, 129–30.

65 Rougier, "The Little Boy Who Wouldn't Smile," *Life*, July 23, 1951.

66 "A Child's Salute," *Chicago Tribune*, April 5, 1964, H11. Other adoptee stories also highlighted citizenship. See, for example, "Korean Orphan Now Citizen," *New York Times*, November 22, 1962, 54; and Sue Lynn Belke, photograph of six-year-old in front of the US Courthouse in Denver after becoming a US citizen, *Denver Post*, July 27, 1969, 37.

67 In 1966 sociologist William Peterson used the term "model minority" to describe the success of Japanese Americans. Similar reports appeared in the *US News and World Report* heralding the successes of Chinese Americans. William Peterson,

"Success Story, Japanese-American Style," *New York Times Magazine*, January 9, 1966, 180; "The Success Story of One Minority Group in the US," *US News and World Report*, December 26, 1966.

68 Wu, *Color of Success*, 111–44; Shah, *Contagious Divides*, 242–50; Cheng, *Citizens of Asian America*, 71–84. For an examination of Japanese Americans and African Americans in postwar Los Angeles, see Kurashige, *Shifting Grounds of Race*.

69 Margaret A. Valk to Oak Soon Hong, November 12, 1954, Box 166, Case 36441, SW109.2, SWHA; December 29, 1954–June 1955, Box 167, Case 37097, SW109.2, SWHA.

70 Transnational adoptees describe the tension between gratefulness and loss. See Trenka, *Language of Blood*; *First Person Plural* and *In the Matter of Cha Jung Hee*, DVDs, directed by Deann Borshay Liem.

71 Susan Pettiss, memorandum, "Conference at Washington Children's Home Society," February 8, 1956, p. 2, Box 10, Folder 3, SW109, SWHA.

72 "Famous Orphan," *Life*; Brenneis, "New American Comes 'Home.'"

73 "Korean Boy Adopted by GI Comes to US," *Los Angeles Times*, November 23, 1953, 6. US secretary of state John Foster Dulles understood how positive stories of successful Chinese refugee settlement in the 1950s could promote US democracy and the abundant opportunities available in the free world, while at the same time maligning communism. He encouraged the humanizing of "individual stories of refugees" to highlight the good work of Americans, but also suggested that cultural producers downplay the far greater US resources allotted to Europeans over Asians. Hsu, *Good Immigrants*, 172–73.

74 "Practical Hints about Your Korean Child," June 1957, Box 10, Folder 34, SW109, SWHA (hereafter "Practical Hints," SWHA).

75 Margaret A. Valk to Letitia Di Virgilio, April 24, 1956, Box 10, Folder 39, SW109, SWHA.

76 "Practical Hints," SWHA; Margaret A. Valk, "Adjustment of Korean-American Children in Their American Adoptive Homes," paper presented at the National Conference on Social Welfare, April 1957, pp. 11–12, Box 10, Folder 2, SW109, SWHA. Studies also reported the rapid adaptability of Korean children. See Dong Soo Kim, "How They Fared"; and Kim, "Issues in Transracial and Transcultural Adoption."

77 "Summary of Adoptive Home," June 21, 1955, Box 26, Case 37708, SW109.2, SWHA.

78 Quotes from Holt International Children's Services child reports, November 16, 1965, and April 14, 1964. Middle quote from letter from S.'s nursemaid to "S.'s Parents," July 1968, translated August 17, 1968, Administrative Records, Holt International Children's Services, Seoul, Korea (hereafter, Holt International).

79 Letter from S.'s nursemaid to "S.'s Parents," July 1968, Holt International.

80 "Child Report," August 11, 1968, Holt International.

81 "Child Report," October 22, 1979, Sangrokwŏn Orphanage, Seoul, Korea.

82 Dove M. Kull, Academy of Certified Social Workers, to Child Welfare Supervisor, January 3, 1964, Box 17, Folder 29, SW109, SWHA.

83 At a 1960 child welfare symposium, a social worker determined that the "Oriental" adoptee should learn American culture so that he would not grow up feeling that he belonged elsewhere. He suggested that they could "see whether later on he might want to inquire more into his own background." "Adoption of Oriental Children by American White Families," SWHA.

84 Lucille C. Evers to Susan Pettiss, October 16, 1956, Box 166, Case 36568, SW109.2, SWHA.

85 I have found no instances of parents using the child's Korean name. The closest was James Lee Paladino, whose surname became his middle name. Elizabeth's story is described by the Ogle County Court probation officer in Oregon who helped place the child. Lillian Llewellyn, probation officer, Ogle County Court, Oregon, Illinois, to Margaret A. Valk, July 18, 1955, Box 20, Case 37133, SW109.2, SWHA.

86 Lucille Evers to Susan Pettiss, July 11, 1956, n.a. redacted case files, Box 166, Case 36585, SW109.2, SWHA.

87 Janet Wilson, caseworker, Department of Social Welfare, California, to Susan Pettiss, August 13, 1956, Box 21, Case 37182, SW109, SWHA.

88 "Home Study," October 8, 1954, pp. 7–8, Box 166, Summary 36201–36900, SW109.2, SWHA. In the end, the Korean girl was placed with another family. Lenore G. Levin, caseworker, Department of Social Welfare, California, to Susan Pettiss, October 8, 1956, p. 2, Box 17, Case 36716, ISS Case Studies, SWHA.

89 Unsigned memorandum to Dr. Edith Jackson, "Concerning Questions Asked by ISS," March 12, 1959, Box 17, Folder "Symposium, 1959," SW109, SWHA.

90 William T. Kirk, "Introduction: The Program of International Social Service," in "Adoption of Oriental Children by American White Families," p. 8, SWHA.

91 Maretski, "Community Attitudes," in "Adoption of Oriental Children by American White Families," p. 26, SWHA.

92 "Are Interracial Homes Bad for Children?," Ebony.

93 Kandice Chuh explains that the model minority could cultivate a divisiveness that deflects attention from systemic conditions that give rise to differential advantage along various identificatory axes (including race, class, gender, and sexuality). Chuh, Imagine Otherwise, 12.

94 Photographs were used in orphanage registries at Holt, Angel's Haven, Sangrokwŏn, and Yŏngnak as early as 1956. The photographs described here are from the first five entries at the Holt Adoption Program (now Holt International Children's Services) in Seoul, where the black-and-white headshots were glued onto notepaper and kept in three-ring binders.

Ulrich Baer's approach to seeing photographs of trauma—of witnessing and looking to find the spectral evidence embedded within them—guides my reading of these photographs. Baer, Spectral Evidence.

PART III. ERASING EMPIRE

1 For example, see Irma Tehnant Materi, "A Night in a Keesang House," in *Irma and the Hermit: My Life in Korea* (New York: Norton, 1949), 212–28.

2 Yuh, *Beyond the Shadow of Camptown*, 17; Enloe, *Bananas, Beaches and Bases*, 84–91.

3 Authorities had to address the pervasive deterioration of US military courtesy toward Koreans. GIs viewed the women as expressly there to entertain them. Seungsook Moon, "Regulating Desire," 43.

4 Ibid., 42; Yuh, *Beyond the Shadow of Camptown*, 17–19. The Japanese military forced Korean, Filipino, and Chinese women to act as "comfort women" for its soldiers during World War II. Soh, *Comfort Women*, 4.

5 Yuh, *Beyond the Shadow of Camptown*, 19–20.

6 Grant E. Meade, *American Military Government in Korea* (New York: King's Crown, 1951), quoted in Seungsook Moon, "Regulating Desire," 45.

7 Enloe, *Maneuvers*, 40.

8 Yuh, *Beyond the Shadow of Camptown*, 30.

9 The ISS president of the board of directors explained that because of the "low status of women and the very limited opportunities" for them, many Korean women turned to prostitution. Morris Hadley, president, board of directors, ISS, to Paul Cherney, "Visit to Korea—June 23–July 9, 1965," Box 35, Folder 2, SW109, SWHA. Also see Katherine H. S. Moon, *Sex among Allies*, 3; Enloe, *Maneuvers*, 39; Ahn, "Double Exposure of the War"; Yuh, *Beyond the Shadow of Camptown*, 30–32; and Cumings, "Silent but Deadly."

10 Lie, "Transformation of Sexual Work," 316.

11 Enloe, *Maneuvers*, 39; Yuh, *Beyond the Shadow of Camptown*, 24–25. With 400,000 to 600,000 American soldiers in US-occupied Japan starting in 1945, the Japanese Home Ministry arranged prostitution in the Recreation and Amusement Association to protect "respectable" Japanese women from rape. Nakamura, "Families Precede Nation and Race?," 37.

12 Yuh, *Beyond the Shadow of Camptown*, 21–22; Katherine H. S. Moon, *Sex among Allies*, 84–103; Cho, *Haunting the Korean Diaspora*, 106–9.

13 UN Civil Affairs monthly summaries 1952, November 1952, p. 50, RG 550, Box 75, Folder "USAFF-Statistical Data 1952 to 'Fight Cold War,'" NA.

14 John L. Murray, "Off Limits Areas," September 14, 1956, RG 338, Box 643, Folder 250.2, NA.

15 One Korean journalist described the need to halt the practice to "salvage the integrity and ways of Korean women." "Yanggongju dŭngnokche" [State registration for Yankee princesses (prostitutes)], *Kyŏnghyang sinmun*, January 29, 1953, 2. Newspapers also reported on the rising problem of STDs. "Sŏngbyŏng tŏuktŏ manyŏn" [STD patients increasing], *Dong-A Ilbo*, January 14, 1956, 3; "Yanggongju dansokkanghwa" [Enforcing harsher regulations against prostitutes], *Kyŏnghyang sinmun*, March 23, 1954, 2.

16 This was the language used in a Korean newspaper reporting on the increase in prostitution and the damage that it inflicted on the military. "Nŭrŏganŭn ch'angnyŏ" [Increase in prostitutes], *Kyŏnghyang sinmun*, March 25, 1956. Journalists also blamed city girls for their indecent interest in American men. "Kwabunhanmomch'arim samgara ilbunamyŏdaehaksaengdŭre cheyŏn" [College girls should refrain from wearing revealing clothes], *Kyŏnghyang sinmun*, September 13, 1955, 2.

17 "Report of Meeting with Dr. Pierce of World Vision," SWHA.

18 Höhn and Moon, "Introduction," 11.

19 Lie, "Transformation of Sexual Work," 316.

20 "GI Guard in Korea Kills Woman Thief," *New York Times*, October 6, 1957, 16. In 1957, Korean newspapers reported that US soldiers killed seventy civilians (including four women and a three-year-old boy) since they signed the armistice on July 23, 1953. Another report stated that eighty-eight people, including eleven women, had been wounded in 158 separate incidents. "Sŏurŭn Mi'gukŭi chumsurŭl maekyŏta" [Seoul scores US], *Dong-A Ilbo*, October 7, 1957. "Chŭnginshimmun kyesong migun yŏinsarhaesagŏn" [US soldier kills woman], *Kyŏnghyang sinmun*, June 21, 1958, 2. Bruce Cumings describes the regular assaults upon young girls and women in camptowns. Cumings, "Silent but Deadly," 171–73.

21 "Chonsŭn hasa chongshinhyŏng" [US soldier charged with life imprisonment in Korea], *Dong-A Ilbo*, November 19, 1956, 3.

22 "Sarinbanghwa mibyŏngch'ep'o" [Killed and set on fire—US soldier arrested], *Dong-A Ilbo*, June 12, 1958, 5.

23 "GI Convicted of Slaying a Korean," *Los Angeles Times*, December 8, 1958, 32.

24 "Ch'angyŏsakpalsagŏnbonhoeŭi pihwa" [Shaving prostitutes' hair], *Dong-A Ilbo*, January 12, 1960, 1.

25 "Migunŭi p'ok'haeng tto saenggyŏnne" [Another assault by US soldier], *Kyŏnghyang sinmun*, April 30, 1957, 3; "Changdananmatnŭn hanmihaptongsusa, migunhŏnbyŏnggwa kongmohan kunyongyŏlch'asagŏn" [Korean Army and US Army unable to cooperate], *Dong-A Ilbo*, April 21, 1957, 3.

26 "Ch'ŏlchomang chubyŏn migunbudaech'onŭi hyŏnshil" [Koreans on the other side of US military barbed wire], *Dong-A Ilbo*, July 23, 1962, 3.

CHAPTER 5. MIXED-RACE CHILDREN AND THEIR KOREAN MOTHERS

1 Mrs. T. to President Rhee, April 27, 1956, Reel P-2, Section 18, Foreign Overseas Adoptions, MoFA.

2 Stoler, *Along the Archival Grain*, 106–11.

3 To borrow A. Naomi Paik's conceptualization of "rightlessness," Korean adoptees were deemed worthy because of the devalued existence of Korean mothers and their mixed-race children in South Korea. The "rightless" are thus a necessary condition of those with rights. Paik, *Rightlessness*, 4.

4 "Chŏnjaeng goanŭn ŏdirogana?" [Where are the war orphans going?], *Dong-A Ilbo*, November 28, 1954; "Chŏnjaeng goa 10-man" [100,000 war orphans], *Kyŏnghyang sinmun*, March 1, 1952.

5   Y. T. Pyun, Korean consulate, San Francisco, to Myo Mook Lee, minister, Korean legation, London, June 22, 1955, File 553, Part VII, Rhee Papers.

6   "Koarŭl wihan jip" [Making homes for orphans], *Chosŏn Ilbo*, November 8, 1956, 3.

7   "Such'unmyŏng koa" [A thousand orphans], *Chosŏn Ilbo*, November 10, 1956, 3.

8   "Han'guk chŏnjaeng koa" [Korean war orphans], *Chosŏn Ilbo*, September 7, 1962, 3; "Herald's Relay: Mendicant Mentality," *Korean Herald*, January 23, 1968; "Haeoeyangjaalsŏn chomdŏ seshimhage" [Strictly monitoring overseas adoptions], *Kyŏnghyang sinmun*, September 20, 1972, 6.

9   "Saranghanŭn gachogŭl ch'akko issnŭn koadŭl" [Orphans looking for a loving family], *Chosŏn Ilbo*, April 24, 1963, 7. Due to the importance of familial bloodlines, domestic adoptions were rare; Kim Don Yŏng, interview by author; Shin Dong Han, interview by author.

10 China, Mongolia, Japan, and the United States had all, at one point, occupied Korea. For more on foreign presence in Korea, see Yur-Bok Lee, "A Korean View." Korean welfare professionals explained that while their women were "defiled," the children born as a result of Chinese and Japanese invasion could pass as Korean. "Welfare of Mixed-Blood Children," p. 2, SWHA.

11 Nak Choong Kim, "Children Born Outside of Marriage," in Children's Survey Sub-Committee et al., *Handicapped Children's Survey*; and Lois McCarthy, director, Department of Child Welfare, Oregon, to Margaret A. Valk, June 6, 1957, Box 34, Folder 20, SW109, SWHA. For a discussion of recent discriminatory laws and policies against mixed-race people in Korea, see Mary Lee, "Mixed Race Peoples," 59.

12 Won, "Study on Korean Adoption Policy," 43; Syngman Rhee to Young Han Choo, December 3, 1953, File 547, Folder "February 1954," Part I, Rhee Papers.

13 Lucile L. Chamberlin to Susan Pettiss, March 23, 1956, Box 10, Folder 29, SW109, SWHA; Social Welfare Society, *5 Decades of SWS*, 18–20; Augusta Mayerson to Helen Wilson, "Adoption of Korean Orphans," February 25, 1953, Box 18, Folder 126/2/01 "Child Welfare," UNKRA 1950–1960, UN.

14 Charles Grutzner, "A Few GIs Abuse Koreans in Seoul," *New York Times*, December 20, 1950, 4; "GI Held in 2 Korean Slayings," *New York Times*, May 29, 1953, 2. Korean women often did not report cases of sexual assault by UN servicemen for fear of bringing shame upon themselves and their families. Though the assaults were not spoken about openly, Koreans were aware of them. Ahn Junghyo's novel *Silver Stallion* chronicles the life of a war widow who was raped by two UN soldiers and subsequently ostracized by Korean villagers. With no other recourse, the widow turned to prostitution in order to support and feed her children. Though a fictional story, it was based on the author's memories of US occupation and the war. Ahn recalled adults telling him that Americans were good and how they cheered for them during the day, but that at night American soldiers would venture into the villages to rape the women. Ahn, *Silver Stallion*; and Ahn, "Double Exposure of the War."

15 Chakerian, *Changing Scene*, 19–20.

16 Social Welfare Society, *5 Decades of SWS*, 18–19.

17 Chae Yu Choi to Dr. Howard L. Brooks, director, American-Korean Foundation activities in Korea, March 29, 1956, Reel P-2, Section 18, 1390/1485.4, Foreign Overseas Adoptions, MoFA.

18 Social Welfare Society, *5 Decades of SWS*, 18–20.

19 "An Airlift for 89 Orphans Flies Korean Children 'Home'to US," *New York Times*, December 18, 1956, 33.

20 "Welfare of Mixed-Blood Children," table 2, p. 6, SWHA.

21 Cable from Ambassador Yang to Syngman Rhee, c. January 6, 1959, Reel P-2, Section 18, 1390/1485.4, Foreign Overseas Adoptions, MoFA. The South Korean government also praised Bob Pierce, Pearl Buck, and Howard Rusk for their work with Korean orphans and mixed-race children. "Segyegi dokkyosŏnmyŏnghoe P'il paksae kamsajang" [Certificate of appreciation awarded to Dr. Pierce], *Dong-A Ilbo*, November 4, 1958, 3; "Sajinŭn koarŭl tolbonŭn p'ŏlbŏng yŏsa" [Photograph of Mrs. Pearl Buck taking care of orphans], *Dong-A Ilbo*, November 19, 1956, 4; "Haeng'unŭi Yŏlsoe Chŭngjŏng Rŏsŭk'ŭssi buch'ŏe" ["Key of Fortune" awarded to Rusk], *Kyŏnghyang sinmun*, March 14, 1953, 2. Koreans commemorated Harry Holt when he passed away. "Irhŏbŏrin koaŭi abŏji" [Father of the forgotten orphans], *Kyŏnghyang sinmun*, April 29, 1964, 3.

22 Dorothy M. Frost, memorandum, November 25, 1958, p. 2, Box 10, Folder 31, SW109, SWHA.

23 Youm, "Press Freedom under Constraints," 869–70.

24 "Ibyang bumoga P'orinarŭl sarangsŭrupke kirŭkoisŭm" [Adoptive parents give love and properly raise orphan Paulina], *Chosŏn Ilbo*, June 10, 1958, 2. News of successful mixed-race placements circulated in South Korea. "Yangyŏn maetko tomihan mui honhyŏlgoa soshik" [Update regarding mixed-race children], March 11, 1957, 3.

25 Sheldon Reed to Mr. Wilbur, December 2, 1957, Box 10, Folder 39, SW109, SWHA. Reed was the author of *Counseling in Medical Genetics* (Philadelphia: W. B. Saunders, 1955). In the 1950s, the views of geneticists, scientists, sociologists, and other specialists varied widely on the topic of race mixture. In 1952 American sociologist Diana Tead synthesized the UNESCO series "The Race Question in Modern Science" to discredit the linkage between race, blood, biology, and culture. She wrote that while some feared that race mixture would lead to "unfortunate biological results," studies proved that there were "no grounds for such fears." Tead, *What Is Race?*, 66.

26 For discussions on race and blood, see Saks, "Representing Miscegenation Law," 47; Pascoe, *What Comes Naturally*; and Haney López, *White by Law*. For an early example of a study that linked race to blood, see Samuel A. Cartwright, "Report on the Diseases and Peculiarities of the Negro Race," *New Orleans Medical and Surgical Journal* 7 (May 1851): 691–713.

27 Yuh, *Beyond the Shadow of Camptown*, 27–28; Katherine H. S. Moon, *Sex among Allies*, 85–92.

28 The earliest recorded case that I found was from Holt International Children's Services dated June 3, 1954; Registry Record No. 4, Holt International.

29 The categories appeared on forms at Holt International Children's Services, Sangrokwŏn Child Care Center, and Yŏngnak Orphanage; all three of these wartime orphanages, located in Seoul, were linked to and partially supported by the United States. "16ire chŏndalshik hapshimwŏne ibalgidŭng" [On the 16th, orphanage received an array of supplies from US donors], *Dong-A Ilbo*, May 26, 1959.

30 Handwritten descriptions often appeared next to photographs of mixed-race children in orphanage registries and files. For example, Registry Record No. 4, June 3, 1954, Holt International.

31 "Dental Record," c. 1959, Administrative Records, Yŏngnak Orphanage; "Dr. Bang's Dental Clinic," January 1971, Administrative Records, Sangrokwŏn Orphanage.

32 Melosh, *Strangers and Kin*, 94–95.

33 Child born February 10, 1953, Box 167, Case 37317, SW109.2 ISS, SWHA.

34 This language can be seen across numerous materials. "Child Report," April 14, 1964, Holt International; "Handicapped Report," April 1, 1964, child born October, 17, 1962, Holt International.

35 *Cong. Rec.*, 84th Cong., 1st sess., June 30, 1955, Miscellaneous Reports on Private Bills, Vol. 5, No. 11: S1216.

36 Oak Soon Hong to Bessie C. Irvin, April 20, 1955, p. 2, Box 10, Folder 37, SW109, SWHA.

37 "Welfare of Mixed-Blood Children," pp. 5–7, SWHA.

38 Cho Kyu Hwan, interview with author.

39 "Chŏn'gugŭi honhyŏra Migugimink'i-ro" [Transferring all mixed-race children to US], *Kyŏnghyang sinmun*, August 8, 1954, 3; "Honhyŏrach'uryangbangan" [Planning to transport all mixed-race children], *Dong-A Ilbo*, March 31, 1961, 3; "Honhyŏraŭi Migugibyang sŏdullŏ" [Rush to send off all mixed-race children to US], *Dong-A Ilbo*, June 16, 1961, 3; "Ch'ŏn-si, kodoksogŭi Han'gugŭi honhyŏra" [Lonely and disregarded children in Korea], *Kyŏnghyang sinmun*, May 1, 1965, 6; "Honhyŏradong 5-baekmyŏng padŭlt'ŏ" [Plan to adopt 500 mixed-race orphans], *Kyŏnghyang sinmun*, March 30, 1956, 3; "Honhyŏra 80-myŏng ch'ŏshi ibyang" [First migration of 80 mixed-race children], *Kyŏnghyang sinmun*, October 31, 1957, 2; "Han'guk honhyŏlgoa 650-myŏng ibyang" [Adoption of 650 Korean mixed-race children], *Dong-A Ilbo*, January 26, 1958, 3; "Han'guk honhyŏra 90-myŏng derigo sanghangdoch'agyejŏng" [Holt set to bring 90 Korean mixed-race orphaned children to the US], *Kyŏnghyang sinmun*, December 11, 1956, 3; "Oeguk honhyŏra sŏnbal suyongsoshinsŏl ch'ujin" [Center needed to gather mixed-race children], *Kyŏnghyang sinmun*, May 21, 1955, 3. Korean newspapers also promoted the adoption of mixed-race children to non-US countries. "P'aragwairodo ibyang

450-myŏng mokp'yoro" [Targeting to send 450 orphans to Paraguay], *Kyŏnghyang sinmun*, February 26, 1964, 4. Newspapers also reported on the financial strains caused by mixed-race children, though it was more accurately all institutionalized children who contributed to postwar economic pressures. "Honhyŏlgoa yangyukpi" [Mixed-race children fostering expense], *Kyŏnghyang sinmun*, September 24, 1954, 2.

40 Oak Soon Hong to ISS, October 1956, Box 166, Case 36585, SW109.2, SWHA.

41 Their first adopted son, Yi In-su, was the son of Li Ki-bung, who ran for vice president in 1956 and lost. Historians suggest that Li and his wife convinced the Rhees to adopt their son with the hopes of bolstering their political power. Kenneth B. Lee, *Korea and East Asia*, 190.

42 Marcia J. Speers to Florence Boester, June 25, 1957, Box 34, Folder 20, SW109, SWHA.

43 Francesca Donner to Pearl Buck, February 21, 1957, Reel P-2, Section 18, 1390/1485.4, Foreign Overseas Adoptions, MoFA.

44 "Report of Meeting with Dr. Pierce of World Vision," SWHA.

45 Solinger, *Pregnancy and Power*, 150–53; Solinger, *Wake Up Little Susie*; Fessler, *Girls Who Went Away*.

46 Social workers described how it was more difficult to uproot an older child from Korea than a young child or infant. Margaret A. Valk to Oak Soon Hong, November 12, 1954, Box 166, Case 36441, SW109.2, SWHA; December 29, 1954–June 1955, Box 167, Case 37097, SW109.2, SWHA.

47 Statement by Chang Whan Sohn, January 19, 1959, Reel P-1, 457/1486, Koa kuho [Orphan Relief], 1958–59, MoFA. In another letter, Minister Chang states that the "general attitude of Korean custom" is that illegitimate children would "never [be] accepted as normal," and that those who appeared mixed would have a "harder social life" should they stay in the "home land." He concludes, "In consideration of these point [sic] most of the mothers come to the conclusion that they should give up their children for adoption by American homes where there should be no such a problem and the children's future will be a much more brilliant than here under normal home life and love given by both parents." Statement by Chang Whan Sohn, January 13, 1959, Reel P-2, Section 18, 1390/1485.4, Foreign Overseas Adoptions, MoFA.

48 Shin Dong Han, interview with author; Kang Ji Yŏng, interview with author.

49 Cho Kyu Hwan, interview with author; Report from Florence Boester for the International Council Meeting, Geneva, May 31 to June 1, 1957, Box 4, Folder 6, SW109, SWHA.

50 Speers to Boester, June 25, 1957.

51 Talisman wrote that Holt and Swedish adoption agencies visited Seoul Babies Home once a week to see whether there were any available children and that "the scene [was] competitive." S. Talisman, "Report on Visit to Korea, June 24–July 2, 1968," p. 5, Box 34, Folder 18, SW109, SWHA.

52 Frost, memorandum, November 25, 1958. For missionaries convincing mothers that the United States was more racially tolerant, see Marcia Speers to Susan Pettiss, October 15, 1957, Box 10, Folder 31, SW109, SWHA. Korean social worker Han Hyun Sook, who worked for the ISS in Korea, recalled that the ISS had three cars that it would use to visit camptowns to find mixed-race children. Han, *Many Lives Intertwined*, 98–99.

53 Korean Social Services continued to pressure the mothers of mixed-race children to surrender children at a younger age, convinced that there was no future for these children in South Korea. The ISS assessed that Korean Social Services did not present the mothers with alternatives to intercountry adoptions. "ISS Report on Korea 1968," p. 10, SWHA.

54 Marcia J. Williams to Margaret A. Valk, May 9, 1958, Box 34, Folder 21, SW109, SWHA.

55 Han, *Many Lives Intertwined*, 98–99.

56 The Pearl Buck Foundation was accused of giving mothers four dollars for relinquishing their mixed-race children, a practice that the ISS feared put a "premium on producing illegitimate children." "Report on Activities of Pearl Buck Foundation," Box 17, Folder 2, SW109, SWHA. Hoping to garner additional government funding, some orphanages paid mothers of "illegitimate children" to care for their children. Susan Pettiss to Roberta Rindfleisch, director, child welfare division, Department of Public Welfare, Minnesota, December 2, 1958, Box 10, Folder 31, SW109, SWHA.

57 Susan Pettiss, "Report Regarding a Meeting with Dr. Rho," June 6, 1958, Box 34, Folder 21, SW109, SWHA.

58 Margaret A. Valk to Marcia J. Williams, May 14, 1958, Box 34, Folder 21, SW109, SWHA. Susan Pettiss of the ISS wrote that an "unmarried mother deserves an opportunity to make her decision about her child's future without pressure and with help in being comfortable about her decision once it is made." Susan Pettiss, "Adoption by Proxy," *Child Welfare*, October 1955.

59 Margaret A. Valk to Oak Soon Hong, January 11, 1955, Box 167, SW109.2, SWHA.

60 "ISS Program for Selection of Children for Adoption under the Refugee Relief Act," June 21, 1954, Box 3, Folder 4, SW109, SWHA.

61 Yngvesson, "'Un Niño de Cualquier Color.'"

62 Valk to Oak Soon Hong, January 11, 1955.

63 Foreign Country Adoption Immigration Permit Paper, Holt International.

64 Relinquishment form, Record 251, Administrative Records, Holt International.

65 "Welfare of Mixed-Blood Children," tables 1 and 2, pp. 4 and 6, SWHA.

66 Valk felt it important that the adoptive couple understand the "closeness of [the] little girl to her natural mother." Margaret A. Valk to Oak Soon Hong, January 11, 1955, Box 167, SW109.2 ISS, SWHA; Box 20, Case 37133; Paul R. Cherney to Morris Hadley, "re: Visit to Korea, June 23–July 9, 1965," p. 15, Box 35, Folder 2, SW109, SWHA.

67 In 1956 a Japanese caseworker requested photographs of the child with her new family to help a Japanese birth mother cope with her loss. "Pictures mean a great deal to our mothers who have given up their children," she explained to the ISS. Kimi Tamura to Margaret A. Valk, "Assistance for Japanese American Orphans," July 16, 1956, Box 167, Case 37163, SW109.2, SWHA.

68 Graves, "Domesticating Foreign Affairs," 221.

69 Crystal Breeding to Geraldine Pogacer, January 25, 1957, ISS, SWHA.

70 In her autobiography, Pak Ok-sun describes how she was conceived when her mother was raped by a white American soldier in 1946. In order to raise her, her mother began to work in military prostitution and moved them both to a town where no one knew them. Seungsook Moon describes the autobiography in "Regulating Desire," 39–40.

71 Han, *Many Lives Intertwined*, 99.

72 "Welfare of Mixed-Blood Children," table 2, p. 6, SWHA; "Haeoeibyang-gil mak'in honhyŏra" [Adoptions for mixed-race children abroad blocked], *Kyŏnghyang sinmun*, March 13, 1963, 7; "Taeriyangjajep'yeji" [Proxy adoption halted], *Kyŏnghyang sinmun*, October 20, 1961, 3. Korean newspapers also informed readers that though the laws had changed, there were still ways to send mixed-race children abroad. "Honhyŏraŭi Migugibyang ap'ŭro-do kyesok" [Sending mixed-race children to US continues], *Kyŏnghyang sinmun*, July 28, 1961, 2.

73 "Meeting of Child Welfare Experts: Intercountry Adoptions," p. 5, January 31, 1963, Box 10, Folder 36, SW109, SWHA.

74 Cherney to Hadley, "re: Visit to Korea, June 23–July 9, 1965."

75 Of the mixed-race children remaining in South Korea, 1,097 were "Caucasian-Korean" and 306 "Negroid-Korean." Hurh, "Marginal Children of War," 14–15. Paul Cherney of the ISS estimated five thousand mixed-race children in South Korea. Cherney to Hadley, "re: Visit to Korea, June 23–July 9, 1965."

76 Anne Davison to Susan Pettiss, November 23, 1961, Box 34, Folder 24, SW109, SWHA.

77 Children's Survey Sub-Committee et al., *Handicapped Children's Survey*, 112. The study cost over 9,175,500 hwan (the equivalent of about US$7,000). Administrators made 400,000 survey forms in anticipation of the great number of disabled children in postwar Korea. The AKF, KAVA, and other agencies contributed to the printing costs. Davison to Pettiss, November 23, 1961. The Korean press commended the survey. "Chwadamhoe pulgujado in'ganida chŏn'guge changaeadong 8-man" [Meeting about the 80,000 handicapped children of Korea], *Dong-A Ilbo*, March 1, 1962, 4.

78 "Introduction," in Children's Survey Sub-Committee et al., *Handicapped Children's Survey*, 14–16.

79 Though Korean professionals outnumbered US ones, the manual reflected the heavy handiwork of the United States. US Reverend George M. Carroll of KAVA trained Korean social workers for the survey. The study was funded in part by the following non-Korean sources: Pearl S. Buck, Aid to the Blind in Korea, Ameri-

can Korean Foundation, Anglican Church in Korea, Canadian Save the Children Fund, Cardinal Francis Spellman, Catholic Relief Services, Chaplain's Fund of the 5th Cavalry Division of 8th US Army, Christian Children's Fund, Foster Parents Plan, International Social Service, Church World Service, Methodist Committee for Overseas Relief, Mission to Lepers, Oriental Missionary Society, Oxford Committee on Famine Relief, Remington Rand International, Salvation Army, Save the Children Fund, YWCA, United Church of Canada, United Presbyterian Church, USA, United States Operations Mission to Korea Women's Club, Mr. Dale Weaver, and World Vision. Children's Survey Sub-Committee et al., *Handicapped Children's Survey*, 5–6.

80 Lucile L. Chamberlin, "Objectives of the Children's Survey of Korea," in Children's Survey Sub-Committee et al., *Handicapped Children's Survey*, 30.

81 Information gathering allowed governments to monitor and thus better discipline their subjects. This US practice was first employed in South Korea during the Occupation period from 1945 to 1948, when US administrators gathered monthly statistics on South Korea's population. Tracking everything from disease rates in various prefectures to the membership numbers of political factions across the countryside, the Supreme Commander of the Allied Powers and Armed Forces Assistance to Korea produced detailed reports with tables presenting the latest statistical data. The techniques used and the kind of information gathered for the *Survey* replicated the methods of the US government, reflecting the shared tactics of colonial governments and the private sector. For colonial statecraft, see Stoler, *Along the Archival Grain*, 28–30, 100–102, especially the discussion of the European Pauperism Commission, 142–44; and Anderson, *Imagined Communities*, 163–86.

82 Korean social workers explained that though ethnic race mixture resulting from past foreign invasions did "harm the pride of [the Korean] race," the "same complexion" of ethnically mixed Korean-Chinese and Korean-Japanese children "did not present any social problem[s]." "Welfare of Mixed-Blood Children," p. 2, SWHA.

83 "Instructions for Conducting the Survey," in Children's Survey Sub-Committee et al., *Handicapped Children's Survey*, 86–93; copy of questionnaire on 91; Hum Yun, "Scope, Design and Instructions for the Survey," ibid., 79–85.

84 Wailoo, *Drawing Blood*, 13.

85 Anne M. Davison, "The Mixed Racial Child," in Children's Survey Sub-Committee et al., *Handicapped Children's Survey*, 72.

86 Soon Yung Kwon, "Handicapped Children and Juvenile Delinquency," in Children's Survey Sub-Committee et al., *Handicapped Children's Survey*, 66, 64.

87 Wacquant, "Wedding of Workfare and Prisonfare," 242.

88 Nak Choong Kim, "Children Born outside of Marriage," in Children's Survey Sub-Committee et al., *Handicapped Children's Survey*, 69.

89 Soon Yung Kwon, "Handicapped Children and Juvenile Delinquency," in Children's Survey Sub-Committee et al., *Handicapped Children's Survey*, 66.

90 "Welfare of Mixed-Blood Children," table 1, p. 4, SWHA; Molly Holt, interview by author.

91 For examinations of US boarding schools for Native American and African American children, see Wexler, *Tender Violence*; Margaret D. Jacobs, *White Mother to a Dark Race;* Adams, *Education for Extinction;* Fear-Segal and Rose, *Carlisle Indian Industrial School;* and Mitchell, "Shadows of Assimilation."

92 Molly Holt, interview by author.

93 "Korean War Orphans," *Chosŏn Ilbo.*

94 Several schools and orphanages for mixed-race children were built after the war. "Honhyŏrae nangbo Sangdodonge pohowŏn'gŏllip" [Good news, facility for mixed-race children built in Sangdo-dong], *Kyŏnghyang sinmun,* September 19, 1955, 3; "Honhyŏragyoyukkigwan Yŏnghwakukmin'gyorŭl shinsŏl" [Newly established Yŏnghwakukmin education institution for mixed-race children], *Dong-A Ilbo,* August 28, 1962, 8; "Yŏngŏshillyŏgi chunghaksaeng saejipkatkedoen honhyŏrahakkyo" [Middle school established for English-speaking mixed-race children], *Kyŏnghyang sinmun,* November 30, 1962, 3; "Sŏuryŏnghwagungminhakkyoesŏ chŭlgŏpkenolgoinnŭn honhyŏradŭl" [Mixed-race children play happily at Seoul English Elementary School], *Kyŏnghyang sinmun,* May 1, 1963. This article included a photograph of Korean-white and Korean-black children playing on a bunk bed, an image that communicated that the children were well cared for.

95 ECLAIR, pamphlet, Box 35, Folder 1, SW109, SWHA.

96 George P. Whitener to supporters of ECLAIR, February 26, 1964, p. 2, Box 35, Folder 2, SW109, SWHA.

97 Untitled note, Box 35, Folder 2, SW109, SWHA. An ISS caseworker was assigned to each child enrolled in ECLAIR. "Notes on ISS Korea," June 15, 1961, p. 8, Box 34, Folder 22, SW109, SWHA.

98 Gardner Munro to Paul Cherney, November 23, 1965, Box 35, Folder 2, SW109, SWHA. Child Placement Service changed its name to Social Welfare Society in 1964, reflecting the shift away from adoption and toward domestic welfare.

99 Claire Lee, "Hard Knock Lives."

100 "Korean War Orphans," *Chosŏn Ilbo.*

101 "Welfare of Mixed-Blood Children," p. 9, SWHA.

102 Adoptee interview with author (name withheld at request of the interviewee), Seoul, Korea, October 2005.

103 "ISS Report on Korea 1968," 11, SWHA.

104 Ibid.

105 Stoler, *Along the Archival Grain,* 137–39.

106 Bob Pierce of World Vision felt that it was "too easy" for GIs to not acknowledge paternity or support mixed-race children. He wanted to pressure the military in Korea "to force the American fathers to some accountability for the children." "Report of Meeting with Dr. Pierce of World Vision," SWHA.

107 The US Department of Defense worked with the ISS and other voluntary agencies to create a pamphlet aimed to either encourage men to adopt their own children or find homes for the children rather than abandoning them outright. Office of Armed Forces Information and Education Department of Defense, "Manual on Intercountry Adoption," Box 23, Folder 23, SW109, SWHA.

108 Enloe, *Bananas, Beaches and Bases; Maneuvers.*

CHAPTER 6. MANAGING KOREAN WAR BRIDES

1 "A War Bride Named 'Blue' Comes Home," *Life*, November 5, 1951, 40–41. During the war, news of the "first" Korean war brides reached Americans. See, for example, "Brings Home Korean War Bride," *Chicago Daily Tribune*, October 19, 1951, 3; "Korean GI Bride," *Chicago Daily Tribune*, July 30, 1951, A1; and "First GI Bride of Korean War Heads for US," *Chicago Daily Tribune*, July 23, 1951.

2 Bok-Lim C. Kim, "Asian Wives of US Servicemen," 99. Statistics from US Commissioner of Immigration and Naturalization, *Annual Reports, 1947–75*, table 6, Washington, DC.

3 Bok-Lim C. Kim, "Casework with Japanese and Korean Wives," 273n2. During this period, 330,975 European women entered as military brides. Between June 22, 1947, and December 31, 1952, 10,517 American citizens, principally armed service personnel, married Japanese women. Over 75 percent of the men were Anglo-American. Strauss, "Strain and Harmony," 280n1.

4 Daniel Boo-Duck Lee, "Korean American Women," 97.

5 Enloe, *Maneuvers*, 160; Seungsook Moon, "Regulating Desire," 44.

6 Friedman, *From the Battlefront to the Bridal Suite*, 26–27. For a discussion of British military brides, see Virden, *Good-Bye, Piccadilly.*

7 Nakamura, "Families Precede Nation and Race?," 4.

8 Ibid., 36–37. The 1790 Naturalization Act excluded Asians from naturalization. These laws were lifted piecemeal in the 1940s. In 1943 the Magnuson Act repealed the Chinese Exclusion Act, granted 105 visas to Chinese immigrants per year, and gave them naturalization rights. In 1946 the Luce-Cellar Act ended exclusion and extended naturalization rights to Filipino and Asian-Indian immigrants (while Filipinos were allowed to enter the country in spite of the 1924 Immigration and Nationality Act that banned the entry of other Asians, the Tydings-McDuffie Act of 1934 restricted their entry to fifty persons per year). The 1952 McCarran-Walter Act eliminated race as a basis of naturalization, but continued to severely limit the entry of immigrants to about 100 visas per Asian group per year.

9 For the process involving Japanese brides, see Nakamura, "Families Precede Nation and Race?," 38–45; and Koshiro, *Trans-Pacific Racisms*, 156–58.

10 Bok-Lim C. Kim, "Asian Wives of US Servicemen," 97. Numerous cases report that tours of duty ended before the men could complete the application process, at which point many abandoned the effort to marry Japanese and Korean nationals. RG 338, Box 644, Folder "Marriage Documents, 1956," NA. Similar strategies were

used for men in the European theater during World War II. In 1942 US military authorities notified chaplain corps that any soldier seeking permission to marry abroad was to be counseled against it. Friedman, *From the Battlefront to the Bridal Suite*, 27–28, 88. Also see Virden, *Good-Bye, Piccadilly*, 32–33.

11 Use of extracts from the family register was grounds for refusal; original and complete documents had to be submitted. L. E. McNutt, memorandum to commanding officer, April 30, 1956, RG 338, Box 644, Folder "Marriage Documents 291.1," NA.

12 "Marriages between American Citizens and Korean Citizens (Nationals)," November 28, 1951, pp. 1–2, RG 338, Box 491, Folder "Marriage Documents 291.1," NA.

13 Correspondence dated July 5, 1956, RG 338, Box 645, Folder 5 "Marriage Documents 291.1," NA.

14 Yuh, *Beyond the Shadow of Camptown*, 46–47.

15 Thornton, "Quiet Immigration."

16 Ota, "Private Matters," 216.

17 December 1956 to June 1959, Box 175, Case 41694, SW109.2, SWHA. In one example, an American serviceman wanted to bring his pregnant fiancée to the United States. The woman was Japanese but working in Korea. Because visas from Korea and Japan were oversubscribed, he would have to return to Korea to marry her there in order for her to immigrate. In the end, he never married his fiancée.

18 George A. McGee Jr., colonel, memorandum, 1958, RG 338, Box 519, Folder 291.1, NA.

19 Robert H. Shell, adjutant general, "Special Interest in Marriage," March 12, 1956, RG 338, Box 643, Folder 291.1, NA.

20 "Legal Implications of Marrying an Alien," November 18, 1955; application for marriage between US serviceman and Korean national, May 11, 1956, RG 338, Box 644, Folder 291.1, NA.

21 Chaplain Dreford J. Devoto, March 3, 1956, RG 338, Box 644, Folder 291.1, NA.

22 RG 338, Box 1888, Folder "Chaplains/Entry A1 234, December 1951," NA. Similar interviews where chaplains tried to persuade couples to give up their quests for marriage took place in Japan. See Nakamura, "Families Precede Nation and Race?," 38.

23 Ms. K., character reference, November 26, 1955, RG 338, Box 643, Folder 291.1, NA.

24 First quote from chief of police, November 24, 1955 (written in Korean and translated into English), RG 338, Box 643, Folder 291.1, NA; second quote from Karl H. Velde, "Background Investigation of Korean National," January 14, 1956, RG 338, Box 644, Folder 291.1, NA. In another statement, the police chief described a potential bride as expressing "clear democratic sentiment." Chief of Seoul Suh Dae Moon Police Station, Report of Police Clearance, RG 338, Box 644, Folder 291.1, NA.

25 In one application, a woman was accused of being part of the Democratic Youth League but was cleared after a background check concluded that she affiliated only to protect her family from Communists. She had two children with a "very

persistent" sergeant, and the application was approved. RG 338, Box 643, Folder 291.1, NA.

26 Bok-Lim C. Kim, "Casework with Japanese and Korean Wives of Americans," 278.

27 Application filed January 23, 1956, RG 338, Box 643, Folder 291.1, NA.

28 Report of Medical Examination was a standard form included in nearly all applications. Hung Sop Shim (translator), October 4, 1955, RG 338, Box 643, Folder 291.1, NA.

29 Most memorandums set the expiration of health exams at sixty days; however, one memo suggested that health reports were valid for six months. The Far East Command asked medical officers to "familiarize themselves with the medical aspects of the Immigration Laws of the US relative to the exclusion of mentally or physically defective or diseased aliens as contained in manual for medical examination for aliens." F. V. Gowen, "Physical Examination for Application for Marriage and Visa Application for Alien Spouse," March 8, 1952, RG 338, Box 519, Folder 291.1, NA.

30 "Marriages between American Citizens and Korean Citizens," November 28, 1951, 1–2.

31 Major General B. to Paul Douglas, August 9, 1956, pp. 1–2, RG 338, Box 65, Folder 291.1, NA.

32 John J. Binns to APO 343, "Congressional Interest in TDY for Purpose Marriage," October 22, 1956, RG 338, Box 645, Folder 291.1, NA.

33 Robert H. Shell, "Marriage of US Military Personnel to Korean Nationals," March 5, 1956, p. 1, RG 338, Box 643, Folder 291.1, NA.

34 George A. McGee to Adjutant General, "Marriage of US Military Personnel to Korean Nationals," April 2, 1956, RG 338, Box 643, Folder 291.1, NA.

35 William T. Kirk to Carter Burgees, Assistant Secretary of Defense, December 23, 1955, Box 23, Folder "US-Armed Services," SW109, SWHA.

36 Mrs. Warren C. Eveland, representative, ISS, to William T. Kirk, "Conference with Air Force Personnel Office," March 12, 1957, Box 23, Folder "Other Organizations," SW109, SWHA.

37 General Headquarters Far East Command, "Return of Brides to United States under Public Law 717," June 25, 1951, RG 338, Box 491, Folder 291.1, NA.

38 Application regarding Japanese bride as beneficiary dated July 5, 1956. Another application includes a statement declaring that the Korean bride was capable of working in the United States. RG 338, Box 644, Folder 291.1, NA.

39 Mrs. M., August 30, 1955, RG 338, Box 643, Folder 291.1, NA. Another application indicates that the serviceman's parents would take care of his spouse in the event that "anything should happen to me or I cannot find immediate employment." Application for a white serviceman and Korean woman dated June 25, 1956, RG 338, Box 519, Folder 291.1, NA.

40 An estimated 125,000 US servicemen abroad married women during World War II. While some Americans viewed the women as "gold-diggers" and others connected

them to prostitution, white war brides did not disrupt the racial status quo. Friedman, *From the Battlefront to the Bridal Suite*, 82; Zeiger, *Entangling Alliances*, 71–91.

41 Yuh, *Beyond the Shadow of Camptown*, 40. Servicemen recount their interactions with Korean women who worked in their offices. In one story, a US serviceman tells of two shy Korean girls who worked as typists in his office. Depew, "Indigenous Girls." After the war when there were few jobs and extreme poverty, women flocked to the cities to find jobs as clerks, seamstresses, waitresses, domestic workers, secretaries, and barmaids. Bok-Lim C. Kim and Michael R. Sawdey, *Women in Shadows*, 25.

42 Bok-Lim C. Kim, "Asian Wives of US Servicemen," 94–95.

43 For an examination of the film and its expression of Cold War anxiety, see Jacobson and González, *What Have They Built You to Do?*

44 Japanese-white couples captured the attention of liberal intellectuals and became a topic of interest in social science research and popular films throughout the 1950s. Many considered the couples to be a "social laboratory" that conveyed the positive possibilities of American race relations—an argument against segregation and for cultural pluralism. Zeiger, *Entangling Alliances*, 190.

45 Simpson, *Absent Presence*, 175–78.

46 McAlister, *Epic Encounters*; Klein, *Cold War Orientalism*. In her study of the United States and Brazil, Micol Seigel shows how cultural exchanges shifted conceptions of race and nation across borders. Seigel, *Uneven Encounters*.

47 These two films have been closely examined by numerous scholars, including Palumbo-Liu, *Asian/American*, 225–32; Marchetti, *Romance and the "Yellow Peril,"* 125–43, 158–75; and Robert G. Lee, *Orientals*, 161–72.

48 Geopolitics made Korea particularly unsuitable for filmmakers in the 1950s. The losses of that war and monitoring by the House Un-American Activities Committee pushed directors to steer clear of films about the still divided peninsula. Hye Seung Chung, *Hollywood Asian*, 123–24.

49 For more on masculinity in 1950s America, see May, *Homeward Bound*, 85–86; and Ehrenreich, *Hearts of Men*, 14–28.

50 Naoko Shibusawa explains how during World War II, Japanese women appeared to be hyperfeminine, childlike, and eager to please American men, a direct contrast to white American women, who were accused of wanting independence, a career, and the ability to change their men. Shibusawa, *America's Geisha Ally*, 41–47. Pate describes the exoticized links between Oriental dolls, Korean prostitutes, and orphans. Pate, *From Orphan to Adoptee*, 92–100.

51 Chester Morrison, "East Meets West . . . ," *Look*, October 29, 1957, 73–75; review of *Sayonara* by Joshua Logan, ibid., 79.

52 Review of *Japanese War Bride*, *Newsweek*, February 11, 1952, 90.

53 "Shirley Yamaguchi Tells of Japanese Married Life," *Pacific Stars and Stripes*, March 23, 1955, 9.

54 William L. Worden, "Where Are Those Japanese War Brides?," *Saturday Evening Post*, November 20, 1954, 133–34; quote on 134.

55 Nakamura, "Families Precede Nation and Race?," 79–80.
56 "GI Brides Go to School in Japan," *New York Times Magazine*, November 7, 1954, 54–56; "Brides to Enroll for Tokyo School," *Pacific Stars and Stripes*, April 1, 1955, 11.
57 Nakamura, "Families Precede Nation and Race?," 104, 131.
58 Zeiger, *Entangling Alliances*, 213.
59 Lawrence Phillips, "Report of Executive Vice President on Operations of USO-Camp," April 30, 1953 p. 30, Box 30, Folder "USO Camp Shows, General Correspondence 51–57," Young Women's Christian Association/United Service Organizations (hereafter YWCA/USO), SWHA.
60 "Bride School Opens" flyer, Taiwan, Taichung: Narrative Reports, 1968, Box 24, SWHA 065, YWCA/USO.
61 Yuh, *Beyond the Shadow of Camptown*, 70–71.
62 "Thanksgiving Buffet and Bride's School," Taegu Bride School, Box 20, Folder "Taegu, Korea: Program and Publicity," SW65, YWCA/USO, SWHA.
63 Ibid.
64 Seungsook Moon, "Regulating Desire," 58.
65 By the 1980s, as Yuh describes, women formed connections through church, on-base military bride organizations, and informal networks of friends. Yuh, *Beyond the Shadow of Camptown*, 191–92.
66 Due to its popularity, the exhibition's original end date of March 30, 1958, was extended a week; it had a total of 35,080 visitors. AKF memo from Patricia Culler, Program Division, to Dorothy Frost, April 11, 1958, Han Mi chaedan [Korean-US Cooperation] 1958, 331/758.22 US, MoFA.
67 World House Gallery showcased thirty-seven modern Korean artists from February 25 through March 22, 1958. Four hundred people attended the preview on February 25, 1958 (the number of invitations sent out were limited due to the small capacity of the galleries). In less than one month, approximately 1,700 people saw the show, and nine pieces were sold. Ibid.
68 Culler to Frost, April 11, 1958.
69 They performed on *The Ed Sullivan Show* more times than Louis Armstrong or Patti Page. Euny Hong, *Birth of Korean Cool*, 112.
70 "Blast from the Past," *Asianlife*, April 11, 2008.
71 "Three Korean Kims and Their Kayagums," *Life*, February 22, 1960, 49.
72 Klein, *Cold War Orientalism*.
73 Lee Kwon, "Interview with Sook-ja Kim," 13.
74 The Kim Sisters were followed by other Asian girl bands that were not as popular but had similar performance styles: Tokyo Happy Coats, a Philippine group called Sunspot, and, from South Korea, Patty Kim, Korean Kitten, Arirang Sisters, Lee Sisters, and Kimchi Kats. Lee Kwon, "Interview with Sook-ja Kim," 38–39; Maliangkay, "Same Look through Different Eyes," 22.
75 "Segyŏmudae chujumchamnŭn pok'ŏlt'im" [Top vocal team in the world], *Kyŏnghyang sinmun*, March 21, 1963, 8. Koreans were familiar with the American

songs performed by the Kim Sisters in large part because of American Forces Network Korea (AFNK). US radio and television channels and the records sold on the black market allowed Koreans to keep up with the latest music and dance trends from Europe and the United States. Maliangkay, "Same Look through Different Eyes," 24.

76 Teszar, "From Seoul to Las Vegas." In 1970, after twelve years overseas, the women were greeted by various celebrities and fans at the airport in Korea. "Kimshisŭt'ŏjŭ, 12-nyŏnmane kwiguk" [Kim Sisters return after 12 years], Kyŏnghyang sinmun, May 19, 1970, 7.

77 "Mi yŏnyegyejŏngsangŭl tallinŭn k'oriŏŭi sejamae, Kimshisŭt'ŏjŭŭi kŭnhwang" [Top of the entertainment industry in US, Kim Sisters], Kyŏnghyang sinmun, May 17, 1967, 8.

78 "Kimshisŭt'ŏjŭe kamsahanmi uŭi chŭngjin kongk'ŏ" [Appreciation and gratitude for the Kim Sisters], Maeil, November 25, 1967, 4.

79 "Kim Sisters."

80 Lee Kwon, "Interview with Sook-ja Kim," 8–10, 59.

81 The show claimed NBC's primetime slot on Sunday nights at 7:00 p.m. between September 1962 and May 1963. It was based on internationalist novelist William Lederer's All the Ships at Sea and Ensign O'Toole and Me, and promoted American acceptance of nonwhite others and US benevolence abroad. Lederer consulted on the show, likely ensuring that the Cold War message of American benevolence, not military power, carried through each episode. Tim Brooks and Earle Marsh, The Complete Directory to Prime Time Network and Cable Shows 1946–Present (New York: Ballantine, 2007), 423.

82 "Ensign O'Toole 1962 Full Episode Operation Benefit Dean Jones."

83 "Three Korean Kims," Life, 55.

84 Lee Kwon, "Interview with Sook-ja Kim," 23–24.

85 Ibid., 24–27, 32–33.

86 "Kimboijŭ t'ansaeng" [New vocal group—Kim Boys], Dong-A Ilbo, December 8, 1961, 4.

87 Lee Kwon, "Interview with Sook-ja Kim," 48.

88 Ibid., 12, 40–46.

89 Toki Schalk Johnson, "Toki Types: God Knows No Difference . . . ," Pittsburgh Courier, April 21, 1951, 10.

90 "Furlough Dries Tears," New York Times, March 5, 1956, 25.

91 Sociologist Bok-Lim C. Kim describes how many Asian wives of US servicemen were physically abused and isolated. Reports from Asian ethnic workers and military chaplains at military bases indicated that there was a high incidence of wife beating among military husbands. Kim goes on to explain that women could not use the existing shelters and services in the United States because of language and cultural barriers. Bok Lim C. Kim, Battered Women, 442; and Kim, "Casework with Japanese and Korean Wives," 274. Asian military brides experienced homesickness, felt estranged from their children due

to their increased exposure to English, and perceived a lack of understanding or support from their military husbands. Kim and Sawdey, *Women in Shadows*, 16–19.

92 Interviewees in Ji-Yeon Yuh's study expressed similar initial fears when remembering their arrival in the States. Yuh, *Beyond the Shadow of Camptown*.

93 "Cemetery Cleared of Refusing Burial of Korean Woman," *Chicago Daily Tribune*, January 12, 1961, D11.

CONCLUSION

1 Loomis to Margaret A. Valk, September 3, 1958, Box 173, Case 40796, SW109.2, SWHA.

2 Loomis to Margaret A. Valk, September 4, 1958, Box 173, Case 40796, SW109.2, SWHA.

3 Ibid.

4 Home visit, November 24, 1958, Box 173, Case 40796, SW109.2, SWHA.

5 Anne M. Davison to Margaret A. Valk, November 6, 1960, Box 173, Case 40796, SW109.2, SWHA.

6 Margaret A. Valk to Loomis, November 14, 1960, Box 173, Case 40796, SW109.2, SWHA.

7 Integration of the armed forces rolled out slowly and unevenly. Several "all-Negro" units remained intact during the Korean War. This changed as the war progressed, when replacing the dead or injured with soldiers of the same race proved nearly impossible. It was not until 1954 that most units were integrated, and even then it remained a hot-button issue. MacGregor, *Integration of the Armed Forces*, 458.

8 For a discussion of "mamasans" and camptown life in South Korea, see Sturdevant and Stoltzfus, *Let the Good Times Roll*, 208–39, 336.

9 Brothels were segregated to appease white US soldiers who demanded that the women uphold the same racial boundaries that existed in the States. Yuh, *Beyond the Shadow of Camptown*, 27–28; Katherine H. S. Moon, *Sex among Allies*, 71–72, 128–29. For the experiences of African American servicemen in Korea and Japan after World War II, see Green, *Black Yanks in the Pacific*; and Phillips, *War! What Is It Good For?*

10 Ch'oe, "Activities of Foreign Voluntary Agencies."

11 "Chǒnjaeng 11-nyǒn huǔi 5-man gucho'ǒnmyǒng isang mimanginkwa koadǔli ajikdo namaissda" [Eleven years since the Korean War but more than 590,000 war widows and war orphans remain], *Chosǒn Ilbo*, March 3, 1961, 3.

12 Morris Hadley to Paul Cherney, "Visit to Korea—June 23–July 9, 1965," p. 16, Box 35, Folder 2, SW109, SWHA.

13 "ISS Report on Korea 1968," 4, SWHA; Marcia J. Williams to Susan Pettiss, April 22, 1958, Box 34, Folder 21, SW109, SWHA; Susan Pettiss to Reuben E. Carlson, February 25, 1960, Box 10, Folder 14, SW109, SWHA; "Activity Report, ISS, Korea," May 22, 1963, p. 4, Box 34, Folder 24, SW109, SWHA.

14 The US military set up schools to train Koreans long-term leading up to, during, and after the war. Brazinsky, *Nation Building in South Korea*, 71–100. Immediately after the war, South Korean officials also urged the US military to stay to enforce security in the unstable peninsula. "Migunch'ŏlsujungjihara" [Stop US military from leaving], *Kyŏnghyang sinmun*, August 20, 1954, 1. Seungsook Moon shows how South Korean modernity that emerged during the Cold War was a mix of Foucauldian discipline and military violence, a pairing tied to the legacies of US imposition. Seungsook Moon, *Militarized Modernity*, 5–7.

15 Young, single Korean women from the countryside made up the majority of factory workers. A previously untapped labor source, the female workforce was expected to put in long hours plus overtime, making it challenging for women to work after marriage. These uneven conditions contributed to women workers' active role in the labor movement. Koo, *Korean Workers*, 36, 39–40, 92–99. For labor movements in the 1960s, also see Ogle, *South Korea*.

16 Hadley to Cherney, "Visit to Korea."

17 Hübinette, "Korean Adoption History," 6.

18 Arissa Oh, *To Save the Children*, 202.

19 Graves, "Domesticating Foreign Affairs," 11–12.

20 Jon Herskovitz, "S. Korea a Lonely Place for Mixed-Race Children," *Washington Post*, March 5, 2006.

21 A 1982 survey found that 95 percent of mixed-race Koreans wished to move to the United States due to social alienation and racism. Claire Lee, "Hard Knock Lives."

22 Lisa Lowe argues that because "culture is the contemporary repository of memory, of history, is it through culture, rather than government, that alternative forms of subjectivity, collectivity, and public life are imagined." Lowe continues that "it is only through culture that we conceive and enact new subjects and practices in antagonism to the regulatory *locus* of the citizen-subject." Lowe, *Immigrant Acts*, 22. Stuart Hall emphasizes that cultural identities and the histories that make them are not fixed, opening up the possibility of resistance and re-positioning. Hall, "Cultural Identity and Diaspora." Korean adoptees and military brides are doing this cultural work, altering the identities that have been imposed on them. See, for example, the work of activist-artist Mihee-Nathalie Lemoine, who produces films, painting, poetry, and photography. "Star~Kim Project." Also see paintings by Kang Tŏk-kyŏong and Kim Sun-dŏk in "Portfolio: Artwork by Former Comfort Women," *positions* 5, no. 1 (Spring 1997): 275–78; and Jieun Lee, "Performing Transnational Adoption."

23 Daniel Boo-Duck Lee, "Korean Women Married to Servicemen," 96–97.

24 Katherine H. S. Moon, *Sex among Allies*, 1.

25 Katharine H.S. Moon, "South Korean Movements," 138–39; Seungsook Moon, "Regulating Desire," 57–58. House of Grace was founded in 1960 by American Presbyterian missionary Eleanor E. Van Lierop as a home for runaway girls and prostitutes. In 1973 it became a home for unwed mothers. In 1983, when Eleanor

Van Lierop retired and returned to the United States, the General Assembly of the Presbyterian Church of Korea took over, and it was subsequently named Ae Ran Won (Planting Love). The organization receives some support from the South Korean government. Dorow, *I Wish for You a Beautiful Life*, 132. Du Rae Bang established a bakery to offer former bar women employment. Kirk and Okazawa-Rey, "Demilitarizing Security," 160. Also see Chai, "Korean Feminist and Human Rights Politics."

26 Kirk and Okazawa-Rey, "Making Connections," 312. Also see Elaine Kim and Chungmoo Choi, *Dangerous Women*.

27 Choe Sang-Hun, "South Korea Illegally Held Prostitutes Who Catered to GIs Decades Ago, Court Says," *New York Times*, January 20, 2017.

28 Yuh, *Beyond the Shadow of Camptown*, 27. For a study of South Korean military labor, including prostitution for US troops and its role in the expansive growth of the national economy, see Jin-kyung Lee, *Service Economies*.

29 Kim Min-kyung, "Court Finds That South Korean Government Encouraged Prostitution," *Hankyoreh*, February 9, 2018.

30 Étienne Balibar's "citizen subject" is useful to consider how the United States government extended US economic and political power to create a new kind of neocolonial subject in Korea during the Cold War. Citizenship in South Korea could not be separated from US military, political, and economic imposition. Balibar, *Citizen Subject*.

31 Jodi Kim, *Ends of Empire*. Also see Heonik Kwon, *Other Cold War*; and Chen, *Asia as Method*. For a study on South Korean intellectual, political, and cultural revival in the 1970s and 1980s in response to not being "subjects of their own history" and to limited civil liberties under a US-backed government, see Namhee Lee, *Making of Minjung*.

32 Dudziak, *War Time*.

33 Man, *Soldiering through Empire*, 4, 17–48.

34 Engelhardt, "Iraq as a Pentagon Construction Site," 136. As of 2001, the United States had 725 recognized overseas military bases that cost $118 billion. Johnson, *Sorrows of Empire*, 190.

35 For a historical examination of how US militarization has become the presumed path to imposing US ideas around the world, and the centrality of militarism in US culture since Vietnam, see Bacevich, *New American Militarism*.

36 Officers explain how they rebuilt hospitals and gave crayons to kids. Soldier John Thurman explains, "Infantrymen—I think by definition we're not supposed to be doing humanitarian things. . . . How are we supposed to beat the Taliban this way?" *Serial* Podcast, season 2, episode 6, "Five o' clock Shadow" (hosted by Sarah Koenig, 2015). Neda Atanasoski considers how human difference became the mode through which redemption and atrocity became coarticulated during the Vietnam War, the Soviet-Afghan War, and the 1990s wars of secession in former Yugoslavia, imperial projects recast as multicultural rescue. Atanasoski, *Humanitarian Violence*.

37 Scholars across many fields have actively and creatively addressed the uneven power dynamics of the archive. See, for example, Stoler, *Along the Archival Grain*; Lowe, *Intimacies of Four Continents*; Camp, *Closer to Freedom*; and Scott, *Domination and the Arts of Resistance*.

38 Avery Gordon, *Ghostly Matters*, 8.

39 "Korean Waif Becomes Real American Boy," *Los Angeles Times*, January 10, 1955, 19.

40 According to the article, Paladino's new wife had two children from a previous marriage and a newborn with Paladino. "Korean Orphan, 9, Gets a Fresh Start," *New York Times*, January 21, 1958, 33.

41 "Children's Choir Here from Korea," *New York Times*, April 13, 1954, 6; "Of Local Origin," *New York Times*, January 28, 1954, 24.

42 Korean adoptees, birth mothers, and military brides are telling their stories. See Trenka, *Language of Blood*; Nicole Chung, *All You Can Ever Know*; Clement, *Unforgotten War*; Arnold, *Litany for the Long Moment*; Cox, *Voices from Another Place*; Elizabeth Kim, *Ten Thousand Sorrows*; Robinson, *A Single Square Picture*; Park Nelson, *Invisible Asians*; Yuh, *Beyond the Shadow of Camptown*; and Prébin, *Meeting Once More*. For documentary films, see *First Person Plural*, *In the Matter of Cha Jung Hee*, and *Geographies of Kinship*, DVDs, directed by Deann Borshay Liem; and *Camp Arirang*, DVD, directed by Diana S. Lee and Grace Yoon Kyung Lee.

43 Lisa Cacho draws upon Derrick Bell's "racial realism" to consider how though acknowledgment of inequality and violence may not lead to "transcendent change," "the fight itself has meaning and should give us hope for the future." Cacho writes that the decision to struggle can be empowering. Cacho, *Social Death*, 32.

BIBLIOGRAPHY

ARCHIVES AND MANUSCRIPT COLLECTIONS

Korea

Angel's Haven Social Welfare Foundation. Administrative Records. Seoul.

Holt International Children's Services. Administrative Records. Seoul.

Ministry of Foreign Affairs, Seoul.

    Han Mi chaedan [Korean-US Cooperation].

    Koa kukŭi ibyang [Foreign Overseas Adoptions].

    Koa kuho [Orphan Relief].

Rhee, Syngman. Papers. Yonsei University, Seoul.

Sangrokwŏn Orphanage. Administrative Records. Seoul.

Yŏngnak Orphanage. Administrative Records. Seoul.

United States

Kurland, Gil. Collection. Margaret Herrick Library, Fairbanks Center for Motion
    Picture Study, Beverly Hills, CA.

Meals for Millions. Foundation Records. Special Collections, University of California,
    Los Angeles.

Military Photographic Collection. Schomburg Center for Research in Black Culture,
    New York Public Library.

National Archives, College Park, MD.

    Record Group 59. US Department of State.

    Record Group 111. US Department of Defense, Department of the Army, and Office
        of the Deputy Chief of Staff for Operations, US Army Audiovisual Center.

    Record Group 331. Supreme Commander for the Allied Powers.

    Record Group 338. US Army Operational, Tactical and Support Organizations.

    Record Group 469. US Foreign Assistance Agencies.

    Record Group 550. US Army, Pacific.

Social Welfare History Archives. University of Minnesota, Minneapolis.

    International Social Service.

    International Social Service, Case Studies.

    Young Men's Christian Association.

    Young Women's Christian Association/United Service Organizations.

Truman, Harry. Files. Manuscript Division, Library of Congress, Washington, DC.

United Nations Korea Reconstruction Agency. Registry Files. United Nations Archives, New York.

World Vision, Inc. Central Records. Monrovia, CA.

Yale University Divinity Archives, New Haven, CT.

China's Children Fund.

Records of the Presbyterian Church, Foreign Missions.

Severance Crippled Children's Center and Elementary School, Yonsei University Medical Center.

INTERVIEWS

Cho Kyu Hwan. President, Angel's Haven Social Welfare Foundation, Seoul, Korea. October 2005.

Holt, Molly. Chairperson, Holt Ilsan Welfare Center, Ilsan, Korea. October 2005.

Im Yong Ok. Director of Overseas Affairs, Social Welfare Society, Inc., Seoul, Korea. October 2005.

Kang Ji Yŏng. Caseworker, Sangrokwŏn Child Care Center, Seoul, Korea. October 2005.

Kim Don Yŏng. Director of International Programs, Holt Children's Services, Inc., Seoul, Korea. October 2005.

No Wŏl Ae. Director, Ethel Underwood Girl's Home Center, Seoul, Korea. October 2005.

Shin Dong Han. Office manager, Yŏngnak Orphanage, Seoul, Korea. September 2005.

Sŏng Kyŏ Hŭi. Staff member, Holt Ilsan Welfare Center, Ilsan, Korea. October 2005.

KOREAN NEWSPAPERS

Chosŏn Ilbo
Dong-A Ilbo
Hankyoreh
Korean Herald
Korean Republic
Korea Times
Kyŏnghyang sinmun
Maeil

US NEWSPAPERS AND MAGAZINES

Atlanta Daily World
Chicago Daily Tribune
Chicago Defender
Christian Science Monitor
Cue
Daily Journal
Ebony
Honolulu Star Bulletin
Jet

Life
Look
Los Angeles Times
McCall's
Miami News
National Geographic
Newsweek
New York Herald Tribune
New York Journal American
New York Times
New York Times Magazine
Pacific Stars and Stripes
Parade
Pittsburgh Courier
Puck
Reporter
Saturday Evening Post
Saturday Review
Time
US News and World Report
Washington Post
Washington Post and Times Herald

BOOKS AND JOURNAL ARTICLES
Adams, David Wallace. *Education for Extinction: American Indians and the Boarding School Experience, 1875–1928.* Lawrence: University of Kansas Press, 1995.
Agamben, Giorgio. *Homo Sacer: Sovereign Power and Bare Life.* Translated by Daniel Heller-Roazen. Stanford: Stanford University Press, 1998.
Ahn, Junghyo. "A Double Exposure of the War." In *America's Wars in Asia: A Cultural Approach to History and Memory,* edited by Philip West, Steven I. Levine, and Jackie Hiltz, 161–71. Armonk, NY: East Gate Book, 1998.
———. *Silver Stallion: A Novel of Korea.* 1986. Reprint, New York: Soho, 1990.
Allen, Stookie. *Keen Teens: 101 Ways to Make Money.* New York: Emerson Books, 1955.
Alstein, Howard, and Rita J. Simon, eds. *Intercountry Adoption: A Multinational Perspective.* New York: Praeger, 1991.
Anderson, Benedict. *Imagined Communities: Reflections on the Origin and Spread of Nationalism.* 1983. Reprint, London: Verso, 1991.
Anderson, Warwick. *Colonial Pathologies: American Tropical Medicine, Race, and Hygiene in the Philippines.* Durham: Duke University Press, 2006.
Appiah, Kwame Anthony. "Global Citizenship." *Fordham Law Review* 75, no. 5 (April 2007): 2375–91. http://ir.lawnet.fordham.edu/flr/vol75/iss5/3.
Appy, Christian G. *American Reckoning: The Vietnam War and Our National Identity.* New York: Penguin, 2015.

Arendt, Hannah. *The Origins of Totalitarianism*. New York: Harcourt Brace Jovanovich, 1973.

Armstrong, Charles. "The Destruction and Reconstruction of North Korea, 1950–1960." *Asia-Pacific Journal* 7 (March 16, 2009): 1–9.

Arnold, Mary-Kim. *Litany for the Long Moment*. Berkeley, CA: Essay Press, 2018.

Atanasoski, Neda. *Humanitarian Violence: The US Deployment of Diversity*. Minneapolis: University of Minnesota Press, 2013.

Axinn, June, and Mark J. Stern. *Social Welfare: A History of the American Response to Need*. 7th ed. Boston: Pearson Education, 2008.

Azuma, Eiichiro. *Between Two Empires: Race, History, and Transnationalism in Japanese America*. New York: Oxford University Press, 2005.

Bacevich, Andrew. *The New American Militarism: How Americans Are Seduced by War*. New York: Oxford University Press, 2005.

Baer, Ulrich. *Spectral Evidence: The Photography of Trauma*. Cambridge: MIT Press, 2002.

Bailkin, Jordanna. *The Afterlife of Empire*. Berkeley: University of California Press, 2012.

Balcom, Karen A. *The Traffic in Babies: Cross-Border Adoption and Baby-Selling between the United States and Canada, 1930–1972*. Toronto: University of Toronto Press, 2011.

Baldoz, Rick. *The Third Asiatic Invasion: Migration and Empire in Filipino America, 1898–1946*. New York: New York University Press, 2011.

Balibar, Étienne. *Citizen Subject: Foundations for Philosophical Anthropology*. New York: Fordham University Press, 2016.

Banet-Weiser, Sarah. "Elián González and 'The Purpose of America': Nation, Family, and the Child-Citizen." *American Quarterly* 55, no. 2 (June 2003): 149–78.

Baughman, James L. "Who Read *Life*? The Circulation of America's Favorite Magazine." In *Looking at Life Magazine*, edited by Erika Doss, 40–51. Washington, DC: Smithsonian Institution Press, 2001.

Bederman, Gail. *Manliness and Civilization: A Cultural History of Gender and Race in the United States, 1880–1917*. Chicago: University of Chicago Press, 1995.

Beeching, Barbara J. "Paul Robeson and the Black Press: The 1950 Passport Controversy." *Journal of African American History* 87, no. 3 (Summer 2002): 339–54.

Belkin, Aaron. *Bring Me Men: Military Masculinity and the Benign Façade of American Empire*. New York: Columbia University Press, 2012.

Belmonte, Laura A. *Selling the American Way: US Propaganda and the Cold War*. Philadelphia: University of Pennsylvania Press, 2008.

Benjamin, Walter. "Thesis on the Philosophy of History." In *Illuminations: Essays and Reflections*, edited by Hannah Arendt, translated by Harry Zohn, 253–64. New York: Schocken, 1968.

Berebitsky, Julie. *Like Our Very Own: Adoption and the Changing Culture of Motherhood*. Lawrence: University Press of Kansas, 2000.

Bergquist, Kathleen Ja Sook, M. Elizabeth Vonk, Dong Soo Kim, and Marvin D. Feit, eds. *International Korean Adoption: A Fifty-Year History of Policy and Practice.* Binghamton, NY: Haworth, 2007.

Bhabha, Homi. *The Location of Culture.* London: Routledge, 1994.

Blight, David. *Race and Reunion: The Civil War in American Memory.* Cambridge: Belknap, 2001.

Bonham, Gordon Scott. "Who Adopts: The Relationship of Adoption and Social-Demographic Characteristics of Women." *Journal of Marriage and Family* 39 (May 1977): 295–306.

Borstelmann, Thomas. *The Cold War and the Color Line: American Race Relations in the Global Arena.* Boston: Harvard University Press, 2001.

Botham, Fay. *Almighty God Created the Races: Christianity, Interracial Marriage, and American Law.* Chapel Hill: University of North Carolina Press, 2000.

Bowman, LeRoy, Benjamin A. Gjenvick, and Eleanor T. M. Harvey. *Children of Tragedy: Church World Service Survey Team Report on Intercountry Orphan Adoption.* New York: Church World Service, 1961.

Bradley, Mark Phillip. *Imagining Vietnam and America: The Making of Postcolonial Vietnam, 1919–1950.* Chapel Hill: University of North Carolina Press, 2000.

Brazinsky, Gregg. *Nation Building in South Korea: Koreans, Americans, and the Making of Democracy.* Chapel Hill: University of North Carolina Press, 2007.

Briggs, Laura. "Mother, Child, Race, Nation: The Visual Iconography of Rescue and the Politics of Transnational and Transracial Adoption." *Gender and History* 15, no. 2 (August 2003): 179–200.

———. *Reproducing Empire: Race, Sex, Science, and US Imperialism in Puerto Rico.* Berkeley: University of California Press, 2002.

———. *Somebody's Children: The Politics of Transracial and Transnational Adoption.* Durham: Duke University Press, 2012.

Byrd, Jodi A. *Transit of Empire: Indigenous Critiques of Colonialism.* Minneapolis: University of Minnesota Press, 2011.

Cacho, Lisa. *Social Death: Racialized Rightlessness and the Criminalization of the Unprotected.* New York: New York University Press, 2012.

Caldwell, John C. *Children of Calamity.* New York: John Day, 1957.

Camacho, Keith L., and Laurel A. Monnig. "Uncomfortable Fatigues: Chamorro Soldiers, Gendered Identities, and the Question of Decolonization in Guam." In *Militarized Currents: Toward a Decolonized Future in Asia and the Pacific,* edited by Setsu Shigematsu and Keith L. Camacho, 147–80. Minneapolis: University of Minnesota Press, 2010.

Camp, Stephanie. *Closer to Freedom: Enslaved Women and Everyday Resistance in the Plantation South.* Chapel Hill: University of North Carolina Press, 2004.

Carp, Wayne. *Family Matters: Secrecy and Disclosure in the History of Adoption.* Cambridge: Harvard University Press, 1998.

Cartwright, Lisa. "Photographs of 'Waiting Children': The Transnational Adoption Market." *Social Text* 21, no. 1 (Spring 2003): 83–109.

Casey, Steven. *Selling the Korean War*. New York: Oxford University Press, 2002.

Chai, Alice Yun. "Korean Feminist and Human Rights Politics: The Chongshinedae/ Jugunianfu ('Comfort Women') Movement." In *Korean American Women: From Tradition to Modern Feminism*, edited by Young I. Song and Ailee Moon. Westport, CT: Praeger, 1998.

Chakerian, Charles. *The Changing Scene: Second Report on Korea*. New York: Church World Service, 1963.

———. *From Rescue to Child Welfare*. New York: Church World Service, 1968.

Chang, In-Hyub. "Korea, South." In *Social Welfare in Asia*, edited by John E. Dixon and Hyung Shik Kim, 176–213. Dover, NH: Croom Helm, 1985.

Chen, Kuan-Hsing. *Asia as Method: Toward Deimperialization*. Durham: Duke University Press, 2010.

Cheng, Cindy I-Fen. *Citizens of Asian America: Democracy and Race during the Cold War*. New York: New York University Press, 2013.

Children's Survey Sub-Committee, Korea Child Welfare Committee, in cooperation with Ministry of Health and Social Affairs. *Handicapped Children's Survey Report*. Seoul, 1961.

Cho, Grace M. "Diaspora of Camptown: The Forgotten War's Monstrous Family." *Women's Studies Quarterly* 34, nos. 1–2 (Spring/Summer 2006): 309–31.

———. *Haunting the Korean Diaspora: Shame, Secrecy, and the Forgotten War*. Minneapolis: University of Minnesota Press, 2008.

Choi, Chungmoo. "The Discourse of Decolonization and Popular Memory: South Korea." *positions* 1, no. 1 (Spring 1993): 77–102. doi: 10.1215/10679847-1-1-77.

———. "The Politics of War Memories toward Healing." In *Perilous Memories: The Asia-Pacific War(s)*, edited by T. Fujitani, Geoffrey M. White, and Lisa Yoneyama, 395–409. Durham: Duke University Press, 2001.

Chong, Denise. *The Girl in the Picture: The Story of Kim Phuc, the Photograph, and the Vietnam War*. New York: Viking, 2000.

Chong, Sylvia Shin Huey. *The Oriental Obscene: Violence and Racial Fantasies in the Vietnam Era*. Durham: Duke University Press, 2012.

Choy, Catherine Ceniza. *Empire of Care: Nursing and Migration in Filipino American History*. Durham: Duke University Press, 2003.

———. *Global Families: A History of Asian International Adoption in America*. New York: New York University Press, 2013.

Choy, Catherine Ceniza, and Gregory Paul Choy. "Transformative Terrains: Korean American Adoptees and the Social Constructions of an American Childhood." In *The American Child*, edited by Caroline Levander and Carol Singley, 262–79. New Brunswick: Rutgers University Press, 2003.

Chuh, Kandice. *Imagine Otherwise: On Asian Americanist Critique*. Durham: Duke University Press, 2003.

Chung, Hye Seung. *Hollywood Asian: Philip Ahn and the Politics of Cross-Ethnic Performance*. Philadelphia: Temple University Press, 2006.

Chung, Kyung Cho. *Korea Tomorrow: Land of the Morning Calm*. New York: Macmillan, 1956.

Chung, Nicole. *All You Can Ever Know: A Memoir*. New York: Catapult, 2018.

Clement, Thomas Park. *The Unforgotten War: Dust of the Streets*. Bloomfield, IN: Truepeny, 1998.

Cohen, Lizbeth. *A Consumers' Republic: The Politics of Mass Consumption in Postwar America*. New York: Knopf, 2003.

Cohen, Stanley. *States of Denial: Knowing about Atrocities and Suffering*. Cambridge: Polity, 2001.

Conn, Peter. *Pearl S. Buck: A Cultural Biography*. Cambridge: Cambridge University Press, 1996.

Conroy-Krutz, Emily. *Christian Imperialism: Converting the World in the Early American Republic*. Ithaca: Cornell University Press, 2015.

Coontz, Stephanie. *Marriage, A History: From Obedience to Intimacy, or How Love Conquered Marriage*. New York: Viking, 2005.

———. *The Way We Never Were: American Families and the Nostalgia Trap*. New York: Basic Books, 1992.

Cooper, Frederick, and Ann Laura Stoler, eds. *Tensions of Empire: Colonial Cultures in a Bourgeois World*. Berkeley: University of California Press, 1997.

Cox, Susan Soon-Keum, ed. *Voices from Another Place: A Collection of Works from a Generation Born in Korea and Adopted to Other Countries*. St. Paul, MN: Yeong and Yeong, 1999.

Cumings, Bruce. *Korea's Place in the Sun: A Modern History*. New York: Norton, 1997.

———. *The Origins of the Korean War*. Vol. 2, *The Roaring of the Cataract, 1947–1950*. Princeton: Princeton University Press, 1990.

———. "Silent but Deadly: Sexual Subordination in the US-Korean Relationship." In *Let the Good Times Roll*, edited by Saundra Pollock Sturdevant and Brenda Stoltzfus, 169–75. New York: New Press, 1993.

Das, Veena. "National Honor and Practical Kinship: Unwanted Women and Children." In *Conceiving a New World Order: The Global Politics of Reproduction*, edited by Faye D. Ginsburg and Rayna Rupp, 212–33. Berkeley: University of California Press, 1995.

Davin, Anna. "Imperialism and Motherhood." *History Workshop* 5 (Spring 1978): 9–65.

Davis, Janet M. "Moral, Purposeful, and Healthful: The World of Child's Play, Body-building, and Nation-Building at the American Circus." In *Body and Nation: The Global Realm of US Body Politics in the Twentieth Century*, edited by Emily S. Rosenberg and Shanon Fitzpatrick, 42–60. Durham: Duke University Press, 2014.

Depew, Donald R. "Indigenous Girls." In *Retrieving Bones: Stories and Poems of the Korean War*, edited by W. D. Ehrhart and Philip K. Jason, 127–33. New Brunswick: Rutgers University Press, 1999.

Diaz, Vicente M. "Deliberating 'Liberation Day': Identity, History, Memory, and War in Guam." In *Perilous Memories: The Asia-Pacific War(s)*, edited by T. Fujitani, Geoffrey M. White, and Lisa Yoneyama, 155–80. Durham: Duke University Press, 2001.

Di Virgilio, Letitia. "Adjustment of Foreign Children in Their Adoptive Homes." *Child Welfare*, November 1956, 15–21.

Donzelot, Jacques. *The Policing of Families*. New York: Pantheon, 1979.

Dorow, Sara K., ed. *I Wish for You a Beautiful Life: Letters from the Korean Birth Mothers of Ae Ran Won to Their Children*. St. Paul, MN: Yeong and Yeong, 1999.

———. *Transnational Adoption: A Cultural Economy of Race, Gender, and Kinship*. New York: New York University Press, 2006.

Dower, John W. *Embracing Defeat: Japan in the Wake of World War II*. New York: Norton, 1999.

Dubinsky, Karen. *Babies without Borders: Adoption and Migration across the Americas*. New York: New York University Press, 2010.

Dudziak, Mary. *Cold War, Civil Rights: Race and the Image of American Democracy*. Princeton: Princeton University Press, 2000.

———. *War Time: An Idea, Its History, Its Consequences*. New York: Oxford University Press, 2012.

Duncan, Patti. "Genealogies of Unbelonging: Amerasians and Transnational Adoptees as Legacies of US Militarism in South Korea." In *Militarized Currents: Toward a Decolonized Future in Asia and the Pacific*, edited by Setsu Shigematsu and Keith L. Camacho, 277–308. Minneapolis: University of Minnesota Press, 2010.

Eckert, Carter J., Ki-baik Lee, Young Ick Lew, Michael Robinson, and Edward W. Wagner. *Korea Old and New: A History*. Seoul: Ilchokak, 1990.

Ehrenreich, Barbara. *The Hearts of Men: American Dreams and the Flight from Commitment*. New York: Anchor, 1983.

Eng, David L. "Transnational Adoption and Queer Diasporas." *Social Text* 21, no. 3 (2003): 1–37.

Engelhardt, Tom. "Iraq as a Pentagon Construction Site." In *The Bases of Empire: The Global Struggle against US Military Posts*, edited by Catherine Lutz, 131–41. New York: New York University Press, 2009.

Enloe, Cynthia. *Bananas, Beaches and Bases: Making Feminist Sense of International Politics*. 1989. Reprint, Berkeley: University of California Press, 1990.

———. *Does Khaki Become You? The Militarization of Women's Lives*. London: Pluto, 1983.

———. *Maneuvers: The International Politics of Militarizing Women's Lives*. Berkeley: University of California Press, 2000.

———. *The Morning After: Sexual Politics at the End of the Cold War*. Berkeley: University of California Press, 1993.

Espiritu, Yên Lê. *Body Counts: The Vietnam War and Militarized Refuge(es)*. Berkeley: University of California Press, 2014.

———. "The 'We-Win-Even-When-We-Lose' Syndrome: US Press Coverage of the Twenty-Fifth Anniversary of the 'Fall of Saigon.'" *American Quarterly* 58, no. 2 (2006): 329–52.

Fear-Segal, Jacqueline, and Susan D. Rose, eds. *Carlisle Indian Industrial School: Indigenous Histories, Memories, and Reclamations.* Lincoln: University of Nebraska Press, 2016.

Fehrenbach, Heide. *Race after Hitler: Black Occupation Children in Postwar Germany and America.* Princeton: Princeton University Press, 2005.

Feldstein, Ruth. "'I Wanted the Whole World to See': Race, Gender, and Constructions of Motherhood in the Death of Emmett Till." In *Not June Cleaver: Women and Gender in Postwar America, 1945–1960,* edited by Joanne Meyerowitz, 263–303. Philadelphia: Temple University Press, 1994.

———. *Motherhood in Black and White: Race and Sex in American Liberalism, 1930–1965.* Ithaca: Cornell University Press, 2000.

Fessler, Ann. *The Girls Who Went Away: The Hidden History of Women Who Surrendered Children for Adoption in the Decades before* Roe v. Wade. New York: Penguin, 2006.

Fieldston, Sara. *Raising the World: Child Welfare in the American Century.* Boston: Harvard University Press, 2015.

Foucault, Michel. *Discipline and Punish: The Birth of the Prison.* New York: Vintage, 1995.

———. "Governmentality." In *The Foucault Effect: Studies in Governmentality,* edited by Graham Burchell, Colin Gordon, and Peter Miller, 87–104. Chicago: University of Chicago Press, 1991.

———. *History of Sexuality: An Introduction.* New York: Vintage, 1990.

Friedman, Barbara G. *From the Battlefront to the Bridal Suite: Media Coverage of British War Brides, 1942–1946.* Columbia: University of Missouri Press, 2007.

Fujita-Rony, Dorothy. *American Workers, Colonial Power: Philippine Seattle and the Transpacific West, 1919–1941.* Berkeley: University of California Press, 2003.

Gaddis, John Lewis. *Strategies of Containment: A Critical Appraisal of American National Security Policy during the Cold War.* New York: Oxford University Press, 2005.

Gallup, George. *The Gallup Poll: Public Opinion, 1935–1971.* New York: Random House, 1972.

Gerstle, Gary. "The Protean Character of American Liberalism." *American Historical Review* 99, no. 4 (1994): 1043–73.

Gilman, Nils. *Mandarins of the Future: Modernization Theory in Cold War America.* Baltimore: Johns Hopkins University Press, 2003.

Glenn, Evelyn Nakano. *Issei, Nisei, War Bride: Three Generations of Japanese American Women in Domestic Service.* Philadelphia: Temple University Press, 1986.

Go, Julian. "The Provinciality of American Empire: 'Liberal Exceptionalism' and US Colonial Rule, 1898–1912." *Comparative Studies in Society and History* 49, no. 1 (2007): 74–108.

Go, Julian, and Anne L. Foster, eds. *The American Colonial State in the Philippines: Global Perspectives.* Durham: Duke University Press, 2003.

Gonzalez, Vernadette Vicuña. *Securing Paradise: Tourism and Militarism in Hawai'i and the Philippines.* Durham: Duke University Press, 2013.

Gordon, Avery. *Ghostly Matters: Haunting and the Sociological Imagination.* Minneapolis: University of Minnesota Press, 1999.

Gordon, Linda. *The Great Arizona Orphan Abduction.* Cambridge: Harvard University Press, 1999.

Gotanda, Neil. "Multiculturalism and Racial Stratification." In *Mapping Multiculturalism,* edited by Avery F. Gordon and Christopher Newfield, 238–52. Minneapolis: University of Minnesota Press, 1996.

Green, Michael Cullen. *Black Yanks in the Pacific: Race in the Making of American Military Empire after World War II.* Ithaca: Cornell University Press, 2010.

Hacking, Ian. *Historical Ontology.* Cambridge: Harvard University Press, 2002.

———. "The Looping Effect of Human Kinds." In *Causal Cognition: A Multidisciplinary Debate,* edited by Dan Sperber, David Premack, and Ann Premack, 351–83. Oxford: Oxford University Press, 1995.

Hall, Stuart. "Cultural Identity and Diaspora." In *Identity: Community, Culture, Difference,* edited by Jonathan Rutherford, 222–37. London: Lawrence and Wishart, 1990.

Halliday, Jon, and Bruce Cumings. *Korea: The Unknown War.* New York: Pantheon, 1988.

Hamamoto, Darrell Y. *Monitored Peril: Asian Americans and the Politics of TV Representation.* Minneapolis: University of Minnesota Press, 1994.

Han, Hyun Sook. *Many Lives Intertwined: A Memoir.* St Paul, MN: Yeong and Yeong, 2007.

Haney López, Ian F. *White by Law: The Legal Construction of Race.* New York: New York University Press, 1996.

Hanley, Charles J. *The Bridge at No Gun Ri: A Hidden Nightmare from the Korean War.* New York: Henry Holt, 2001.

Herman, Ellen. *Kinship by Design: A History of Adoption in the Modern United States.* Chicago: University of Chicago Press, 2008.

Hing, Bill Ong. *Making and Remaking Asian America through Immigration Policy, 1850–1990.* Stanford: Stanford University Press, 1993.

Hirsch, Marianne, ed. *The Familial Gaze.* Hanover, NH: University Press of New England, 1999.

———. *Family Frames: Photography, Narrative, and Postmemory.* Cambridge: Harvard University Press, 1997.

Hochfield, Eugenie. "Across National Boundaries: Problems in the Handling of International Adoptions, Dependency and Custody Cases." *Juvenile Court Judges Journal* 14, no. 3 (Fall, October 1963): 3–7.

Hoganson, Kristin L. *Consumers' Imperium: The Global Production of American Domesticity.* Chapel Hill: University of North Carolina Press, 2007.

———. *Fighting for American Manhood: How Gender Politics Provoked the Spanish-American and Philippine-American Wars*. New Haven: Yale University Press, 1998.

Höhn, Maria, and Seungsook Moon. "Introduction: The Politics of Gender, Sexuality, Race, and Class in the US Military Empire." In *Over There: Living with the US Military Empire from World War Two to the Present*, edited by Maria Höhn and Seungsook Moon, 1–36. Durham: Duke University Press, 2010.

Holt, Bertha. *Bring My Sons from Afar*. Eugene: Holt International Children's Services, 1986.

Hong, Euny. *Birth of Korean Cool: How One Nation Is Conquering the World through Pop Culture*. New York: Picador, 2014.

HoSang, Daniel Martinez. *Racial Propositions: Ballot Initiatives and the Making of Postwar California*. Berkeley: University of California Press, 2010.

Hsu, Madeline Y. *The Good Immigrants: How the Yellow Peril Became the Model Minority*. Princeton: Princeton University Press, 2015.

Hübinette, Tobias. *Comforting an Orphaned Nation: Representations of International Adoption and Adopted Koreans in Korean Popular Culture*. Seoul: Jimoondang, 2006.

———. "Korean Adoption History." In *Community 2004: Guide to Korea for Overseas Adopted Koreans*, edited by Eleana Kim. Seoul: Overseas Koreans Foundation, 2004. http://www.tobiashubinette.se/adoption_history.pdf.

Huebner, Andrew J. "Kilroy Is Back: Images of American Soldiers in Korea, 1950–1953." *American Studies* 45, no. 1 (Spring 2004): 103–29.

Hunt, Michael H., and Steven I. Levine. *Arc of Empire: America's Wars in Asia from the Philippines to Vietnam*. Chapel Hill: University of North Carolina Press, 2012.

Hunter, Jane. *The Gospel of Gentility: American Women Missionaries in Turn-of-the-Century China*. New Haven: Yale University Press, 1984.

Hurh, Won Moo. *The Korean Americans*. Westport, CT: Greenwood, 1998.

———. "Marginal Children of War: An Exploratory Study of American-Korean Children." *International Journal of Sociology of the Family* 2, no. 3 (1972): 10–20.

Hurtado, Albert L. *Intimate Frontiers: Sex, Gender, and Culture in Old California*. Albuquerque: University of New Mexico Press, 1993.

Imada, Adria. *Aloha America: Hula Circuits through the US Empire*. Durham: Duke University Press, 2012.

Iriye, Akira. *Pacific Estrangement: Japanese and American Expansion, 1897–1911*. Cambridge: Harvard University Press, 1971.

———. *Power and Culture: The Japanese-American War, 1941–1945*. Cambridge: Harvard University Press, 1981.

Jacobs, Margaret D. *White Mother to a Dark Race: Settler Colonialism, Maternalism, and the Removal of Indigenous Children in the American West and Australia, 1880–1940*. Lincoln: University of Nebraska Press, 2009.

Jacobs, Seth. *America's Miracle Man in Vietnam: Ngo Dinh Diem, Religion, Race, and US Intervention in Southeast Asia, 1950–1957*. Durham: Duke University Press, 2005.

Jacobson, Heather. *Culture Keeping: White Mothers, International Adoption, and the Negotiation of Family Difference*. Nashville: Vanderbilt University Press, 2008.

Jacobson, Matthew Frye. *Barbarian Virtues: The United States Encounters Foreign People at Home and Abroad, 1876–1917*. New York: Hill and Wang, 2000.

Jacobson, Matthew Frye, and Gaspar González. *What Have They Built You to Do? "The Manchurian Candidate" and Cold War America*. Minneapolis: University of Minnesota Press, 2006.

Jelly-Schapiro, Eli. *Security and Terror: American Culture and the Long History of Colonial Modernity*. Berkeley: University of California Press, 2018.

Jerng, Mark C. *Claiming Others: Transracial Adoption and National Belonging*. Minneapolis: University of Minnesota Press, 2010.

Johnson, Chalmers. *The Sorrows of Empire: Militarism, Secrecy, and the End of the Republic*. New York: Henry Holt, 2004.

Jung, Moon-Ho. *Coolies and Cane: Race, Labor, and Sugar in the Age of Emancipation*. Baltimore: Johns Hopkins University Press, 2006.

———. "Seditious Subjects: Race, State Violence, and the US Empire." *Journal of Asian American Studies* 14, no. 2 (June 2011): 221–47.

Kaplan, Amy. *Anarchy of Empire in the Making of US Culture*. Cambridge: Harvard University Press, 2002.

Kauanui, Kēhaulani J. *Hawaiian Blood: Colonialism and the Politics of Sovereignty and Indigeneity*. Durham: Duke University Press, 2008.

Kerber, Linda. "The Republican Mother: Women and the Enlightenment—An American Perspective." *American Quarterly* 28, no. 2 (Summer 1976): 187–205.

Kim, Bok-Lim C. "Asian Wives of US Servicemen." *Amerasia* 4 (1977): 91–115.

———. *Battered Women: Issues of Public Policy*. Washington, DC, A consultation sponsored by the United States Commission on Civil Rights, January 30–31, 1978.

———. "Casework with Japanese and Korean Wives of Americans." *Social Casework* 53 (May 1972): 273–79.

Kim, Bok-Lim C., and Michael R. Sawdey. *Women in Shadows: A Handbook for Service Providers Working with Asian Wives*. La Jolla, CA: National Committee Concerned with Asian Wives of US Servicemen, 1981.

Kim, Claire Jean. "The Racial Triangulation of Asian Americans." *Politics and Society* 27, no. 1 (March 1999): 105–38.

Kim, Dong Soo. "How They Fared in American Homes: A Follow-up Study of Adopted Korean Children in the United States." *Children Today* 6, no. 2 (March–April 1977): 2–6.

———. "Issues in Transracial and Transcultural Adoption." *Social Casework* 59, no. 8 (1978): 477–86.

Kim, Elaine H., and Chungmoo Choi, eds. *Dangerous Women: Gender and Korean Nationalism*. New York: Routledge, 1998.

Kim, Eleana. *Adopted Territory: Transnational Korean Adoptees and the Politics of Belonging*. Durham: Duke University Press, 2010.

———. "Our Adoptee, Our Alien: Transnational Adoptees as Specters of Foreignness and Family in South Korea." *Anthropological Quarterly* 80, no. 2 (2007): 497–532.

Kim, Elizabeth. *Ten Thousand Sorrows: The Extraordinary Journey of a Korean War Orphan*. New York: Doubleday, 2000.

Kim, Hosu. *Birth Mothers and Transnational Adoption Practice in South Korea*. New York: Palgrave Macmillan, 2016.

———. "Mothers without Mothering: Birth Mothers from South Korea since the Korean War." In *International Korean Adoption: A Fifty-Year History of Policy and Practice*, edited by Kathleen Ja Sook Bergquist, M. Elizabeth Vonk, Dong Soo Kim, and Marvin D. Feit, 131–53. New York: Routledge, 2007.

Kim, Hosu, and Grace M. Cho. "The Kinship of Violence." In *Mothering in East Asian Communities: Politics and Practices*, edited by Patti Duncan and Gina Wong, 31–52. Bradford, ON: Demeter Press, 2014.

Kim, Jan Rae. "Waiting for God: Religion and Korean Adoption." In *Religion and Spirituality in Korean America*, edited by David K. Yoo and Ruth H. Chung, 83–99. Urbana: University of Illinois Press, 2008.

Kim, Jodi. *Ends of Empire: Asian American Critique and the Cold War*. Minneapolis: University of Minnesota Press, 2010.

Kim, Jung Ha. "Cartography of Korean American Protestant Faith Communities in the United States." In *Religions in Asian America: Building Faith Communities*, edited by Pyong Gap Min and Jung Ha Kim, 185–214. Walnut Creek, CA: Altamira, 2002.

Kirk, Gwyn, and Margo Okazawa-Rey. "Demilitarizing Security: Women Oppose US Militarism in East Asia." In *Frontline Feminisms: Women, War, and Resistance*, edited by Marguerite Waller and Jennifer Rycenga, 157–70. New York: Routledge, 2001.

———. "Making Connections: Building an East Asia-US Women's Network against US Militarism." In *The Women and War Reader*, edited by Lois Ann Lorentzen and Jennifer Turpin, 308–22. New York: New York University Press, 1998.

Klein, Christina. *Cold War Orientalism: Asia in the Middlebrow Imagination, 1945–1961*. Berkeley: University of California Press, 2003.

Koo, Hagen. *Korean Workers: The Culture and Politics of Class Formation*. Ithaca: Cornell University Press, 2001.

Korean Mission, Commission on Ecumenical Mission and Relations, and United Presbyterian Church in the United States of America. *An Evaluation of "An Advisory Study."* July 1962.

Koshiro, Yukiko. *Trans-Pacific Racisms and the US Occupation of Japan*. New York: Columbia University Press, 1999.

Kozol, Wendy. *Life's America: Family and Nation in Postwar Photojournalism*. Philadelphia: Temple University Press, 1994.

Kramer, Paul A. *The Blood of Government: Race, Empire, the United States, and the Philippines*. Chapel Hill: University of North Carolina Press, 2006.

Kurashige, Scott. *The Shifting Grounds of Race: Black and Japanese Americans in the Making of Multiethnic Los Angeles*. Princeton: Princeton University Press, 2008.

Kwon, Heonik. *The Other Cold War*. New York: Columbia University Press, 2010.

Kwon, Tai-Hwan. "Demographic Trends and Their Social Implications." *Social Indicators Research* 62, no. 1–3 (April 2003): 19–38.

LaFeber, Walter. *America, Russia, and the Cold War, 1945–1996*. 8th ed. New York: Wiley, 1997.

Lasker, Bruno. *Filipino Immigration to the Continental United States and Hawaii*. Chicago: University of Chicago Press, 1931.

Lederer, William J., and Eugene Burdick. *The Ugly American*. New York: Norton, 1958.

Lee, Daniel Boo-Duck. "Korean Women Married to Servicemen." In *Korean American Women Living in Two Cultures*, edited by Young In Song and Ailee Moon, 94–123. Los Angeles: Academia Koreana, Keimyung-Baylo University Press, 1997.

Lee, Erika. *At America's Gates: Chinese Immigration during the Exclusion Era*. Chapel Hill: University of North Carolina Press, 2003.

Lee, Jieun. "Performing Transnational Adoption: Korean American Women Adoptees' Autobiographical Solo Performances." *Theatre Annual* 70 (2015): 60–80.

Lee, Jin-kyung. *Service Economies: Militarism, Sex Work, and Migrant Labor in South Korea*. Minneapolis: University of Minnesota Press, 2010.

Lee, Kenneth B. *Korea and East Asia: The Story of a Phoenix*. Westport, CT: Praeger, 1997.

Lee Kwon, Myoung-ja. "An Interview with Sook-ja Kim." Las Vegas Women in Gaming and Entertainment Oral History Project. University of Nevada, Las Vegas, 1997. www.library.unlv.edu.

Lee, Mary. "Mixed Race Peoples in the Korean National Imaginary and Family." *Korean Studies* 32 (2008): 56–85.

Lee, Namhee. *The Making of Minjung: Democracy and the Politics of Representation in South Korea*. Ithaca: Cornell University Press, 2007.

Lee, Robert G. *Orientals: Asian Americans in Popular Culture*. Philadelphia: Temple University Press, 1999.

Lee, Yur-Bok. "A Korean View of Korean-American Relations, 1882–1910." In *Korean-American Relations, 1866–1997*, edited by Yur-Bok Lee and Wayne Patterson, 1–10. Albany: State University of New York Press, 1999.

Leffler, Melvyn. *A Preponderance of Power: National Security, the Truman Administration, and the Cold War*. Stanford: Stanford University Press, 1992.

Lentz, Richard, and Karla Gower. *Opinions of Mankind: Racial Issues, Press, and Propaganda in the Cold War*. Columbia: University of Missouri Press, 2010.

Leong, Karen. *The China Mystique: Pearl S. Buck, Anna May Wong, Mayling Soong, and the Transformation of American Orientalism*. Berkeley: University of California Press, 2005.

Lie, John. "The Transformation of Sexual Work in 20th-Century Korea." *Gender & Society* 9, no. 3 (1995): 310–27.

Liem, Ramsay. "History, Trauma, and Identity: The Legacy of the Korean War for Korean Americans." *Amerasia Journal* 29, no. 3 (January 2003): 111–30.

Lim, Shirley Jennifer. *A Feeling of Belonging: Asian American Women's Public Culture, 1930–1960*. New York: New York University Press, 2006.

Lipman, Jana. "'Give Us a Ship': Vietnamese Repatriates on Guam, 1975." *American Quarterly* 64, no. 1 (March 2012): 1–31.

Lovelock, Kirsten. "Intercountry Adoption as a Migratory Practice: A Comparative Analysis of Intercountry Adoption and Immigration Policy and Practice in the United States, Canada and New Zealand in the Post WWII Period." *International Migration Review* 34 (Fall 2000): 907–49.

Lowe, Lisa. *Immigrant Acts: On Asian American Cultural Politics*. Durham: Duke University Press, 1997.

———. *The Intimacies of Four Continents*. Durham: Duke University Press, 2014.

Luce, Henry. *The American Century*. New York: Farrar and Rinehart, 1941.

MacGregor, Morris. *Integration of the Armed Forces, 1940–1965*. Washington, DC: Center of Military History Press, 1981.

Maliangkay, Roald. "Same Look through Different Eyes: Korea's History of Uniform Pop Music Acts." In *K-Pop: The International Rise of the Korean Music Industry*, edited by JungBong Choi and Roald Maliangkay, 19–34. New York: Routledge, 2014.

Man, Simeon. *Soldiering through Empire: Race and the Making of the Decolonizing Pacific*. Berkeley: University of California Press, 2018.

Marchetti, Gina. *Romance and the "Yellow Peril": Race, Sex, and Discursive Strategies in Hollywood Fiction*. Berkeley: University of California Press, 1993.

Marre, Diana, and Laura Briggs, eds. *International Adoption: Global Inequalities and the Circulation of Children*. New York: New York University Press, 2009.

Marsh, Margaret, and Wanda Ronner. *The Empty Cradle: Infertility in America from Colonial Times to the Present*. Baltimore: Johns Hopkins University Press, 1996.

Masuda, Hajimu. *Cold War Crucible: The Korean Conflict and the Postwar World*. Cambridge: Harvard University Press, 2015.

Matsumoto, Valerie J. *Farming the Homeplace: A Japanese American Community in California, 1919–1982*. Ithaca: Cornell University Press, 1993.

Mauldin, Bill. *Bill Mauldin in Korea*. New York: Norton, 1952.

May, Elaine Tyler. *Barren in the Promised Land: Childless Americans and the Pursuit of Happiness*. Cambridge: Harvard University Press, 1995.

———. *Homeward Bound: American Families in the Cold War Era*. New York: Basic Books, 1988.

McAlister, Melani. *Epic Encounters: Culture, Media, and US Interests in the Middle East, 1945–2000*. Berkeley: University of California Press, 2001.

McCann, David R. "Our Forgotten War: The Korean War in Korean and American Popular Culture." In *America's Wars in Asia: A Cultural Approach to History and Memory*, edited by Philip West, Steven I. Levine, and Jackie Hiltz, 65–83. Armonk, NY: East Gate Book, 1998.

McClintock, Anne. *Imperial Leather: Race, Gender, and Sexuality in the Colonial Contest*. New York: Routledge, 1995.

McCune, George M. *Korea Today*. Cambridge: Harvard University Press, 1950.

McCune, George, and John A. Harrison, eds. *Korean-American Relations: Documents Pertaining to the Far Eastern Diplomacy of the United States*. Vol. 2, *The Period of Growing Influence, 1887–1895*. Berkeley: University of California Press, 1963.

McKee, Kimberly, *Disrupting Kinship: Transnational Politics of Korean Adoption in the United States*. Urbana: University of Illinois Press, 2019.

McMahon, Robert J. *Colonialism and Cold War: The United States and the Struggle for Indonesian Independence, 1945–1949*. Ithaca: Cornell University Press, 1981.

Melosh, Barbara. *Strangers and Kin: The American Way of Adoption*. Cambridge: Harvard University Press, 2002.

Miller, John, Jr. *Korea, 1951–53*. Washington, DC: Department of the Army, 1953.

Miller, Stuart Creighton. *"Benevolent Assimilation": The American Conquest of the Philippines, 1899–1903*. New Haven: Yale University Press, 1982.

Min, Pyong Gap. "Korean Americans." In *Asian Americans: Contemporary Trends and Issues*, edited by Pyong Gap Min, 199–231. Thousand Oaks, CA: Sage, 1995.

Moon, Katharine H. S. *Sex among Allies: Military Prostitution in US-Korea Relations*. New York: Columbia University Press, 1997.

——. "South Korean Movements against Militarized Sexual Labor." In *Militarized Currents: Toward a Decolonized Future in Asia and the Pacific*, edited by Setsu Shigematsu and Keith L. Camacho, 125–46. Minneapolis: University of Minnesota Press, 2010.

Moon, Seungsook. *Militarized Modernity and Gendered Citizenship in South Korea*. Durham: Duke University Press, 2005.

——. "Regulating Desire, Managing the Empire: US Military Prostitution in South Korea, 1945–1970." In *Over There: Living with the US Military Empire from World War Two to the Present*, edited by Maria Höhn and Seungsook Moon, 39–77. Durham: Duke University Press, 2010.

Myrdal, Gunnar. *An American Dilemma: The Negro Problem and Modern Democracy*. New York: Harper and Brothers, 1944.

Ngai, Mai. *Impossible Subjects: Illegal Aliens and the Making of Modern America*. Princeton: Princeton University Press, 2004.

Nguyen, Mimi. *The Gift of Freedom: War, Debt, and Other Refugee Passages*. Durham: Duke University Press, 2012.

Nguyen, Viet Thanh. *Nothing Ever Dies: Vietnam and the Memory of War*. Cambridge: Harvard University Press, 2016.

Nitz, Paul H., and S. Nelson Drew. *NSC-68: Forging the Strategy of Containment*. Washington, DC: National Defense University, 1995.

Nkrumah, Kwame. *Neo-Colonialism: The Last Stage of Imperialism*. New York: International Publishers, 1965.

Office of Public Information, Republic of Korea. *Letters to Tall Soldiers from Small Koreans*. Seoul: Office of Public Information, 1951.

Ogle, George. *South Korea: Dissent within the Economic Miracle*. London: Zed Books, 1990.

Oh, Arissa. *To Save the Children of Korea: The Cold War Origins of International Adoption*. Stanford: Stanford University Press, 2015.

Oh, Chae Kyung. *A Handbook of Korea*. New York: Pageant Press, 1957.

Okihiro, Gary O. *Margins and Mainstreams: Asians in American History and Culture.* Seattle: University of Washington Press, 1994.

Oliver, Robert T. *50 Facts about Korea.* Washington, DC: Korean Pacific Press, 1948.

———. *The Republic of Korea Looks Ahead.* Washington, DC: Korean Pacific Press, 1948.

Omi, Michael, and Howard Winant. *Racial Formation in the United States from the 1960s to the 1990s.* New York: Routledge, 1994.

Onishi, Yuichiro. *Transpacific Antiracism: Afro-Asian Solidarity in 20th-Century Black America, Japan, and Okinawa.* New York: New York University Press, 2013.

Orenstein, Dara. "Void for Vagueness: Mexicans and the Collapse of Miscegenation Law in California." *Pacific Historical Review* 74, no. 3 (August 2005): 367–408.

Ortiz, Ana Teresa, and Laura Briggs. "The Culture of Poverty, Crack Babies, and Welfare Cheats: The Making of the 'Healthy White Baby Crisis.'" *Social Text* 21, no. 3 (Fall 2003): 39–57.

Ota, Nancy K. "Private Matters: Family and Race and the Post-World-War-II Translation of 'American.'" *IRSH* 46 (December 2001): 209–34.

Paik, A. Naomi. *Rightlessness: Testimony and Redress in US Prison Camps since World War II.* Chapel Hill: University of North Carolina Press, 2016.

Paik, George L. *The History of Protestant Missions in Korea, 1832–1910.* 1927. Reprint, Seoul: Yonsei University Press, 1970.

Paik, Wondam. "The 60th Anniversary of the Bandung Conference and Asia." *Inter-Asia Cultural Studies* 17, no. 1 (2016): 148–57. doi: 10.1080/14649373.2016.1150246.

Palumbo-Liu, David. *Asian/American: Historical Crossings of a Racial Frontier.* Stanford: Stanford University Press, 1999.

Pardue, Austin. *Korean Adventure.* New York: Morehouse-Gorham, 1953.

Park Nelson, Kim. *Invisible Asians: Korean American Adoptees, Asian American Experiences, and Racial Exceptionalism.* New Brunswick: Rutgers University Press, 2016.

Pascoe, Peggy. *Relations of Rescue: The Search for Female Moral Authority in the American West, 1874–1939.* New York: Oxford University Press, 1990.

———. *What Comes Naturally: Miscegenation Law and the Making of Race in America.* New York: Oxford University Press, 2009.

Pate, SooJin. *From Orphan to Adoptee: US Empire and Genealogies of Korean Adoption.* Minneapolis: University of Minnesota Press, 2014.

Patterson, Wayne. *The Ilse: First-Generation Korean Immigrants in Hawai'i, 1903–1973.* Honolulu: University of Hawai'i Press, 2000.

Patton, Sandra. *BirthMarks: Transracial Adoption in Contemporary America.* New York: New York University Press, 2000.

Peterson, Nicolas. "The Changing Photographic Contract: Aborigines and Image Ethics." In *Photography's Other Histories,* edited by Christopher Pinney, 119–45. Durham: Duke University Press, 2003.

Phalen, Peggy. *Unmarked: The Politics of Performance.* London: Routledge, 1993.

Phillips, Kimberly L. *War! What Is It Good For? Black Freedom Struggles and the US Military from World War II to Iraq.* Chapel Hill: University of North Carolina Press, 2011.

Pierce, Bob. *The Korean Orphan Choir: They Sing Their Thanks.* Grand Rapids, MI: Zondervan, 1965.

Plummer, Brenda Gayle. "Brown Babies: Race, Gender, and Policy after World War II." In *Window on Freedom: Race, Civil Rights, and Foreign Affairs, 1945–1988,* edited by Brenda Gale Plummer, 67–91. Chapel Hill: University of North Carolina Press, 2003.

Potter, Sarah. *Everybody Else: Adoption and the Politics of Domestic Diversity in Postwar America.* Athens: University of Georgia Press, 2014.

Pratt, Mary Louise. *Imperial Eyes: Travel Writing and Transculturation.* London: Routledge, 1992.

Prébin, Elise. *Meeting Once More: The Korean Side of Transnational Adoption.* New York: New York University Press, 2016.

Quinsaat, Jesse, ed. *Letters in Exile: An Introductory Reader on the History of Pilipinos in America.* Los Angeles: UCLA Asian American Studies Center, 1976.

Rafael, Vicente L. *White Love and Other Events in Filipino History.* Durham: Duke University Press, 2000.

Ragoné, Heléna, and France Winddance Twine, eds. *Ideologies and Technologies of Motherhood: Race, Class, Sexuality, Nationalism.* New York: Routledge, 2000.

Renda, Mary. *Taking Haiti: Military Occupation and the Culture of US Imperialism, 1915–1940.* Chapel Hill: University of North Carolina Press, 2000.

Rhee, Syngman. "Re-Establishment of Korean Nation." In *Korea's Fight for Freedom,* edited by Robert T. Oliver, 10. Washington, DC: Korean Pacific Press, 1951–1952.

Rifkin, Mark. "Debt and the Transnationalization of Hawai'i." *American Quarterly* 60, no. 1 (March 2008): 43–66.

Robinson, Katy. *A Single Square Picture: A Korean Adoptee's Search for Her Roots.* New York: Berkley Books, 2002.

Roediger, David R. "Gook: The Short History of an Americanism." *Monthly Review* 43 (March 1992): 50–54.

Saenz, Rogelio, Sean-Shong Hwang, and Benigno Aguirre. "In Search of Asian War Brides." *Demography* 31, no. 3 (1994): 549–59.

Said, Edward. *Orientalism.* New York: Vintage, 1978.

Saks, Eva. "Representing Miscegenation Law." *Raritan* 8, no. 2 (Fall 1988): 39–69.

Saranillio, Dean Itsuji. *Unsustainable Empire: Alternative Histories of Hawai'i Statehood.* Durham: Duke University Press, 2018.

Saxton, Alexander. *Indispensable Enemy: Labor and the Anti-Chinese Movement in California.* Berkeley: University of California Press, 1971.

Scarry, Elaine. *The Body in Pain: The Making and Unmaking of the World.* New York: Oxford University Press, 1985.

Scott, James C. *Domination and the Arts of Resistance: Hidden Transcripts.* New Haven: Yale University Press, 1990.

Seigel, Micol. *Uneven Encounters: Making Race and Nation in Brazil and the United States.* Durham: Duke University Press, 2009.

Sekula, Allan. "The Traffic in Photographs." *Art Journal* 41, no. 1 (Spring 1981): 15–25.

Serlin, David. *Replaceable You: Engineering the Body in Postwar America.* Chicago: University of Chicago Press, 2004.

Shah, Nayan. *Contagious Divides: Epidemics and Race in San Francisco's Chinatown.* Berkeley: University of California Press, 2001.

Shibusawa, Naoko. *America's Geisha Ally: Reimagining the Japanese Enemy.* Cambridge: Harvard University Press, 2006.

Silva, Noenoe K. *Aloha Betrayed: Native Hawaiian Resistance to American Colonialism.* Durham: Duke University Press, 2004.

Simmons, LaKisha Michelle. *Crescent City Girls: The Lives of Young Black Women in Segregated New Orleans.* Chapel Hill: University of North Carolina Press, 2015.

Simpson, Caroline Chung. *An Absent Presence: Japanese Americans in Postwar American Culture, 1945–1960.* Durham: Duke University Press, 2001.

Singh, Maina Chawla. *Gender, Religion, and "Heathen Lands": American Missionary Women in South Asia (1860s–1940s).* New York: Garland, 2000.

Singh, Nikhil Pal. "Culture/Wars: Recoding Empire in an Age of Democracy." *American Quarterly* 50, no. 3 (1998): 471–522.

Social Welfare Society. *The 5 Decades of SWS (Since 1954–2003).* Seoul: Social Welfare Society, 2004.

Soh, C. Sarah. *The Comfort Women: Sexual Violence and Postcolonial Memory in Korea and Japan.* Chicago: University of Chicago Press, 2008.

Solinger, Rickie. *Pregnancy and Power: A Short History of Reproductive Politics in America.* New York: New York University Press, 2005.

———. *Wake Up Little Susie: Single Pregnancy and Race before Roe v. Wade.* New York: Routledge, 1992.

Sontag, Susan. *Regarding the Pain of Others.* New York: Farrar, Straus and Giroux, 2003.

Spickard, Paul. *Mixed Blood: Intermarriage and Ethnic Identity in Twentieth-Century America.* Madison: University of Wisconsin Press, 1989.

Spivak, Gayatri. "Can the Subaltern Speak?" In *Marxism and the Interpretation of Culture,* edited by Cary Nelson and Lawrence Grossberg, 271–313. Chicago: University of Illinois Press, 1988.

Stephens, Sharon. "The 'Cultural Fallout' of Chernobyl Radiation in Norwegian Sami Regions: Implications for Children." In *Children and the Politics of Culture,* edited by Sharon Stephens, 292–318. Princeton: Princeton University Press, 1995.

———. "Nationalism, Nuclear Policy and Children in Cold War America." *Childhood* 1, no. 4 (February 1997): 103–23.

Stoler, Ann Laura. *Along the Archival Grain: Epistemic Anxieties and Colonial Common Sense.* Princeton: Princeton University Press, 2010.

———. *Carnal Knowledge and Imperial Power: Race and the Intimate in Colonial Rule.* Berkeley: University of California Press, 2002.

———. *Race and the Education of Desire: Foucault's "History of Sexuality" and the Colonial Order of Things.* Durham: Duke University Press, 1995.

————. "Tense and Tender Ties: The Politics of Comparison in North American History and (Post) Colonial Studies." *Journal of American History* 88, no. 3 (December 2001): 829–65.

Strauss, Anselm L. "Strain and Harmony in American-Japanese War-Bride Marriages." In *The Blending American: Patterns of Intermarriage*, edited by Milton L. Barron, 268–81. Chicago: Quadrangle Books, 1972.

Stueck, William. *Rethinking the Korean War: A New Diplomatic and Strategic History.* Princeton: Princeton University Press, 2004.

Sturdevant, Saundra Pollock, and Brenda Stoltzfus, eds. *Let the Good Times Roll: Prostitution and the US Military in Asia.* New York: New Press, 1993.

Sturken, Marita. *Tangled Memories: The Vietnam War, the AIDS Epidemic, and the Politics of Remembering.* Berkeley: University of California Press, 1997.

Sueyoshi, Amy. *Discriminating Sex: White Leisure and the Making of the American "Oriental."* Urbana: University of Illinois Press, 2018.

Suh, Sang-Mok, and David Williamson. "The Impact of Adjustment and Stabilization Policies on Social Welfare: The South Korean Experiences during 1978–1985." In *Adjustment with a Human Face: Country Case Studies*, edited by Giovanni Andrea Cornia and Richard Jolly Frances Stewart, 218–37. Oxford: Clarendon, 1987.

Tagg, John. *The Burden of Representation: Essays on Photography and History.* Amherst: University of Massachusetts Press, 1988.

Tang, Eric. *Unsettled: Cambodian Refugees in the New York City Hyperghetto.* Philadelphia: Temple University Press, 2015.

Tchen, John Kuo Wei. *New York before Chinatown: Orientalism and the Shaping of American Culture, 1776–1882.* Baltimore: Johns Hopkins University Press, 1999.

Tead, Diana. *What Is Race? Evidence from Scientists.* Paris: UNESCO Department of Mass Communication, 1952.

Thornton, Michael C. "The Quiet Immigration: Foreign Spouses of US Citizens, 1945–1985." In *Racially Mixed People in America*, edited by Maria P. P. Root, 64–76. London: Sage, 1992.

Trenka, Jane Jeong. *The Language of Blood: A Memoir.* St. Paul, MN: Borealis Books, 2003.

Trenka, Jane Jeong, Julia Chinyere Oparah, and Sun Yung Shin, eds. *Outsiders Within: Writing on Transracial Adoption.* Cambridge, MA: South End Press, 2006.

Trouillot, Michel-Rolph. *Silencing the Past: Power and the Production of History.* Boston: Beacon, 1995.

Truman, Harry S. *Questions about the Battle in Korea.* Revised May 1951. Washington, DC: Congress of Industrial Organizations, Political Action Committee.

Tuan, Mia. *Forever Foreigners or Honorary Whites: The Asian Ethnic Experience Today.* New Brunswick: Rutgers University Press, 1998.

Underwood, Horace Horton. *Tragedy and Faith in Korea.* New York: Friendship Press, 1951.

Van Kirk, Sylvia. *Many Tender Ties: Women in the Fur-Trade Society in Western Canada, 1670–1870.* Winnipeg: Watson and Dwyer, 1980.

Varg, Paul. *Missionaries, Chinese, and Diplomats: The American Protestant Missionary Movement in China, 1890–1952*. Princeton: Princeton University Press, 1958.

Varzally, Allison. *Children of Reunion: Vietnamese Adoptions and the Politics of Family Migrations*. Chapel Hill: University of North Carolina Press, 2017.

Vaughan, Megan. *Curing Their Ills: Colonial Power and African Illness*. Stanford: Stanford University Press, 1991.

Virden, Jenel. *Good-Bye, Piccadilly: British War Brides in America*. Urbana: University of Illinois Press, 1996.

Volkman, Toby Alice, ed. *Cultures of Transnational Adoption*. Durham: Duke University Press, 2005.

Von Eschen, Penny. *Race against Empire: Black Americans and Anti-Colonialism, 1937–1957*. Ithaca: Cornell University Press, 1997.

———. *Satchmo Blows Up the World: Jazz Ambassadors Play the Cold War*. Cambridge: Harvard University Press, 2004.

Wacquant, Loïc J. D. "The Wedding of Workfare and Prisonfare in the 21st Century." *Journal of Poverty* 16, no. 3 (2012): 236–49. doi: 10.1080/10875549.2012.695540.

Wadlington, Walter. "The *Loving* Case: Virginia's Anti-Miscegenation Statute in Historical Perspective." In *Mixed Race America and the Law: A Reader*, edited by Kevin R. Johnson, 53–55. New York: New York University Press, 2003.

Wailoo, Keith. *Drawing Blood: Technology and Disease Identity in Twentieth-Century America*. Baltimore: Johns Hopkins University Press, 1997.

Wexler, Laura. *Tender Violence: Domestic Visions in an Age of US Imperialism*. Chapel Hill: University of North Carolina Press, 2000.

Williams, William Appleman. *The Tragedy of American Diplomacy*. New York: Norton, 1959.

Wong, K. Scott. *Americans First: Chinese Americans and the Second World War*. Philadelphia: Temple University Press, 2005.

Woo, Susie. "When Blood Won't Tell: Integrated Transfusions and Shifting Foundations of Race in 1950s America." *American Studies* 55, no. 4 (2017): 5–28.

Wu, Ellen D. *The Color of Success: Asian Americans and the Origins of the Model Minority*. Princeton: Princeton University Press, 2013.

Yamashita, Karen Tei. *Letters to Memory*. Minneapolis: Coffee House Press, 2017.

Yngvesson, Barbara. *Belonging in an Adopted World: Race, Identity, and Transnational Adoption*. Chicago: University of Chicago Press, 2010.

———. "'Un Niño de Cualquier Color': Race and Nation in Intercountry Adoption." In *Globalizing Institutions: Case Studies in Regulation and Innovation*, edited by Jane Jenson and Boaventura de Sousa Santos, 169–206. Aldershot, UK: Ashgate, 2000.

Yoneyama, Lisa. *Hiroshima Traces: Time, Space, and the Dialectics of Memory*. Berkeley: University of California Press, 1999.

Yoo, David K., and Ruth H. Chung. "Introduction." In *Religion and Spirituality in Korean America*, edited by David K. Yoo and Ruth H. Chung, 1–17. Urbana: University of Illinois Press, 2008.

Yoshihara, Mari. *Embracing the East: White Women and American Orientalism*. New York: Oxford University Press, 2003.

Youm, Kyu Ho. "Press Freedom under Constraints: The Case of South Korea." *Asian Survey* 26, no. 8 (August 1986): 868–82.

Young, James E. *The Texture of Memory: Holocaust Memorials and Meanings*. New Haven: Yale University Press, 1993.

Yu, Henry. *Thinking Orientals: Migration, Contact, and Exoticism in Modern America*. Oxford: Oxford University Press, 2001.

Yuh, Ji-Yeon. *Beyond the Shadow of Camptown: Korean Military Brides in America*. New York: New York University Press, 2002.

———. "Moved by War: Migration, Diaspora and the Korean War." *Journal of Asian American Studies* 8, no. 3 (October 2005): 277–91.

———. "Moving within Empires: Korean Women and Trans-Pacific Migration." In *Gendering the Trans-Pacific World: Diaspora, Empire, and Race*, edited by Catherine Ceniza Choy and Judy Tzu-Chun Wu, 107–13. Leiden: Brill, 2017.

Zeiger, Susan. *Entangling Alliances: Foreign War Brides and American Soldiers in the Twentieth Century*. New York: New York University Press, 2010.

DISSERTATIONS AND THESES

Ch'oe, Wŏn-gyu. "Oeguk min'gan wŏnjo danch'e hwaltonggwa han'guk sahoe saŏp palch'ŏne mich'in yŏnghyang" [Activities of foreign voluntary agencies and their influences upon social work development in Korea]. PhD diss., Seoul National University, 1996.

Graves, Kori A. "Domesticating Foreign Affairs: The African-American Family, Korean War Orphans, and Cold War Civil Rights." PhD diss., University of Wisconsin–Madison, 2011.

Kelso, Julianne N. "Pictorial Korea: Visualizing the Nation for a Foreign Audience in Cold War Photobooks." MA thesis, University of Toronto, 2015.

Kim, Whanyung. "Political Economy of Development and Religions in America." PhD diss., Stanford University, 1996.

Mitchell, Susan. "The Shadows of Assimilation: Narratives and Legacies of the Carlisle Indian Boarding School, 1879–1918." MA thesis, California State University, Fullerton, 2018.

Nakamura, Masako. "Families Precede Nation and Race? Marriage, Migration, and Integration of Japanese War Brides after World War II." PhD diss., University of Minnesota, August 2010.

Park, Bong Soo. "Intimate Encounters, Racial Frontiers: Stateless GI Babies in South Korea and the United States, 1953–1965." PhD diss., University of Minnesota, 2010.

Won, Yŏng-hi. "Han'guk ibyang chŏng ch'aeke kwanhan yŏngu" [A study on Korean adoption policy]. PhD diss., Ewha Women's University, Seoul, 1990.

Yi, Mi Son. "Haeoeibyanginŭi simrisahoejŏgjogŭnge yŏnghyangŭl mach'inŭn yoinŭ kwanhan yŏngu" [Research on the factors influencing the psycho-social adjustment of overseas adoptees]. PhD diss., Seoul Women's University, 2001.

FILMS

Battle Hymn. Directed by Douglas Sirk. Los Angeles: Universal Pictures, 1957. DVD.

Camp Arirang. Directed by Diana S. Lee and Grace Yoon Kyung Lee. New York: Third World Newsreel, 1995. DVD.

First Person Plural. Directed by Deann Borshay Liem. San Francisco: National Asian American Telecommunications Association, 2000. DVD.

Flower Drum Song. Directed by Henry Koster. Los Angeles: Universal International Pictures, 1961. DVD.

Geographies of Kinship–The Korean Adoption Story. Directed by Deann Borshay Liem. Berkeley, CA: Mu Films, 2012. DVD.

History and Memory: For Akiko and Takashige. Directed by Rea Tajiri. New York: Women Make Movies, 1991. DVD.

In the Matter of Cha Jung Hee. Directed by Deann Borshay Liem. Berkeley, CA: Mu Films, 2010.

Japanese War Bride. Directed by King Vidor. Los Angeles: Twentieth Century Fox, 1952. DVD.

The Manchurian Candidate. Directed by John Frankenheimer. Los Angeles: Metro-Goldwyn-Meyer, 1962. DVD.

Memory of Forgotten War. Directed by Deann Borshay Liem and Ramsay Liem. Berkeley, CA: Mu Films, 2015. DVD.

Sayonara. Directed by Joshua Logan. Los Angeles: Warner Brothers, 1957. DVD.

A Thousand Men and a Baby. Directed by Marcus Cole. Los Angeles: Columbia Broadcasting System, 1997. TV film.

Three Stripes in the Sun. Directed by Richard Murphy. Los Angeles: Columbia Pictures, 1955. Film.

WEBSITES

"America's War." US Department of Veterans Affairs, Office of Public Affairs. Accessed July 28, 2018. https://www.va.gov/opa/publications/factsheets/fs_americas_wars.pdf.

"Blast from the Past: Kim Sisters Rock the States." *Asianlife*, April 11, 2008. Accessed April 8, 2019. http://www.asianlife.com/magazine/view/articles/id/645838630.

"Catalog of *The Big Picture*." Army Pictorial Center: Signal Corps Photographic Center. Accessed April 4, 2019. www.armypictorialcenter.com/Catalog_of_the_Big_Picture.htm.

"*Ensign O'Toole* 1962 Full Episode Operation Benefit Dean Jones." Classic Friday Night TV. Accessed January 12, 2017. https://www.youtube.com/watch?v=WPAX_DqQVoA.

"Fact Sheet: An Overview of the US Army in the Korean War." US Army Center of Military History. Accessed July 17, 2018. http://www.nj.gov/military/korea/fact sheets/army.html.

Gibson, Campbell, and Kay Jung. "Historical Census Statistics on Population Totals by Race, 1790 to 1990, and by Hispanic Origin, 1970 to 1990, for the United States, Regions, Divisions, and States." US Census Bureau, September 2002. Accessed January 8, 2018. https://census.gov/content/dam/Census/library/working-papers/2002 /demo/POP-twps0056.pdf.

"Immigration and Nationality Act of 1952." US Department of State Office of the Historian. Accessed April 16, 2019. https://history.state.gov/milestones/1945-1952 /immigration-act.

Kang, Shin-who. "Shin Named Honorary President of Overseas Adoptees' Network." *Korea Times*, May 23, 2010. Accessed March 5, 2019. www.koreatimes.co.kr/www /nation/2018/07/719_66350.html.

Kim, Min-kyung. "Court Finds That South Korean Government Encouraged Prostitution Near US Military Bases." *Hankyoreh*, February 9, 2018. Accessed June 14, 2018. http://english.hani.co.kr/arti/english_edition/e_international/831625.html.

"Kim Sisters." Accessed April 14, 2019. https://www.youtube.com/watch?gl=SN&page =1&hl=fr&v=nPfOil8KoF8.

"Korean War Children's Memorial." Accessed April 2, 2019. www.koreanchildren.org.

"Korean War Fast Facts." CNN Library, April 30, 2018. Accessed April 15, 2019. https:// www.cnn.com/2013/06/28/world/asia/korean-war-fast-facts/index.html.

Lay, James S. "A Report to the National Security Council." National Security Council, April 14, 1950, 4. Accessed April 1, 2019. https://www.trumanlibrary.org/whistle stop/study_collections/coldwar/documents/pdf/10-1.pdf.

Lee, Claire. "Hard Knock Lives of Koreans Born to US Soldiers." *Korean Herald*, April 30, 2016. Accessed May 23, 2018. http://www.koreaherald.com.

Rhem, Kathleen T. "Korean War Death Stats Highlight Modern DoD Safety Record." US Department of Defense. Accessed April 5, 2019. https://archive.defense.gov /news/newsarticle.aspx?id=45275.

Shin, Paull. "Senator Paull Shin's Speech at KACF (Korean American Community Foundation) Fundraiser." Korean American story.org, January 2011. Accessed April 5, 2019. www.koreanamericanstory.org/senator-paull-shins-speech-at-kacf-fundraiser-3/.

"Star~Kim Project" (Kimura Byol-Nathalie Lemoine). Accessed February 2, 2018. https://starkimproject.com/.

Teszar, David. "From Seoul to Las Vegas: Story of the Kim Sisters." *Korea Times,* September 21, 2011. Accessed November 2, 1018. http://www.koreatimes.co.kr/.

Wilz, John Edward. "United States Policy Vis-a-vis Korea, 1850–1950." United States Air Force Academy Harmon Memorial Lecture 35, 1992. Accessed April 5, 2019. www .usafa.edu/app/uploads/Harmon35.pdf.

INDEX

Acheson, Dean, 35

adopters, 228n32; alternative child offered to, 102; barriers for African American, 126–30, 255n50; as Cold War internationalists, 15–16; HAP accepting unaccredited, 91, 121, 245n16; HAP requiring Christianity, 90–91, 245n12, 245n14; ISS criteria for, 117, 119–20; state transferring responsibility to, 116–17; US servicemen as, 39, 53–55, 106, 237n79, 238n90; white American figured as ideal, 89, 100

adoption: American narrative on, 141–42, 258n94; Americans inquiring about, 89–90, 245n6; barriers to African American, 125–30, 155–56, 255n48, 256n56; barriers to Korean-black placement, 128–29, 155, 168–69; biological likeness in US, 99–100, 121–22, 254n32; challenges of US military, 53–54, 237n80; as Christian duty, 85; Christian family clubs and, 91, 246n17; democracy and, 15–16; difficulty placing mascots, 52, 237n71; DoD preventing, 55; DoD response to demand for, 107–8; framed as Cold War internationalism, 15–16, 105; by GIs, 53–54, 106, 238n90; HAP numbers in, 121, 151; immigration laws and proxy, 90, 108–9, 252n105; as intercountry or overseas, 1–2, 2, 3, 225n3; ISS criteria for, 117, 119–20; from Japan, 106, 251n87; Korean mothers and severed ties to child, 161–62; Korean shame surrounding, 210; media

on Japanese, 254n33; orphanages as institutes for, 153, 156; photography used in, 100, 141, 249n65; professionalization of social welfare field through, 118, 253n21; Rhee facilitating overseas, 101–2, 150–52; Rhee's personal, 157–58, 264n41; RRA and demand for, 106–8; South Korea and US laws on, 106–9, 114–17, 251n94, 251n98, 253n16; transnational, 1–2, 2, 3, 88–89, 225n3; US domestic adoption, 99; World Vision sponsoring, 75, 86, 120, 253n27. *See also* relinquishment; transnational adoptions

AFAK. *See* Armed Forces Assistance to Korea

African Americans: adoption efforts by, 127–30, 205–7, 255n50; barriers to adoption, 126–30, 155–56, 256n56; coloration matching, 126, 255n50; constructed as "unfit" mothers, 125–30; discrimination against, 8, 18, 127–28; Holt, H., on Korean-black adoptees, 86, *87*, 88; Korean-black children categorized as, 124, 130; low numbers of adopters, 125–26, 255n48; McCarthyism constraining activism, 98–99; photographs used to screen adopters, 129–30; segregation in military, 154, 275n7, 275n9. *See also* black mothers; Korean-black children

Afro-Asian Conference, Bandung, Indonesia, 65, 240n38

AKF. *See* American-Korean Foundation

American civilians: adoption inquiries from, 89–90, 245n6; adoption narrative for, 112, 141–42, 257n70; appeals to, 60–61; assimilation expectations of, 111, 113, 134–35, 137–38, 174, *175*, 188–89, 191–92; black-white color line policed by, 125; children choirs embraced and supported by, 67–70, 73–77, *76*, 242n68; Cold War duty of, 101; criticism of US government regarding GI babies, 105; figured as members of a global family, 13–17, 104–5; immigration policy opened by, 109–10, 208, 215; Korean adoptees becoming, 112, 131–33, 256n66; Korean children figured as cowboys for, 48–49, *49*, 56, 236n55; Koreans as different from, 104, 250n75; as makers of international families, 4–5, 74, 80–81, 89; missionary women communicating with, 97–98; news of orphans from GIs to, 50–51; newsreels selected for, 40–41, 55–56; Orientalism and perceived superiority of, 61–63, 101–2; Orientalist imaginings by, 58–59, 103–4; orphanages operated by, 15–16, 57, 64, 84, 94, 96, 110, 119–20; orphan caretakers figured as, 50–51, 81; rescue by, 14–15, 64–65, 79–80, 101; RRA pushed by, 107, 251n98; support for Korean War, 35, 233n14; US empire changed by, 109–11; US global reach expanded by, 64–65, 98; on whiteness in Korean adoption placements, 122–23, 254n34

American empire, 2, 5–6, 20–21, 167, 173; administration of, 27; children as lens on, 8; "citizen subject" of, 212, 277n30; claims of "liberation" in, 11, 228n23; expansion and, 5–6; international criticism of, 10–11, 18, 109; "invisible government" and, 24, 230n55; Japanese incarceration in context of, 11, 184; Korean-black child experience in, 205–7; Korean War reconfiguring, 20–21, 207–8; Korean women and children altering, 5, 85, 202, 215; mixed-race children reminders of, 23, 150, 207; nongovernmental organizations participation in, 85; paternalism as tool of, 9, 34; post WWII shifts in, 5, 11; race ordering, 6, *7*, 8–9; South Korea as central to, 10, 212; sparking immigration fears, 6–9, *7*, 16; subjects of, 9, 16; US civilians changing, 16, 109–11, 208; US military and, 212, 277n34; US missionaries and, 85, 98; violence and care partnering in, 12, 20–21, 215

Americanization: of adoptee Lee, 1–4, *2*, *3*, 213; of immigrants, 18–19, 137–38; of Korean children, 46, 46–47, 70, 73–74, 112, 131–33, *133*, 136–38, 258n83; naming Korean adoptees, 136, 138, 258n85; transnational project beginning in Korea, 96, 136–37, 190–92

American-Korean Foundation (AKF), 58, 62; Children's Choir, political aims, 69–70; Children's Choir and, 67–74, *72*, 241nn50–51; *Masterpieces* Metropolitan Museum opening with Korean hostesses, 192–93, 273nn66–67; *Masterpieces of Korean Art* exhibit, 192–93, 273nn66–67; South Korean government support for, 241nn50–51; US government support for, 68–69

American Red Cross (ARC), 189

Angel's Haven Social Welfare Foundation, Seoul, 43, 57, 152, 159, 258n94

Anti-Asian sentiment, 8–9, 134–35

Armed Forces Assistance to Korea (AFAK), 34, 40, 84, 244n9

Armed Forces Radio Korea, xi, 273n75

Armstrong, Louis, 194, 230n54, 273n69

Asians: rejection of US imperialism, 10, 227n19; US racial discrimination against, 8–9, 134–35; as wards of

American empire, 6–9, 7, 12, 227n16, 228n25

assimilation: American things and actions as evidence of, 4, 77, 113, 133, 135, 197; coerciveness of, 25, 138; Korean adoptees experiences with, 17–18, 111, 257n70; to mitigate fears of non-white immigrants in American homes, 134–35, 137–38, 174, 175, 188–89, 191–92; in model minority scripts, 17–19, 113, 131–36; in narratives about Japanese war brides, 188–89; in narratives about Korean adoptees, 2, 3, 4, 133, 141; in narratives about Korean orphans, 76–77, 243nn78–79; in projects of US imperialism, 8–9, 189, 192; transnational processes of, 16, 136–37, 190–92

atomic bombs: deployed by US in Japan, 11; *Hiroshima Maidens Project* as US effort to repair damage, 13–14; nuclear family as security against, 13

Baer, Ulrich, 258n94

Battle Hymn, 77–80, 243n80

black mothers: constructed as "unfit," 125–30, 256n56; excluded from Korean rescue, 127; need to exceed standards in place for white adopters, 129–30; US agencies denying, 122–28

black-white color line, 124–30, 153–56, 255n42

Blaisdell, Russell, 77, 243n80

boarding schools, 8–9, 168–69, 268n91, 268n94

Bonesteel, Charles H., 10

Bowles, Chester, 10

brides schools, 16, 191–92, 273n65; transnational project of assimilation, 189–90

British military brides, 176, 269n6, 271n40

Buck, Pearl S., 105, 120, 158, 170, 246n25, 253n27, 268n97; censored for decrying US racial discrimination, 230n54; on

INS screening, 115; Korean controversy over mixed-race children "dropping like flies" comment, 92–93, 246n26; Korean mothers paid by, 160, 265n56; on "Negro-Korean" adoptions, 125, 255n47; South Korea praising work of, 262n21

Cambodia, 26

camptowns: in Korea, 30, 144, 144–45, 211; women, children hidden in, 147, 152, 160, 163, 206

CARE. *See* Cooperative for American Remittances to Everywhere

Catholic Committee for Refugees, 106

CCF. *See* Christian Children's Fund

censorship, 36, 40, 230n54, 233n16

Chicago Daily Tribune, 87, 132

Child Placement Service (CPS): Korea, 101–2, 151, 170, 268nn97–98. *See also* Social Welfare Society

children: evidencing US democracy through transformation of, 8–9, 75–76, 76, 131, 132, 133; navigating US empire through, 8, 11–12; photography of suffering, 60–61, 63–65, 240n28; US as saviors of, 14, 71, 228n30

China, 6, 9–10, 32, 35, 62, 227n16, 239n23, 248n45

China Doll Review, 194

Chinese Americans, 8–9, 17, 62, 134, 139, 229n38, 239n23 256n67

choirs. *See* Korean Children's Choir; Korean Orphan Choirs

Chosŏn Ilbo, 93, 152

Christian Children's Fund (CCF), 63–64, 240n27, 240n36, 244n9

Christians, 63, 78, 85; adopting from Korea, 90–91, 245n12; AFAK assisting missionaries in construction of orphanages and schools, 84, 244n9; choristers figured as, 74–77, 76, 79–80, 242n68; Christian adoptive family clubs, 91, 246n17;

Christians (*cont.*)
    converted Korean, 16, 31, 83–84;
    domestic and foreign missions, 95,
    248nn41–42; Korean Christian im-
    migration to Hawai'i, 95, 248n40;
    orphans and Christmas celebrations,
    41–42; proselytizing tactics in foreign
    missions, 94–95, 247nn34–35; US oc-
    cupation administration appointing
    Korean, 84; views on Korean ancestry,
    31–32, 232n3; women administrating
    Korean orphanages, 89, 95–98, 248n45.
    See also missionaries; missionary
    women
Christian Science Monitor, 90
Christian Women's Association (CWA),
    189
"citizen subject," 212, 277n30
Civil Rights, 88, 99, 134
"clean slates," 8, 134
coercion, 110–11, 160–64, 265nn52–53,
    265n58
Cold War, 2–5, 11–12, 63, 68, 70; democ-
    racy and, 15–16, 135, 257n73; family
    scripts and geopolitical needs of, 14,
    146–47; hidden Korean women and
    mixed-race children to uphold scripts
    of, 149, 260n3; increased defense
    spending and military build-up dur-
    ing, 35; international rescue and, 15–16,
    105; Korean adoptees supporting
    scripts of, 2, 2–3, 3, 113; Korean women
    disrupting scripts of, 176; making of
    international families during, 18–19;
    medical advancements as evidence of
    US prowess during, 13, 56; mother-
    hood as tool of, 95–96, 100–101; race
    conceptions and, 3, 16, 272n46; racial
    discrimination as liability in, 18; racial
    liberalism in, 19, 23; social workers
    aligning with, 118; US altruism to
    counter military force during, 20–21.
    See also communism

colonialism, 20–22, 51, 212, 230n52, 267n81
    277n30; Asians rejecting, 10, 227n19;
    intimacy and, 21–22, 149
"comfort women," 143–44, 259n4
commodities, Korean Children as Cold
    War, 18–19, 74, 104
communication, between Americans in
    Korea and the US, 50–51, 97–98
communism, 59, 63, 68, 84, 119, 184,
    257n73; INS screening for, 114–15,
    252n7; plight of GI babies and criti-
    cism of US, 105–6, 250n83; Soviets and,
    35, 234n21; US fight against, 1–2, 13–14,
    21, 36, 38, 238n5
Cooperative for American Remittances to
    Everywhere (CARE), 51
Cousins, Norman, 13
cowboys, 48–49, *49*, 56, 236n55
CPS. *See* Child Placement Service
Cuba, 228n23
CWA. *See* Christian Women's Association

Dean Martin Show, 199
decolonization: post-WWII, 10–11, 20; US
    policies in decolonizing countries, 35
democracy: Asian war brides evidenc-
    ing US, 179, 270nn24–25; children's
    choirs alignment with, 69–70; Cold
    War and, 15–16, 135, 257n73; families
    and, 12–13; HAP claims of racial, 88,
    108; INS screening for, 114–15, 252n7;
    through international adoption,
    102–3, *103*, 112–13; Japanese war brides
    evidencing racial, 184, 272n44; for
    Korea, 1, 67, 69; Korean children and
    future of, 18–19, 23, 45, 50, 55–56, 59,
    67, 69, 81, 98, 100, 112; missionary
    claims to, 84; South Korea upheaval
    and, 209, 276n15
Department of Defense (DoD), 51, 182,
    236n66; on adoption demand, 107–8;
    adoptions prevented by, 55; on GI
    babies, 268n107; on houseboys, 51–53;

orphan films by, 29, 34, 40–45, 44, 55–56; supervision of USO, 190

Department of the Army (DoA): on Korean children, 51, 236n55; on requests for adoption, 55; on requests for marriage, 180–81

disabled children, 97–98, 164–66, 266n77, 266n79, 267n81; mixed-race as, 166–68

Displaced Persons Act (1948), 250n85, 253n16

DoA. See Department of the Army

DoD. See Department of Defense

donations, 14, 64, 71, 73, 97, 197; CCF eliciting, 63–64, 240n36; global citizenry through, 59–60, 67; international bonds through, 22; rescue through, 15, 22, 65, 131; during war, 40–41, 51

Dong-A Ilbo, 39, 146

Ebony, 92, 125, 140

ECLAIR. See Eurasian Children Living as Indigenous Residents

The Ed Sullivan Show, 75, 194, 196, 273n69

Eisenhower, Dwight D., 57–58, 64, 68–70, 73, 238n5, 253n20

Eisenhower, Mamie, 70, 73

Ensign O'Tool, 197, 274n81

"ethnic cleansing," Korea's policy on mixed-race children as, 171

Eurasian Children Living as Indigenous Residents (ECLAIR), 169–70, 268n97

European military brides, 176–77, 269n6, 271n40

exceptionalism, 10; during Korean War, 36, 135, 140–41

families, 29; Americans constructing transnational, 4–5, 14–18, 80–81, 89; children's choirs evoking international, 71, 72, 73–74; Cold War containment and, 12–14, 146–47; democracy and, 12–13, 55, 74; empire undone by immigration resulting from transnational

families, 208; global reach through scripts of, 14, 16, 18, 58, 74, 81, 95–96; Korean adoptees and making of transnational, 17, 80–81, 89, 123–24; Korean mothers, mixed-race children denied, 160–63; Korean mothers struggle to maintain, 163–64; Koreans imagined as part of American, 14, 28–29; regulation of socially engineered, 99–100, 249n58

Family of Man, 13–14

First World, 100–102

Flower Drum Song, 17, 194

gender, 143, 191; expectations of Asian brides, 16, 174, 175, 187, 187–89, 191; expectations of Korean adoptees, 1–4, 2, 3, 136–37; GI absolution and, 172–73; militarized constructions of Korean boys, 1–2, 2, 44–53, 46, 47, 49; paternalism and girl choristers, 69, 71–73, 72; protecting Korean girls, 43–44; scripts for Korean orphans, 42, 69; threatened masculinity, 6, 185–87, 227n11, 272nn49–50

GI babies, 226n9; DoD on, 172, 268n107; efforts to remove from Korea, 157–58; evidence of well-cared for, 152, 157, 266n67, 268n94; GIs omitted from narratives about, 172–73; Korean adoptee narratives supplanting, 112–13; Korean mothers omitted from adoptee narratives, 146–47, 157; as mixed-race, 27, 86–89, 87; as outside US history of race mixture, 123; publicizing plight of, 89–90, 92–93; US demand for, 90, 93, 159; US military criticized for, 105–6, 250n83; US military responsible for creating, 5, 149, 206–7; US stories of abandoned, 105, 156–58. See also Korean-black children; Korean-white children; mixed-race adoptees; mixed-race children

GI brides. *See* European war brides; Japanese military brides; Korean military brides; war brides

GIs, 226n9. *See also* US servicemen

"global citizenship," 59–60, 231n67

Global Overseas Adoptees' Link, 54

global reach: through structures of domesticity, 14, 16, 18, 81, 96; of US, 2, 13, 21–22, 36, 57, 238n5

"Gook," 233n16

Guam, 228n23, 229n46

Haiti, 34

Handicapped Children's Survey Report Korea, 164–68, 266nn77–79

HAP. *See* Holt Adoption Program

Hawai'i, 4, 6, 21, 95, 143, 227n14, 229n47, 230n59, 248n40

Hess, Dean, 77–80, 243n80

Hiroshima Maidens Project, 13–14

Hollywood, California, 77, 79, 118, 152

Hollywood Palace, 196

Holt Adoption Program (HAP), 89–90, 108, 245n7; breakdown cases involving, 91, 120; children placed by, 93, 120, 121, 247nn30–31; competition by, 159–60, 264n51; ISS criticism of, 120–21; Korean mothers not informed by, 162–63, 265n64; mothers coerced by, 160–61, 265n52, 265n58; news of happy placements affirming, 152, 262n24; partnership with CPS, 151; race identifying practices of, 154–55, 263n34, 263nn28–30; social welfare agency criticism of, 91–92; South Korea awarding, 151–52, 262n21; South Korea supporting, 151–52, 263n39; unaccredited adopters by, 91, 121, 245n16, 254n30

Holt, Bertha, 89, 108

Holt, Harry, 55, 85, 86, 89, 155; Christianity requirement for adoptions, 90–91, 245n12, 245n14; on Korean-black

children, 86, *87*, 88, 155; lobbying for mixed-race adoptions, 108, 155, 251n98; on plight of mixed-race children, 86–88, *87*, 90, 155, 245n7, 254n33; proxy adoptions, 120–21; publicity efforts to promote Korean adoptions, 86–88, *87*, 89–90

Holt, Molly, 89, 90, 96, 118, 160, 245n6

houseboys, 48–50, 51–55, 236n53, 236n66; colonial context of, 51; military heterosexuality and masculinity learned by, 52; US military efforts to prevent, 52–53; as US military translators and spies, 47, 48, 51–52

humanitarianism, 159, 212, 215, 235n37; as proselytizing tactic in US foreign missions, 63, 91, 94–95; and US Cold War policy, 21, 40–41, 59, 107, 110

immigration, 29–30, 210; adoptee placement and, 114–17; Americanization in, 18–19, 138; Cold War pressures and opening of US, 113; from Japan, 106, 251n87; from Korea, 4, 16, 19; Korean children and women made safe for, 16; provisions to stop chain migration, 115–16; proxy adoptions and laws on, 90, 108–9, 252n105; resulting from US empire, 6, 9, 16; US restrictions on, 4, 88, 113, 225n6, 244n3 (chapter 3), 252n1, 269n8

Immigration and Naturalization Service (INS), 113; Buck on screening by, 115; denying entry of Korean birth mothers, 161; ISS partnering in placements of mixed-race children, 117, 121; protections against brides becoming public charges, 182–83, 271nn38–39; screening of adoptees, 113–16, 252n7; screening of military brides, 179–80, 270nn24–25

imperialism, 20, 165, 229n46; accusations against US, 10; administering, 34–35, 213, 278n37; anti-conquest narratives in service to, 28; Asians as wards of, 5, 9, 12, 227n16, 228n25; assimilation and projects of, 189–90, 192; care and kin allaying accusations of, 207–8; colonialism and US, 21–22, 230n52; First World superiority and, 100–102; intimacy in, 21–23, 27; ISS as against, 119; Japan resisting white, 229n41; Korean adoptees softening appearance of, 24, 112; liberal claims in, 18–19, 229n42; mixed-race children as reminders of US, 5, 23, 150, 207; motherhood and, 100–102, 228n31; overlapping projects of, 20, 36, 84; race and, 6–9, 7; rescue to allay accusations of, 13, 22, 212, 277n36; South Korea and US, 20–21; Truman response to, 36, 233n20; US expansion as, 5–6, 24, 230n55; war brides softening appearance of, 14, 174, 184. *See also* American empire

India, 10

INS. *See* Immigration and Naturalization Service

integrated schools, 170–71, 268n98

integration: by African Americans, 134; assimilation to whiteness as pretense for, 18–19, 123; by Chinese and Japanese Americans, 134; intercountry adoption as evidence of racial, 4, 105; international rescue and claims of, 64–65; KAVA, ECLAIR for, 169–70; as outcome of Korean War, 5; South Korea need for, 171; US failures in, 18, 88, 125, 184, 244n3 (chapter 3); welfare agencies not helping, 125, 130

internationalism: assaults by US servicemen and damage to, 146–47; choir children embodying, 67–77, 72, 76; Cold War scripts of, 149; to counter anti-imperialist stance of Japan, 229n41; Holt, H., as representative of, 88; immigration problems resulting from, 29–30; Kim Sisters embody-

ing, 196–97, 201; Korean adoptions as evidence of, 3, 3–4, 5, 86, 100, 105; Korean-black children and limits of, 124–25; military general as representative of, 68–69, 71, 72; Orientalism for, 61; otherness supporting, 70; overshadowing experiences of Korean mother and child, 19–20, 147; put into practice by Americans, 27; white mothers and, 15; white women missionaries and, 96

International Social Service (ISS), 92, 106, 117, 121; adoptee adjustment reported in home studies, 122–23; adoption criteria by, 117, 119–22; anti-imperialist approach of, 119; black-white color line upheld by, 125; on closeness between Korean mother and child, 163, 265n66; cooperation with other agencies, 117–19; criticism of Holt, H., 92, 120; DoD marriage communications with, 182; efforts to find mixed-race children, 160; GI marriage assistance from, 181–82; INS partnering with, 116–17; Korean-black adoption concessions by, 126–27, 255n52; Korean branch of, 117, 119; obstacles to Korean-black placements, 127–28, 256n58; professionalization of social welfare, 118–19; relinquishment concerns by, 160–62, 265n58; transnational adoptions overseen by, 117–18, 247n31, 253n17; views on Korean mixed-race children, 92, 105, 163; WAIF and, 117–18, 253n20

interracial families: barriers to Asian-black adoptive, 126–30, 205–7; barriers to black-white, 124–25; biological likeness within, 121–23, 254n38; Korean-white as acceptable, 122–24, 254n34; miscegenation laws, 177, 178, 255n39; supporting Cold War scripts, 3, 16; US rejection of, 123

ISS. *See* International Social Service

Japan: adoption from, 106–7, 251n87; African Americans and adoption from, 128–30; birth "mother's sorrow," 163, 266n67; colonization of Korea, 9, 11, 20, 35, 36, 67, 83, 144, 234n25; "comfort women," 143–44, 259n4; compared against Koreans, 31–32, 66; filmed instead of Korea, 185, 272n48; GIs visit orphanages in, 38; prostitution sanctioned by, 145, 251n11; spy trials against, 52, 237n69; turned into US ally, 17, 38; Western imperialism resisted by, 229n41; during WWII, 17, 36

Japanese Americans, 11, 184; as model minorities, 17, 133–34, 256n67, 257n68; transnational identities of, 231n67

Japanese military brides: assimilation of, 188–89; brides schools for, 189–90, 191; cultural pluralism through, 184, 187, 272n44; differentiated from Korean women, 190; films depicting, 185–88; INS and war bride fees for, 182–83, 271n38; marriage process for, 177–79, 269n9; supplanting narratives of Korean brides, 30, 184; white masculinity affirmed by, 185–89, 187, 272nn49–50

Japanese War Bride (1952), 185–88, 272n47

Jim Crow laws, 5, 11, 153–54, 232n72

Jimmy Pusan (Pon Son See), 44–47, 46, 47, 48, 50

juvenile delinquency, 45, 167

Kang Koo Rhee, 131, 132, 133

KAVA. See Korean Association of Voluntary Agencies

KCAC. See Korea Civil Assistance Command

"Keen Teens," 45–47, 46

Kim, Kathy, 131–33, 256n66

Kim Sisters, 193–201, 195, 198, 199, 273n69; childhood innocence and sexuality of, 199, 199–201; connected with Korean orphans, 197–99, 198, 274n81;

connected with Korean war brides, 201; as internationalists, 196–97, 201; as Korean cultural ambassadors, 196, 273nn74–76; photography showing, 195, 197–99, 198, 199

Korea: Christianity in, 16, 31, 83–84; division of, 9–10, 21, 23, 31, 37, 272n48; mass migration within, 34, 57; US militarization altering, 23, 205–7, 215; US occupation of, 9–10, 31, 34–37, 150, 234n21, 261n10; US views on, 31–32, 232n1 (part 1); war starting in, 10, 227n18. See also South Korea

Korea Civil Assistance Command (KCAC), 34–35

Korea family registries, 115, 120, 123, 150, 177, 252n10, 261n9

Korean adoptees: Americanization of, 70, 73–74, 112, 131, 135–38, 258n83; American names for, 136, 138, 258n85; assimilation of, 134–37, 141; Battle Hymn actors becoming, 80–81; Christian family clubs with, 91, 246n17; as "clean slates," 8, 134; as commodities, 18–19, 74, 104, 110, 209; community and empowerment of, 25, 215, 278n43; as cowboys in US media, 48–49, 49, 236n55; on "first day" in America, 1–4, 2, 3, 112, 131, 133, 135; as "full-blooded" in US media, 1–4, 2, 3, 80–81, 112, 131–33, 135; HAP competition for, 159–60, 264n51; HAP placement of, 93, 120, 247nn30–31; infants versus children as, 158–59, 264n46; INS management of mixed-race, 117; INS rejecting "defective," 114–15; isolation from Asians benefitting, 134–35; Korea erased for, 8, 134, 138, 213; as Korean ambassadors, 23; as Korean "exports," 110, 150, 209; lack of Korea social personhood for, 116, 252n10; militarized constructions of boy, 1–2, 2; model minorities, 131–36, 256n67; narratives about mixed-race,

152, 262n24; narratives crafted for US, 17, 112, 141–42; numbers of, 4, 25, 93, 209–10, 247nn28–31; perspectives of, 17–18, 25, 111, 170, 215, 231n63, 257n70, 258n94, 276n22, 278n42; photography and trauma of, 140–42, 258n94; placed into existing constructions of family, 16–18, 123–24; presumed adaptability of, 135–36, 257n76; racial difference contained in home, 140–41; as refugees, 25–26; return tours, reunions for, 210; trauma for, 111, 138, 141, 213–14, 278n40; as US citizens, 131–33, 256n66; US demand for, 89–90, 93, 157; US gendered expectations of, 136–37; war brides disrupting narratives of, 176; whiteness for, 99–100, 123. See also Korean-black children; Korean-white children; mixed-race adoptees

Korean adoption: alternative children offered in, 102, 249n69; challenges to domestic, 149–50, 261n9; change of citizenship in, 116; Cold War aims of, 104–5, 113; expanding US notions of family, 89, 123–24; family lineages lost by, 115–16, 161–62; as First World responsibility, 100; gatekeeping practices in, 114–17, 119–20; Holt, H. popularizing, 86–88, 87, 254n33; as immigration breach, 16; ISS and, 120–23, 163, 265n66; Korea media promoting overseas, 152, 157–58, 263n39; as legacy of Korean War, 211–12; legislation for, 106–9, 250n85; Orientalist framework in, 71, 103–4, 122–23; parent search before, 116, 252n13; race intermixing through, 88, 138–40, 258n88; racial discrimination and, 88, 112, 138–40, 258n88; racial liberalism and, 88, 105; softening appearance of imperialism, 24, 104–5, 112, 230n55; to unaccredited homes, 91, 121, 245n16, 254n30; US military barriers against, 53–55. See

also Holt Adoption Program; International Social Service; World Vision

Korean Association of Voluntary Agencies (KAVA), 169–70, 266n77

Korean-black children, 226n9; boarding schools for, 168–69, 268n91, 268n94; Buck on adoptions of, 93, 125, 255nn47–48; categorized as African American, 124, 130; effects of US militarization upon, 205–7, 275nn7–9; examinations to identify race of, 152–56; experiences of, 170, 205–7; institutionalization of in Korea, 30, 128, 147, 155–56; internationalist limits on, 124–25; ISS adoption concessions for, 126–27, 255n52; ISS challenges placing, 127–29, 256n58; Korean family registries excluding, 115, 123, 150, 261n9; as "Negro-Korean," 124–26, 255n47; numbers of, 109–10, 163, 164, 252n108, 266n75; "patient identity" for, 155, 166; racial discrimination against, 124, 125, 130, 168, 170; transnational adoption "preferred solution" for, 168; US requests for, 93, 247n30; white parents raising, 124, 255n44

Korean children: Americanization of, 45–47, 46, 70–71, 73–74, 131–33, 136–38; American women caring for, through donations, 51, 248n44; assimilation of, 2, 3, 4, 18, 111, 141; in Battle Hymn, 77–81; as bridge between Korea and US, 1–4, 2, 3, 55–56, 58; choirs of, 67–77, 72, 76, 242n68; Christian missionaries and needs of, 84, 94–98, 119, 247nn34–35; 248n51; in constructions of US postwar power, 11; father preventing relinquishment of, 100–101; girls protected among, 43; GIs interacting with, 39–50, 46, 47, 234n33; GIs recast with, 34, 49–50; Korean sovereignty and, 65, 196, 273nn74–76; militarized construction of boys, 43–47, 46, 47;

Korean children (*cont.*)
numbers emigrating, 4, 225n7; Orphan
Adoption Special Law for, 116; photography of, 2, 3, 44, 46, 47, 49, 71–73, 72,
76, 87, 132, 133; politicizing of, 1–4, 11,
212–13; as representatives of democracy, 18–19, 23, 45, 50, 59, 67, 74, 81, 98,
100, 112; rescue deserved by, 12, 58–61;
scant wartime documents by, 213,
278n37; search for biological parents
of, 116, 252n13; as South Korean "exports," 110, 150; US aid transforming,
70–71, 76–77; US Cold War aims and,
12, 59, 67–68, 149; US empire changed
by, 5, 215; US gendered constructions of, 48–50, 49, 69, 136–37; waif
imagery of, 59–61, 132, 239n15; white
women global reach via, 95–98. *See
also* Korean adoptees; Korean-black
children; Korean orphans; Korean-
white children
Korean Children's Choir: AKF for, 67–69,
241nn50–51; families evoked by, 71,
72, 73; as Korea ambassadors, 67, 74,
241nn50–51; political aims of, 67–69;
US civilians supporting, 67–70, 73–74;
US paternalism and girls of, 69; Van
Fleet and photography of, 71, 72, 73
Korean Crippled Children's Center, 97–98
Korean military brides, 4, 17–18, 226n9;
activism of, 211; brides schools and, 16,
189–92, 273n65; as charges of military husbands, 182–83, 271nn38–39;
community for, 192, 211, 273n65; to
Hawai'i, 230n59; as hidden, 19, 147;
immigration stemming from, 19, 210;
imperialism allayed by "first," 174, 175,
269n1; INS screening of, 113–14, 179–
80, 270nn24–25; McCarran-Walter
Act of 1952 permitting, 178, 269n8;
numbers of, 4, 174, 225n7; perspectives of, 215, 278n42; as prostitutes,
190; as refugees, 25–26; supplanted by

narratives of Japanese brides, 30, 184;
trauma for, 203, 274n91, 275n92; US
gendered expectations of, 174, 175, 191;
US military efforts to prevent, 177–82,
269nn10–11, 271n29; War Brides Act of
1947, 16, 182; working on US military
bases, 183, 271n41
Korean mothers: adoption agreements as
binding, 161; assumed prostitutes, 55,
104, 150; as erased in order to sustain
Cold War scripts, 149, 157–64, 260n3;
GI babies and omission of, 146–47, 157;
HAP coercing, 160–61, 265n52; ISS on
child and, 160–62, 163, 265n58, 265n66;
ISS search for mixed-race children,
160, 265n52; Korean views on, 159;
mixed-race children and, 148–49,
164, 260n3; mother of Korean-black
child, 205–7; mother of Korean-white
child, 148; orphanages not informing,
162–63, 265n64; Pearl Buck foundation
paying, 160, 265n56; perspectives of,
215, 278n42; prostitution after rape,
163, 266n70; rescue not including,
19–20, 157; state pressure to relinquish
children, 157–59, 160, 264n47, 265n53;
white mothers substituted for, 102–3,
103, 161–62
Korean Orphan Choirs, 74; *Battle Hymn*
echoing, 79–80; Christianity alignment for, 74–77, 76, 79–80, 242n68; by
World Vision, 74–75, 76, 242n68
Korean orphans: aid to meet needs of, 15,
62–64, 239n24; Americans figured as
caretakers, 50–51, 81; *Battle Hymn* acting by, 77–80; choirs of, 67–77, 72, 76,
241nn50–51, 242n68; Christianity for,
16, 98, 135; Christmas unfamiliar to,
41–42; DoD filming of, 29, 34, 40–41,
43–45, 44; figured as waifs, 59–61, 64,
132; GIs raising money for, 50, 236n58;
as houseboys, 48–50, 51–55, 236n53,
236n66; Kim Sisters connected with,

197–99, *198*, 274n81; Koreans finding homes for, 149–50; as mascots, 44–46, *49*, 49–50; numbers of, 14–15; perceived adaptability of, *76*, 76–77, 243nn78–79; prostitution to support themselves, 144–45; resulting from Korean War, 14–15, 57–58; South Korea unable to support, 37, 57, 94; trauma for, 42; US war violence creating, 5, 11, 32, 36, 42, 207; white women caring for, 50–51

Koreans: anti-communist stance of, 1, 61, 270n24; Christianity embraced by, 16, 31, 83–84; criticism of US military, 36–37, 145–46, 232n3, 260n16, 260n20; effort to remove mixed-race children, 150–53, 171, 210, 263n39; finding local homes for orphans, 149–50; importance of family lineage, 92, 115, 150, 261n9; Kim Sisters as, *195*, 195–96; missionary women and needs of, 94–98, 247nn34–35; population in US, 4, 18; positive views on US, 39; representations of Koreans by, 65–66, 192–93; on US missionaries, 149; US Orientalist views on, 31–32, 35, 104, 232n1 (part 1), 232n3 (part 1), 250n75; wartime images of, 4, 43–50, *44*, 59–61, 64, *132*

Korean War, 1, 10, 33; American disapproval of, 33, 35–36; American support for, 35, 233n14; armistice, 1, 11; civilian deaths in, 32, 36; as civil war, 35; feared to be start of WWIII, 33; as forgotten, 24, 214; losses in, 1, 11, 225n2; military force and aid in, 21; napalm used in, 11, 36; North Korea guerilla tactics, 33, 143; numbers of ROK servicemen in, 35; numbers of UN allies in, 35; numbers of US servicemen in, 32, 234n30; as opportunity for global reach of white women, 15–16, 95–98; prostitution, orphanages, adoptions stemming from, 10, 227n18; as test of

US power, 33, 35–36, 233n14; Truman selling, 36, 233n20; US bomb used in, 11, 32, 36, 228n22, 233n16; US empire reconfigured by, 207–8; US financial commitments in, 32, 35; war brides from, 211–12; "war time" result of, 212, 277n35

Korean-white children, 226n9; adjustment in adoptive homes, 122–23; completing US families, 102–3, *103*; as exotic, 122–23; as "half-American," 106, 123, 150–52; HAP competition for, 159–60, 264n51; HAP placement of, 93, 120, 247nn28–31; INS management of, 117, 125; integrationist aims through, 123–24; Korean discrimination against, 168, 170; narratives about, 152, 262n24; numbers of, 109–10, 163, 164, 252n108, 266n75; "patient identity" for, 155, 166; requests for, 93, 122, 247n30; schools for, 168–69, 170, 268n91, 268n94; surprise acceptance of in US, 18–19, 65, 123; white parents resembling, 122–23, 254n36, 254n38. *See also* mixed-race children

Korean women: activism and empowerment of, 163–64, 192, 211, 215, 278nn42–43; as AKF hostesses, 193, 273n66; assaulted by US servicemen, 37, 146, 151, 160, 209, 234n23, 260n20, 261n14, 276n15; as assumed prostitutes, 104, 150, 180–81, 183, 190; in camptowns, 147, 160–61, 163, 205–7; as "comfort women," 143–44, 259n4; scant wartime documents by, 213, 278n37; US empire changed by, 5, 215; US militarized prostitution and, 144–46, 259n9, 260n16; US military discouraging relationships with, 176; US nation-building efforts and erasure of, 146–47, 157, 202; as war widows, 48, 59, 144, 145–46, 275n11. *See also* Korean military brides; Korean mothers

Lady Liberty, 71–72, *72*

Lee, Kyung Soo (Paladino, James Lee), 1–4, *2*, *3*, 56, 131, 213–15, 225n1, 278n40

liberalism, 18–19, 22–23, 112–13, 130, 184, 194, 229n40, 229n42

Life, xi, xii, 1–4, *2*, *3*, 70, 80–81, 104–5, 131, *131*, *132*, 174, *175*, 194, 197–99, *198*, *199*, 200, 214, 225n4

Look, xi, 131, 187, *187*

Los Angeles Times, 76, *76*, 213, 214

"mamasans," 205–7, 275n8

The Manchurian Candidate, 183–84, 272n43

mascots, 44–50, *46*, *47*, *49*, 52, 236n53, 236n55, 237n71; adoption difficulty for, 52, 237n71; model qualities of, 46–47; as US military translators and spies, 47, 48, 51–52

masculinity, 6, 78, 227n11; GIs teach Korean boys, 44–46, *46*, *47*, 52; Japanese women affirming white, 185–87, 272nn49–50; as threatened, 6, 18

Masterpieces of Korean Art, 192–93, 273nn66–67

McCall's, 60, 100, 131

McCarthyism, 98–99

media: "full-blooded" Korean adoptees in US, 1–4, *2*, *3*, 80–81, 112, 131–33, 135, 256n66; Japanese adoptions in US, 254n33; Korean self-representation for US, 65–66, 192–93, 240nn38–39; Korea promoting adoption, 152, 157, 263n39; plight of GI baby in US, 86–88, *87*, 89–93; South Korea censorship, 39–40, 152, 235n36; South Korean propaganda, 37–38; US censorship, 36, 40, 233n16; US newsreels, 40–41, 55–56; war brides in US, 174, *175*, 185–89, *187*, 269n1

Miami Daily News, 46, *46*

miscegenation laws, 123, 177, 178, 255n39, 262n26

missionaries: Korean incompetence perceived by, 209; orphanages administered by, 94, 96, 135; proselytizing mission in Korea, 83–84, 94–95, 247n36; relationship with US occupation government, 84–85; US held accountable through, 151; views on Koreans, 31–32. *See also* Christians; missionary women

missionary women, 248n41; communication with American donors, 97–98; at forefront of foreign missions, 95–99, 248n42, 248n45; implementing Bible and Western modes of care in Korean orphanages, 89, 95–98, 248n51

mixed-race adoptees, 226n9; adjustment in adoptive homes, 122–23; breakdown cases involving, 91–92, 120; Buck on, 92–93, 105; demand for, 93, 122, 247n30, 254n34; "ethnic cleansing" of, 150, 171; "full" Korean adoptee narrative supplanting, 112–13; GI adoptions of, 54–55, 238n92; GIs omitted from narratives about, 172–73; HAP competition for, 159–60, 264n51; HAP placement of, 93, 120, 247nn30–31; as hidden, 19–20, 147; Holt, H., on, 86–88, *87*, 120–21, 254n29; INS management of, 117; Korea family registries excluding, 115, 150; Korean media promoting, 152, 157, 251n94, 262n24, 263n39; Korean mothers omitted from narratives about, 146–47, 157; need for Korean policies to protect, 168; numbers of, 4, 29–30, 93, 112, 163, 210, 247nn28–31; perspectives of, 170, 171, 215, 278n42; photographs of, for Korean mothers, 27, 207, 266n67; proxy ban reducing, 164, 266n72; publicizing plight of, in US, 89–90, 92–93; racial discrimination against in Korea, 92, 164, 261n11, 264n47; as "social handicaps," 30, 166–68, 267n82; US and responsibility for,

105, 159–60; US demand for, 90, 93, 159, 254n34. *See also* Korean adoptees; Korean-black children; Korean-white children

mixed-race children: boarding schools for, 168–69, 268n91, 268n94; ECLAIR school for, 169–70; examination and blood of, 152–56, 262nn25–26; GI fathering responsibility for, 88, 105, 109, 150, 153, 172–73, 183; hidden in camptowns, 147, 152, 160, 163; Korean-Chinese and -Japanese mixture, 150, 166; Korean mothers and, 148–49, 163–64, 205–7; numbers in Korea, 93, 163, 164, 210, 247nn28–29, 266n76; perspectives of, 170, 171, 215, 276n21, 278n42; presumed criminality of and intervention for, 166–68; racial discrimination against, in Korea, 92, 164, 261n11, 264n47; as reminders of US intervention, 23, 27, 30, 150, 207; searched for in camptowns, 159–60; as "social handicaps," 30, 166, 171, 267n82; social welfare solutions for, 166–68; South Korea and, 23, 30, 86–88, *87*, 93, 148–51, 159–60, 166–67, 171, 210, 246n26, 247nn28–29, 276n21; stateless and without rights, 150; troubling US liberal claims, 149, 260n3; as "unwanted," 23, 92, 128, 150–51, 157, 159–60, 210, 276n21

model minorities, 140, 256n67; Chinese Americans as, 17, 134, 229n38, 256n67; as divisive, 140, 258n93; Japanese Americans as, 17, 133–34, 256n67, 257n68; Korean adoptees as, 17–19, 113, 131–35; photographs communicating, *2*, *3*, *46*, *72*, *76*, *133*, 140, *175*, *187*, *198*; war brides as, 174, *175*, 179, 184–89, *187*

motherhood: American *versus* Korean, 88; appeals to, 60; black, 125–30; Koreans denied, 19–20, 157–64; as tool of Cold War internationalism, 96,

100–104, *103*; transnational adoptions and mobilization around, 109–10; and US citizenship, 100, 102; white imperial, 100–102. *See also* black mothers; Korean mothers; white mothers

National Geographic, 43, 48, *49*

nationalism: Korean, 23, 149–50; preserving US and South Korean, 167, 172–73

National Security Council Report 68 (NSC-68), US military build-up as a result of, 35

National Urban League (NUL), 126, 255n50

nation-building: Korean, 23, 65–66, 74; US, 6, 21

Native Americans, 5, 8–9

neo-colonialism, 20

Newsweek, 40, 79, 188, 194

New York Times, 36, 37, 58, 66, 68, 71, 72, 73, 80, 92, 93, 203, 214

Nkrumah, Kwame, 20

No Gun Ri, 33

nongovernmental organizations: aid by, 27, 57–58, 238n4; CCF, 63–64, 240n27, 240n36; as extension of American empire, 22, 85, 208; Korean children and communism connected by, 58–59; for Korean women, 211, 276n25; photos of suffering children and, 59–64, 240n28

North Korea, 1, 10, 32, 33, 36, 209, 234n21

NSC-68. *See* National Security Council Report 68

NUL. *See* National Urban League

Oliver, Robert, 31

Orientalism, 16–17; access to Asia and Asian women, 143, *144*, 259n3; anti-Chinese sentiment in, 62, 239n23; blending of "Oriental" things, 104, 195, 200; female gendered, 17, 143, 188, 200, 272n50; internationalism unable to supplant, 140; Kim Sisters and, 193–96, *195*;

Orientalism (*cont.*)
post-WWII shifts in US, 17, 61; pretext for US intervention, 35, 209; in rescue, 61–62; in US representations of Koreans, 31, 58–59, 62–65; US superiority assumed in, 31, 71, 209, 276n14; white women and, 102–4, *103*

Orphan Adoption Special Law (1961), 116, 253n14

orphanages, 26–27; choir children and *Battle Hymn* actors from, 74, 78, 80; director signature authorized for adoptions, 162–63, 265n64; domestic adoption efforts in Korean, 150; GIs visiting in Japan, 38; GIs visiting in Korea, 29, 39–42, 50–51; as institutions for adoptions, 153–56, 158; as legacy of Korean War, 209, 211–12; as location for transnational assimilation projects, 16, 96–98, 136–38; photographs in administrative files, 141–42; racially segregated, 30, 147, 156; as US-operated and supported, 15–16, 20, 37, 57–58, 64, 84, 94, 96, 110, 119–20, 208–9

Orphan Bill (1957), 108

orphans. *See* Korean orphans

Packwood, Norval E., 143, *144*

Paladino, James Lee. *See* Lee, Kyung Soo

Paladino, Vincent, 1–3, *2, 3*, 131, 213–14, 225n1, 278n40

paternalism, 9, 11; choir girls and US, 69; donations and, 14, 71, 73; problematized for GIs, 52–53; as veil and vehicle of American empire, 34

"patient identity," 166

Philippines, 6–9, *7*, 21, 227n16, 228n23, 229n46

photography, 60–62; of adoptees: Kang, 131, *132, 133*; of adoptees: Kim, 131–33, 256n66; of adoptees: Lee, 1–4, *2, 3*; adoptee trauma seen in, 140–42, 258n94; in adoptions, 100, 249n65;

capturing "first day" in America, 1–4, *2, 3*, 131, *133*, 135, 174, *175*; CCF and Cold War constructions, 63; contradictions in family, 29; framing and narrative in, 28–29; "ghostly matters" in, 213; global understanding through, 2, 3, 13–14; Kim Sisters, *195*, 197–99, *198, 199*; of Korean children, *47, 49*, 59–60, *132*, 239n15; of mixed-race adoptees, 86, *87*; model minorities communicated through, 140; for mothers to evidence happy placements, 27, 163, 266n67; pain communicated though, for purpose of rescue, 60–61, 239nn17–18; to screen prospective adoptive parents, 129–30; Van Fleet and Children's Choir in, 71, *72, 73*

Pierce, Bob, 78, 86, 92, 243n79; on GI culpability, 172, 268n106; South Korea praising, 262n21

Pittsburgh Courier, 202

propaganda, 38, 40–41

prostitutes, 144–46, 259n9; activism and resistance, 163–64, 211, 215; after rape, kidnapping, 144, 163, 261n14, 266n70; blaming Korean women, 145, 260n16; camptowns, 30, 144–45, 147, 160–61, 163–64, 205–7, 211; connected to "comfort women," 143, 259n4; denied rights and protections, 145–46; health examinations for military brides, 180, 271nn28–29; INS screening to deny, 178–79; Kim Sisters evoking, *199*, 199–201; Korean mothers and, 55, 104, 163, 166–67; legacy of Korean War, 211–12; "mamasans," 205–7, 275n8; military brides as assumed, 175–76, 183, 190, 271n40; monitored for disease, 145, 259n15; mothers as assumed, 55, 104, 190; organization among and settlement for, 211, 276n25; racial segregation and, 206, 275n9; registration of, 145; sanctioning of Japanese, Korean,

145, 259n11; South Korea rejecting, 23, 26, 145; as unseen, 19–20, 147; US militarization root cause of, 143–46, *144*, 168, 170, 183–84, 230n58, 260n16, 277n28; war brides as assumed, 178, 183; war widows, orphans as, for survival, 144, 145–46, 259n9, 275n11

proxy adoptions: ban reducing, 164, 266n72; Buck use of, 253n27; Holt use of, 120–21, 151, 254n30; ISS criticism of, 92, 120; laws on, 90, 108–9, 252n105

Puck magazine, 6–9, *7*

Puerto Rico, 21, 228n23

race, 8; Cold War and conceptions of, 3–4, 15–16, 272n46; Holt, H., on, 86, *87*, 88, 155; Kim Sisters and US Orientalism, 193–96, *195*; Korean adoptions and intermixing, 88, 138–40, 258n88; Korean-white children as closer to white, 122–23; liberalism and Korean adoptions, 88, 104–5; limits of liberalism, 17–18, 112–13, 130, 140; linked to blood, 255n42, 262nn25–26; matching in domestic adoptions, 99–100, 121–22; mixing as "social handicap" in Korea, 166–68, 267n82; US fears on interracial families, 123; US internationalism and, 22–23, 88, 103, *103*, 109, 112–13, 184

racial democracy: during Cold War, 18–19, 103, *103*, 112–13, 229n40; limits of, 130, 229n42

racial discrimination: against Asian Americans, 134–35; against Asian war brides, 176–77, 269n6, 271n40; against black mothers, 127–28; civil rights constrained by McCarthyism, 98–99; Cold War internationalism as cover for ongoing, 3–4, 16, 272n46; in discussions of adoptees intermarriage, 138–40, 258n88; in Korea, 92, 152–53, 164, 261n11, 264n47; against Korean-black children and adopt-

ers of, 124–30; in Korean integrated schools, 171; against Korean military brides, 202; Korean-white children made safe through whiteness, 122–23; as marring US claims to democracy, 18; miscegenation laws as, 123, 178, 255n39, 262n26; in practices to identify Korean-black children, 153–56, 262nn25–26, 263nn28–30; in US, 110, 184; US transferred to Korea, 153–56

racial segregation: in Korea, 30, 154, 156, 206, 275n9; in US, 18, 109, 244n3 (chapter 3)

Refugee Relief Act (RRA), 106–8, 114, 251n98

refugees, 25–26, 33, 57, 77, 238n1, 252n7; Chinese, 107, 113, 257n73

relinquishment: of children *versus* infants, 158–59, 264n46; in domestic US adoption, 99, 158; forms used in Korea, 252n13, 265n64; ISS regarding, 160–62, 265n58; Korean father refusing, 100–110; Korean mothers coerced by Americans, 160–64, 265n58, 265nn52–53; Korean mothers pressured by Koreans, 157–59, 264n47; Pearl S. Buck foundation paying for, 160, 265n56. *See also* Korean adoption

Reporter, 48

Republic of Korea Army: build-up as result of US occupation, 35; numbers in, 35; trained by US military advisors, 35

Republic of Korea Office of Public Information (OPI), 37–38, 78

rescue: as an American right, 100–102; Americans enacting internationalism through, 64–65; black mothers excluded from participation in, 127; CCF campaigns, 63–64, 240n36; covering US imposition, 22, 32, 41–43, 212, 277n36; global citizenry by, 59–60, 67; of Korean child as cover for US war violence, 32, 34; Koreans as deserving of, 12, 58–61;

rescue (*cont.*)
Korean women ineligible for, 19–20, 157; Orientalism in scripts of, 61–63; photography and narratives of, 13–14, 60, 239n17; unintended responses to, 41–43; through US donations, 14–15, 40–41, 51, 64–65, 80, 97, 131; US narrative on, 12, 14–15, 22, 24–26, 34, 41–45, 44; visualizing pain for purpose of, 60–61, 235n46, 239nn17–18, 240n28

resemblance: of Korean-white children to adoptive mothers, 122–23, 254n36, 254n38; race-matching in US domestic adoptions, 99–100, 121–22, 254n32

Rhee, Syngman, 209; censorship of newspapers by, 235n36; directive to remove mixed-race children, 92–93, 150, 157–58, 210, 246n26; facilitating overseas adoptions, 54, 100–102, 151–52; on his marriage and adoption of Korean children, 158, 264n41; praise for Buck, Holt, Pierce, Rusk, 151–52, 262n21; promoting Korean sovereignty, 65–67, 74, 78

ROK army. *See* Republic of Korea Army

RRA. *See* Refugee Relief Act

Rusk, Dean, 10

Rusk, Howard, 58–59, 67, 69, 73, 262n21

Russell, Jane, 117–18, 253n20

Samoa, 6, 229n46

Saturday Evening Post, xii, 43, 131, 189

Saturday Review, 13, 105

Sayonara (1957), 185–88, 272n47

SCAP. *See* Supreme Commander for the Allied Powers

segregation. *See* racial segregation

"social handicaps," 30, 166, 169, 171, 267n82. *See also* mixed-race children

Social Welfare Society, Korea (formerly Child Placement Service), 57, 170, 268n98. *See also* Child Placement Service (CPS)

social welfare workers, American: biological likeness and adoptions by, 99–100, 121–22, 254n32; establish programs in Korea, 135, 209, 253n21; offering solutions for mixed-race children in Korea, 164–67, 266n79; professionalize field through globalization, 118–19, 253n21; upholding black-white color line in Korean adoptions, 125, 127, 130

South Korea, 22, 207–8; adoptees, protections for, 116–17; adoptees Americanization beginning in, 135–37; adoptees as ambassadors of, 23; adoptees lacking personhood in, 116, 252n10; adoption, challenges of domestic, 149–50; adoption protocols for, 107; adoption race identifying practices in, 154–55, 263nn28–30; adoption shame for, 149–50, 209–10; Americans and rights over, 100–102; *Battle Hymn* supported by, 78; children "exported" by, 110, 150–52; children's choirs and, 67, 74, 241nn50–51, 242n68; Christianity and Hawai'i immigration, 95, 248n40; civil liberties limited by, 212, 277n31; Cold War family of US and, 137; democracy for, 1, 31, 67, 69; disabled children treatment by, 97–98, 165–66, 267n81; HAP awarded by, 151–52, 262n21; Independence Day commemoration for, 37, 231n66, 234n25; industrialization in, 66, 209; integrated schools in, 169–71, 268n98; Japan as stand-in for, 185, 272n48; Kim Sisters of, 196, 273nn74–76; Korean-black children segregated by, 30, 128–29, 147, 156; Korean-black examinations in, 152–56; Korean women and settlement from, 211; mass migrations to, 34, 57; media and mixed-race adoptees of, 152, 157, 251n94, 262n24, 263n39; missionary women and needs of, 94–96, 247nn34–35; mixed-race children and, 23, 30, 86–88, 87, 148–51, 159–60, 163, 166–67, 171, 210, 247nn28–29, 276n21; mixed-race discrimination in, 152–53; mixed-race protestations by, 93, 246n26; mothers erased by, 156–57, 163–64; mothers pressured to relinquish by, 157–59, 264n47; nationalism of, 23, 150, 167, 173; newspapers controlled by, 39, 235n36; nongovernmental organizations aid for, 27, 57–58, 230n53, 238n4; Orphan Adoption Special Law of, 116; orphanages for adoption, 152–53, 156, 159, 264n51; orphanages operated by, 50, 94, 136, 141, 150, 209; orphan numbers overwhelming, 37, 57, 94; political upheaval in, 209, 276n15; population of, 34, 57, 244n4; prostitutes regulated by, 145; prostitutes sanctioned by, 23, 145, 259n11; on race mixing, 166–68, 267n82; racial discrimination in, 87–88, 92, 154, 168, 170, 267n21; refugees into, 57, 238n1; reliance upon US aid, 37–38, 57, 94; return tours, reunions offered by, 210; self-representation by, 65–67, 196, 240nn38–39; sovereignty, 9–10, 23; students from, 225n7; tourism, investing guide on, 65–66, 241nn44–45; transnational adoption and, 24–25, 209–10, 231nn60–63; US accountability by, 37, 146, 151, 260n20; on US adoption laws, 106–7, 116–17, 251n94; US ally in, 1; as US "citizen subject" of, 212, 277n30; US empire, central to, 10, 212; US imperialism in, 20–21, 229n46; US military during occupation, 34–35, 36, 234n21; US military instructing, 35, 208–9, 248n49, 276n14; US military numbers in, 19, 146, 212, 229n45, 234n30; US missionaries, welfare workers

instructing, 96, 208–9; USO brides schools for, 190–92; US on perceived Korean incompetence, 35, 98, 208–9, 249n56; US race identifying practices transferred to, 153–56, 263nn28–31, 263nn33–34; US suppression and protests in, 36–37, 234n21

Soviets, 10, 35, 184, 234n21. *See also* communism

Stars and Stripes, 45, 46, 47, 52, 143, 188

storks, delivering adoptees, 90, 102–3, *103*, 109

Supreme Commander for the Allied Powers (SCAP), 34, 38, 234n21

Third World, 100, 105; consciousness, 11, 65, 240n38; construction of, through aid for, 61–64, 135, 240n28; photography of, 13–14; survival for, 62–64, 239n24

Time magazine, 79, 92, 93, 225n4

transnational adoptions, 1–2, 2, 3, 88–89, 225n3; Americans accepting, 122–23, 254n34; assimilation narratives for, 134–37, 141; Buck on, 92–93, 105, 246nn25–26; foreign mission goals complicated by, 94–95; GIs introducing, 1–2, 2, 3, 54–55; ISS overseeing, 117, 119, 253n17; Korea beginning, 24–25, 209, 231n60, 231n63; as Korean welfare solution, 167–68, 209; lack of available US children prompting, 99, 249n62; missionary women administering, 96, 98; race difference contained in private home, 17–18, 140–41; race views not expanded by, 117–18, 140; Truman support for post-WWII "eligible orphans," 106, 250n85; by US, 22–23, 106–8; US gendered expectations in, 69, 136–37; US legislation for, 106–9, 114–16, 251n94, 251n98, 253n16; white American families with, 102–4, *103*. *See also* Korean adoption

trauma: for Korean adoptees, 111, 138,
141, 214; for Korean children, 42, 60,
141; for military brides, 203, 274n91,
275n92; photography showing, 59–60,
140–42, 258n94; silencing effects of, 17;
as spectacle over engagement, 60–61
Treaty of Peace, Amity, Commerce, and
Navigation, 31
Truman, Harry: integration of military
under, 206, 275n7; intercountry adoption under, 53, 106, 250n85; Korean
War, 10, 35–36, 232n2 (chapter 1),
233n20; Truman Doctrine and Marshall Plan, 36, 238n5; War Brides Act
by, 176–77

The Ugly American, 89, 244n4
Underwood, Horace Grant, 83–84
Underwood, Horace Horton, 32
United Nations, 1, 10; allied forces in
Korean War, 35
United Nations Korean Reconstruction
Agency (UNKRA), 34, 238n1, 238n4
United Services Organizations (USO), 16,
190–92
United States (US), 85, 208, 215; abdica-
tion of responsibility for adoptees
by, 114; adoptees and exceptionalism
for, 135, 140–41; altruism and military
force of, 20–21; American citizens
and RRA of, 107, 251n98; American
civilians and empire of, 109–11; *Battle
Hymn* promoting internationalism,
77–78; black-white color line and,
124–30, 153–54, 156, 255n42; bombing
by, 11, 33, 36, 228n22, 233n16; children
bridging Korea and, 56, 58; children
for Cold War needs of, 11–12, 113; choir
children evidencing power of, 70–71;
"citizen subject" of, 212, 277n30; Cold
War and adoptions by, 15–16, 100, 105;
displays of military prowess, 40–41;
domestic adoption, 99; exceptionalism supported by adoptee narratives,
135, 140–41; expansionism of, 5–6, 20,
230n55; fight against communism, 1–2,
21, 35–36, 238n5; gatekeeping policies
of, 113–14; GI babies and race fears in,
123; GI babies narrative in, 86–88, *87*,
105–6, 250n83; as global leader, 2, 21,
36, 57, 238n5; global military presence
of, 212, 277n34; immigration restricted
by, 4, 113, 225n6, 244n3 (chapter 3),
252n1, 269n8; imperialism, 5–9, *7*,
20–22, 34, 229n46; international
adoption legislation of, 106–9, 114–16,
251n94, 251n98, 253n16; internationalism as Americanism, 23, 112–13;
Korean children and paternalism
of, 11; Korean children supporting
US militarized democracy, 1–4, *2*,
3, 45; Korean children transformed
by, 70, *76*, 76–77; Korean incompetence perceived by, 98, 209, 249n56;
Korean War and, 11, 13, 23, 32, 33,
35–37, 228n22, 233n14, 233n16; Korean
women barriers to entry, 114, 180–83;
Korean women omitted by, 146–47,
157; Korea viewed by, 31, 232n1 (part
1); liberal claims of, 18–19, 22–23, 113,
130, 229n42; military prostitution
sanctioned by, 145, 259n11; mixed-race
adoption relieving military responsibility, 159–60, 172–73; nation-building
efforts of, 6, 21; occupation of South
Korea, 10, 34–35, 261n10; Orientalism and assumed superiority of, 31,
71, 209, 276n14; photography of "first
day" in, 1–4, *2*, *3*, 131, *133*, 135, 174, *175*;
as post-WWII superpower, 2, 14, 21,
33, 57; race-matching in domestic
adoptions, 99–100, 121–22, 254n32;
race practices transferred to Korea,
154–56, 263nn28–30; racial democracy
of, 18–19, 103, *103*, 112–13, 229n40;
racial harmony claims of, 3–4, 81,

105; racial segregation in, 18, 109, 125, 244n3 (chapter 3), 272n44, 275n9; refugees and, 25–26, 231n64; rescue narrative of, 12, 14–15, 40–41, 43–50, 44, 79; rescue of Korean child as cover for war violence, 32, 34; rescue of "Third World" by, 61–63; South Korea ally for, 1; South Korea and adoption laws of, 106–7, 251n94; South Korea on accountability of, 151; transnational adoption by, 22, 137; unwed teen mothers in, 158; US missionaries and accountability of, 151; US wealth *versus* Korean poverty, 50, 61–63; welfare practices applied to children in Korea, 97–98, 165–67, 267n81; white family and security of, 4–5, 12–13; white motherhood in, 14, 101, 228n31

US Army chaplains: Blaisdell and "Operation Kiddie Car," 77, 243n80; coordinating GI visits to orphanages, 39; counseling against marriage, 178–79, 181, 270n22; organizing Christmas parties, 39

US Army Military Government in Korea (USAMGIK), 36–37

US Department of State, 53, 78, 230n54; censorship by, 230n54; Office of Public Affairs, 40

US Eighth Army: mandating contact between GIs and children, 38–39; preventing marriage, 177; public relations officers in, 40; response to adoption requests, 53, 237n79

US-Korean families, 16

US military: against adoptions, 53–54; African American GIs treatment in, 154, 206, 275n7, 275n9; AKF and ties to, 68; base numbers of, 212, 277n34; *Battle Hymn* supported by, 78; camptowns near, 147, 160, 163, 206–7; civilian deaths caused by, 32, 33; concerns about GIs playing fathers to Korean children, 52–53; encouraging GIs to choose wholesome activities, 172, 268n107; GI babies and criticism of, 105–6, 250n83; GI babies as outcome of, 5, 149, 207; houseboys as spies for, 47, 48, 51–52; houseboys prevented by, 52–53; intimate fallout from, 26–27, 147, 171, 215; Korea divided by, 9–10; Koreans criticizing, 37, 146, 260n20; Korean War damage wrought by, 11, 13, 23, 32, 36, 228n22, 233n16; Korean women and jobs in, 174, 271n41; against marriages, 176–82, 270n11, 270n17, 270n22, 271n29; mixed-race children identified by, for purpose of adoption, 159; number of servicemen in Korea, 19, 24, 32, 146; during occupation of South Korea, 34–35; prostitution and, 143–46, 144, 175–76, 183–84, 230n58, 259n11, 260n16, 277n28; prostitution and culpability of, 172–73, 211, 268n106; prostitution regulation by, 145, 259n15; refugees and, 25–26, 231n64; reputation improved through aid for children, 39–40; schools and orphanages built by, 34–35, 39, 236n61; show of force by, 20–21, 40; training ROK army, 35, 209, 248n49, 276n14

US missionaries. *See* Christians; missionaries; missionary women

USO. *See* United Services Organizations

US occupation of South Korea, 9–10; build-up of ROK Army during, 35; economic aid to South Korea during, 31; former Japanese colonial practices continued in, 20, 36; KCAC construction and civil affairs during, 34–35; Korean protests suppressed by, 36–37, 234n21; mass migration South during, 34, 84; US missionary support for, 84

US racial harmony: claims to, 4, 81, 105; erasures required to sustain, 149, 260n3

US servicemen (GIs): adoption by, 1–3, 2, 3, 39, 53–54, 106, 237n79, 238n90; adoption of girls, 54; adoption requests by, 53–54, 205–7; African American, 154, 205–7, 275n7, 275n9; aid for Korean children, 40–41, 50, 236n58, 236n61; appeals to Americans for orphan aid, 50–51; brides as charges of, 182–83, 271nn38–39; civilian death caused by, 32, 33; culpability of, 14, 88, 105, 109, 172–73, 210–11, 268n106; efforts to marry, 180–83; European military brides of, 176, 269n6, 271n40; humanitarianism of, 40–41, 235n37; interactions children in Korea and Japan, 38–39, 43–50, 46, 47, 234n33; as internationalist caretaker, 68–69; ISS marriage assistance for, 181–82; Japanese military brides of, 187, 188–90; Korean boys as houseboys for, 48–50, 51–55, 236n53, 236n66; Korean boys as mascots for, 44–50, 46, 47, 236n55; Korean boys receive lessons on masculinity, militarization by, 44–50, 46, 47; Korean children recasting, as saviors, 34, 49–50, 55–56, 78; Korean civilians assaulted by, 37, 143–46, 144, 151, 209, 234n23, 260n20, 261n14, 276n16; in Korean War, 176, 234n30; military disapproval of fatherly role of, 52–53; mixed-race adoptions by, 54–55, 238n92; mixed-race children linked to, 150–51, 260n3; number stationed in Korea, 19, 24, 32, 146, 229n45; orphanages operated by, 37, 39; orphanages visited by, 29, 38–42, 50–51, 172–73; orphans not understood by, 41–43; orphans thanking, 37–38; propriety and violence required of, 33–34, 40–41; prostitution and, 24, 145–46, 168, 170, 260n16; US Marines, 41, 45–48, 49, 143, 144, 212. See also US military

Van Fleet, James A., 67–69, 71, 72, 73, 87
violence: and care in US empire, 11–12, 215; GIs balancing propriety and, 33–34, 40–41; of Jim Crow laws, 11, 18, 232n72; against Korean women, 37, 143–46, 144, 151, 209, 234n23, 260n20, 261n14, 276n16; photographs separating children from state violence, 2, 2, 3, 60–61, 239n18; US military, 11, 13, 21–22, 23, 32, 33, 36, 228n22, 233n16

WAIF. See World Adoption International Fund
war brides, 30, 226n9; assimilation of, 17–18, 188–90; assumed to be prostitutes, 176, 180–81; as charges of military husbands, 182–83, 271nn38–39; European, 176–77, 269n6, 271n40; as evidence of US pluralism, 18–19, 272n44; as hidden, 19–20, 147, 202; imperialism softened by, 14, 174, 175; INS screening of, 179–80, 270nn24–25, 271nn28–29; ISS and DoD communications on, 182; Japanese, 184, 272n44; Korean, 4, 17–18; as legacy of Korean War, 211–12; numbers of, 174–75, 184, 269nn2–3, 271n40; schools for, in Japan and Korea, 189–92; US military against Asian, 177–81, 269n10, 270n11, 270n17, 270n22, 271nn28–29; in US news, 174, 175, 202–3, 269n1; US representations of, 184–89, 272n47. See also European military brides; Japanese military brides; Korean military brides
War Brides Act (1945), 176–77, 269n8
War Brides Act amended (1947), 16, 182
"war time," 212, 277n35
white American families: as adopters, 89, 99; Cold War internationalist constructions of, 13–14, 80–81, 89; domestic constructions of, 12–13; heroism reserved for, 127; making transnational

families, 4, 89, 102–4, *103*; securing democracy through, 12–13

white American men, as saviors to Korean children, 3, *3*, 15, 55–56, 77–78, 87

white mothers, 88–89; adoption for, 102–4, *103*; Cold War internationalism of, 15–16, 95–96, 101–4, *103*; expectations of adoptee assimilation by, 137; global reach via Korean children, 98–99; imperialism and, 100–102; Korean-black children raised by, 124, 255n44; Korean mothers substituted with, 161–62; Korean-white children resembling, 122–23, 254n36, 254n38; Lady Liberty cast as, 71, *72*; proper citizenship for, 12–13, 127–28, 228n31; rescue reserved for, 127; as stay-at-home, 121

whiteness: family heroism and, 127; Korean adoptees and, 18–19, 99–100, 123–24; Korean-white children, 122–23, 254n36, 254n38; as path to inclusion, 18–19, 129, 134–35; segregation and upholding, 123

white women: access to citizenship through adoptions, 99, 102–4, *103*; aid for Korea, 50–51, 248n44; Christian missionaries, 89, 95–96, 248nn41–43, 248n45; global reach via Korean children, 95–96, 98–99, 100, 248n31; Korean War enabling reach of, 15, 96, 99–100; McCarthyism and containment of, 98–99; perceived right to Korean children, 100–102; and professionalization through social welfare, 118–19, 253n21; as threat to white masculinity, 185–87, 272n50; transferring US lessons to Korea, 96–98. *See also* missionary women; white mothers

World Adoption International Fund (WAIF), 117–18, 253n20

World Vision, 158; adoption sponsored by, 75, 86, 253n27; on GI culpability, 268n106; Korean Orphan Choirs by, 74–77, *76*, 79–80, 242n68

Yamaguchi, Shirley, 188

ABOUT THE AUTHOR

Susie Woo is Associate Professor in the Department of American Studies at California State University, Fullerton. Her essays have appeared in *American Quarterly*, *American Studies Journal*, and the edited volume *Pacific America: Histories of Transoceanic Crossings*.